Under an Open Sky

Under
an Open Sky

Rethinking America's
Western Past

———————

Editors

WILLIAM CRONON

GEORGE MILES

JAY GITLIN

W · W · NORTON & COMPANY
New York   London

Printed in the United States of America

First Edition

The text of this book is composed in Janson
with the display set in Goudy Handtooled and Goudy Old Style.
Manufacturing by The Maple-Vail Book Manufacturing Group.
Book design by Jacques Chazaud.

Library of Congress Cataloging in Publication Data

Under an open sky : rethinking America's Western past / editors, William Cronon, George Miles, Jay Gitlin.
p.   cm.
Includes index.
1. West (U.S.)—Historiography.   2. West (U.S.)—History.
I. Cronon, William.   II. Miles, George.   III. Gitlin, Jay.
F591.U53   1992
978—dc20   91–23557

ISBN 0-393-02993-X

W. W. Norton & Company, Inc., 500 Fifth Avenue, New York, N.Y. 10110
W. W. Norton & Company Ltd., 10 Coptic Street, London WC1A 1PU

1 2 3 4 5 6 7 8 9 0

For
Howard

Contents

CONTENTS

Preface

Not long ago fashionable academic historians predicted that interest in the history of the American frontier had spent itself. Books and articles on the history of the American West seemed destined for oblivion, along with other western genres that seemed irrelevant to postmodern Americans. But like western movies, literature, art, and music, the history of the American frontier has confounded pundits with its popularity and durability.

The essays in this rich anthology suggest one of the reasons: Historians have continued to find new meanings in the western past that have kept it relevant to the interests and concerns of this generation. The provocative lead essay by the editors of *Under an Open Sky*, William Cronon, Jay Gitlin, and George Miles, and the variety of other fine essays in this collection provide eloquent testimony to the field's continuing vitality.

The historians in this anthology speak clearly for themselves without need of prefatory elaboration. My task is to point out that all of them honed their skills under the direction of one remarkable individual, Howard Roberts Lamar, and to join his former students in celebrating the extraordinary influence he has had in fostering and shaping the study of western history.

Howard Lamar has made a profound impact on the study of the West in a variety of ways—as teacher, scholar, editor, and adviser—and he has done so from the unlikely vantage point of New Haven,

Connecticut, where, for over four decades, he has taught history at Yale University. He began there as an instructor of history in 1949 and advanced through the ranks to hold the distinguished William Robertson Coe Professorship of History in 1970. Along the way he also assumed a number of burdensome but essential administrative duties, including chairman of Yale's large and vigorous history department (1967–70) and dean of Yale College (1979–85).

As a teacher Howard has directly influenced generations of students through his popular graduate and undergraduate courses. Even while serving as dean, he maintained his strong commitment to teaching. For the first time in living memory at Yale, the dean taught an undergraduate lecture course. Despite the fact that class began at the unpopular hour of eight-thirty in the morning, Howard's course in western history drew so many students that it provoked comment on the editorial page of the *New York Times*. Graduate students, too, continued to receive Howard's attention during his deanship. No fewer than fifteen students completed their Ph.D. dissertations during those six years. All in all, fifty-seven students have earned or are pursuing Ph.D.'s under Howard's direction. Twelve of them are represented in this anthology.

Through his writing Howard Lamar has also taught many of us who did not study under his immediate direction. Initially he contributed to a growing understanding of the major role the federal government and the politics of colonialism played in frontier development—an understanding that challenged prevailing assumptions about frontier individualism and self-reliance. His *Dakota Territory, 1861–1889: A Study of Frontier Politics* (1956) and his magisterial study *The Far Southwest, 1846–1913: A Territorial History* (1966) suggested new frameworks for understanding western expansion and became models for subsequent explorations of the relatively neglected subject of territorial politics.

In addition to his books, Howard has enlightened a wide readership through his many essays in scholarly journals, anthologies, and introductions to books. In essays too numerous to mention, he has examined a wide range of topics, from American Indian policy to the cowboy and from ethnic labor to the historiography of the West. Like his books, Howard's suggestive essays are studded with insights and connections between specific and general, past and present. His broad view of context and pattern has made his work essential reading for those who have followed him. No student of the Indian trade on the frontier, for example, can ignore Howard's extended essay *The Trader on the American Frontier: Myth's Victim* (1977), in which he explores the murky region between what actually happened in the past and what we suppose happened. Specialists on the frontier process, to take another example, have found their horizons extended by the sweeping vistas Howard Lamar and Leonard Thompson offered in the introductory and concluding essays of their anthology *The Frontier in History: North America and Southern Africa Compared* (1981). Finally, in stimulating examinations of western historiography, such as "Persistent Frontier: The West in the Twentieth Century" (1973), Howard successfully challenged frontier historians to venture into the twentieth century.

As an editor Howard Lamar has also made a deep imprint on the field of western history. On the editorial board of the Yale Western Americana Series, he helped make accessible such classics as Susan Shelby Magoffin's *Down the Santa Fe Trail* and Joseph T. Downey's *The Cruise of the Portsmouth, 1845–1847* (each of which appeared with a new introduction by Lamar), and he contributed a previously unpublished memoir to the series, *Gold Seeker: Adventures of a Belgian Argonaut during the Gold Rush Years*, by Jean-Nicolas Perlot (1985). Since 1981 Howard Lamar has served as the chief editor of Ray Billington's Histories of the American Frontier Series, with its growing list of the most authoritative and readable books on the key themes of frontier expansion. And as editor of the massive *Reader's Encyclopedia of the American West* (1977) he coordinated the work of some two hundred historians and the production of over twenty-four hundred articles on nearly every person, place, institution, event, and idea of significance to the western experience.

Directly and indirectly, then, students of the West have felt the impact of Howard Lamar's scholarship. Indeed, his name has come to be so closely identified with the field that in one recent book a historian confused a president of the short-lived Republic of Texas, Mirabeau Buonaparte Lamar, with Howard Lamar and asserted that Howard, in an expansionist frenzy, had "claimed all lands north and east of the Rio Grande as part of the Texas domain." (The relationship, Howard later told me, was not entirely fanciful; Mirabeau Buonaparte Lamar was his grandfather's uncle.)

Under an Open Sky celebrates more than Howard Lamar's scholarship and reputation. It also testifies to the deep appreciation and affection that many of us in the profession hold for this gentle, genial, and unassuming man—whether we were his students or not. Over the years Howard has made himself unselfishly available to read manuscripts critically, give shrewd advice, and offer enthusiastic encouragement to young scholars. Whatever the cost to his own research and writing, he has profoundly influenced the work of others. The essays in this volume offer eloquent testimony to his effectiveness as a teacher and to his immense contribution in keeping western history a more vital field than pundits once supposed possible.

DAVID J. WEBER
Robert & Nancy Dedman Professor of History
Southern Methodist University

Editors' Acknowledgments

The editors and contributors would like to thank Yale's Beinecke Rare Book and Manuscript Library and its director, Ralph Franklin, for the institutional and financial support that made this collection possible. The Beinecke sponsored a major conference in April 1989 at which our authors had an opportunity to discuss their initial drafts with one another and with a panel of outside critics. All of us would like to thank those critics for the many ways they improved these essays. Richard Maxwell Brown, Ann Butler, David Thelen, David Weber, and Richard White all have left a significant mark on *Under an Open Sky*, even though their names do not appear on any of the essays. The same is true of our editor at W. W. Norton & Company, Steven Forman, without whose enthusiastic support this book might never have come into being.

Finally, we would like to thank Howard and Shirley Lamar, and their daughters Susan and Sarah, for many years of hospitality and friendship. This book is our way of saying thanks to all four of them.

Under an Open Sky

Becoming West

Toward a New Meaning
for Western History

WILLIAM CRONON, GEORGE MILES, JAY GITLIN

Does the western past have a future?

Half a century ago no one would have thought to ask such a question. Whether they encountered it in the novels of Owen Wister or Zane Grey, the paintings of Frederic Remington or Charley Russell, or the B westerns that poured out of Hollywood in a seemingly endless stream, most Americans could hardly doubt that the nation's western part was very much alive. No other phase of U.S. history—with the possible exceptions of the Revolution and the Civil War—was more beloved by Americans. Professional historians belonging to Frederick Jackson Turner's "frontier school" were nearly unanimous in arguing that "the westward movement" had given Americans their democratic values and their special character as a people. Although a few critics complained that the Turner school made too much of the frontier experience, they were a distinct minority. Most Americans—historians and lay people alike—agreed that one could not hope to understand the United States if one overlooked its frontier, its western past.

Times have changed. In the years following World War II, professional historians lost much of their interest in Turner's frontier thesis. They abandoned it for the best of reasons: It was fraught with error. American democracy had not begun on the frontier. Far from inventing the American character, westerners had borrowed most of their cultural values and their notions of government from Europe and the older settlements back East. The "free land" of the frontier was nothing of the sort, having passed into European hands only through the violent conquest of its earlier Indian owners. Although the quintessential frontier hero who had loomed so large in earlier stories of western life had been white, Anglo-Saxon, and male, many of those who actually settled western regions just did not fit the description. By the 1960s traditional frontier historiography struck many as racist, sexist, and imperialist in its depiction of western settlement. On a more theoretical level, many critics argued that the frontier thesis was muddled and contradictory, so much so that it was fatally flawed as an analytical tool. Any explanation that purported to answer so many questions about so much of American history in the end risked being so broad as to explain nothing.

Perhaps most important, the issues of the twentieth century that loomed largest in the minds of historians after World War II—communism, the atom bomb, civil rights, urban poverty, racism, feminism—seemed to have no obvious connection to the rural past of the western frontier. As historians of the 1950s and 1960s sought to explore the problems that mattered most to them, the western past seemed at best an irrelevant distraction. It was no longer on the cutting edge of historical research. The number of scholars studying the field declined. Universities stopped offering courses in western history. One even heard stories of professors discouraging graduate students from studying western history with the advice that the field had "no future." From the time half a century before when the frontier and the West had been among the most creative centers of American historical scholarship, academic interest waned to the point that many historians had no time for either.

Understandable as these changing scholarly enthusiasms may be, there remains something odd about them. Even as many historians were abandoning the West, it remained a much-beloved subject for ordinary Americans. The reasons for this have as much to do with the myths Americans live by as with the actual history they remember and preserve.

The West of the popular imagination, unlike the West of the scholars, is an almost timeless sort of place. At some point in our lives,

4

often when we were very young, we came to know it as a landscape peopled with brave men and women, unforgettable pioneer heroes who helped build the nation. We know some of them by name and can tell their stories by heart: Daniel Boone, Lewis and Clark, Kit Carson, George Armstrong Custer, Buffalo Bill Cody. Others are anonymous, yet we know their stories just as well. We require little effort to picture in our minds thousands of families clearing forests and plowing prairies to make America a Jeffersonian nation of small farmers. We can easily conjure up the bittersweet feelings of women loading all they owned into wagons that would carry them and their families across the continent to farms in Oregon and gold mines in California. Each fragment of the western past evokes a familiar image. Irish and Chinese laborers work under the hot sun to lay down the ties of transcontinental railroads. Prostitutes gaze through dusty windows on the main streets of Kansas cattle towns. Indians fight tragic battles amid dwindling herds of bison to defend homes they will finally lose to the invaders.

However bored historians may be with such images, they retain a strong hold over our collective imaginations. We grew up with them. We recognize in them something of ourselves, for from them we learned the fantasies—and fears—that the less cynical among us might still call the American Dream. If the presidency of Ronald Reagan taught us nothing else, it surely affirmed the continuing power of western symbolism to express the identity and vision of ordinary Americans. The historians might be writing fewer books about it, and Hollywood might even be filming fewer movies beneath its dry hillsides, but the West as a landscape of dream and desire is very much alive.[1]

As we survey the field of western history in the 1990s, then, fully a century after the U.S. census declared the frontier era over, an odd paradox confronts us. For many historians the western past has lost its fascination because there seems to be nothing new or important to say about it. For many ordinary Americans, on the other hand, the western past has lost none of its excitement—for much the same reason. It is so well known, so reassuringly familiar, that it feels like home, albeit a home we may have left long ago. We don't *want* it to change. We hardly question the reality of the myths and histories we locate there. Historians and nonhistorians thus find themselves at odds. What has become a cliché for the scholars remains an icon for most other Americans.

And so our question—does the western past have a future?—is more than just a coy play on words. It arises as much from scholars' doubts as from the popular myths that helped create those doubts in the first place. We should declare at the outset that we regard the question as an unhappy one, and our chief task in this essay is to try to lay it to rest. We wish to argue that the West offers rich opportunities for anyone—scholar and nonscholar alike—who wishes to grasp the broad outlines of American history. We would go further still: We believe that one cannot understand the modern United States without coming to terms with its western past.

In making this claim, we of course repeat the chief argument of Frederick Jackson Turner. Although our differences with Turner will rapidly become clear in the pages that follow, we believe that Turner's critics ultimately went too far in their attacks on his work. Whatever the contradictions and errors of his scholarship, Turner was surely right to see the long European (and African and Asian) invasion of North America—and the resistance to it by the continent's existing inhabitants—as the pivotal event in American history.[2] "Up to our own day," he wrote in 1893, "American history has been in a large degree the history of the colonization of the Great West."[3]

We see no reason to modify that sentence. In pursuing our own vision of western history, we start where Turner did, with "the colonization of the Great West." One of Turner's most fruitful suggestions was that invasion, settlement, and community formation followed certain broad, repeating patterns in most, if not all, parts of North America. Turner's greatest achievement in defining western history as he did was to center the field not on a single region but on many regions undergoing parallel historical change. It was the *parallelism* of Turner's regional histories that made his interpretation seem so rich and suggestive. His most compelling argument about the frontier was that *it repeated itself.* Much as our own approach may differ from Turner's, we share his belief that a comparative study of parallel regional changes—"frontier processes"—has much to offer. Without it, regional history loses much of its broader significance. By coupling western history with the idea of sequential frontiers, Turner showed that the history of "the West" was in fact the history of the entire nation. It would be a shame to lose the power of that insight just because Turner surrounded it with a lot of erroneous, misleading, and wrongheaded baggage. Even if Turner's proposed sequence of frontier changes was entirely false—and it nearly is—his idea of sequential regional change would still be worth preserving and exploring.

We have no sympathy for Turner's model of a universal frontier process that was everywhere and always the same. Turner, good progressive that he was, thought he saw in the West a social evolution from hunter to fur trader to cattle raiser to farmer to merchant and manufacturer. Things were never so simple or clear-cut. Frontier colonies followed no such linear, Darwinian sequence. Their histories did not recapitulate the stages of civilization, nor did their societies evolve according to some inevitable march of progress. This is not to deny, however, that common social and economic processes repeated themselves as invading peoples "discovered" and colonized the many Wests that America eventually became. They did. Among these processes, probably the broadest and most important was the tendency for different parts of the continent to make the long transition from frontier to region.

Over and over again Indians and Old World invaders met, traded, and fought, sometimes with each other, sometimes with themselves. As they struggled to control a particular corner of the continent, they created new landscapes, new property systems, new social relationships, and new political institutions. In the process, zones of fluid, ongoing conflict and opportunity gave way to the stabler, more coherent areas we know today as the regions of North America. How this happened—how different regions and local communities precipitated out from the general tide of Euro-African-Asian settlement—is still one of the great questions of American history.

One should analyze frontier and region not as isolated, alternative ways of viewing the American past but rather as phases of a single historical process. We should worry less about trying to define precisely when a frontier ends and a region begins than about analyzing how the one moved toward the other. The narrative we have in mind carries us from frontier invasion and land taking to the settlement and formation of new communities—processes often at odds with one another—bringing us to the gradual emergence of local and regional identities with their attendant problems of community reproduction, conflict, and change. Out of these broad processes have come locales and regions as different as the fishing villages of Nova Scotia, the hill country of Appalachia, the Corn Belt of the Midwest, the cattle lands of the High Plains, the Navajo sheep pastures of the desert Southwest, and the irrigated agroindustrial empire of Southern California. Explaining how regional differences like these could emerge from common frontier processes is a key task of western history.

Among the many virtues of this approach is the sense of direction it lends to American history without tempting us to worship the false god "progress." It gives to local history a much more than antiquarian significance, for it links ordinary life to much larger historical processes. It tells us that communities in America have never been wholly united—our national republican ideology to the contrary—for geographic divisions have always masked divisions of gender, class, and ethnic identity. Just as important, it locates the history of American communities on the land, reminding us that the continent itself has been both the principal object of human struggle and the stage on which that struggle has taken place.

By keeping close to the land, frontier and regional history can move back and forth between the nitty-gritty details of ordinary life—activities like growing crops, raising children, building homes—and the larger meanings people have attached to such activities. It can embed people and their communities in the most abstract of historical processes without losing sight of what it was like to live through those processes. The abstraction of conquest becomes an abandoned tepee on the hill behind a newly built cabin. The abstraction of community formation becomes a town meeting in which citizens vote to sell public land as a way of paying for a new school where their children will learn republican values from McGuffey Readers. The abstraction of cultural conflict becomes a young woman in such a schoolhouse teaching English to Hispanic and Indian children against the wishes of their parents. Because each of these small, local images leads to much larger questions about the meaning of America, we see the public affection for western history as one of its greatest strengths. The continuing struggle among different communities to impose ordered boundaries and regional identities on the landscapes of North America remains one of the most powerful themes in our nation's history. That theme is our common heritage—as beautiful as it is ugly, as tragic as it is triumphant—and we believe Americans would do well to explore it together.

If the transition from frontier to region has taken place, however incompletely, in all the various "Wests" that today compose the United States of America (not to mention Canada and the rest of the Americas as well), what can we say about their common history? How should we describe the repetitive patterns that will help us understand the frontiers and regions of this nation? What might a new history of the West(s) look like?

In contrast to Turner's frontier school, a new approach to this history is likely to stress the *connectedness* of frontier areas more than their isolation. Western history makes sense only when we see the complex linkages that tied frontier areas to other parts of the world. One cannot hope to understand colonies without exploring their empires. If North American frontiers emerged when Europeans invaded Indian territory, then frontier history is anything but the unique story that earlier scholars made of it. The frontier that Turner portrayed as "isolated" was instead part of the worldwide expansion of European economies and nation-states that traces back to the fourteenth century and before. As such, we can best know the history of the American West if we read it as a chapter in the much larger history of European colonialism.

The parallelism we see as the major strength of frontier history is largely a function of this common European background. Europeans around the world (and soon many of the people they colonized as well) invaded other continents in similar ways and brought similar baggage with them. In the early stages of this expansion, the emergent merchant classes and newly ambitious national courts of Europe were pivotal in creating colonies in the New World. Equally important was the tumultuous change in the European countryside. The separation of peasants from their common lands, the growth of mercantile cities, and the new schisms in western Christendom all fostered the demographic shifts that gave the colonies their new inhabitants. The point holds for the later stages of expansion as well, even after the formation of American nations like the United States, Mexico, and Canada. Migrants to the West chose to go there mainly to escape their circumstances in Europe or the East.

To tell the history of the West without pursuing these Old World linkages is to miss a simple but powerful truth: Connections matter. From them came the chief puzzle facing all frontier communities: whether to reproduce the ways of the old world or abandon them for the new. Areas that Euroamericans had only recently entered had a peculiar fluidity that characterized frontier communities around the world. Resources, wealth, and power, although hardly within reach of all, were nonetheless more up for grabs here than in the more rigidly hierarchical societies the invaders had left behind. When displaced migrants made homes in frontier areas, they tried to hang on to the familiar world they remembered from before, but they also sought to change and improve it. Their effort to pick and choose between the known and the unknown as they shaped their new settlements was one of the most common features of frontier life, and the

9

experience of being able to pick and choose—for those who had that opportunity—could carry with it an unexpected feeling of empowerment.

For many people, living in a frontier area evoked the feeling that one was somehow present at the creation of a new world. It is striking that Turner and those who have followed him have so easily used words like "freedom" and "opportunity" when speaking of frontier life. People who moved to frontier areas carried a whole world inside their heads, but they transformed that world in the very act of bringing it to a new place. As migrants made choices about the sorts of communities they wanted to construct, they started to travel down paths from which there would be no return. The act of exercising the freedom to change old ways laid the foundations that would create new old ways and eventually restrict the very freedom that had created them. By making choices—often unknowingly—frontier inhabitants began constructing the regional identity that would be their chief historical legacy to the future.

Frontier connections mattered immensely, not least because they were usually so tenuous. Frontier areas were remote places, far distant from the centers of wealth and power out of which many of their inhabitants had come. They existed on the outer colonial edge of Old World empires. This suggests one important way of defining frontier settlements: as peripheries whose dependence on imperial metropoles helped define local society. Perennially short of labor and capital, frontier economies were usually extractive, transferring nonindustrial resources to more populous areas nearer the center of empire. However open their social systems might seem, their inhabitants could never attain the same status as elites in the metropolis.

The converse of this argument, however, was that remoteness also undermined hierarchy. Living at the edge of empire generally meant living where the power of the central state was weak, where economic activity was poorly regulated, and where cultural innovation met few obstacles. Far from bearing the iron imprint of empire, many frontier communities fostered a genuine mixture, or at least coexistence, of European and native traditions (and eventually African and Asian traditions as well) in which no side enjoyed clear cultural superiority. European migrants were by no means solely responsible for cultural mingling. The people they met in their journeys, and those in whose midst they settled, were also responsible for remaking their familiar worlds to accommodate their new neighbors.

The Europeans saw themselves as "discovering" the Indians, but

10

of course, the discovery was mutual. Just as colonists gathered information about "new" frontier lands and their inhabitants, Indians soon learned the opportunities and threats the invaders offered. The Europeans held out many attractions: rich chances for trade, access to new tools and ways of living, help against old enemies, and general cultural ferment. Time and again Indian peoples made their own choices about what to preserve and what to abandon from traditional ways. A time eventually came when Euroamerican coercion severely limited their options, but even then Indian peoples found ways to assert autonomy and the right to choose what kind of world they wanted to inhabit. No two Indian groups made precisely the same choices, but all shared responsibility with the Europeans for shaping the transition from frontier to region.

Having recognized the connectedness and remoteness of frontier areas and the choices their residents faced between reproducing old ways or embracing new ones, we can begin to compare their movement toward regional identity. As we do so, we start to recognize certain broad processes of frontier change that have recurred everywhere in North America, a half dozen of which we will offer in this essay as non-Turnerian foundations for a new frontier and regional history. Although these processes share with Turner's frontier stages the virtue of lending a sense of movement and direction to western history, they are neither linear nor sequential. Unlike Turner's crude teleologies, in which the triumph of American nationalism was the inevitable end of frontier settlement, the processes we have in mind have all been open-ended. They imply nothing about "progress" or "the march of civilization." Because they have mingled with each other in complex ways that have rarely been predictable, they imply widely differing outcomes to the frontier-regional story. Their results have been the diverse peoples and landscapes of North America as we know them today.

One of these simultaneous processes we can call *species shifting*, the movement of alien organisms into ecosystems from which they were once absent. Such organisms were the most visible proof that a frontier area had become linked to the rest of the world in a new way. Europe, Africa, and Asia were now reproducing themselves—quite literally—in America. We now know that human colonists were by no means the most challenging opponents the Indians faced. More important, at least at the outset, were the nonhuman invaders that accompanied the Old World migrants: strange crops, new weeds, tame animals, and—worst of all—lethal microorganisms. The modern world

11

has seen nothing like the epidemics that killed millions of Indians in the wake of Old World contact. No people has ever suffered a worse epidemiological disaster. The demographic collapse of the tribes forced the survivors to make a complex series of social, economic, and political adjustments that we have just begun to understand.

But microbes were only the cutting edge of a much more general biological invasion that has continued right down to the present. Hundreds of Old World organisms took part in the Old World settlement of North America, and each had a frontier history all its own. Some migrants, like the horse, encouraged dramatic changes in the lives of Indians who acquired them. Others, like the bluegrass or the pig, the dandelion or the rat, had more quietly sinister implications as they began to replace various native plants and animals. Old World organisms had greater success in some ecosystems than in others, with predictable consequences for the prosperity of new settlements: Europeans thrived best where their organisms did. The familiar frontier tension between reproducing the old and embracing the new expressed itself in new settlement landscapes that increasingly resembled those of Europe and in new political economies better adapted to New World ecosystems. Regional histories began to diverge right from the start as groups of human inhabitants responded differently to the changing environments around them. But despite regional variations, no frontier phenomenon was more universal than the process of species shifting. By working to reproduce the world they had left behind, Europeans brought massive ecological changes to New World environments. Ecology and empire went hand in hand, and we are only just starting to understand their relationship.

However universal species shifting might be, it was a slow, gradual process that usually—apart from the epidemics—gave Indians time to adapt to the changes around them. The frequency with which they turned those changes to their own advantage suggests the fallacy in regarding them solely as powerless victims of invasion. More often than not, Indians became active partners of the Europeans they met. The exchange of organisms between the Old World and the New was part of another frontier process—*market making*—in which Indians could often wield just as much power as the Europeans. For many years Europeans, Africans, and Asians were present only in small numbers in most parts of the continent. They came less as settlers or conquerors than as resident traders intending only to sojourn for a while with Indian communities. Wherever trade thrived, Indians and Europeans developed intimate social ties, more complicated cultural mixing, and more evenly balanced political power than in areas with little trade activity.

For Indians and the early traders who dealt with them, the market became a common space, a middle ground that both sides had to interpret according to the cultural traditions of the other. If Indians chose to see the exchange of goods as gifts passing between intimate friends, then European traders had little choice but to enter into this cultural convention. The different peoples who engaged in trade in frontier areas had to arrive at a mutual understanding of what constituted a market, so much so that the exchange relationship could sometimes be indistinguishable from the way of life that surrounded it. Traders of Indian and European descent married into each other's families. They borrowed each other's rituals. Always they sought to accommodate each other's cultural universe so that the market between them might thrive.

The common ground was not, however, easy to maintain, for trade produced its own conflicts. Markets made friends of those who took part in them and enemies of those who did not. Supply lines, trade routes, and market centers became the objects of fierce competition, so that Europeans fought with one another—at least as much as Indians did—to gain favored access for themselves. Wherever cross-cultural trade predominated, conflict tended to occur most often between those whose exchange relations were weakest. The potential for violence swirled always just beyond the edges of the common ground.

In the long run, however, the very market that had brought Indian and European traders together eventually helped drive them apart. Because the new lands of North America became colonies just as a capitalist market economy was emerging in Europe, settlement brought with it new markets and the relationships between land and people they implied. The economies that appeared on the periphery of European settlement more often than not were extractive. They took the natural products of the landscape and moved them in the simplest possible way to metropolitan markets. Animals had prices placed on their skins, and in the resulting exchange earlier Indian trade networks became linked to the mercantile economy of the North Atlantic. From that start market making gradually grew so that more and more elements of North American ecosystems became tradable commodities. Products like wheat, lumber, livestock, and gold moved great distances across the continent and ocean in order to travel from hinterland periphery to metropolitan core. Market making and species shifting thus combined to produce ever more extensive ecological and economic change in frontier areas. Together they helped establish the boundaries within which new regional identities would gradually emerge.

Peaceful trade relations between Indians and Europeans could persist only so long as European demand for commodities did not interfere with Indian subsistence. But sooner or later it did interfere, and the timing of when it did depended on a third frontier process: *land taking*.[4] The hunting economy of the fur trade exerted market pressure on only a small portion of the natural resources in an area. As more settlers moved into that area, their economic activities proliferated across other parts of the ecosystem, attaching new prices to new sets of resources. Most important, the arrival of permanent settlers generally turned the land itself into a commodity. Now Euroamericans sought to purchase not just furs but the very foundation of Indian subsistence.[5] As settlers began to acquire Indian land, the common ground contracted almost to the vanishing point, and new frontier conflicts—this time involving survival itself—began to appear.

The rate and form of land taking by European settlers depended on the economy and community they intended to create in an area. If they meant to support themselves by any means other than trading with the people who already lived there, they also intended to control the land on which their new life would depend. New England village, Virginia plantation, Spanish hacienda—each implied a dramatically different way for colonists to occupy land, but all brought fierce conflicts with erstwhile Indian neighbors. Land taking invariably involved complex changes not just in ownership rights over property but in class relations among the different people who would work that property. Property and class further buttressed the foundations on which new regional identities would grow.

Everywhere Europeans came up with one device or another for denying Indian claims to land. They pointed to the supposed savagery of Indians and invented the myth that Indians raised no crops. Set against the agricultural and "civil" societies of the Europeans, such myths became pretexts for land taking. Similar devices could also work against other Europeans, as when Americans in New Mexico or California sought to usurp the rights of Hispanic landowners. The climax of this ideological exercise came in the teachings of Frederick Jackson Turner himself. Turner's "free land," in defining the frontier, "explained" American history only by erasing the legitimacy of Indian

· 14

claims to the continent. Just so could history rationalize conquest and empire.

"Settlement" meant land taking, and land taking meant violence. Violence was central to the frontier experience. Sometimes it was perpetrated by individuals, and sometimes by the military power of the state. Always it drew dark lines on a landscape whose newly created borders were defended with bullets, blades, and blood. Although it is easy to exaggerate the military superiority of the Europeans, the evolving military technologies that the invaders employed—and the industrial systems that stood behind those technologies—were eventually pivotal to their success.

Behind the borders where the threat of violence was greatest, a much subtler but ultimately more powerful cultural invasion continued the work of those who wielded the weapons. Land taking blended imperceptibly into the fourth of our frontier processes: *boundary setting*, the very essence of frontier life. Every activity contributed to this process. Ways of defining property, ways of killing animals, ways of planting fields, ways of building houses, ways of rearing children, ways of praising God: all became symbols of difference between those who stood on opposite sides of frontier boundaries. Even so simple and benign a process as building a house and raising a family became a part of the contested terrain of the frontier.

These simple activities were perhaps even more effective than overt violence in moving Indians off their lands, for they justified land taking by giving the invaders a permanent sense of entitlement to the landscape around them. The more settlers invested their labor and their dreams in the land, the more they belonged to that land and the more the land belonged to them. Indeed, the longer they (and their children and their grandchildren) perceived themselves in such terms, the less one could even call them invaders. Before very many years had passed, they too were defending the homes of their ancestors. "Europeans" and "Africans" and "Asians" had become "Americans." In killing and being killed to preserve their homes, frontier inhabitants shed the blood that created sacred ground, lending an almost religious authority to their claims of ownership.

Lands that belong to me, lands that belong to you: the history of the West is the story of how the American map came to have the boundaries it shows today. Colonization, at its most basic level, was a struggle to define boundaries on the landscape. The first such boundaries were terrestrial, defining whether Indians or Europeans controlled a tract of land or whether one European monarch or another had laid claim to it. Once such territories had been established, those in power set about creating property systems for transferring land into private ownership. National boundaries thus helped delimit the more personal boundaries that marked the fields or pastures or mines that individual farmers or proprietors owned.

Formal divisions of land became the foundation for new systems of ecological use and political economy. Within the general boundaries of the land itself emerged the economic boundaries of trade and production; the social boundaries between kin groups, tribes, and communities; and the political boundaries that defined who had power over whom. Some of these expressed themselves in geographic space. Others had more to do with social distinctions among peoples. All, however, were part of an emerging network that was fundamental to the general shift of landscape and community from frontier toward region. Out of a frontier world of unstable boundaries would come a regional world in which the human terrain of conflict and difference was more definite and familiar, if no less serious or deadly.

Boundary setting is so inclusive a frontier and regional process that it encompasses all the others; all social life is in some sense a struggle to define the difference between ours and theirs, mine and yours, self and other. But the most clear-cut of social boundaries came into being through a fifth process that defines the transition from frontier to region more precisely than any other: *state forming*. Just as the market exerted a pivotal influence on the form of frontier life, so too did the state. North American frontiers were classically areas where the authority of the state was weak, where law was either the result of customary practice or makeshift invention. Indian polities were generally less bureaucratic and institutionalized than those of the Europeans, so native encounters with the invaders were also encounters with new forms of political governance. Moreover, since the era of colonial expansion was also the period during which European nation-states came into being for the first time, frontier areas became virtual testing grounds for new institutions of state power.

Frontier inhabitants typically looked to multiple sources of political authority, acknowledging allegiance to more than one leader or government. This tended to strengthen the common ground that trade and the market had already produced, for without effective state power—and the institutionalized violence it could muster—no single group was likely to dominate others completely. In much the same way, groups living on the margins between imperial systems—for instance, the Iroquois in the Northeast or the Tlingits in coastal Alaska—derived considerable power from their ability to play European groups off against one another. But interstitial power of this sort relied on a balancing act that no Indian group could maintain indefinitely. Once European empires extended their hold over the continent and stabilized the boundaries among themselves—once regions and nations began to be delimited—law flowed more and more from state authority and coercion. Although the state system of New France, for example, differed radically from that of Canada, the power of a central government to assert its rule over vast territories in each case represented a decided break from the political systems of their Indian predecessors.[6]

The United States is in some ways a special case of the growth of colonial authority over North American peoples. Just as American frontiers were capitalist in their economy by the end of the eighteenth century, so too were they republican and federal in their politics. The United States took the earlier colonial assumptions of the European powers and gave them a new face. From 1787 on, imperial expansion would be formally democratic in character, following the model of state formation articulated in the Northwest Ordinance. Once frontier territories had been brought within the boundaries of the United States, they would receive an extended tutelage in the traditions of republican democracy. During this stage the familiar structures of American government would be reproduced within their boundaries. Once their schooling was over, the territories would enter the United States as full partners with the original thirteen. By this device, the United States sought to escape the paradox of its own imperial ambitions. Invasion seemed more palatable if the territories a republic seized eventually became equal participants in their own democratic rule. The republican empire, so the theory went, had the moral authority of manifest destiny to extend its rule, whether or not the people it absorbed wished to become citizens.

The extension of state power was the clearest possible indication of successful invasion and a retreating frontier. In frontier areas, peoples of different cultures confronted one another as independent political nations, but only for a time. Whenever native peoples found their freedom of action effectively constrained by the laws of another state, their frontier independence gave way to political dependency. They began to inhabit a region within the boundaries of a single nation. (In much the same way, inhabitants of other European empires—the French in the Mississippi Valley or Spanish-speaking mestizos in the Southwest—could find themselves suddenly within the boundaries of an expansionist United States, thereby posing long-term questions about the meaning of citizenship and ethnicity in a multicultural nation.) State-forming processes like those specified in the Northwest Ordinance might continue, but the end was in sight. By the time a territory became a state, it had left its frontier era behind and was well on its way to defining its regional relationship to the rest of the nation.[7]

Once a central government had extended its authority over the entire territory of a nation like Canada or Mexico or the United States, a powerful force for national homogeneity began to exert its influence through the institution of citizenship. The invention of an "American" or a "Mexican" or a "Canadian" nationalism was one result of this process. No less important, however, were the conflicting local and regional identities that emerged at the same time. Together, these constitute one final frontier-regional process that in fact occurs at all times in all human societies: *self-shaping*. As people constructed new homes for themselves in different parts of North America, drawing new boundaries on the landscapes around them, they also erected boundaries that defined themselves as members of particular communities in particular places at particular times. Self-shaping was part of the very earliest frontier encounters and continues as a central challenge of regional life right down to the present. The different identities of individuals and groups blended and contested in frontier areas to produce the peculiar mixtures that eventually gave regions and subregions their special cultural identities. Similar as our frontier processes may have been as they repeated themselves across the continent, they finally yielded very different results: one nation, but many regions and many selves. Despite certain common backgrounds, French separatists in Quebec, Chicano migrants in California, Navajo shepherds in Arizona, German dairy farmers in Wisconsin, and black tobacco workers in North Carolina continue to assert their separateness as groups and as individuals. From similar frontier experiences have come the very different regions and cultures we find today across the map of North America.

Boundaries on the land are ultimately boundaries between people, for each implies a different way of shaping and experiencing the self. In this sense, the divide between Indians and non-Indians was only the most dramatic case of a far more general phenomenon. Apart from certain broad cultural traits, Europeans and Africans and Asians were no more monolithic in their self-identities than the Indians. Settlers coming to frontier areas from different American regions or Old

World countries formed communities that often wanted little to do with one another. Complex national and ethnic divisions typified many North American frontiers. German, Scotch-Irish, and English settlers lived side by side with only limited mixing in the valleys of the Appalachians, just as Indians, Hispanics, and Anglos did in New Mexico's Rio Grande Valley. In some western areas the coming of regional identity was often accompanied by the formation of ethnic enclaves. This was especially true where the boundaries of ethnic selfhood expressed themselves in terms of racial difference, as in Chinatown, the barrio, and the reservation. In such places, disempowered communities often preserved considerable autonomy for themselves by maintaining control over an isolated geographic space. The evolution of such enclaves, and of their complex relations to the society around them, is a crucial story that scholars are just beginning to explore.

In the shift toward regionalism, ethnic difference easily became the terrain on which old frontier encounters continued to act themselves out. The various communities in a frontier area sometimes succeeded in blending ethnic traditions, but as often as not they displayed a fierce loyalty to the places they had fled. The very opportunity that frontiers offered people to abandon their old ways often put a premium on maintaining them, so that self-shaping reproduced within individuals the very conflicts between old and new that were already embedded in the cultural history of a people. This was as true of Indians as it was of Europeans, Africans, and Asians. Frontier areas were fertile ground for conservative social movements seeking to resist both cultural change and those who promoted it. Religious revivals, nativist movements, and similar efforts at cultural revitalization occurred with some frequency on the frontier. Most expressed a nostalgia for the imagined traditions—many of them newly invented—of a supposedly older way of life. Frontier encounters might even create new ethnicities by building the traditions that legitimated them. Something of this sort happened to the mixed-race Seminoles in Florida and the Mormons in Utah. Whether conservative or not, the ethnic self would emerge as a pivotal phenomenon in American regional life. Once ethnic difference expressed itself geographically—and frontier processes made this almost inevitable—it could evolve and reproduce a personal sense of selfhood that was both ethnic and regional at the same time.

Even in ethnically homogeneous communities, the transition from frontier to region brought new self-identities based on the social

19

boundaries of class or gender. Once frontier land had come under non-Indian control and was being bought and sold as a commodity, migrants were usually struck by its initial abundance in comparison with more densely settled areas like Europe, the American East, or Asia. The relative openness of frontier communities and the mobility of their social hierarchies rested in no small way on the favorable ratio of population to resources. One could buy land cheap and sell one's own labor dear—exactly the opposite of conditions that prevailed in large parts of the Old World. If Turner's "free land" had any legitimate basis, this was it. So long as conditions of frontier abundance persisted, social divisions and class systems might remain weaker and less elaborate than in older metropolitan areas.

But frontier abundance inevitably declined. Whether because the population of an area grew so as to bring its resource base under increasing pressure or because property systems permitted individuals to monopolize control of resources, the land/labor ratio fell. As it did, and as a political economy based on wage labor expanded, new class divisions came to characterize regional life. Those who owned land and capital increased their fortunes by hiring those who did not. Although there might be considerable movement back and forth between the two groups, a fundamental social boundary nonetheless emerged. The general tendency was for class systems to become more multitiered and hierarchical—gaining new layers at both the top and bottom of society—as frontier areas aged and began to develop regional identities. As that happened, individuals became increasingly conscious of the class identity—the self—implied by their birth, their work, their social status, even their dreams.

It would be wrong, of course, to assert that the movement from frontier to region created class divisions where none had existed before. Quite the contrary. Frontiers generally reflected the class structure of the societies that produced them, albeit in simplified form. Frontier settlements in seventeenth-century New England tended to reproduce the mercantile and peasant communities the colonists had left in England. The missions and ranches of Hispanic New Mexico reflected the traditions of the Roman Catholic Church and the Spanish bureaucracy. Corporate mining operations in the nineteenth-century Rocky Mountains tended to reproduce the capitalist social relations of wage labor that typified American industry at the time. A region's class divisions ultimately depended on the resource markets, relations of production, cultural traditions, and state structures that shaped its economy. Although such divisions might produce intense conflict within a regional community, they also defined the social identities of those who declared their membership in that community and thereby helped define the region itself.

Gender was at least as pervasive and subtle as class in shaping regional identities. However intimately men and women might be joined within a single community, they often experienced frontier life from radically different perspectives. At the most overt level, the physical production of community life—whether in obtaining food, making shelter, or raising children—was invariably embedded within an intricate sexual division of labor. Together women's and men's work made daily life possible even as they transmitted the values and practices of one generation to the next. As in all human communities, the frontier goal of transmitting an older cultural world into a new one finally depended on the roles men and women played in the reproductive process itself, so that marriage, love, and family—however defined—lay at the very heart of the transition from frontier to region.

The activities of men and women on opposite sides of an intercultural divide became a particularly rich source for conflict or cooperation. Frontier violence usually evoked fears, some of them almost pornographic, about the depredations that enemy men might commit against the women of a frontier community. Sexual fantasy thus helped enforce the boundary between "savage" and "civil" society in ways that amplified frontier hostilities. On the other hand, bonds of gender could sometimes cross cultural boundaries in ways that contributed to a more inclusive sense of community in frontier areas. Indian women, for instance, often chose to attach themselves to non-Indian male traders, becoming wives who were also partners in production. By doing so, they reinforced ties of trade with ties of blood. The children of such unions found their self-identities in new métis communities that existed in a third regional world on the boundaries between the worlds of their parents.

Inside particular communities, gender boundaries helped define regional self-identity. To take just one example, in certain commodity frontiers of the nineteenth-century West—especially those involving minerals, livestock, and lumber—a disproportionate number of immigrants were male. This simple fact bore a host of implications for received notions of gender. Lonely frontier men might so exaggerate their longing for the "feminine ideal" that their actions when meeting a woman became a caricature of nineteenth-century ideologies of domesticity. The few women who lived in such areas—many of whom were nonwhite—found that traditionally unremunerated women's work suddenly had a market and could earn a money wage. Restaurants, boardinghouses, laundries, and brothels all represented an extension of the market into the domestic sphere. All prospered from unbalanced frontier sex ratios. In much the same way, men without women found themselves having to take on roles that would never ordinarily have been theirs, so that male gender identities also had to undergo subtle shifts in frontier circumstances. As with ethnicity and class, the gender boundaries that emerged in such places helped shape new regional selves that were distinct from each other and from their common ancestors.

It would be wrong, however, to leave the impression that self-shaping was merely a process whereby divisions of gender, class, and ethnicity reproduced themselves on the North American landscape. These divisions did proliferate during the long transition from frontier to region, but there also developed a more collective sense of local and regional identity. The very differences that divided the inhabitants of a particular place were ways of life they understood and shared more intimately with each other than with people anywhere else on the continent. Their conflicts and divisions—like their hardships and celebrations—also defined their particular home. By belonging to that place and that community, people intertwined their moral universe in a web of familiar values that supplied the reference points of the self. Here too there emerged a feeling of difference, but it was one separating their community from other communities located elsewhere in geographic space. One's own region was home; everywhere else was not. From that simple fact would come the great patchwork of regional communities and identities we recognize as we travel across the continent today. They more than anything else are the legacy of the nation's frontier past.

And so we come full circle, back to the larger question of how to see in the Great West a story of colonial frontiers becoming national regions. In proposing a unified telling of frontier and regional history, we seek to embrace a central paradox of American life. Just as frontier inhabitants struggled with the problem of choosing between the old and the new, so too do the inhabitants of today's regional America struggle with the task of defining and narrating their separateness in the midst of our collective oneness.

The frontier-to-region processes we have been describing—species shifting, market making, land taking, boundary setting, state forming, and self-shaping—have produced results that point in opposite directions. On the one hand, each has contributed to a general process of homogenization that has tended to make the different parts of the United States more like each other than ever before. Converging ecosystems, an all-encompassing market, lands seized from Indians to be held under one legal system, social boundaries defined on a single national map, a unified state, and the sense of citizen selfhood that flows from American nationalism—all these suggest the success of the Old World invasion in producing similar results in all parts of the continent.

And yet these same processes have also defined what we do not share as Americans, the things that mark us as somehow belonging to special places called "Quebec" or "New England" or "the West" or "the Great Plains" or "the Spanish Borderlands" or "California"—places that are not at all the same. Much as our mobility as a people may complicate our regional identities, it has by no means ended them. The places we recognize as our regional homes distinguish themselves from one another by the same markers that otherwise seem to suggest the universal victory of the frontier invasion. The weather around us, the plants and animals by which we recognize the seasons of our year, the local products that no one else can buy so readily, the place-names that echo the presence of Indian peoples still very much alive on their diminished lands, the social divisions that mark the people in whose midst we live, the peculiarities of our local government—all come together to produce the uniquely regional selves we recognize as our own.

At its heart the transition from frontier to region was a process of creating new, stabler geographic identities in the midst of landscapes that people chose to perceive as homes. Despite what some scholars seem to believe, it is no easier to define a region than a frontier, and we have no interest in pursuing what long ago became a sterile debate about the relative merits of frontier versus regional history. We have already argued that the two are in fact inextricably entangled with each other and that each is best understood when seen in light of the other. Rather than offer a fixed definition of either, we propose to recognize their common story by placing them next to each other. We might describe their relationship as a shift from relative newness to relative oldness or from flux to fixity. Perhaps the most telltale sign of the transition was a feeling among the inhabitants of a place that they were no longer inventing a world but inheriting one. The more people felt this way about their home landscape, the more we think of that place as a "region" rather than a "frontier."

The transition from frontier to region has been implicit in "western" or "frontier" history since its founding, as these often interchangeable labels suggest. One of the peculiarities of the field has been its tendency to study "frontiers" as they migrate all the way across the continent, but to study only one large region—the trans-Mississippi West—in the twentieth-century period after the territorial frontiers of the United States had ceased most of their movement. Perhaps this makes pragmatic sense when considered in light of the academic division of labor. The South surely has not needed the services of frontier historians. One can hardly argue that the Northeast has suffered from having its history written as if it were the history of the nation as a whole. Only the Middle West seems to get left out in this regional division of scholarly turf. Midwestern historians (like Turner himself) often consider themselves frontier or even western historians, but their more westerly colleagues tend to scoff when they do. Most scholars who call themselves western historians study the region west of the Mississippi River. Some would place it still farther west, beyond the Missouri or perhaps even beyond the front range of the Rockies (thus enlarging even more the capacious boundaries of the Middle West).

We will not in this essay try to offer a separate analysis of the trans-Mississippi West as a modern region. It undoubtedly has special characteristics that mark its regional identity and set it apart from the rest of the continent: its general aridity, its low population density, its intense contrast between urban and rural landscapes, its love-hate relationship to the federal government's money and power. For our purposes, the modern West brings us back to a final problem about the general transition from frontier to region. The West as we know it today is not just a region; it is also the last frontier. More than anywhere else in North America, the regional self-identity of the West flows from its ties to the frontier past. It is the place where Americans suddenly realized that frontier expansion could not continue forever.

Like Turner's, their response was to regret its passing and to try to slow or stop the very processes that elsewhere carried communities ever farther from their frontier past. The West would be a region where at least the memory of the frontier would be held close to the hearts of most who called the region home—by no means all of them westerners. It would be a place where problems that had once been "solved" by moving them or oneself somewhere else could no longer be escaped so easily. In the trans-Mississippi West the fiction could no longer hold that people like Indians or Mormons or racial minorities could be driven to entirely different regions. Instead, the West would become a region not of moving on but of settling in, where enclaves would replace frontiers as expressions of community identity and conflict. The "free land" that elsewhere passed so quickly into private hands would now be "conserved" or "preserved" in the West by government bureaucrats. Next to the frontier booster's vision of regional development would stand a monument to antidevelopment, the wilderness landscape that some now hope to save as a symbol of the frontier world they have nearly lost. And in tourist meccas from Disneyland to Six Flags over Texas, false vestiges of a frontier past would be lovingly reconstructed so that no one would forget whence this particular region supposedly came.

One might almost say that the trans-Mississippi West has appropriated to itself—rather illegitimately—the entire frontier history of the continent. In the minds of most westerners, and many other Americans as well, the West is the classic, the only, frontier landscape. Popular icons of the frontier are a jumbled collage of Texas cowboys, boomtown prostitutes, families on overland trails, California miners, Plains Indians, and cavalry soldiers. Hollywood's West is almost always a dry sagebrush landscape, fixed at a timeless moment distantly resembling the 1870s or 1880s, in which men wearing cowboy hats ride horses past the false-fronted buildings of a town where they will reenact the eternal struggle between good and evil. Earlier frontiers—the Wests of Daniel Boone or the Canadian voyageurs or the prairie farmers or the Mississippi slaves—have no such hold over the popular imagination.

Why this should be so remains one of the most intriguing problems of western history. The modern regional West has become the repository for a national frontier past. In this sense, the history of the frontier has never ended but continues to this day as a key element in the mythology and ideology of American nationalism. For good or for bad, the frontier is where many Americans continue to locate a central core of their identity. The meaning of heroism, the relation of the individual to family and community, the nature of patriotism, the value of freedom, the challenge of making a home: however abstractly we state these things, it takes but an instant to think of frontier icons that express them. We have covered this ground before. Davy Crockett at the Alamo. George Armstrong Custer at Little Bighorn. Families on the Oregon Trail. Would-be miners walking thousands of miles in hopes of finding a golden Eldorado in the Sierra Nevada. Spanish-speaking Californios sinking into poverty as they lose their lands. Black families fleeing their southern homes to build an Exoduster paradise

25

in Kansas. Chinese sojourners on the Pacific coast working the margins of an Anglo economy in the hope of improving their family's lot back home.

Some such icons are nostalgic and sentimental, inventing a fictitious golden age when men and women better understood their roles in life, when good and evil seemed easier to recognize, when life itself seemed simpler. Except insofar as they capture old longings that Americans have cherished for a long while, they tell us more about modern anxieties and fantasies than they do about past reality. Other icons are more genuinely ambivalent, precisely because they express the paradoxes of the present in the very act of representing the past. The wilderness we try to lock away in a timeless place refuses to remain unchanged and soon comes to symbolize the very opposite of the thing it ostensibly preserves. Rather than a landscape of boundless freedom, it is a walled-off preserve in which the very act of experiencing the wild proves how tame it has become. The men who wear cowboy hats in downtown Houston or Denver now manage the institutions that drive ranchers and cowboys bankrupt. Oldest of all, there is the tragic frontier icon of "noble but doomed" Indian warriors making their "last stand" as a "vanishing race." Like all the others, this one cuts both ways, especially since it encourages one to forget that Indian men and women continue to struggle for dignified lives in the modern world: they have neither vanished nor made their "last stand." But even the myth of a doomed race suggests the hard truth that the America we know today was built on the bones of those who never wanted it to exist. The moral ambiguity of that fact is not likely ever to vanish.

The West, then, is many things, and one cannot define away its complexities by fiat. This is where Turner's critics went awry. The problem they thought they saw in his definition of western history was, in fact, the central problem of that history. The West may be the region lying somewhere beyond the Mississippi River, but it is also the experience of going there. It is the westering (and northering and southering and eastering) that carried new peoples into new lands all across the continent, whether from the East or Europe or Mexico or Canada or Africa or Asia. There have been many geographic Wests, even if most of them have now changed their names so that we no longer recognize them as such. Just so did Northwest become old Northwest, and that in turn become Middle West and even—for some—East. Much of western history has always been about ceasing to be west—that is to say, making the long transition from frontier to region.

And because the experience of ceasing to be west has happened everywhere, even in the West itself, the icons of the western frontier express
the common history not of a particular region but of America itself.
Whether we begin with the myths, the history, the region, or the
frontier, sooner or later we find ourselves wandering through all of
them because together they are where we came from. To try to separate them is to miss their most important message. Dancing somewhere in their midst is the creative center that has kept western history
vibrantly alive for over a century. That same center, we believe, holds
the promise of its future as well.

Kennecott Journey

The Paths out of Town

WILLIAM CRONON

Kennecott: It is one of the most unlikely ghost towns in the United States. The way there is long and hard, and you are not apt to stumble upon it by accident. About eighty miles north of Valdez in south-central Alaska, you turn east off the main Richardson Highway and drive thirty miles on deteriorating asphalt to the tiny hamlet of Chitina, with its bar, post office, and thirty-odd inhabitants. There, the pavement gives out altogether and you had better buy gasoline, for you will not get the chance to do so again. As you continue east across the Copper River, the roadbed suddenly narrows, changes to gravel, and shows increasing evidence of being exactly what it is: an abandoned railroad bed. The ties have been removed to make the going easier for cars, but each winter the frost still heaves up a few of the old spikes that once held rails and ties together. Locals will suggest that you check your spare tire before proceeding, lest one of these historical artifacts put a premature end to your journey.

You are on the McCarthy Road, which will carry you some 63 miles into the heart of the Wrangell Mountains. You will see few people or buildings along the way, but everywhere there are quiet indications that this corridor was once much busier than it is today. Despite its state of abandonment, the roadbed has obviously had great labor and capital expended upon it; although the countryside dips and rolls around you, the grade of the road is virtually a dead level, reflecting the engineering skill of its builders. At times decaying wooden trestles tower 50 or more feet above you, and you wonder who went to so much trouble to erect such structures in so remote a land. Your most exciting moment (some would say terrifying) is likely to come when the road crosses 283 feet above the gray-green waters of the Kuskulana River, on an eighty-year-old steel bridge that spans the narrow canyon with only the most casual of guardrails. That such a construction has survived the earthquakes and winter storms of three-quarters of a century is testimony to the care that went into building it. You can try to reassure yourself with this thought as you inch your car across it.

The McCarthy Road finally comes to an abrupt end at the foot of the Kennicott Glacier, where the dirty torrent emerging from beneath the ice has washed away all traces of the route. Your journey is still not over. Here you must leave your car behind and pull yourself across the river in a tiny hand-powered cable car suspended fifteen or twenty feet above the churning water. Once you've relocated the old railbed, it is a few hundred yards' walk to the village of McCarthy, where perhaps a dozen people still make their homes. You may want to pause before continuing, for the town is a rather haunting shadow of its former self. The streets have become little more than foot trails if you can find them at all beneath the dense foliage. Most of the buildings have not seen a coat of paint in half a century. More than a few are being actively reclaimed by the vegetation around them, as sagging roofs and collapsing walls return to the soil.

If you know the West, you have seen such abandonment before; it is all too familiar a place. As such, it conjures up the sorts of questions one often asks in the presence of romantic ruins. The people who built these empty structures, where did they come from? What sorts of lives did they lead, and why did they leave their homes in this sorry state? Why were they here, what did they do, where did they go? The solutions to such riddles lie like tracings in the landscape around you, for the past of these people is written in the marks they made upon this land.

To understand what happened to McCarthy, you must complete the final leg of your journey. The old railroad bed does not end here. It leads you yet another six miles north, skirting the edge of the vast

29

dirty glacier, to your ultimate destination: Kennecott. Here, so the story goes, Jack Smith and Clarence Warner wandered up the valley in August 1900 and spied on a high hillside an outcropping of malachite so green that they mistook it for grass to feed their horses.[1] In fact, it proved to be ore so pure that it assayed in at better than 70 percent copper, the richest vein the world has ever seen.[2]

If McCarthy impresses one mainly with its state of collapse, Kennecott gives an opposite impression. The buildings and equipment that formed the heart of this company town have survived remarkably intact. At the center of everything is the enormous crushing mill and leaching plant, a sprawling structure that hugs the hillside as it drops in a series of steps 180 feet down toward the valley floor. Ore entered the mill via a tramway descending from the peaks above and then dropped through ever finer crushers and sifters until it spilled out the bottom into ammonia vats, where it was readied for shipment.[3] The building's dozen or more stories reflect the multistaged refining process within, piled on top of each other in an oddly Gothic jumble like something out of a Charles Addams cartoon. The red walls and white window trims have faded, but one gets little feeling of decay or collapse. It is a ghost factory in a ghost town, yet its haunting could almost have begun yesterday. In the bunkhouse where the millmen slept and ate, linen is still on the beds, and plates are still on the cafeteria tables. Open account books lie scattered about the storerooms and offices, protected from decay only by the coldness of the northern climate. Even the machinery is remarkably well preserved: Lift the cover of the sifting mechanisms, and beautifully clear oil still bathes the gears with lubricant.

Kennecott was once one of the greatest copper milling centers in the world, yet its rise and fall spanned less than three decades. It began as the brainchild of Stephen Birch, a young mining engineer just out of Columbia University, though the money for its development soon came from people with names like Guggenheim and Morgan. Their Alaska Syndicate, initially capitalized at ten million dollars, finally grew to an investment more than ten times that amount.[4] Out of that money (and the labor it bought) came Kennecott's mines, crushing mill, company town, and railroad. The mines themselves, which were located 4,000 feet above the mill, eventually included 40 miles of underground tunnels, in rock so cold that the temperature at which men worked never rose more than a degree or two above freezing. An extensive network of aerial trams delivered ore to the mill, and the railroad then carried the concentrated product 196 miles to

Cordova on the south coast, where a fleet of company-owned steamships carried it on to Tacoma, Washington. The first shipment arrived in that city on April 14, 1911, and was valued at a quarter of a million dollars.[5] Over the next twenty-seven years Kennecott produced ore worth somewhere between two and three hundred million dollars, earning its owners approximately one hundred million dollars in profits.[6]

And then it ended. Like so many other western colonies, Kennecott's days of promise and abundance were numbered. The depressed markets of the 1930s knocked the bottom out of world copper prices at the same time that Kennecott's fabulously wealthy veins finally began to give out. By 1938 Kennecott Copper Company (founded after the Alaska Syndicate had reorganized in 1915) had closed its Alaskan mines and shifted operations to Utah, Chile, and other more promising sites. Almost overnight, the machinery at Kennecott fell silent. Within a few months the population of the area had dwindled to a mere handful of people, so that not much remained but the buildings, the piles of blue-green tailings, and the deserted railroad. The Kennecott boom was over, though the corporation it had spawned would outlive its namesake to become the largest copper producer in the world. On

The abandoned mill at Kennecott. *Courtesy of William Cronon.*

November 11, 1938, the last locomotive completed its run from Kennecott to the coast, leaving behind it an abandoned pair of rails leading to an abandoned pair of towns in a remote but extraordinarily beautiful Alaskan valley.[7]

What is one to make of this place and of the memories that lie so visibly on its landscape?

The thing that initially most strikes one about Kennecott is just how *western* it is. Despite its far northern location, nearly everything about it evokes the West. Its remote rocky valley, ringed by snow-capped peaks, could lie only on the sunset side of the Mississippi River. Although it inverts the dryness that characterizes large parts of the arid West, it shares with the rest of the region a more fundamental trait: a climate of extremes. It has too much cold, too much rain and snow, too much and too little sun to be mistaken for anywhere else on the continent. People living under these conditions must adopt very different survival strategies from those in the gentler East. Because the climate is so severe, relatively few people can live here. Even at the height of its mining operations, the population density of the valley was minuscule, with virtually all its inhabitants clustering in two towns and four mines. This distribution of people mimicked in miniature the West as a whole, where large cities remain separated by vast stretches of relatively empty land. In much the same way Kennecott's resource-extractive economy mimicked that of many other parts of the region. Finally, these ruins evoke one of the most familiar patterns of western settlement, the boom-and-bust economy that can create and destroy communities almost overnight. If one wanted a case study for thinking about environmental change in the West as a whole, one could do a lot worse than to make the long journey to Kennecott.

What happened at this place, and the way it became connected to the rest of the world, provide a classic study in the environmental history of western North America. In exploring Kennecott's changing environment, we ask questions that have a significance beyond this place, for they point to new ways of thinking about the West as a region, new ways of approaching environmental history in other times and other places.[8] In posing them, we seek to integrate three broad elements: the ecology of people as organisms sharing the universe with many other organisms, the political economy of people as social beings reshaping nature and one another to produce their collective life, and the cultural values of people as storytelling creatures struggling to find the meaning of their place in the world. Our goal in peering through these three lenses is to see how environmental change relates to other changes in human societies. The special task of environmental historians is to tell stories that carry us back and forth across the boundary between people and nature to reveal just how culturally constructed that boundary is—and how dependent upon natural systems it remains. As we seek to understand Kennecott, the questions we ask must show us the paths out of town—the connections between this lonely place and the rest of the world—for only by walking those paths can we reconnect this ghost community to the circumstances that created it.

One starting point, obviously, is the environment itself. It makes good sense to follow the geographer's lead and ask questions that map the natural features of the place called Kennecott. One looks at its climate to determine its temperatures (cold), its total precipitation (high), its annual growing season (short). One learns about its bedrock, its minerals, its soils. One identifies the plant species that make up its vegetation and the animal species that constitute its food chain. One gathers data about the microorganisms that infect the people and other creatures that live here. One maps out the flow of its rivers, the depth of its water table, the slopes of its topography, and all the other physical characteristics that might somehow be relevant to human life. The end product is a kind of atlas showing what is distinctive about the environment of this particular place.[9]

The chief danger in this approach is that it all too easily produces an endless accumulation of details with no order, no hierarchy, no analytical value beyond mere description. All too many regional histories and geographies, in the West and elsewhere, begin with a dry, dead chapter on "environment" that recites innumerable minutiae about climate, soil, and vegetation without the slightest indication of why they matter to history. Often they *don't* matter: the author forgets most of them as soon as the chapter is over, never bothering to explore their relevance to the rest of the narrative. The bankruptcy of such an approach should be self-evident. The chief innovation of environmental history has been to assert that discussions of natural context cannot be relegated to an isolated chapter but must be integral to the human history of which they are so fundamental a part.

Cataloging the environment, then, is only the beginning of our work. The deeper task is to connect it to the people who live within it. To do so, we might simply ask what those people eat. The food we put in our mouths, digest in our intestines, and excrete back into the environment is one of our most intimate ties to the natural world. Much of our social life is devoted to acquiring and consuming it. Our survival depends on it. Every article of food reaches our stomachs via a different route, and is thus a kind of pathway—out of town and back into nature—for an environmental historian to trace. Ecologists speak much of the energy flows and nutrient cycles that define an ecosystem, and these apply no less powerfully to human societies. Energy and nutrition are what food is all about. But because people inhabit cultures as well as ecosystems, the choice of what to eat has as much to do with filling the soul as with filling the gut. Two different communities inhabiting the same ecosystem can make radically different choices about which parts of it will enter their stomachs. In so doing, they say much about who they are and what they believe.

Take, for instance, the native people who inhabited the Copper River watershed before Kennecott ever existed. Called the Ahtnas—after the Russian name for the river itself—they relied entirely on local plants and animals for their survival.[10] Salmon, caribou, and ground squirrels were among their most important foodstuffs. But to describe such creatures only as "food" would be to miss their most vital qualities, for they were also fellow beings who shared a complex moral universe with the people who hunted them. Long ago, in myth time, there had been no boundary between people and animals, so that beings could shift form from human to raven to fish and back again as suited their purposes.[11] "Once all was man," the Ahtna storytellers said, and their tales of those former times reminded children of the essential qualities that people and animals shared with one another.[12]

Even now the animals still had great power. They understood human speech and were always watching from just beyond the edges of the camp to see whether people were acting as they should. To understand the Ahtnas' environment—and the environment of most native peoples in North America—one has to see it as they did, as a moral space inhabited by spiritual beings. The forest was everywhere alive with eyes, all of them watching.[13] "Good luck" and "bad luck" were no mere superstitions in such a place; rather, they defined success or failure in the hunt, which in turn marked the boundary between survival and death. One could kill and eat animals, but only after properly thanking them for acquiescing in their own deaths. Some were so powerful that to harm them at all brought great peril. Wolves, for instance, were among the greatest of animal hunters, and it was dangerous even to touch their tracks in the snow. If anyone was foolish enough to kill a wolf, the resulting bad luck was so strong that one would never kill anything else again. Unless one atoned for the death with a great gift to the animal, one would die a slow death oneself—by starvation.[14]

Death by hunger is, of course, not merely a spiritual event but a profoundly material one. The Ahtnas had good reason to worry about it. For them, the threat of starvation was an annual affair. This suggests further questions we need to ask even about more forgiving environments. Any geographical description, no matter how static, can be set in motion by asking, "How does this place *cycle?*"[15] As the planet rotates on its axis, how does the life of the day differ from that of the night? As the earth revolves around the sun, how does the flux of solar energy shift from month to month? During what period is life most exuberantly abundant, and for how long does the local world slumber in the winter cold? Most critically, at what time of year is sheer survival most at risk, and how do people respond to the dangers they face?

The Ahtnas dealt with the extreme seasonal cycling of their ecosystem in several ways. For one thing, they kept their total population very low, no more than a few hundred people in the entire Copper River valley south of Chitina. In the seventy-mile stretch of country between Chitina and Kennecott, perhaps thirty individuals made their homes.[16] Even this small group could not always live together, for during the worst winter months the food supply was too sparse to feed so many people. The Ahtnas solved this difficulty by regularly shifting locations and changing the size of their settlements. Like most people and animals, they also stored surplus food to use when nature's larder would be nearly empty. In spring they lived in relatively large, permanent villages along the banks of rivers where they could fish the salmon runs, drying and storing their catch for later use. Toward midsummer they headed upslope to smaller meat camps where they could trap and hunt everything from caribou to squirrels. Fall found them back at their larger village sites to eat the stored salmon they had cached earlier in the year.

But the annual flow of solar energy is weak in Alaska, and even animals have difficulty storing enough summer fat in their bodies to make it through the long dark winter. Human beings faced the same problem, and their success or failure depended on that of the animals. By January or February Ahtna food caches usually began to give out and families were forced to disperse once again in search of whatever food remained. Late winter was always the hardest of times. If luck was good—if people were scrupulous in attending to their rituals and

35

if the animals were generous in their gifts—a small band could capture enough ground squirrels and the occasional emaciated moose to make it through the winter without great suffering. If not, starvation was a constant possibility. In 1828 the winter failure of the caribou herds brought death to more than one hundred natives in the Copper River valley.[17] When Lieutenant Henry Allen made the first American exploration through this country, during the late winter of 1885, he found hungry native families scrounging for food wherever he went. Allen's own group, dizzy with hunger and barely able to crawl, was eventually reduced to eating rotten moose meat, which they consumed as eagerly as the starving natives. As one member of the expedition reported, "it tasted good, maggots and all."[18]

Not just food is affected by the seasonal cycling of the ecosystem. Virtually everything a human community does—its shelter, its clothing, its work, its rituals—reflects the wheel of the seasons. An environmental historian needs to track each of these elements and reconstruct their connections to the natural world. Take travel, for instance. Alaska's peculiar climate and soils make it extremely difficult to move through the interior during spring and fall, when mud, floods, and unreliable ice encourage everyone to stay at home. (In this it has much in common with other parts of the West; migrants on the famed Oregon and California trails faced many of the same seasonal problems.) Alaskan travel is easiest when rivers are open and not so flooded that boat travel becomes too dangerous, or in deep winter, when the rivers are frozen and can serve as highways for sled travel. This meant that groups like the Ahtnas could make extended journeys only at well-defined times of the year. When Lieutenant Allen set out from the mouth of the Copper River, traders there were expecting upstream natives to appear any day with their winter fur catch, taking advantage of the last reliable ice before the river broke up and travel became impossible.[19]

Allen himself faced the same challenge. He and his men began their journey with nearly half a ton of supplies but quickly learned that there was no way to move so heavy a burden on sleds across the unreliable snow and ice of the March landscape. Within three days of starting, they had jettisoned nearly half their load. All that remained in the way of food were 150 pounds of flour, 100 pounds of beans, 40 pounds of rice, two sides of bacon, 15 pounds of tea, and small quantities of beef extract, deviled ham, and chocolate.[20] The list of provisions is ecologically suggestive, for there is nothing Alaskan about it. Allen's food quickly gave out, so that he and his men soon found themselves, as Alaskans said, "living upon the country," but his original intention had been to survive on the stored food he had imported from Outside.[21] This in turn opens up a profoundly important set of questions for environmental history and the history of the West.

Living upon the country or importing from Outside: These are the two most basic human choices about how to live in a particular place. From the many objects and organisms around them, people identify a certain subset as "resources," things to be drawn into the human community and turned to useful ends. Some become food, some are burned for warmth, some are fabricated into clothing and tools, some serve as markers of wealth and status, some express beauty, some become holy, and most become a mixture of these things. Asking how people partition an ecosystem into a resource base shows us the boundaries they draw between useful and useless things. Just so do they define a unique human place in nature, a unique way of being in the world.

Some of these resources are of interest to more than just local people. Among the many human actions that produce environmental change, few are more important than trade. When people exchange things in their immediate vicinity for things that can only be obtained elsewhere, they impose a new set of meanings on the local landscape and connect it to a wider world. In so doing, they invent what one might call new paths out of town. These increase the chance that the local environment will begin to change in response to outside forces, so that trade becomes a powerful new source of ecological change.

When transport systems and markets are limited, the resources that enter into them and travel farthest tend to be light, low in bulk, and highly valuable. It is no accident that early trade networks in many parts of the globe concentrated on spices, rare foods, precious metals, and furs. This was true throughout the West—one finds salt, coffee, alcohol, gold, and skins being traded everywhere—and it was true in the subarctic North.[22] Natives from interior Alaska exchanged furs and fish with natives in coastal areas long before Europeans ever visited the region, thereby linking the resources of two broad ecological zones.[23] Such exchanges were not necessarily peaceful. Coastal Chugach Eskimos from time to time made raiding expeditions nearly to the source of the Copper River to pillage Ahtna settlements, rob food caches, and kidnap women.[24] Viewed ecologically, raids and conflicts of this sort often express many of the same values that underpin trade.

Although these "exchanges" might link communities hundreds of miles apart, native trade and its ecological consequences were limited because goods could move only in packs, sleds, or boats. When the Russians arrived in their sailing craft and sought to purchase furs, they pulled Alaska into a much larger Eurasian market.[25] This meant that a certain share of Alaska's resources—particularly its fur-bearing mammals—began to be extracted from the region and shipped half-way around the planet to meet the demands of people with dramatically different cultural needs. Russian and native traders started operating along the coast and throughout interior Alaska. In response, the Ahtna made regular excursions to the mouth of the Copper River, traveling in boats made of caribou skins, which they dismantled, tanned, and sold after arriving at the trading post.[26]

The ecological implications of such encounters were by no means simple. The Russian demand for furs no doubt encouraged natives to kill animals for different purposes than before, putting new population pressures on species that were now being exported from the local ecosystem. A new market-oriented logic began to exist side by side with the older gift-giving rituals that previously characterized native relations with animals. But such changes were rarely absolute. Natives managed to respond to market demands without abandoning their older spiritual relationships with the world around them.[27] As long as the fur trade depended for its work force solely on the small local population, hunting pressure on animals remained limited in scale.

This was less true on the coast. There marine mammals had special vulnerabilities that meant they could be exploited in much more intensive ways. Unlike other ocean dwellers, marine mammals had to breathe, opening themselves to human attack each time they surfaced for air. More important, several species—especially seals and sea otters—spent key periods of their reproductive cycles in coastal rookeries, where cows and calves could escape the attacks of predators. There they were easily slaughtered in the thousands by any human hunters who had clubs and the will to use them. To create that will, the Russians conquered native populations on the coast, especially the Aleuts, and reorganized them into a mobile labor force capable of exploiting seals and sea otters at levels far beyond their natural reproductive rates. By quite early in the nineteenth century market hunting was devastating marine mammals.[28]

Trade linked the resources of one ecosystem with the human demands of another. Alaskan villages that had no sugar, alcohol, or tobacco obtained such things by trading with communities that had no furs. The net result was to redefine the resources of the Alaskan landscape, pushing them beyond the needs of local subsistence into the realm of the market, where any good could be transformed into any other. At the same time the act of economic consumption came to be increasingly separated from the place of ecological production, distancing people from the consequences of their own acts and desires. A kind of alienation from nature was the almost inevitable result.

In many parts of the world, one element in this process was simple population density. Trade redefined ecosystems by moving resources from places with few people to places with many. Certainly this happened in most parts of the American West. Natives of the Copper River valley had lived in relative balance with their fellow organisms partly because their numbers were small, and stayed so because a larger population would very likely have starved by winter's end. Local game animals were not likely to suffer serious depletion as long as they helped limit human numbers. Providing fur coats to the citizens of Moscow or Peking or New York City, on the other hand, was an entirely different matter. Wild game populations could hardly help failing in the face of such demand.

But population density by itself is almost never an adequate explanation for environmental change, for it leads willy-nilly to the much more complicated riddle of *why* human beings number as they do. Any environmental history must inevitably touch upon this question, if only implicitly. The answer has partly to do with the natural abundance of the ecosystem but has even more to do with social organization and political economy. Farming folk tend to be more numerous than hunting and gathering folk the world over. When farmers produce more food than they themselves consume, they can support individuals and groups that do not raise their own food. The result is not just greater human numbers but more elaborate human hierarchies. Agriculture thus supports the rise of cities, supplying their dense nonfarming populations with imported food. Although we too easily tend to forget this fact, every urban culture also farms. Industrial revolutions presuppose agricultural ones, so that city and country grow together.

Kennecott and the American West are hardly the places to explore human social evolution writ large, but they did supply distant cities whose inhabitants rarely gave a second thought to their existence. The process of linking sparsely populated regions with densely populated ones has been central to the entire course of western history. It takes little effort to write the history of the frontier West as a story of peripheral areas becoming ever more integrated into an urban-industrial economy. Because city dwellers were fed by an agricultural system that they themselves controlled and because they could look to so many different parts of the world to supply themselves, their needs were in no way limited by their local ecosystem. Indeed, no one place was essential to their survival, for they could always use their wealth and capital to look elsewhere if the resources of any one place began to run out. The same was true of frontier agriculture: If farmers exhausted the soil, they could move on to greener pastures and start again. The result was a dynamic, unstable system that constantly threatened to push beyond the limits of the ecosystems that supported it.

The story of Kennecott is a classic case in point. When Lieutenant Allen visited the area in 1885, the natives showed him copper knives, bullets, and jewelry, all of local manufacture. The Ahtna chief Nicolai explained that he and his people made these things from nuggets in a local river and that he knew of a vein of ore high above his settlement that he would be happy to show to his visitors after the snow melted. Ahtna villages had been trading copper goods south to the coast for generations.[29] Although the local Indians clearly regarded their copper as valuable and depended on it for trade, their uses for it were limited. Weapons, tools, and jewelry were all they made with it, so their demand for the metal was considerably smaller than the supply. What made copper valuable was the human labor and skill that fashioned it into useful objects. The raw metal itself had much less intrinsic value, so the Ahtnas could afford to be generous in sharing it. "I do not believe," wrote Allen, "that the natives guard as a secret treasure the copper or other mineral beds, but think they would willingly reveal to the white man their knowledge in the matter."[30]

Allen, of course, saw the veins of blue-green ore with different eyes. For him, they had greater intrinsic value, for a reason that would have meant nothing to Nicolai: copper's ability to conduct electricity. The culture Allen represented was discovering a new need for this ability, and so began to draw Nicolai's world into its orbit. Allen's party embarked on its journey just as an increasing number of American prospectors were scouring the area for gold, a mineral they valued so highly that it could attract immigrants far in excess of the local ecosystem's ability to feed them. Already the increased numbers of people, armed with rifles and other weapons, were putting new pressure on local game species. In 1884 an army officer had issued clothing to natives on the Copper River because "it was quite plain to the casual observer that the immigration of so many white people into the Copper River Valley meant the driving out of the greater part of the large game. . . ."[31] The long-term consequence was the same in the Copper River valley as in so many other parts of the West: Game disappeared.[32]

Conflict seemed likely under such circumstances, and the army, remembering what had happened ten years before at Little Bighorn, was careful to make plans for winning any violent encounter that might occur. This was why Lieutenant Allen had been sent on his journey. The orders authorizing his expedition bluntly predicted that "the conflicting interests between the white people and the Indians of the Territory may in the near future result in serious disturbances between the two races. . . ."[33] Allen's assignment was to explore what might be called the military ecology of the region. If the army invaded, it would bring a massive human influx to the region. Such a force would face the same choice as any other human population—living upon the country or importing from Outside—so army officials asked Allen to report on the local food sources and outside supply lines that would feed the troops.[34] Although the Ahtna had heretofore been entirely peaceful in their dealings with Americans, the United States was planning for violence. It was an old frontier story. One way or another, an invasion was in the offing.

The ecological nature of Allen's reconnaissance is best suggested by the order that directed him to pay special attention to any grass species he encountered along the way. "You will examine," his superior told him, "especially as to the kind and extent of the native grasses, and ascertain if animals ordinarily used in military operations can be subsisted and made of service there."[35] Did the Copper River valley contain enough grass to feed soldiers' horses? On the basis of their experiences elsewhere in the West, Allen's superiors were asking shrewd ecological questions, which historians would do well to emulate. Every human community depends for survival on its relationships with other species. If people migrate to a new location, other species do too. These in turn have all sorts of unexpected effects on ecosystems in which they gain a foothold.

The introduction of alien plants, animals, and diseases is one of the fundamental stories of environmental history throughout the American West. Although the process was more limited in Alaska than elsewhere because of its harsh climates and soils, migration went on even in the Far North. The most famous instance in the nineteenth century was Sheldon Jackson's effort to encourage Eskimos living on the Bering Strait to start raising Siberian reindeer as a substitute for

Alaskan caribou. Good missionary that he was, Jackson saw the reindeer as a way of introducing natives not just to a replacement source of food, but to a new pastoral way of life that would be more conducive to the Christian religion he sought to promote, proving again the intimate linkage of environment, economy, and cultural belief systems.[36]

Most such introductions, however, occurred without the help of self-conscious missionaries like Jackson. When a Euroamerican community did finally develop at Kennecott, residents managed to supply part of their food needs with the alien species they brought with them. Inger Jensen Ricci, who spent her childhood in the town, remembered how her parents supplemented family meals with cabbages, onions, and turnips from a backyard garden. The Jensens kept chickens so as to have fresh eggs and raised rabbits for fresh meat.[37] These mimicked in a small way the much more extensive migration of agricultural species in the West as a whole. But the Jensens' garden was hardly a farm. It contributed only a small share of the family's food because Kennecott's climate and terrain were poorly suited to the meat and grain crops of a typical American diet. The only viable alternative was for residents to import food from Outside.

The problem was how to do so. Lieutenant Allen's hardships in traveling across the Alaskan terrain demonstrated that no large-scale military movements were likely to be successful there, and none in fact ever took place. Instead, it was Nicolai's copper that finally brought a Euroamerican invasion to the region, enabling Outsiders to build a railroad that overcame the seasonal mud and ice of Alaskan travel to supply an urban-industrial colony by the side of the Kennicott Glacier. Fifteen years after Allen had visited the area, prospectors finally staked a claim to the blue-green vein that the Ahtna chief had described. In so doing, they introduced a new legal definition of property to the valley. Before Kennecott's copper could be used, before it could tempt anyone to pour millions of dollars into its development, it had first to be *owned*. Nicolai and his people claimed important rights of occupancy to the lands around their villages and when necessary defended them against intruders. But their shifting settlement patterns, and their reliance on the hunt, left them little concerned about drawing sharp property boundaries upon the landscape. When Jack Smith and Clarence Warner filed their claim to the copper vein that eventually became the Bonanza Mine, they had in mind a completely different way of owning and occupying the terrain. And therein lay the origin of the community called Kennecott.

Another group of questions about environmental history, then, has to do with property. How do people imagine they own the land and creatures around them? How does their legal system express this sense of ownership, and what consequences does it have for the environment? The legal history of the western economy, particularly as regards property, remains a largely unexplored field, badly in need of more theoretically sophisticated studies that will place the law in its cultural and ecological context.[38] Law is the foundation on which property rests and is therefore the formal expression of a community's relationship to nature.[39]

Kennecott came into being through a wide variety of legal mechanisms. Land laws enabled prospectors to claim ownership rights over any resources they "found." Laws of bankruptcy and limited liability allowed the Kennecott Copper Company to come into being and protected its owners from the full consequences of their actions. Contract laws governed trade and established the rules whereby managers and laborers worked together. Tort laws defined responsibility for accidents or environmental damages. Together they created a series of relationships between land and community that broke radically with the gift-giving spirituality of the Ahtnas. The law defined political and economic power in the West and is crucial to any systematic understanding of environmental change in the region.

Because Stephen Birch's Alaska Syndicate was able to buy up the legal rights to subsurface copper in the mountains above Kennecott, the company's owners knew they could sell and profit from that copper if only they could bring it to market. Toward that end they invested millions of dollars in the mining technology that brought ore out of the ground, the processing technology that purified it, and the transport technology that delivered it to the smelters where it finally became a commodity that people would buy. Collectively these technologies—along with the mineral in the ground and the money paid to workers—became the company's capital, which would henceforth determine the fate of the town it had called into being.[40] The story is familiar to every mining community in every part of the American West.

Capital invested at Kennecott was driven by outside forces that had nothing to do with the local community or ecosystem of the Copper River valley. The syndicate's profits required it to earn the best rate of return on its investments. Those who capitalized the town knew from the beginning that its key resource would eventually be extracted so completely as to destroy the community's raison d'être.

43

They could do this because their own survival in no way depended on conserving Kennecott's resources for the long run. Quite the contrary. Unlike the hunter-gatherer communities that preceded them, the owners of Kennecott had little interest in maintaining a self-sustaining relation to their resource base. Once it was used up, they could simply throw the remnants away.

In the Copper River valley a human population that depended almost entirely on the local landscape was invaded by a population that depended virtually not at all on that landscape. The same process happened to varying degrees throughout the nonagricultural West. Because the railroad liberated Kennecott's miners from the seasonal food cycles of the local ecosystem, it permitted a much denser and more sedentary population to live there. Kennecott's inhabitants lived in Alaska by converting copper into cash. Market hunters might shoot wild game in the surrounding valleys, but the residents of Kennecott and McCarthy purchased their meat in local butcher shops without ever encountering the animals whose flesh they ate. Local gardens might yield onions, turnips, cabbages, and other northern produce, but such crops mainly supplemented a more southerly diet of rail-borne fish, grain, and meat from distant ports and farms.

Historians writing about the past of any particular western place would do well to remember that its history is tied to many other regions undergoing parallel changes at the same time. The canned salmon that Kennecott's workers consumed in their cafeteria presupposed the prior development of a commercial fishery along the Pacific coast and the creation of dozens of packing plants scattered up and down the Alaskan shoreline.[41] The bread they ate came to them via Seattle from the vast agricultural areas of Washington and Oregon, where family farms followed the time-honored frontier practice of selling wheat—much as the mine owners sold copper—to buy supplies from the metropolitan economy.[42] The coffee that the miners drank, and the sugar they used to sweeten it, reflected a broader international trade with tropical areas far to the south, each of which was undergoing its own peculiar encounter with the forces of capital and empire.[43] Interregional trade networks such as these had been part of frontier history right from the beginning. Each trade linkage was also a new interface between ecosystems in remote parts of the world, and each raises possible lines of investigation—new paths out of town—for environmental historians seeking to place the history of the American West in its larger context.[44]

But what of the smaller context? Kennecott was not simply the end of a trade route; it was also a world in its own right, a place where people made homes for themselves. Questions on a different scale suggest themselves here. Once people have chosen to call a place home, how do they arrange their lives within it? How does the physical form of their community reflect their relationships to each other and to the natural world? The shifting settlements of the Ahtnas responded to natural cycles of abundance and scarcity but also reflected the Ahtnas' sense that certain social groups should try to stick together. When a large summer village broke down into smaller camps, it did so along clearly defined lines of kinship, gender, and authority. Access to resources, political power, participation in rituals: all followed a carefully codified set of rules that expressed themselves as spatial patterns.[45]

The same was true of Kennecott. Complex boundaries of class, gender, and ethnicity produced an intricate social geography between the mines on the ridgetops, the processing mill in the valley, and the private town of McCarthy at the foot of the glacier. Most ridgetop inhabitants were single men, wage employees of the company, who lived in bunkhouses where the ordinary domestic activities of eating, playing, and sleeping took place in an unusually public setting. Few of the men had families, and turnover was high. Miners came from widely different ethnic backgrounds and did not always speak the same language. Under such circumstances, "community" was a tenuous thing, defined partly by the corporation and partly in opposition to the corporation.

Mapping out the geography of gender, class, race, and ethnicity remains one of the most important but least studied aspects of environmental history. More questions to answer: Why do people live where they do? How do they declare their differences from one another in the locations and forms of their homes? How do their dealings with one another and with nature reflect their positions in society? What does it mean to be a single man in this place? A married woman? A middle-class child? A person of color? An immigrant who speaks no English? A tourist? How do the many categories into which people divide themselves define the ways they experience and affect the landscape? Who has power over whom in this place, and how does the land reflect that power?

In the Alaskan copper region a clear class hierarchy overlapped with gender to create the very different communities of Kennecott, McCarthy, and the mines. The mines were entirely male and working-class, save for the few foremen and managers—also male—who

45

directed the mining process. The male world of the mines was matched by the more female world of McCarthy, although even there men constituted the larger share of the population. McCarthy was a "private" town, independent of the copper company, and it existed mainly as a market for the men on the ridgetops. A few miners had wives in McCarthy and conducted their family lives at long distance on an irregular cycle of meetings; the children of such unions might see their fathers only rarely. The rest of the miners visited McCarthy as well, but their relationships to the women of the town had a more commercial flavor. Sex and affection were usually filtered through the markets of the saloon and brothel. McCarthy had a middle class of store owners and their wives, but its customers made it a working-class town in which single men and women were a disproportionate share of the population.

This was less true of Kennecott, which residents knew simply as "camp." Camp had little to offer the miners, who rarely even stopped there on the trip down to McCarthy. Camp did not feel like nearly so working-class a place as McCarthy or the mines. The millworkers were single men much like the miners on the ridgetops, but they were more highly paid and had a higher status. More important, camp was where the company's manager and superintendent lived. They, along with the doctor, teachers, nurses, and office workers, constituted the highest social class in the community. They had a separate dining hall for themselves and were provided with all the appurtenances of middle-class life: comfortable single-family houses with leather furniture, fine china, silver service, wall hangings, and other markers of elite status. Somewhat below them in rank were the various foremen who oversaw the operations of the mill, but they too got houses that set them apart from the wageworkers in the bunkhouses.

The consequences of this class hierarchy were manifold. In Kennecott, to be working-class was to be single and male. To be a woman or child, on the other hand, was to be middle-class—very different from the situation in McCarthy. Women and children lived in the one-family dwellings that Americans saw as the ideal environment for middle-class life; indeed, children were told to stay away from the working-class bunkhouses "for fear of exposure to the hardened life."[46] Then again, even the middle class had gradations; not all single-family dwellings were equal in status. The less desirable ones were a steep walk up the hillside next to the mill and did not have indoor plumbing. They had running water only until pipes froze in winter, whereupon a family had to carry its water in pails until spring. Only those

in the most elegant buildings—and the workers in the bunkhouses—
had the luxury of indoor toilets. Everyone else used outhouses. As
Inger Jensen Ricci remembered it, "camp had a very definite class
distinction."[47]

Not surprisingly, camp's relation to the surrounding environment was very different from that of Nicolai's village. The whole point
of this community, after all, was to carve a maze of tunnels beneath
the slopes where men in heavy woolen clothing wearing carbide lamps
worked in a constant icy fog to extract ore from the mountains' heart.
Other than copper, little in the local ecosystem was essential to Kennecott's survival. Nature therefore became what it was for many other
urban Americans: a place of outdoor recreation, in stark contrast with
the mines' underground place of work. One symbol of this was the
cantilevered tennis court perched on the hillside above camp, where
those who had permission were allowed to play. (Unfortunately the
mosquitoes became such a problem for the players that the court finally
had to be covered over with netting.) Inger's father went hunting and
maintained a trapline, but more as a hobby than anything else. He
was an amateur taxidermist who enjoyed stuffing animals in his spare
time—not something the Ahtnas would have thought to do with their
animal neighbors. Some miners made a practice of drifting back and
forth between underground wage work and "living upon the country"
by hunting for part of the year, but most middle-class excursions from
camp were more for play than anything else. Berry-picking time was
a great favorite of the children, though the food it added to family
tables was hardly a necessity of life. Come summer, families took their
children on holiday to Long Lake, a modest middle-class tent resort
about a dozen miles down the railroad from McCarthy. There, they
could get out into "nature"—not the nature of the Ahtna hunters, but
a nature of genteel leisure and romantic retreat, far from the noisy
industrial world of Kennecott. It was as if a little bit of the Adiron-
dacks had been transplanted to the Far North.

In the end, the abstract questions we ask about environmental
history resolve themselves into small human actions at very particular
times and places: Ahtna hunters setting aside caribou meat as an offering by the fire, miners digging copper in frozen tunnels, middle-class
families fishing by a lake. It is the details that matter. Imagine Inger
Jensen as a ten-year-old Kennecott child out for a sunny walk along
the railroad tracks to gather mountain cranberries so her mother could
make pie—perhaps using an old Scandinavian recipe—as dessert for
the family's dinner table.[48] Then imagine an Ahtna girl doing much

the same thing just a few years before—gathering the same favorite berry because it ripens so late in the year and stores so well through the winter months that it will still be nutritious when the snow melts, still provide color for dyes, still be useful as a medicine against sore throats and colds.[49] Two children, both gathering food, both enjoying their useful play. Imagine the differences between them. Imagine their worlds.

Big questions, small answers.

The story of how Kennecott became a twentieth-century ghost town suggests much about the environmental history of the West. Like so many other historical sites in the region, what happened at Kennecott found its roots in the depths of the earth. Without the chalcocite and malachite that had concentrated copper in the fissures of Kennecott's dolomite, the human past of this place would have been entirely different. And yet the mere existence of these minerals did not in and of itself determine the events that took place here. Far from it.

For large-scale exploitation of Kennecott's copper to occur, a human community organized on an entirely different basis had first to find it. Before chalcocite and malachite could become significant "determinants" of human history, electricity had to be discovered as a form of energy capable of being transmitted over copper wire. Economic demand for electricity required that it have some practical application, so that the invention of electric lights, motors, and telecommunication devices went hand in hand with electrical generating stations in fostering the market for an inexpensive base metal capable of wiring them together. Just as necessary was the concentration of human populations into cities where economies of scale for the first time made it possible to sell lights, telephones, electricity—and therefore copper—at a profit.

To realize such profits, there had to be still other conditions. The community had to have people interested in reading past the ordinary hours of daylight and workers whose factories no longer closed at sunset or depended on belts and shafts for their primary power transmission. Scientists had to understand enough about geography, geology, and chemistry to know where copper occurred and how to extract it. Transportation systems had to be able to move heavy, low-priced metals cheaply over great distances from western mines to urban markets. Food supplies had to come from an agricultural system capable of moving foodstuffs to mines that were otherwise incapable of feeding themselves. And not least, the economy required the capitalist social relations and corporations capable of mobilizing immense amounts of wealth to assemble the workers and equipment without which copper could neither be mined, turned into wire, nor installed in houses, offices, and factories.

Kennecott's emergence as a great copper-mining complex in the first two decades of the twentieth century was thus neither a historical accident nor a case of geographical determinism. At no prior moment in the history of the West would it have been possible for capitalists in New York to hire engineers and workers in Alaska to construct a railroad, mine, and crushing mill deep in the interior of that remote territory so that the nation's cities could purchase a metal they hardly knew they needed just half a century before. A particular vein of a particular mineral created an opportunity, and a particular culture with particular social and technical needs then seized that opportunity for its own purposes. Kennecott thus emerges as a near-perfect example of the environmental processes that scholars of western history most need to study and understand.[50]

The mills at the end of the old railroad bed now stand silent, and the buildings are finally beginning to lean at crazy angles as the glacial

The face of Kennecott. *Courtesy of William Cronon.*

49

till gradually shifts beneath them. The people who erected this vast complex inserted themselves into the local ecosystem, built a community, transformed the local economy, and extracted the only resource that mattered to them on behalf of urban markets thousands of miles away. Kennecott exists because a myriad of historical forces joined together to reshape the hillsides above a dirty glacier in an obscure Alaskan valley. It was called into being at the behest of such forces, and it was turned into a ghost town in much the same way. Its copper was used up, demand declined, markets disappeared, and there was no longer any reason to maintain so remote and expensive a colony in so cold and northern a place. And so, overnight, like so many western ghost towns before it, it all shut down.

The story, of course, does not quite end there. There is still the long drive over the abandoned railroad bed on which you began your journey to this place, and the reason you yourself bothered to come at all. Curiously, these too are among the central questions of environmental history in the American West. Your very presence is proof that Kennecott remains a kind of colony attached in a new but not altogether unfamiliar way to the outside world. The old mill now lies within the bounds of Wrangell-St. Elias National Park, the largest such park in the entire United States. The property has been deeded over to the federal government (though the corporation still retains subsurface rights to the copper—just in case). The old railroad bed has lost its ties, so that tourists can travel the seventy-odd miles from Chitina, across the Kuskulana River Bridge, by cable car across the river, and by foot from McCarthy to the red mills of Kennecott, to see this symbol of abandoned industrialism within one of the largest "wilderness" areas of the continent.

That this wilderness is honeycombed with underground tunnels, pockmarked by blue-green piles of tailings, and still shows traces of aerial tramways leading from mines to mills, hardly matters to the backpackers and mountain climbers who visit it today. For them, escapees from an urban world who are willing to pay dearly to travel to the outer edges of civilization, this place has become a symbol of romantic decay in the midst of deep wilderness. Your journey here has more than a little in common with the trip Kennecott families once made to the tent resort on Long Lake in their efforts to get away from town and closer to nature. As you scramble about the ruins of the place, admiring the icy sublimity of the mountains and reflecting on the more ambiguous beauty of the mill, you would do well to place yourself as one of the figures in this ghost landscape. You too are part of its environmental history, bringing with you—even as a reader—assumptions about nature and humanity that have led you to choose this particular place as the object of some desire. The paths out of town have brought you to Kennecott on the very road that once created it to send copper to the outside world. The end of the journey is also its beginning: in the wilderness that is culture's creature, the place where nature and history have met and turned, and turned again.

To Hear an Old Voice

Rediscovering Native Americans in American History

GEORGE MILES

On his sixteenth day out of St. Joseph, Missouri, as he traveled west of Salt Lake City on his way to the silver mines of Virginia City, Nevada, at the start of the Civil War, Mark Twain came upon a band of Gosiute Indians. Twain, who proclaimed himself "a worshipper of the Red Man," declared the encounter a great disappointment. Instead of the articulate, "scholarly savages" about whom he had read in Cooper, he found the Gosiutes "a silent, sneaking, treacherous looking race, taking note of everything, covertly, like all the other 'Noble Red Men' that we (do not) read about, and betraying no sign in their countenances." After some reflection Twain decided that he had been misled, the the sinister silence of the Gosiutes typified all Indians and that "wherever one finds an Indian tribe he has only found Goshoots more or less modified by circumstance and surroundings—but Goshoots, after all." For Twain, the Gosiutes' inability or unwillingness to communicate became a sign and proof of the subhuman and irredeemable condition of all Indians.[1]

The silent Indian is a familiar image in American culture. Sometimes, as in Maynard Dixon's 1912 oil painting *What an Indian Thinks*, in which a solitary Indian peers across a majestic desert scene, or in the late 1960s antilittering campaign in which an Indian cries silently by the side of a trash-covered highway, the image carries positive connotations of quiet nobility. Frequently, however, the image conveys a message similar to Twain's, of the Indian as inarticulate and unknowable, as someone destined to be excluded forever from civilized discourse.

Working a century after Twain and in a different medium, another American entertainer and social critic, Robert Altman, attempted to reshape our image of the uncommunicative Indian. In *Buffalo Bill and the Indians, or Sitting Bull's History Lesson*, Altman proposed that Indians are not so much silent as silenced. In the film, which is a fictional account based loosely on the single season Sitting Bull toured with the Wild West Show, Altman depicts the Sioux leader as a dignified man who quietly suffers the insults of Cody and his associates because he has dreamed that as a member of the show he will meet the president and deliver a plea on behalf of his people. When the opportunity presents itself, however, a pretentious, bureaucratic president refuses to allow Sitting Bull to speak and insists that he must talk only to the agent at his reservation.

Altman skewers politicians for their callous indifference to Indians, but the film's subtitle suggests that he is seeking bigger game. His principal targets are mythmakers who justify the conduct of politicians by distorting the past. Throughout the film he depicts Cody and his partner Nate Salsbury as popular historians, men creating a story of the past to tell America. They want Sitting Bill to play a crucial part in their tale, but he refuses to accept the caricature they assign him. After Sitting Bull dies at Wounded Knee, Cody encounters his spirit in a vision. Still angry that Sitting Bull would not cooperate with his plans, Cody complains, "You ain't even the right image." Yet Cody understands the tension between the reality that he and Sitting Bull lived and the story he wants to peddle. Contemplating his own image in an oversize portrait that hangs above his desk, he wonders aloud why everyone has taken him for a king. In the end Cody embraces the myth. As the movie concludes, he stages a show in which he, as Buffalo Bill, confronts and kills a dangerous, savage Sitting Bull. In his own way the mythmaker silences the Indian as effectively as any political bureaucrat.[2]

Historians and other scholars may feel comfortably removed from the criticism that Altman directs at the purveyors of popular culture. After all, the last three decades have seen Native American history grow as rapidly as any field in American history. Working together, historians and anthropologists have created an important journal, *Ethnohistory*, and a major research center, the D'Arcy McNickle Center for the History of the American Indian at the Newberry Library, and have written scores of award-winning essays and books about Indian history and culture. But the past quarter century has also brought disappointments for students of the Native American experience. In his essay "Some Thoughts on Colonial Historians and American Indians,"[3] James Merrell points out that although ethnohistorians have made numerous valuable discoveries about Native Americans and their role in American history, they have enjoyed little success in persuading colleagues in colonial history to revise their image of Native Americans or to integrate them within their general studies. Furthermore, Merrell suggests, the impact of ethnohistory on American history seems to be waning. Whereas in the 1970s books like Gary Nash's *Red, White, and Black* and Edmund Morgan's *American Slavery, American Freedom* incorporated the latest scholarship on Native Americans in their exploration of the colonial origins of the American nation, the 1980s saw Bernard Bailyn explicitly reject the inclusion of the Native American experience in *The Peopling of British North America*.[4]

Merrell focuses on colonial history, but a similar tale can be told about western history. Although scholars have written important tribal and topical histories as well as major interpretive essays about western Native Americans, most authors of regional and general histories of the West have failed to integrate Native Americans into their accounts any better than their colonial cousins. Indian history remains an interesting sideshow worthy of a preliminary chapter (or introductory lecture), after which the main act of white history takes the stage. Perhaps American historians have not progressed as far beyond Altman's Cody as we would like to believe.

As tempting as it is to explain the failure of ethnohistorians to exert greater influence on American history by blaming their colleagues for not listening, a major part of the problem lies in the way ethnohistorians have structured their tales of the Indian experience. Since the turn of the century most North American ethnographies and ethnohistories have employed one of two basic plots. As Edward Bruner has pointed out, through World War II most accounts of Indian life depicted "the present as disorganization, the past as glorious, and the future as assimilation." Scholars generally attempted to identify and depict an idealized traditional culture, which they anticipated would soon vanish along with all traces of Indians as distinct people. After

World War II, when intellectuals around the world began to attack the concept of assimilation as a product of colonial ideology, a new scheme emerged. Postwar studies envisioned the Indian present "as a resistance movement, the past as exploitation and the future as ethnic resurgence." The new plot emphasized how Indians had survived pressures to adopt white ways and preserved islands of traditional culture in the midst of the modern world.[5]

Each plot provides a framework for scholars to investigate important elements of the Indian experience, but by depicting Indian and white cultures in antiethical terms, they make it virtually impossible to imagine an approach in which Indian history can be incorporated into the mainstream of American historiography. The plots render Indians more interesting and important as foils for white history than as significant participants in it. Indian history becomes a tragic chapter in the creation of modern America, with the inevitable clash between incompatible cultures the price of America's glory or the source of its shame, and Indians the necessary enemy or victim. The process reduces American history to a moral fable in which Native Americans become little more than abstract components of an ideological agenda. They serve as convenient tools for cultural critics of modern white society, from which the plots exclude them, and the Indian's own voice, which so many ethnohistorians have struggled to hear, never reaches the general audience for American history.[6]

The failure of historians to transmit Indian voices has meant that most modern Americans remain unaware that Native Americans have been reading and writing in their own languages and in English for more than three hundred years. The exaggerated response of many Americans to the Red Power movement of the 1960s and 1970s reflects the depth of their ignorance about the historical range of Indian literacy. Book titles heralded the arrival of *The New Indians* and *The Emergent Native Americans* as if Indians had, for the first time, discovered a voice.[7] Newspapers such as *Akwesasne Notes* were described as prototypes of an independent Indian journalism by people unaware that the first Native American newspapers had been published in the 1820s. Reviewers hailed as unprecedented the work of Sioux author Vine Deloria without recognizing that his aunt Ella Deloria had herself published a series of books a quarter of a century earlier.[8] It does not diminish the accomplishments of modern Indian activists, writers, and editors to suggest that American popular culture badly misunderstands their historical roots. They represent not an unprecedented flourishing of Indian literacy but the continuation of a tradition of

Native American self-expression that antedates the American Revolution.

There are perhaps no greater examples of the vitality of that tradition than the *Cherokee Phoenix and Indian Advocate* and its successor, the *Cherokee Advocate*. The publication of the first issue of the *Phoenix* at New Echota, Georgia, in January 1828 marked a culmination of events that had begun nearly two decades earlier, when a young Cherokee named Sequoyah (also known as George Guess) determined to provide his people with a means of writing their language. Sequoyah, who could neither read nor write English, initially experimented with a glyphic system of several thousand signs, each of which represented a unique Cherokee word. When his wife's relatives, suspicious that he was practicing witchcraft, burned his cabin and papers, Sequoyah discovered that he himself could remember few of the signs. He then focused on representing not full words but the far fewer unique syllables constituting them. By 1819 he had identified and created symbols for eighty-five basic sounds. When his six-year-old daughter successfully read a statement that a group of Cherokee leaders had dictated to Sequoyah in her absence, Cherokees throughout Georgia were persuaded of the system's practicability. Within a few years thousands of Cherokees had learned to read and write their language. The Reverend William Chamberlain, a missionary to the Cherokees, observed, "The knowledge of Mr. Guess's Alphabet is spreading through the nation like fire among the leaves."[9]

Sequoyah developed his syllabary too late for it to halt the spread of English as a second language within the Cherokee Nation, but it soon became apparent to the national Council and to interested whites that bilingual literacy had become a permanent feature of Cherokee culture. In 1827 the Council, with the assistance of the American Board of Commissioners for Foreign Missions, obtained a printing press and arranged for a Massachusetts foundry to forge type of the syllabary.[10] The next January Cherokee editor Elias Boudinot distributed the inaugural issue of the *Cherokee Phoenix and Indian Advocate*, the first Native American national newspaper. Printed in both Sequoyan and English, the *Phoenix* served for six years as an effective propaganda tool promoting Cherokee resistance to removal and recruiting support from sympathetic whites around the United States. The press at New Echota published a variety of titles in Sequoyan, including portions of the Bible, hymnals, almanacs, annual laws, and political tracts. The printing office was so effective that Georgia authorities arrested its editors and ultimately confiscated the press. In 1834, with removal

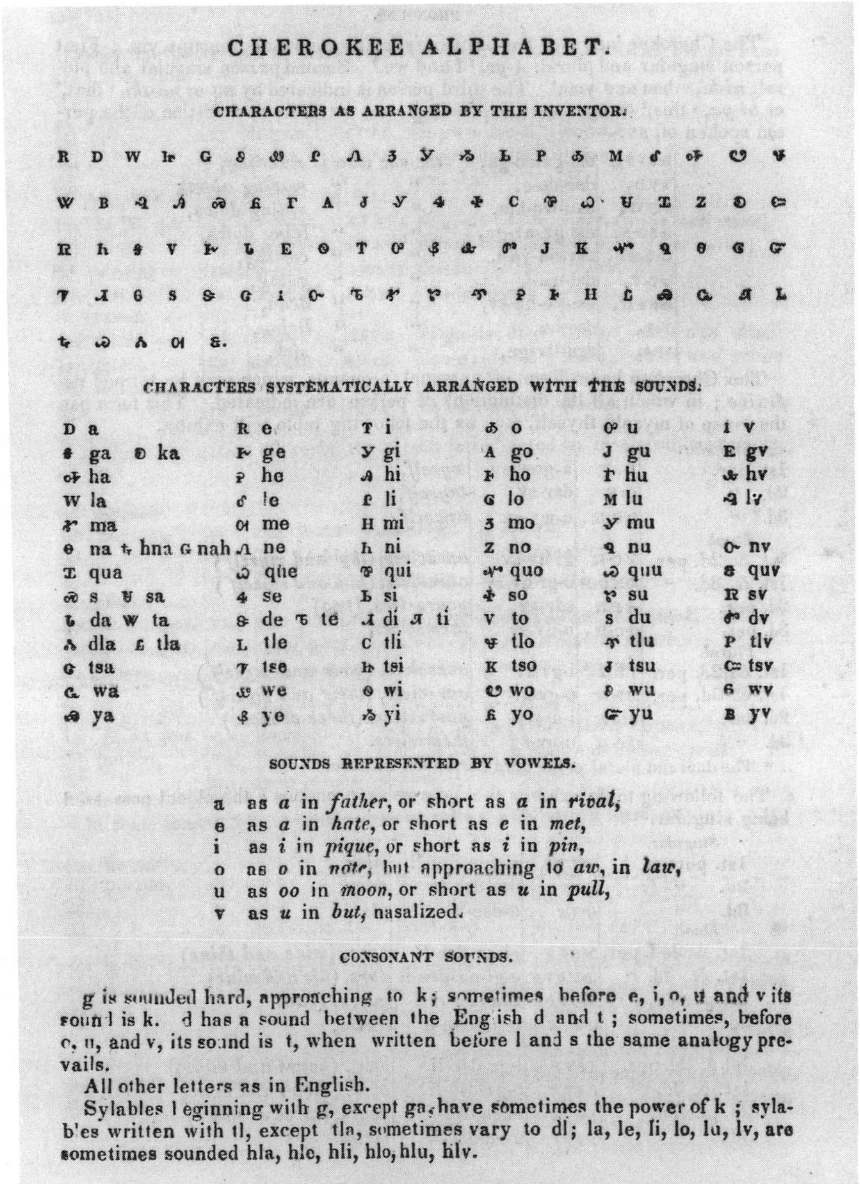

CHEROKEE ALPHABET.

CHARACTERS AS ARRANGED BY THE INVENTOR.

Ꭱ Ꭰ Ꮃ Ꮵ Ꮐ Ꮽ Ꮺ Ꮅ Ꮑ Ꮌ Ꭹ Ᏹ Ꮟ Ꮲ Ꭳ Ꮇ Ꮄ Ꭽ Ꮼ Ꮰ

Ꮤ Ᏼ Ꮈ Ꭿ Ꮝ Ᏺ Ꮁ Ꭺ Ꮷ Ꮍ Ꮞ Ꮠ Ꮯ Ꮘ Ꮚ Ꮜ Ꮖ Ꮓ Ꭷ Ꮸ

Ꮢ Ꮒ Ꭶ Ꮩ Ꭸ Ꮣ Ꭼ Ꮻ Ꭲ Ꭴ Ᏸ Ꮂ Ꮫ Ꭻ Ꮶ Ꮙ Ꮔ Ꮎ Ꮳ Ᏻ

Ꮴ Ꮧ Ꮾ Ꮪ Ꮥ Ꮆ Ꭵ Ꮕ Ꮦ Ꮉ Ꮡ Ꮱ Ꭾ Ꮀ Ꮋ Ꮭ Ꮿ Ꮹ Ꮨ Ꮮ

Ꮏ Ꮗ Ꮬ Ꮊ Ꮛ.

CHARACTERS SYSTEMATICALLY ARRANGED WITH THE SOUNDS.

Ꭰ a	Ꭱ e	Ꭲ i	Ꭳ o	Ꭴ u	Ꭵ v
Ꭶ ga Ꭷ ka	Ꭸ ge	Ꭹ gi	Ꭺ go	Ꭻ gu	Ꭼ gv
Ꭽ ha	Ꭾ he	Ꭿ hi	Ꮀ ho	Ꮁ hu	Ꮂ hv
Ꮃ la	Ꮄ le	Ꮅ li	Ꮆ lo	Ꮇ lu	Ꮈ lv
Ꮉ ma	Ꮊ me	Ꮋ mi	Ꮌ mo	Ꮍ mu	
Ꮎ na Ꮏ hna Ꮐ nah	Ꮑ ne	Ꮒ ni	Ꮓ no	Ꮔ nu	Ꮕ nv
Ꮖ qua	Ꮗ que	Ꮘ qui	Ꮙ quo	Ꮚ quu	Ꮛ quv
Ꮜ s Ꮝ sa	Ꮞ se	Ꮟ si	Ꮠ so	Ꮡ su	Ꮢ sv
Ꮣ da Ꮤ ta	Ꮥ de Ꮦ te	Ꮧ di Ꮨ ti	Ꮩ to	Ꮪ du	Ꮫ dv
Ꮬ dla Ꮭ tla	Ꮮ tle	Ꮯ tli	Ꮰ tlo	Ꮱ tlu	Ꮲ tlv
Ꮳ tsa	Ꮴ tse	Ꮵ tsi	Ꮶ tso	Ꮷ tsu	Ꮸ tsv
Ꮹ wa	Ꮺ we	Ꮻ wi	Ꮼ wo	Ꮽ wu	Ꮾ wv
Ꮿ ya	Ᏸ ye	Ᏹ yi	Ᏺ yo	Ᏻ yu	Ᏼ yv

SOUNDS REPRESENTED BY VOWELS.

a as *a* in *father*, or short as *a* in *rival*,
e as *a* in *hate*, or short as *e* in *met*,
i as *i* in *pique*, or short as *i* in *pin*,
o as *o* in *note*, but approaching to *aw*, in *law*,
u as *oo* in *moon*, or short as *u* in *pull*,
v as *u* in *but*, nasalized.

CONSONANT SOUNDS.

g is sounded hard, approaching to k; sometimes before e, i, o, u and v its sound is k. d has a sound between the English d and t; sometimes, before o, u, and v, its sound is t, when written before l and s the same analogy prevails.

All other letters as in English.

Sylables beginning with g, except ga, have sometimes the power of k; syllables written with tl, except tla, sometimes vary to dl; la, le, li, lo, lu, lv, are sometimes sounded hla, hle, hli, hlo, hlu, hlv.

The Sequoyan syllabary as published in the *Cherokee Messenger*, vol. I, No. 1 (August 1844). *Courtesy Yale Collection of Western Americana, Beinecke Rare Book and Manuscript Library.*

unavoidable and national funds virtually extinguished, the Council suspended its effort to publish the *Phoenix*. In its absence Cherokee officials employed the syllabary to distribute handwritten communiqués throughout the nation.[11]

The tumult and distresses of removal interrupted but did not destroy Cherokee printing. The Cherokees' enthusiastic response to printing in the syllabary so impressed the American Board of Commissioners for Foreign Missions that it moved to assure that printing could resume when the Cherokees and their southern Indian neighbors relocated in Indian Territory. In 1835, before most of the Cherokees had moved west, the board sent Samuel Worcester to Union Mission, Indian Territory, with a press and type sufficient to publish not only for the Cherokees but also the Creeks and Choctaws. In 1837 Worcester moved the press to Park Hill, where it served a broad audience among the "Civilized Tribes." In addition to many missionary tracts, the press printed Cherokee-language editions of the national Constitution and collected laws.[12]

After using the Park Hill press for several years, the Cherokee Council decided to establish its own press at Tahlequah, the new national capital. On October 25, 1843, the Council voted to publish a weekly newspaper, the *Cherokee Advocate*, to promote "the diffusion of important news among the Cherokee people, the advancement of their general interests, and [the] defense of Indian rights." The Council reserved the power to appoint the paper's editor and provided that a translator, responsible for preparing the Sequoyan segments of each issue, be appointed by the principal chief. In addition to his journalistic duties, the editor would be responsible for supervising all government printing. William Potter Ross was selected as the paper's first editor, with James D. Wofford as translator. A new press and set of type were purchased, and on September 26, 1844, the first issue of the new national paper was published.[13]

As was the case with virtually every nineteenth-century American newspaper, the *Cherokee Advocate* was an intensely partisan operation that generally reflected the views of whatever faction held control of the Council.[14] From the first, however, the paper's editors, whatever their political persuasion, strove to reach both their English- and Cherokee-speaking audiences. For much of its existence the *Advocate* was distributed free or at a significant discount "to those who read Cherokee only." Although the amount of Sequoyan typeface in the paper varied from one editor to the next, it increased steadily over time. In 1881 the Council provided that at least one page of each issue be printed in Sequoyan, and by the turn of the century it was common for half the paper to appear in the syllabary.[15] In 1905 the editor, Wiley James Melton, observed, "There is hardly a citizen in the Cherokee Nation over the age of ten years but what is able to read and write, either in English or Cherokee,"[16] and boasted that Cherokee-speaking full bloods were, "as a whole, better posted on current events than their white tenants, and their information has been derived wholly from the Cherokee Advocate."[17]

The *Advocate*'s political orientation was not the only feature it shared with other American newspapers. Like that of most of them, its existence was tenuous, subject to a variety of economic and social pressures, and assured only to the extent that it served the needs of its readers. The *Advocate* did not, in its early years, face the overt hostility from white authorities that contributed to the death of its predecessor, the *Phoenix*. In September 1853, however, for reasons that have never been fully explored, the Council suspended its publication. Whatever its motives, the Council recognized the value of a national press because it retained and cared for the *Advocate*'s equipment. When it revived the paper seventeen years later, it put the press and Sequoyan type back to work.[18] A fire in February 1875 destroyed the original equipment and interrupted publication for more than a year, but a new press began operating on March 1, 1876, and the *Advocate* prospered for several decades.[19] By the turn of the century it faced competition from Kansas newspapers whose editors hoped to capitalize on the likely incorporation of Indian Territory and Oklahoma into a new state, but the *Advocate* endured. Its editor observed that when the *Kansas City Journal* proposed to address the Cherokee market, he had cooperated in the hope that the *Journal*'s circulation might increase the news and information available to Cherokee citizens. He "went so far as to lend them a lot of Cherokee type—Sequoyan's alphabet and some other things," but "they didn't even send us our type back, neither did they send us a copy of their paper. They can work us once, but once only. The people of this Territory have their eye on all these outside advertising schemes."[20]

By 1902 the *Advocate* occupied a "large, old-fashioned square brick building, two stories high, and located in the central part of . . . town."[21] Over the preceding half century its presses had printed not only some two thousand issues of the *Advocate* but hundreds of political and legal tracts in Cherokee and English. Within a few years, however, the *Advocate* would be still, its office building and press sold at auction, and its trays of Sequoyan typeface retired to the Smithsonian Institution.[22] Like the *Phoenix* before it, the *Advocate* fell victim to the hostility of American governmental officials. In 1893 Congress authorized the president to name a commission to implement severalty among the Five Civilized Tribes of Indian Territory. Under Chairman Henry Dawes, the committee dismantled the national government and with it the *Advocate* and its bilingual press. The action transformed hundreds of Cherokee speakers from informed readers into virtual civic illiterates. In one of his final editorials, in February 1906, *Advocate* editor Melton appraised the situation:

> The matter resolves itself into quite a serious question. Here are some eight to ten hundred people who read the Cherokee that are unable to read English. They are as much interested in what is transpiring, especially in the proposed changes in their affairs. They get the news weekly. Everything that pertains to this country is published in the Cherokee for their benefit. They read it and are as well posted as their white and mixed blood brothers. But what will be their condition after March 4th? It will be this: Here are one thousand intelligent people, with their only means of keeping posted taken away, and in a little while they will know nothing of what is going on.[23]

A week later, in an editorial that restated his concerns, Melton observed that closing the *Advocate* press would render the Sequoyan syllabary worthless. In his opinion, the consequences were clear. "Here is a people well educated in their native language, but with no paper printed in that language, they will soon lapse into a condition of ignorance and instead of improving and rising to a higher plane they will go backwards."[24]

In his dire prediction that the syllabary would become "utterly useless" Melton exaggerated. Even after the demise of the *Advocate* the syllabary remained valuable for personal communication among Cherokee speakers and as a means of recording traditional medical formulas. Literacy in Sequoyan declined over the ensuing decades, but in 1961, when John White explored the possibility of reviving Sequoyan printing, he discovered a small but enthusiastic group of readers.[25] The closing of the *Advocate* did, however, dramatically curtail the political value of the syllabary as a tool for developing and expressing Cherokee perspectives on important issues and as a means of fostering community within the nation. In this regard Melton underestimated the significance of the *Advocate* for English-speaking

Cherokees, for although they could keep abreast of news through other papers, they would no longer have available to them a Cherokee editorial voice. In one act the federal government rendered some thousand Cherokees illiterate for most public purposes and effectively silenced the nation.

The basic history of the *Advocate*'s demise has been known for several decades, but historians have undertaken little research about the paper or its personnel. We do not know, for example, why the *Advocate* and its equipment were taken by the government rather than converted to a private operation. Did the Cherokee Nation or the Bureau of Indian Affairs explore alternative arrangements that might have enabled the paper or its press to function after the dissolution of the Cherokee national government? What became of its editor, Melton, and his translators? Nor do we know much about the reaction of other Indian Territory and Oklahoma newspapers to the demise of the *Advocate*. Did they change their editorial or news policies in an attempt to address the *Advocate*'s readers? To which, if any, papers did *Advocate* readers turn?

Similar lacunae exist concerning nearly every aspect of the paper's history. Most of what is known about Cherokee publishing has been discovered by bibliographers as they surveyed the history of Oklahoma printing or Native American publishing. Their spadework has laid a valuable foundation, but few historians have chosen to build upon it. We know little about most of the paper's editors, translators, and printers beyond their names and dates of service. We know even less about the paper's circulation, the extent to which the national Council subsidized it, or the nature of its nonnewspaper business. No one has published a translation of its Sequoyan columns or even attempted to analyze over time the content of its English columns.

Why have American historians done so little to rescue the *Advocate* and Cherokee publishing from the silence into which the federal government cast them nearly a century ago? One reason is that so many of our studies of federal Indian policy focus more on the history of white ideas than on the lives of Indians. Accounts like Francis Paul Prucha's *Great Father* explore in depth, often with brilliant insight, the attitudes of policy makers and the origins of their views. Rarely do they investigate to a commensurate degree what happened to Indian communities as the government enforced its programs. Policy formulation, not implementation, is the principal interest of such studies, and the story of the Native Americans whose lives were changed by government action becomes a secondary rather than primary sub-

61

ject. Prucha, in particular, is aware that policy studies ignore much of the Indian story and defends the approach by pointing out, correctly, that "no history of a tribe can be understood without a detailed consideration of treaties, land cessions, the reservation system, and Indian educational programs, for example, which formed the substance of government policy and action."[26] On the other hand, no history of federal Indian policy that does not explore fully the political implications of its day-to-day administration within specific communities ought be considered complete. Only then will it be possible to appraise the actual consequences, as opposed to the professed goals of policy decisions.

Another source of apathy regarding the *Advocate* lies in the Anglophonic character of much American history, especially Native American studies. Eighty years ago Franz Boas sought to persuade his colleagues of the importance of learning Indian languages by reminding them:

> Nobody would expect authoritative accounts of the civilization of China or Japan from a man who does not speak the languages readily, and who has not mastered their literature. The student of antiquity is expected to have a thorough mastery of the ancient languages. A student of Mohammedan life in Arabia or Turkey would hardly be considered a serious investigator if all his knowledge had to be derived from second hand accounts.[27]

Unfortunately most American historians, however uncomfortable they may feel to be associated with Commissioner of Indian Affairs J. D. C. Atkins, have adopted positions close to the one he expressed in 1887, when he declared that because Indians lived "in an English-speaking country, they must be taught the language which they must use in transacting business with the people of the country."[28] For the most part, American historians have expected Indians to present themselves for study in English documents (or occasionally, for the Far Southwest, in Spanish texts). The lack of writing systems in pre-Columbian North America, which ensured that there were no Indian-language texts for the earliest periods of Indian-white exchange, has contributed to the linguistic laziness of American historians. Since the greater part of the documentary record of Indian-white relations for the sixteenth through the nineteenth centuries is in European languages, English in particular, scholars have generally excused their lack of competence in Indian languages as a minor inconvenience and have overlooked opportunities to make use of Indian-language material such as the Sequoyan columns of the *Advocate*.[29]

Finally, American historians may fail to appreciate the significance of the *Advocate* because they cannot bring themselves to accept the Cherokees as real Indians. In this regard they resemble a young man from Indiana who visited Indian Territory in 1905. Mr. Brown, the *Advocate* reported, sought to discover the "wild and woolly west" but found instead "an Industrious, Prosperous Community of Civilized People." Rather than revise his notions of the West, Brown moved on in what the paper characterized as "his fruitless search of his dreamland west."[30] Whatever the West might have been to Mr. Brown, he clearly expected it to be radically different from life in Indiana. In similar fashion, most white Americans, scholars included, have always insisted that Indians be radically different from themselves. For better or worse, in positive as well as negative images, Indians have always been for whites the alien other against whom they define themselves. Cherokees who read and write, whose ancestors held slaves and intermarried with whites, who speak English, practice Christianity, and employ contemporary agricultural practices challenge not only Twain's image of Indians as silent, uncommunicative savages but all the many different images that define Indians as not-white. Like Mr. Brown, most scholars have preferred not to rethink their preconceptions and have chosen to regard the Cherokees as *sui generis*, a people set apart whose behavior cannot be compared to that of "real" Indians. The history of the *Advocate* becomes an interesting but idiosyncratic story signifying nothing.[31]

Every reason for ignoring the *Advocate* impoverishes our understanding of American history by erasing its Indian component, but the last reason carries the most pernicious consequences. Scholars who focus too narrowly on policy formulation or limit their sources to English texts overlook important aspects of our past, but historians who dismiss the Cherokees as ersatz Indians and the *Advocate* as irrelevant to Native American history embrace an untenable definition of Indians that fundamentally distorts the historical record. Indian and white cultures have always differed in many respects, but a negative definition of what constitutes Indians—that they are not whites—imposes a simplistic, inaccurate uniformity upon the many diverse Native American communities of North America. It also denies Indians the possibility of defining themselves independent of white cultural forms. Furthermore, to consider the manner in which the Cherokees embraced literacy in their own language as unrepresentative of "real" Indian behavior is to ignore contrary evidence from across the continent.

Nearly seventy-five years before the Cherokees adopted their syllabary, the Mohawks of New York had undertaken to instruct their children to read and write in Mohawk and English. Paulus Sahonwadi, a son of the famous Mohawk leader Hendrick, began to teach at the Mohawk village of Fort Hunter as early as 1753. Two years later the British missionary Judge Ogilvie described Paulus as "diligent in his Office as Schoolmaster; he teaches above 40 Children everyday, several begin to read, and some to write."[32] Many of the Fort Hunter Mohawks who had joined the Church of England requested that translations of the Bible and the Book of Common Prayer be printed in Mohawk. A selection of prayers had been published in Mohawk in 1715, but by mid-century only a few copies remained available.[33] As British missionaries prepared a second edition, a young Mohawk named Joseph Brant, likely a former student of Paulus, undertook to translate the Gospel of Mark.[34]

The chaos of the American Revolution delayed the publication of Brant's translation until 1787 but failed to quell the Mohawks' enthusiasm for teaching their children to read and write. In 1780, when most of the Fort Hunter Mohawks had moved into a refugee camp outside Montreal, Paulus helped proofread and collate a third edition of the prayer book. Despite the handicap that neither he nor his fellow teachers had primers or spelling books "but were obliged to make use of Manuscript Scraps with the Alphabet, etc., wrote upon," Paulus conducted school on a regular basis.[35] Enthused by the Mohawk response to the third edition of the prayer book and impressed by their effort to continue schooling their young, Assistant Superintendent of Indian Affairs Daniel Claus, one of the most distinguished Indian translators of the eighteenth century, composed a short primer for Paulus. The book's English title, which appeared opposite its Mohawk translation, describes it well: *A Primer for the use of the Mohawk Children, To acquire the Spelling and Reading of their own: As well as to get acquainted with the English Tongue, which for that purpose is put on the opposite Page.* The ninety-eight-page primer so pleased the Mohawks at Montreal that their countrymen from the village of Canajoharie, who were living in a camp outside Niagara, requested copies. Claus prepared a second edition, which features a frontispiece illustrating a Mohawk teacher (Paulus?) instructing his pupils.[36] Unlike the Cherokees, the Mohawks did not obtain their own press, but Mohawk translations of biblical texts continued to be published throughout the early nineteenth century. The Claus Papers in the Public Archives of

Canada contain a variety of letters in Mohawk written by Paulus, Joseph Brant, John Deserontyon, and other Mohawks that document the spread of literacy within the nation.[37]

It is not always possible to trace the origins of Indian literacy as clearly as in the Cherokee or Mohawk cases, but numerous examples attest to the literary facility of Native American communities. In 1788 Jonathan Edwards, Jr., published a word list and the "Our Father" in Mahican. Three decades later two Stockbridge Indians, John Quinney and Hendrick Aupaumut, translated *The Assembly's Shorter Catechism* into Mahican. A few years later Aupaumut sent a letter in Mahican to friends in the East inviting them to join him at his new home on the White River in Indiana.[38]

Few more dramatic examples of Native American linguistic ingenuity and commitment to literacy exist than the story of an Ottawa orthography and its adaptation by Indian communities throughout the Midwest. The origins of the orthography remain obscure but seem to date from the second quarter of the nineteenth century. Andrew Blackbird, an Ottawa who published his autobiography (accompanied by a grammar of the Ottawa language) in 1887, claimed that his father, Black Hawk, created the system.[39] No direct evidence has been discovered to substantiate Blackbird's claim, but the orthography, which was based on a cursive form of the Roman alphabet featuring vowels with French rather than English phonetic values, took hold not only among the Ottawas but also their neighbors the Potawatomis and Foxes who applied it as a syllabary for their closely related Algonquian languages.[40] Later a community of Siouan-speaking Winnebagos learned of the Fox syllabary and quickly turned it to their own use. In 1885 the agent assigned to the Winnebago reservation reported that "the tribe have suddenly taken to writing their own language, and people who have never learned English have acquired this art."[41] The Winnebago version of the syllabary seems never to have been used for printed material, but Sam Blowsnake, author of one of the most famous of Native American narratives, *Crashing Thunder: The Autobiography of a Winnebago Indian*, recorded his story in it. When Paul Radin published an English translation of Blowsnake's account in 1920, he worked with a Siouan text written in an Algonquian syllabary based on the French alphabet.[42]

Nearly every era and region of American history provide similar examples of Native American communities embracing opportunities to write and read their languages. From the Micmacs of Newfoundland to the Sioux of the plains, from the Apaches, Navajos, and Yaquis of the Southwest and the Luiseños of California to the Aleuts and Eskimos of Alaska, Indian communities eagerly adopted unique writing systems.[43] We have much to learn about their motives, but many of the cases suggest they were seeking, among other goals, to foster public communication and the exchange of information. Some communities, like the Creeks and White Earth Chippewas, emulated the Cherokees and published national newspapers. Unofficial papers appeared in many communities, and individual Native Americans embarked on private careers in journalism. In their pathbreaking bibliographic survey *American Indian and Alaskan Native Newspapers and Periodicals, 1826–1924*, Daniel Littlefield and James Parins identify fifty newspapers that Native Americans founded, edited, or maintained. Their work suggests that the most traveled Indian journalist of the nineteenth century was John Rollin Ridge, a Cherokee who moved to California during the gold rush and owned or edited ten different papers, including the Sacramento *Daily Bee*, the Marysville *California Express*, the *Grass Valley Daily National*, and the San Francisco *Daily Herald*. Under the name of Yellowbird, Ridge published a volume of verse and the *Life and Adventures of Joaquin Murieta*. Ridge's countryman Edward Bushyhead founded and operated the San Diego *Union*, while Elias C. Boudinot, the son of the founding editor of the *Cherokee Phoenix*, founded the Fayetteville *Arkansan*.

Native Americans who chose to edit or publish English-language newspapers for a predominantly white audience clearly saw themselves differently from their colleagues who worked for Indian-language papers, but rather than dismiss their Indian roots and character, consider that between 1772 and 1924 some two thousand Native American writers published in English more than sixty-seven hundred pieces of work, ranging from articles in local newspapers to lengthy academic studies.[44] Many more nineteenth-century Native Americans read and wrote English than American popular conceptions of the Indian accommodate. They wrote to share their concerns, hopes, ideas, and interests not only with each other but with all America. Instead of adopting the procrustean solution of denying such men and women their identity as Indians, we might consider alternative ways of thinking about Native Americans, ways that can accommodate the fact of Indian literacy in both native languages and English. Perhaps then we can discover an approach to Indian history that accurately reflects the historical record and allows us to create new plots for American history that incorporate rather than silence the Indian voice.

Americans' fascination with Indians as the "other" has helped create ahistorical models of Native American and white cultures as stable, autonomous structures composed of mutually exclusive elements: Rational whites worship science and technology while spiritual Indians worship nature; Indian cultures regard history as cyclical while whites believe in linear progress; white society is based on literacy while Indians belong to oral cultures. The story of Indian literacy and the dialogue that Indian authors attempted to establish among their own people and with white Americans refutes such facile oppositions. It challenges us to recognize that although cultures may be conservative, they are neither inherently stable nor rigidly bound. Rather, they are geographically, chronologically, and intellectually fluid. They express history as well as structure and are always evolving. Paulus Sahonwadi, Sequoyah, Wiley James Melton, and Sam Blowsnake followed their own paths to literacy, paths that few or none of their ancestors had followed but paths that they created or identified through a personal synthesis of their heritage and their experience. In the process they embraced their past to organize their present and provide for their future. They did not question their identities as Indians nor did they retreat in silence from the whites they encountered. Instead, they sought to identify and employ the tools that would allow them to converse and debate with whites about the world they both inhabited.[45]

By releasing Indian and white cultures from the lockstep opposition that so many twentieth-century accounts have imposed upon them, historians can move beyond the sterile demarcation of the American historical landscape into isolated Indian and white spheres. They can recognize that Indians and whites often engaged in lengthy, complicated conversations about themselves and their futures, conversations that reveal much not only about Native Americans but also about the emergence of modern America. The correspondents of the Mohawk leader Joseph Brant, for example, ranged from Mohawk political allies to Anglican church leaders, form local white neighbors on the Grand River in Canada to American financier Robert Morris, from small-town militia leaders in the Mohawk Valley to major government officials in America and Britain. Over the course of nearly fifty years they discussed issues that affected thousands of people from the banks of the southern Ohio River to the halls of Parliament. Were Brant's scattered papers organized and published in a modern scholarly edition, every student of the revolutionary era would benefit.[46]

Few Native Americans of the early nineteenth century carried on as extensive a correspondence as Brant, but at least nine Indians published autobiographies or tribal histories before 1862. A portion of one or two may have been ghostwritten, but the remainder represent an effort by literate Native Americans to attract a predominantly white audience to reflect upon the condition of Native Americans. The story of how Native American authors and white publishers cooperated to print and distribute the autobiographies in an era when government policy promulgated the segregation of Indians would reveal much about the social tensions and contradictions of antebellum America.[47] In similar fashion, H. Craig Miner's work demonstrates that many of the eight hundred-odd broadsides, tracts, pamphlets, and books printed within Indian Territory between 1835 and 1890, as well as extensive documents preserved in the national archives of the Civilized Tribes, attest to joint efforts by Oklahoma Indians and American business-men to develop Indian Territory after the Civil War. The records reveal a world in which Indians were far from silent partners, and they offer a different perspective on the history of American economic growth and industrialization.[48]

Just as more Native Americans learned to speak in "white" ways to a white audience than our traditional historiographic and ethno-graphic models predict, so more whites learned to speak in "Indian" ways than is generally assumed. A cursory review confirms that whites as well as Indians helped create a cross-cultural dialogue by adapting their practices to Native American customs. Throughout the eigh-teenth century men like Daniel Claus and his official colleagues among the British and French learned not only how to speak the words of Iroquois languages but also to employ the protocols, forms, and met-aphors of Iroquois diplomacy in their relations with northeastern Indians. In similar fashion, to enhance the profit of its operations, the Hudson's Bay Company adapted its trading procedures to the expec-tations and demands of its Native American partners. Individual trad-ers learned the language of kinship and frequently married into the communities in which they worked. Even missionaries, often criti-cized as the most ethnocentric of all whites, contributed to the dia-logue. Across the continent, from the Mayhews of Martha's Vineyard to Gerónimo de Zárate Salmerón at Jemez Pueblo, from Ivan Venïaminov in Alaska to the Riggs family among the Sioux, mission-aries learned to understand and speak Native American languages. Many of their works remain essential documents in the study of Indian linguistics.[49]

The history of Indian literacy and of white efforts to learn Indian "languages" suggests that when Native Americans and whites attempted to speak with each other, they were not merely shouting into a void but trying in ways both ingenious and imperfect to bridge the distance between them. In no discussion or debate is there perfect communication among participants, and the history of Indian-white conversations includes disappointment, misunderstanding, and deliberate deception; but time and again, by chance and by design, Indians and whites exchanged information about themselves in ways each understood. When we fail to see this and accept instead the image of an impassable gulf between Indian and white, we distort our history by imagining Americans—Natives and whites—to have lived far more fragmented and isolated lives than they did. When we fail to recognize that the "Silent Indian," like the "Vanishing American," is an imaginative construction of a particular epoch of white cultural history, not a fact of Native American history, we contribute to the historical amnesia of twentieth-century popular culture. We perpetuate an image of Indians that denies the historical evolution of their heritage, ignores their participation in the making of America, and leaves us surprised and unprepared to respond when they address us today. By contrast, when we comprehend the literary traditions of Indian communities, we can begin to appreciate the flexible, innovative character of Indian cultures. We can see the ways they shaped not only their own destinies but also the lives of contemporary whites and how modern Native American authors and orators, be they tribal leaders, political activists, lawyers, poets, novelists, or historians, represent a continuing tradition of Indian commentary on the American experience.

The challenge confronting American historians today is to recognize and explore the significance not only of Indian literacy but of the many ways that Native Americans expressed themselves to each other and to their white neighbors. Informed by the example of Indian journalism, we should seek to understand better the ways Indians attempted to speak to whites through the languages of material culture, diplomacy, trade, and legal documents.[50] To appreciate fully the significance of the intercultural dialogue that characterized much of America's past, we must ask who chose to speak to whom, under what circumstances, and for what reasons. When, like Mark Twain, we come upon uncommunicative Indians, we must resist the temptation to cast them as props emblematic of all Native Americans in all circumstances and instead investigate the sources of their silence. Only then can we begin to develop a historiographic tradition that integrates the Native American experience into the broader story of America.

We should also recognize that Indian voices are not merely relics of the past. Around the country Indian men and women—some of them historians—have much to say about themselves, their people, their culture, and their history. The questions they ask about American history may not be the same ones that interest white historians, nor will their answers always be the same. But just as Sequoyah's syllabary allowed Americans to share more fully in the wisdom and insights of Cherokee culture, so Native American historiographic traditions will allow us to see and appreciate more fully the diverse origins of our society. As we come to appreciate the presence of Indian voices in America's past, perhaps we will recognize, in the spirit of Samuel Worcester and Daniel Claus, the humane value of fostering similar voices today, so that sometime soon the descendants of Sitting Bull might indeed teach all Americans a "History Lesson."

On the Boundaries of Empire

Connecting the West
to Its Imperial Past

JAY GITLIN

In the drama of American frontier history, historians have traditionally considered the period of imperial struggle in North America as
the prelude to the main saga of settlement—a story of resourceful
pioneers creating a new society in a landscape free of encumbrances,
notably the claims of empires and Native American polities. Frederick
Jackson Turner saw the struggle between "western" creators and
"eastern" controllers as the central dynamic of the frontier movement.[1] Europe, the headquarters of empire, was the "East" for Turner,
the essence of what he wished to avoid in his efforts to locate the heart
of the American historical narrative in American soil. Ray Allen Billington followed the master's cues in his popular textbook *Westward
Expansion*, which briefly describes the various empires in the West as
so many "barriers." Even chapters on the "colonial frontier" contain
only casual references to imperial relationships.[2] Small wonder that
the traditional narrative of frontier expansion so happily coincided
with the history of American national expansion.

Over the last fifty years historians have gradually abandoned
Turner's notion that the West was somehow created in isolation.[3] We

have come to accept the idea that frontier places, chronically short of labor and capital, were often dependent on imperial or national metropoles. Economic development usually began with the exploitation of extractive, nonindustrial resources in demand in distant marketplaces. From this perspective, North American frontier areas are best understood as hinterlands, edges of the worldwide expansion of European economies, chapters in the history of European colonialism. In this new story of economic linkages between empire and frontier, urban settlements become the spearheads of western settlement.[4] Urban merchants in the metropole and the periphery kept in constant communication to determine how economic and political conditions would affect their investments and, ultimately, the future of a frontier area. Although this new reading of frontier history has yet to penetrate the thick hide of western lore, someday, perhaps, schoolchildren will know that French merchants in St. Louis were reading Voltaire while, far to the east, Daniel Boone was "trailblazing" in the supposedly unmarked wilderness. (The real Daniel Boone was no fool. He moved from Kentucky to Spanish Missouri, received a land grant from a kindly imperial official, and served as a local comandante. Señor Boone's son Daniel Morgan Boone married a French Creole, Constantine Philibert. Their daughters, Elizabeth and Eulalie, were baptized in the Catholic Church, raised in Creole Kansas City, and presumably spoke French.)[5]

With our new emphasis on "connectedness," historians are paying more attention to the cultural baggage, even the animals and plants, that newcomers—whether easterners, immigrants, or displaced native peoples—brought with them to the frontier. Although living in a frontier area evoked in new settlers a sense of freedom and opportunity, pioneers rarely abandoned their ties to distant friends and family. Homes in the New World were often made habitable by memories of the Old. Turner's notion of a frontier as a line of settlement tended to blur these complex relationships. His two-dimensional model not only flattened our view of the circle of connections maintained by an intrusive society in a frontier area but also minimized the indigenous society's reactions to that settlement process. Leonard Thompson and Howard Lamar proposed an alternative model in *The Frontier in History*.[6] They suggested that we view the frontier not as a line but rather as a "zone of interpenetration between two previously distinct societies."

The effort to reexamine the history of native/nonnative interaction makes it all the more important to look closely at the role of empires in the American West. As the American frontier expanded, state and settlers alike agreed that native political and cultural distinctiveness must disappear. (The question of how best to achieve this—by assimilation, removal, enclavement, or genocide—was sometimes a bone of contention.) In contrast, the agents of empire on the various imperial frontiers often promoted alliances with native peoples. Often their aim was to protect trade relationships or to inflate jurisdictional claims vis-à-vis rival empires or colonies. Curiously, had native peoples in North America been able to establish independent states, the role of empires on the frontier might have loomed large in their historiographies. The historiographical tradition of the United States is quite different. The conquest of the continent, the "winning of the West," figures so prominently in our account of the formation of the national character that our revolution against the British Empire seems, at times, to be reduced to a quarrel in the family.[7] Indians appear frequently, but usually as straw men. Indians are portrayed either as victims of progress or as hostile opponents who tested the mettle of the westering pioneers. Neither portrayal acknowledges Indian people to have played an active, meaningful role in the shaping of the western past.

So it is that ethnohistorians and others, determined to bring Indian history back into the mainstream of American history, have also reopened the debate on the role of empire on the frontier.[8] One such historian is Francis Jennings. In his first book, *The Invasion of America*, Jennings unraveled the complex struggle to shape New England's colonial boundaries.[9] Imperial agents, colonists, and Indians each had a variety of goals and often exploited one another as best they could to achieve those goals.[10] The work of Jennings and others has important implications for historians investigating other areas of the Anglo-American settlement frontier. We must also try to unravel the complex transoceanic and cross-cultural connections that shaped those areas of the West claimed by the Spanish, the French, and the Russians. (At one time or another, most of the American West lay within the boundaries of those empires.) We must try to integrate the histories of those non-Anglo imperial frontiers with the narrative of Anglo-American settlement for those various frontiers converged throughout the period of national expansion. Those non-Anglo imperial frontiers not only affected the course of events but also altered the social and economic landscape of the West. Try as they might, the citizens of the young Republic who encountered that altered landscape could never fully avoid its consequences.

To begin the task of integrating the imperial frontiers into our accounts of western settlement, there are at least three problems that historians must recognize. We must first broaden the scope of our investigations. A precondition of writing the history of North American imperial frontiers is a thorough understanding of the political culture of early modern Europe and the distinctions between empires. Second, we need an analytical framework that will allow us to capture the interplay of local and global interests in our local histories. Finally, there is the third and central problem. How do we incorporate the story of imperial frontiers into the overall narrative structure of western history? We cannot be satisfied with narrating the story of a settler nation. Our histories must have an international and multinational awareness.

Our Anglocentric tendency too often leads us to forget that empires were not all alike. The Spanish Empire, for example, had a distinctive bureaucratic style. The Hapsburg Empire was very much a personal domain, an accumulation of disparate political entities that, despite their *fueros* or privileges, were effectively under the supervision of a host of imperial officials. Even after the Bourbon reforms in the reign of Charles III, the Spanish American Empire was characterized by an elaborate administrative structure, legalistic detail, and government-sponsored surveys—for which historians can be thankful. An inclusive and formal system, the Spanish Empire considered native peoples subjects of the Crown. From this fact flowed debates on the nature of native peoples, laws designed to protect them, a strong commitment to Catholic missionizing efforts, and widespread exploitation of native labor. Even in distant New Mexico, where natives had some success in resisting inclusion, a royal official, the protector de Indios, stood guard over cross-cultural relations to prevent fraudulent land transfers.[11] In Spanish Louisiana, traditional Indian land tenure was protected by law, and Christian natives held land on an equal footing with Europeans.[12] Throughout Spanish America, Indian slavery was forbidden, although other forced labor systems obtained. When Spain acquired Louisiana from France in 1763, royal officials did not abolish Indian slavery, but they did their best to destroy the market for Indian slaves.[13]

By way of contrast, Indian communities in British America had no standing in the empire, and until 1756 they enjoyed no royal agency charged with the protection of their interests. At best, tribal polities hoped to maintain a diplomatic and military rapprochement. Once Indian communities became enclaves in a zone of British settlement, they were at the mercy of their colonial neighbors. The Mohegans sought royal protection from Connecticut several times in the first half of the eighteenth century, but their appeals were never crowned with success despite an initial favorable ruling from a special commission appointed by Queen Anne.[14] There simply was no mechanism for including Indian communities in the fabric of the state. British imperial ideology did not sanction inclusion, and British colonists did not desire it. A strong core state lay at the heart of the British Empire, and North American Indians remained outsiders. By contrast, the Spanish Empire evolved as an amalgam of peoples and places, and Native American communities had standing in that heterogeneous polity.

Empires differed not only in their ideologies and their structures but in the indigenous cultures and landscapes they encountered. The dominant position of the fur trade and the tiny European population of Canada forced the French Empire in North America to operate through a network of Indian alliances. The French had no choice but to recognize the sovereignty of Indian tribal communities and observe the boundaries of legal jurisdiction.[15] Just as any discussion of imperial frontiers must acknowledge distinct imperial structures and the ways they changed over time, so it must also keep in view that New World situations influenced imperial responses.

This brings us to our second problem, one that points to a direction in which future research might head. The traditional historiography of imperial frontiers has been profoundly "metrocentric." We have studies of the ways conditions in the periphery affected metropolitan policy, and we have many histories of frontier areas as the staging grounds for grand contests for empire. All such works are written through the lens of the metropolis, a lens that is capable of distortion. The Seven Years War provides a good example. Despite the change it brought in imperial control from France to England, there was surprising continuity in the cis-Mississippi frontier. Patterns of accommodation between Indian and French communities shifted, expanded, and reacted, but they were not fundamentally altered until the next century.

Economic histories are also guilty of this metropolitan bias, viewing frontier production from the vantage point of value to European markets. It is true that overseas markets determined the amount of capital available to frontier merchants, but if we are interested in frontier development, we must know how such capital was invested. What was its place in the local economy? The fur trade, for example, often stimulated local growth out of proportion to its percentage of total Atlantic trade. At the same time the fur trade did not effect a total transformation of the social context of production and consumption, and even if it had, such a transformation and the connections that sustained it would constitute merely an episode in local history as well as be an episode in the history of a developing world system.[16] In our study of frontier economic development we tend to label activities as capitalist or not according to the criteria of the metropole. In so doing, we ignore what Daniel Usner has labeled "frontier exchange," the "small-scale, face-to-face" markets that contributed to the formation of a regional economy. What can we learn from Indian grain sur-pluses, the trade in bear oil or in mococks of maple sugar?[17] Did Anglo-American pioneers covet the Indian share of this barter economy as much as they coveted their land?

What I am arguing for here is not simply local studies of frontier areas but studies that combine a local perspective with an awareness of the metropolitan/periphery context. We tend to forget that the agency of empire in America often operated through locals with their own agendas, agendas that resonated with metropolitan policy but were quite distinct. Consider, for example, the founding of Louisiana. W. J. Eccles has observed that Louis XIV sanctioned the establish-ment of colonies at Detroit and in Louisiana in 1701 to block settle-ment by the English. Imperial policy makers hoped that missionaries and fur traders could bring Indian nations in these areas into the French fold and that fees derived from the fur trade would help defray gov-ernment expenses. But Canadian merchants and royal officials at Que-bec were, in Eccles's words, "bitterly opposed to both these settlements, declaring that they would be the ruin of Canada. . . . Eccles con-cludes that "the fur trade was now definitely subordinated to a politi-cal end."[18]

From the perspective of the metropole, this statement seems quite accurate, yet an entirely different story emerges if we look at the same situation from a "local" point of view. Support for imperial policy came from a group of Canadian-born soldiers and entrepreneurs who were entrusted with implementing that policy—namely, the Le Moyne clan. Pierre Le Moyne (Iberville), the leader of the Louisiana expedi-tion, brought along with him several brothers and cousins: Brother Jean-Baptiste (Bienville) became the governor of the new province; cousin Pierre Dugué de Boisbriant later became commandant in the Illinois country; cousins Louis and Charles Juchereau de St. Denis pursued imperial power and personal profit on the Louisiana-Texas border and along the Ohio River respectively; and a cousin by mar-riage, Pierre-Charles Le Sueur, joined this family venture and used the opportunity to market furs from his Minnesota concession illegally. (Eccles himself notes that merchants back in Canada feared the possibility that traders in their debt would default and ship their furs from this alternate port as a way of avoiding seizure.) Oddly, historians have noted many of these details in passing but have never seen them as constituting a story worth telling. What an incredible family business venture! Seen from the local perspective, imperial policy became the Le Moyne clan's personal tool for gaining royal concessions, forging cross-cultural alliances, outmaneuvering political rivals, and making a buck. The family thrived on the interplay between the local and metropolitan worlds. Bienville was born in Montreal and founded New Orleans. He lived the last twenty-five years of his life in comfortable retirement in Paris. Iberville invested his profits from the fur trade in a cocoa plantation in St. Domingue and several estates in western France.[19]

Local connections to the metropole reflected the fragmented nature of power in an emerging world system. French merchants in North America, for example, responded more readily to Bordeaux, the center of French transatlantic commerce, than to Versailles, the political headquarters of the empire. And if local interests were ready to exploit their connections to a metropole of their own *patria*, imagine the masquerade we must decipher when explaining the situation in the cis-Mississippi frontier from 1760 to 1815. Spanish officials in the Floridas maintained good relations with the Creek Indians through the offices of Panton, Leslie and Company, a group of Scottish merchants. During the American Revolution the British at Detroit sent out militia companies to defend French and French-Indian settlements being held by American forces. The "British" troops contained Frenchmen who had recently been defeated by the British. The "American" troops were composed, to some degree, of other Frenchmen. William Henry Harrison appointed Robert Dickson, a rabid partisan of the British cause during the War of 1812, an American justice of the peace in the newly organized Indiana Territory in 1802. Is it any wonder that local merchants and officials in this arena became extraordinarily skillful at manipulating this complex chain of connections? This cis-Mississippi frontier was not simply the periphery of one empire; it was the periphery of many. The locals in this arena of boundaries knew this well; their letters deal as much with world news as they do with the availability of bear oil. The challenge to historians is to understand the different contexts in which local actors operated and to produce regional studies that consider the ways in which both complex local conditions and a crazy quilt of metropolitan interests shaped the landscape.[20]

It is easy to look at this "mess" in the cis-Mississippi frontier and conclude that it was a world of transience and duplicity, but to do so would be to miss an important story about community formation and to misread the cultures of that period. The political cultures of eighteenth- and early-nineteenth-century imperial frontiers contained ideological assumptions, both Indian and European, that differed in many respects from the ideology of the settler frontier to the east. The settler nation was a republic, and sovereignty resided in the people. Those who spoke a different language or practiced polygamy were both an annoyance and a potential political threat. Empires, on the other hand, were not as dependent on a common culture. It was quite common for an Irishman to serve in the Spanish Army or an Italian to occupy a key role in a French imperial action. Imperial frontiers tended to be more compatible with the multinational social landscape of North America. The imperial frontiers in the Mississippi Valley, the Spanish Borderlands, and Russian Alaska comprised discrete ethnic communities. (They were usually described as "nations," in an older usage of this word.) These communities were connected in certain ways and influenced each other, but they remained discrete. They were frontier zones in suspension, not in solution. The Mississippi Valley throughout the eighteenth century was no harmonious universe—there were struggles for political and economic dominance—but this frontier was shaped and shared by many nations, and perhaps its most distinguishing feature was its heterogeneity. In the words of one Pennsylvanian visiting Fort Wayne in 1823, it was a "real Babel."[21]

To understand how a French Creole in St. Louis could serve the Spanish Empire, send his son to West Point, and all the time further his own interests, we must attend to power and the structure of government in the eighteenth century. First of all, private and public spheres overlapped in ways that may seem quite odd to us. Canadian historian J. F. Bosher cites the royal treasury in New France as an example. The royal treasury was part of a semiprivate banking system. Although the intendants authorized payment, neither they nor the royal councils could control the treasury's operations. When a treasury agent died, his widow and children were responsible for accounts. Not surprisingly, the Crown sometimes had difficulty recovering its funds.[22] This may seem like an inefficient system, but at the time France, Spain, and England were evolving only slowly toward more centralized bureaucratic systems. The state's quest for authority had been challenged at every step by local elites whose offices and privileges, sustained by the Crown, constituted their liberties. Politics was profoundly personal—a chain of patrons and clients in which connections mattered and were both private and public. Politics was theater; every community, a *tableau vivant*. In such a world, Louis XIV could expect Pierre Le Moyne to pursue his own interest while also pursuing the state's interest. The Crown might have been annoyed—and, in fact, was—at the extent to which its priorities were being subverted. Corruption was endemic to this system.

The potential that agents of empire had for independent maneuvering in North America was just about limitless. This was especially the case after the Seven Years War in the cis-Mississippi frontier. The Spanish and British empires, having acquired a vast new territory from France, had to rely in large measure on men and women of substance already on the scene who had connections to local Indian groups. Thus the stage was set for developing a complex set of personal connections crossing national and ethnic lines and containing multiple agendas. Such a political culture resonated with the system of accommodation then emerging between Indian and European communities and between different tribal polities in this same territory. For Indian peoples in this arena, the period between 1760 and 1820 was also a time for building new bridges and finding ways to accommodate differing but compatible agendas. Indian groups already established in Indiana, western Ohio, and Illinois had to find room—socially and geographically—for Shawnee and Delaware immigrants from eastern Ohio and Pennsylvania. Indian leaders such as Blue Jacket and Pacanne had to learn how to negotiate with Europeans and with former Indian rivals. Behind the emergence of cluster settlements at Miami Towns (Kekionga, Fort Wayne) and "The Glaize" (northwestern Ohio) lay a carefully constructed set of arrangements—clan adoptions, marriages, and the like—allowing individuals to pass freely between communities. These communities shared cultural traits and pursued joint objectives, but they remained distinct. It was an international landscape in a local context.[23] Individuals who had the right personal connections and could act successfully as double agents stood to gain the most. One such individual was the Miami chief Jean-Baptiste Richardville, whose position within the tribe and ties to traders and government agents allowed him to amass one of the largest fortunes in Indiana by the time of his death in 1841. From both an Indian and a European perspective, this frontier was very much a multinational stage featuring actors who were skillful interpreters and negotiators.

Although the task of writing the history of North American imperial frontiers may seem daunting, much good history is indeed being written about the pre-1900 international frontiers in Russian Alaska, the Spanish Southeast, and the French Mississippi Valley.[24] ("Russian Alaska" is a convenient shorthand for "Russian-Native Alaska" and so on.) But the challenge remains to incorporate such work into the overall narrative structure of western history. Our narrative still follows Turner, moving from east to west while relating the transformation of the landscape and the political conquest of the country. It provides, in William Cronon's words, a "rhetorical structure" for organizing the "transition of economies and communities from one form of activity to another."[25] It makes a damn good story, but it is not the whole story.

In practical terms, how can a course that attempts to cover the history of westward expansion and settlement take in the stories of these imperial, multinational frontiers in a less awkward way? The standard practice seems to be as follows: Discuss various imperial "intrusions" at the beginning; let the "Great War for Empire" (1756–1763) serve as a sort of clearinghouse event—we remove the French and prefigure the irrelevance of the British, then come back to the Spanish briefly in time for Texas and the Mexican War.[26] The heart of the problem seems to be that our traditional narrative framework minimizes the significance of these international frontiers ("international" is used here as a shorthand for "metropolitan" and "cross-cultural"), concentrating instead on a story of national expansion culminating in the triumph of capitalism, liberal democracy, and the hegemony of our mainstream, Anglo-American Protestant culture.[27] But shortchanging the history of international frontiers in Louisiana, the Great Lakes, the Spanish Southwest, and Alaska, we only encourage future nearsightedness. Adopting a more regional approach might be a way out, but a regional approach might obscure the connectedness between regions that is such an important factor on these frontiers and in the interaction between them.

Solving this dilemma may require that we adopt both a narrative framework, which permits us to explore the interplay between regions, and a comparative approach. Begin a survey course with the formative period of the Anglo-American settlement frontier. I think it is fair to say that on this frontier the story of *accommodation* between Indians and Europeans does not constitute a central theme. Indian people are still important in this narrative, and mutually beneficial cross-cultural relations did exist.[28] Nonetheless, the Indian trade was, with some exceptions, a backcountry phenomenon. Its place in the developing colonial economy may not have been unimportant, but it was not primary. Moreover, on this frontier the agency of empire was mediated by a host of local political institutions, most of which had a stake in promoting further land sales and colonization.

Then turn to another region with a very different history—the French imperial frontier, for example. Because of its geographical proximity, this was the first frontier zone to converge with the Anglo-American settlement frontier. (Note: This use of "convergence" should not imply coordination.) Too often we have presented these imperial or international frontiers as passive landscapes. Without overstating the differences between frontiers, each might be shown to respond characteristically to such typical frontier issues as cross-cultural exchange and the setting of boundaries. On the French imperial frontier, for example, we would note the emergence of a French-Indian middle border in the Great Lakes region and the Mississippi Valley. We would discuss the centrality of the fur trade and the patterns of accommodation that developed between French and Indian villages in this region. A deeper understanding of the French frontier would probably lead us to rethink aspects of the Anglo-American settlement frontier.

Moving away from abstractions, let us take a closer look at the Mississippi Valley-Great Lakes frontier zone after the Seven Years War and suggest various themes that might help us achieve a fresh perspective. The aftermath of the Seven Years War, for example, looks very different when viewed in the context of the French-Indian frontier. The victorious British Empire was forced to recognize the staying power of this frontier. The policies of Lord Hillsborough and Lord Halifax, the two royal officials in London with primary responsibility for administering British North America at the conclusion of the Seven Years War, were aimed at promoting British settlement in Quebec and reducing the influence of French traders in the Illinois country. The Quebec Act of 1774 recognized the failure of those policies and restored Canada's former boundaries.[29] The British had, in effect, become the guardians of the very imperial system they had defeated. Although London was now the primary metropole, and the Montreal bourgeoisie had gained an Anglo-Scottish component, the French continued their cultural hegemony on the local scene. In Detroit Scottish merchants married into influential French families. The children of such unions usually spoke French and were raised in the Catholic Church.[30] In the Indian villages south of Detroit and in the Illinois country, the French retained their favored position, much to the chagrin of a number of Anglo-American merchants.

The French maintained their influence in a broad area reaching in an arc from Detroit to St. Louis to New Orleans. The withdrawal of the French Empire from the Great Lakes and the Mississippi Valley in 1763 should not be equated with the sudden disappearance of local French interests. Far from it. French-speaking immigrants from Canada, France, and the West Indies continued to arrive in the area for over fifty years, and they reinforced the survival of French culture.[31] French towns continued to expand, and several bourgeois kinship groups assumed the status of local elites. The Chouteaus of St. Louis and the Campaus of Detroit maintained that status and increased their wealth into the American regime. One can also observe a maturing urban hierarchy in this period. By the 1790s the Creole women of St. Louis were poking fun at the naiveté of their counterparts in Ste. Genevieve.[32]

The growth of French interests in this period was intimately tied to the extension of their trade with the Indians of this vast region. British officials often noted with exasperation that the French seemed to "inhabit every Indian village."[33] French traders encouraged such exasperation by drinking toasts to the golden bygone days of the French regime with their Indian friends.[34] As older tribal boundaries gave way to new multinational cluster settlements, a growing métis population served as useful intermediaries.[35] The complex human landscape of this frontier deserves further study. Perhaps an urban geographer with training in ethnohistory will discover some pattern in the distribution of Indian communities, French villages such as Kaskaskia and Ste. Genevieve, larger trading towns such as Peoria and small trading posts such as Chevalier's at St. Joseph, pan-Indian neutral "exchange zones" such as Prairie du Chien and Portage des Sioux, and incipient cities such as St. Louis and Detroit.

The persistence of the French, and of French-Indian commerce, in the Great Lakes and the Mississippi Valley created a most unusual situation. On the one hand, there developed a common French provincial culture influenced by Indian and African customs; black slavery existed throughout the region. On the other hand, this was a region on the boundaries of two empires, those of Spain and England. How did the French respond to this situation? For one, contraband activities were ongoing. Creoles (French speakers born in America) continued to cherish their cultural and commercial ties to France, but Montreal and London provided goods and credit for merchants on both sides of the Mississippi River. Creole businessmen viewed the Spanish Empire at first as an economic disaster, and they lodged many protests against restrictions of trade in New Orleans. In St. Louis a small group of merchants obtained monopolistic fur trade concessions from Spanish officials. Those who did not so benefit called for free trade. Although domination by "foreign" empires brought some advantages to the locals, neither state provided welcoming imperial communities. The British Empire offered few patronage opportunities. The Spanish Empire was equally uninviting at the beginning of its rule.

There were signs that the French in America desired some form of political self-determination, but what shape would it take? The famous Louisiana revolt of 1768 is suggestive. In their petition to the French Crown, the inhabitants of New Orleans asked to be saved from Spanish wine ("Catalonian poison") and a "simple diet of tortillas." (How appropriate for them to use food imagery in their political manifestos.) And what did they want? They asked for *free trade* as patriotic *citizens* and a return of their *liege lord and master*—a curious combination.[36] The idea of a republic was briefly proposed, but cooler heads realized that the region had neither the resources to maintain such a state nor the proper geopolitical landscape, given the acknowledged sovereignty of the various Indian nations. Republican ideas were also heard in the Illinois country, where the inhabitants, on the verge of being evicted from their villages by the British military in 1772, petitioned for a civil government patterned after "some Republican Model, a good deal similar to that of the Colony of Connecticut."[37]

It seems clear that the French, like their Indian neighbors, were in a delicate situation. One British observer, Henry Hamilton (lieutenant governor at Detroit during the American Revolution), thought "the French are fickle and have no man of capacity to advise or lead them. . . ."[38] The French themselves attempted to pursue their own interests as best they could, given the distribution of power in the region. Hamilton wrote in the same letter: "The Spanish are feeble and hated by the French. . . ." While this statement had some truth in the fall of 1778, when it was written, it was decidedly less true a decade later. Over the forty-year period of their rule the Spanish managed to attach the Creoles of Louisiana to their interest. In fact, Spanish policies changed over time, and the Spanish Empire took an active role in promoting the development of its newly acquired colony.

Although historians of Louisiana have generally recognized the active agency of Spanish rule, there are problems with the traditional historiography of the Spanish Empire in North America that merit a digression. The historiography is still dominated by the work of Herbert E. Bolton and his students. The very term we use to refer to the various regions within this imperial frontier—Spanish Borderlands—resonates with the perspective of this school of historians. Unlike Turner, Bolton did not and could not portray a frontier developing in isolation; he recognized that imperial policy and metropolitan agendas—religious, economic, and the like—played a critical role in the evolution of frontier societies within the borderlands. Bolton argued that the Spanish Borderlands were managed by the metropole for the primary purpose of protecting Spain's more valuable Mexican possessions from the republican beast to the east. This argument formed the core of his narrative.

Just as Louisiana, Texas, New Mexico, and California were to be engulfed by the Anglo-American frontier of national expansion, so historiographically was Bolton's borderlands narrative destined to be swallowed up by the Turnerian framework. By emphasizing the defensive nature of the Spanish imperial frontier, the Bolton school has allowed this frontier to be seen as simply a "barrier," an obstacle to manifest destiny. Although Spanish policy was formulated, in part, in reaction to a perceived threat of English and Anglo-American aggression, there was more to the Spanish Borderlands than presidios and missions. (Bolton's missionaries and soldiers also curiously resemble Turner's archetypes: solitary figures moving through a grand moral,and rather static, landscape.) Bolton and his many productive students did note the continuing influence down to the present day of Spanish culture and institutions not only in Mexico but in those areas of the borderlands that became part of the United States. As Bolton himself observed, immigrants from the "States" to the "borderlands found the backbreaking work of pioneering already done for them. . . . They could hardly be called pioneers. They entered an established community."[39] Nevertheless, the Bolton school concentrated its work on studies of royal officials, military and diplomatic history, and the like. It is history written from the metropolitan perspective, with few community studies, few analyses of the interplay of imperial policy and local development.

Recent scholarship has begun to redress this imbalance. Whereas older studies described a frontier "holding action" and a "borderland in retreat," newer studies have investigated the Spanish contribution to community formation and Indian relations.[40] These studies stress the positive aspects of Spanish policy and reveal Spain's commitment to urban growth and economic development. Spain promoted city planning, its royal officials being active in the regulation of urban life.

In Louisiana, Spanish land and immigration policy became increasingly attractive to United States citizens. Although the lure of Spanish land grants tempted a relatively small number of emigrants from the United States, some members of Congress in the 1790s saw it as a serious threat to the loyalty of their western citizens and the success of federal land policy. We should reexamine Spanish, and later Mexican, land policy from a local perspective. It was, after all, a viable alternative in the West for over half a century. (And on the Spanish frontier there were no taxes.) Compared with United States land policy before the Homestead Act, Spanish and Mexican land policy was at once more generous and more conservative, promoting the formation of a landed elite and favoring a hierarchical chain of responsibility. Given the competitive nature of these land policies at various times in western history, we ought to devote more attention to the interaction between Spanish and Anglo-American frontier zones.

Spain was well aware of the competition it faced when the United States became its neighbor across the Mississippi. The liberalization of its land policy and commercial regulations for Louisiana were due in no small measure to the young Republic's emergence as a force on the continent.[41] (To this extent, the positive aspects of Spanish policy can still be regarded as reactive or defensive.) Spanish efforts to strengthen French-speaking Louisiana required an investment of both financial and human resources.[42] For Spanish authority to be realized, it was necessary to create a local Spanish interest. It is not surprising that the most popular Spanish governors of Louisiana married local Creole ladies from prominent New Orleans families or that French-speaking lieutenant governors like Zenon Trudeau and Charles de Hault Delassus were instrumental in keeping the allegiance of St. Louis Creoles to Spain. Social alliances and the pursuit of patronage were among the ties that bound this political culture. To understand this Spanish "borderland," we must see how it operated on a local level. Again, empires had their uses; local and imperial agendas informed each other. Only by viewing the Spanish regime as a *significant* episode in local history can we move away from the notion of a defensive borderland. At the same time historians must know the metropolitan context that shaped Spanish rule from "above."

Two other aspects of the Spanish imperial frontier and the French urban "crescent" from Detroit to New Orleans merit mention here because of the distinctiveness they lent to this "alternative" frontier zone: the civil law and Roman Catholicism. Operating as both intellectual and social systems, the civil law and Roman Catholicism were essential components of the culture of this frontier. The substance and procedure of civil law contained a set of operating assumptions about family relations, property, and authority that shaped the communities that adhered to it. Civil law formed part of a community's experience and served as a source of historical allegiance. Recent studies by George Dargo on Louisiana, David Langum on California, and Morris Arnold on Arkansas have investigated the political struggles between adherents of different legal "cultures" that ensued when the Anglo-American settler nation assumed control over a frontier zone under civilian jurisdiction. These studies help identify the social values that inhabitants of distinct frontiers thought worth defending in a period of convergence.[43] As Langum and Dargo point out, by the late colonial period common law procedures were becoming adversarial. This costly, time-consuming system held that "each litigant should look out for his own interests, conduct a vigorous examination of the witnesses, and the judge's role ought to be limited to that of an umpire." Each trial was conducted as a "struggle until there is a clear winner." By way of contrast, civil law procedures on this frontier emphasized the paternalistic authority of the judge and the ideal of reconciliation. Lawsuits were considered a disruption of the community and were to be settled as rapidly and amicably as possible.[44] French and Hispanic merchants especially feared the use of jury trials in civil cases. As one French merchant of Baton Rouge said of the Anglo-Americans: ". . . they will bring with them, in a free and peaceful country, the discord and disunion of families through lawsuits and taxation. Lawyers, sheriffs, and constables will come crowding in here. . . ."[45] Common law was also disliked for its "fragmented notions of property—the relativity of title, the competing claims of present and future property holders, and the difference between legal and equitable ownership."[46] Neither legal tradition had a monopoly on flexibility in the face of changing "commercial and technological realities."[47] And common-law advocates and civilians alike thought the others' legal world to be detrimental to "liberty." The issue of law in these two frontier zones clarifies the meaning of liberty to the respective inhabitants and helps us move away from our traditional ethnocentric view of American expansion and political ideology on the frontier.

The role of Roman Catholicism on this frontier also deserves rescue from the standard ethnocentric historiography. While we possess a number of institutional histories of church-related activities on the frontier, especially those of the Jesuits, who dominate the historiography, we need further studies of the social role of the church, its agency in community formation and regionalization. Like the various governments involved in the American West, the Catholic Church paid attention to the needs of evolving communities and recognized and ordered emerging regional networks through its own, distinct set of progressive boundaries. The Catholic Church was, indeed, a colonial authority with Rome—literally the metropole. Unlike most Protestant sects, the Catholic Church was a great source of what we might call social capital on the frontier, providing funds and manpower that might not otherwise be available. It played an important role in many frontier towns—small and large—sending spiritual leaders who also served as administrators, educators, and nurses. Their services, especially in the many educational institutions supported by the church, were used by Catholics and non-Catholics alike from St. Louis to Detroit, Davenport to Natchez. It is fair to say that Roman Catholicism loomed larger on this "alternate" frontier zone than in any other part of the present-day United States, with the possible exception of the Maryland-Washington, D.C., area, throughout the first half of the nineteenth century. Did its highly visible role force a certain degree of toleration?[48] Did it reinforce the multinational character of this frontier and provide a useful bridge between Indian and non-Indian communities? (One band of Potawatomi Indians on their way to Kansas came across two women, one Catholic and one Protestant. Upon discovering that the Protestant woman did not know how to make the sign of the cross, the Potawatomis shook their heads in pity.)[49] Did the Catholic Church reinforce a sense of social hierarchy and international connectedness? These are most fruitful areas for future research. We should also recognize once and for all that Catholics were no more "slavish" in their devotion to the church—a Parkmanesque term—than Protestants. Priests and ministers alike noted the freethinking tendencies of the Creole elite in St. Louis, and priests who were refugees from revolutionary France, an important group in the West, found to their dismay that many of their parishioners were ardent Bonapartists.[50]

The frontier that emerged in the Mississippi Valley-Great Lakes area was distinct in many ways from the frontier of national expansion that moved from east to west roughly from the 1750s to the end of the nineteenth century. The brief sketch of that French-speaking frontier has obviously glossed over the similarities between the French and the Anglo-American frontiers and neglected other "alternate" frontiers in the Spanish Southwest and Alaska. The point remains: We cannot view most of the American West simply as a frontier zone in which an intrusive society and an indigenous society meet. It is much more accurate to view the historical situation as the meeting of various distinct frontier zones, each with its own dynamic, its own pattern of change. We cannot, for example, understand Tlingit culture in late-nineteenth-century Alaska without taking into account the frontier experience that helped shape it before the United States and its agents arrived on the scene. To the chagrin of many Jeffersonian bureaucrats and land policy historian Paul Wallace Gates, private land claims made a difference in Louisiana, Missouri, and Florida. They also made a difference in the Spanish Southwest. The clients of empire in Missouri and Illinois applied their skills and their connections to other regions in the West. Moses Austin moved easily from Spanish Missouri to Texas. Ceran St. Vrain, the nephew of the last Spanish lieutenant governor of Upper Louisiana (Charles Delassus), moved to New Mexico, as did a host of other "career" double agents. Were they operating as agents of manifest destiny or were they simply entrepreneurs steeped in the political culture of the imperial frontier? Is it merely a coincidence that Pierre Menard of Illinois had a nephew, Michel, who became one of the founders of Galveston, and a grandson, Lucien Maxwell, who received the infamous Maxwell Grant in New Mexico? A closer examination of these alternate frontiers may lead us to a more nuanced interpretation of national expansion.

A new western narrative should include the evolution of these "alternate" frontiers and recognize their persistence in the regionalization process. We may come to know the traditional frontier as a graft or overlay on the history of some regions rather than a transformation. Because the frontier experience, be that myth or reality, still figures so prominently as a source of our national identify, we should reexamine the impact of that traditional frontier. How pervasive was the frontier of national expansion?[51] Which frontier narrative—imperial or national—explains the attraction of Irish and German Catholic immigrants to western places with an already established Catholic support system rooted in French and Spanish communities? Did the shape of the federal Indian business—the operations of powerful merchants who served as brokers between tribesmen and the government—that emerged in the 1820s owe more to republican ideology and practice or to the traditional political culture of the imperial frontier?[52] (St. Louis Creole businessman Auguste Chouteau fancied himself a western Napoleon.) Our traditional frontier history fails to explain too many aspects of our past. Either we endow a new narrative framework with a sense of process that can include the imperial frontier experience, or else we acknowledge that our favorite western was, indeed, a double feature.[53]

Americans, Mexicans, Métis

A Community Approach to the Comparative Study of North American Frontiers

JOHN MACK FARAGHER

Frontier historians once told a simple story, in the words of Theodore Roosevelt, a story of "a bold and hardy race" of English, Scottish, and Irish pioneers, "the love of freedom rooted in their very heart's core," who "thrust ever westward" to win and settle "the immense wilderness which stretched across to the Pacific." Frederick Jackson Turner praised Roosevelt's *The Winning of the West* for the "graphic vigor" with which the author "portrayed the advance of the pioneer into the wastes of the continent." Roosevelt and Turner read frontier history through the narrow lens of nineteenth-century American nationalism.[1] The power of this narrative lay in the way it linked cherished values such as opportunity and freedom with the unfolding of national destiny, the certainty of white supremacy, and the development of rugged, individualistic masculinity. It served the social and political agenda of an aggressive national elite, including presidents like Roosevelt or, in a later time, Kennedy and Reagan, each of whom explicitly called upon this frontier vision. Today, after a quarter century of social history from the bottom up, few supports for that traditional interpretation remain intact. The frontiers of North America encom-

90

passed a multitude of cultures with divergent views. They had "many pasts," and no single group of actors knows their history. The picture emerging from current historical research of diverse, multifaceted frontiers is instructive. It is also intimidating, for it requires that historians now imagine a new narrative.

To move in that direction, we must first assiduously avoid the error of focusing on one phase of the drama, or on a single group of actors, at the expense of others. The history of the North American frontier took place on a vast continental stage and necessitates a continental perspective. It begins with thousands of indigenous communities in a variety of finely tuned adaptations to environmental possibilities and constraints, with over two hundred distinct languages and thousands of dialects. Nothing so belies the European construct "Indian" as the array of distinctions among these communities. We can impose useful order on their variety through the heuristic tool of culture areas: gatherers and hunters in mobile bands on the plains and deserts, in the mountains and subarctic; Pacific coastal gatherers and fishers in high-density sedentary villages; irrigation farmers in tightly structured towns or pueblos along the Rio Grande and other desert rivers; farmers of the great Mississippi Valley organized into elaborate chiefdoms; eastern woodland hunters and horticulturalists in village communities from which they migrated seasonally to key resource sites. This preconquest distribution of the early sixteenth century was the product of a rich history of migration, discovery, invention, and diffusion over many millennia.[2]

To this complex continent, beginning in the sixteenth century, European colonizers forcibly added colonial outposts populated with their own subjects or with minority populations, often including the enslaved men and women from a variety of African culture areas. The invasion of America was not simply a process of "westering" but a movement that took place at virtually all points of the compass. Working north from their colonial core in the Caribbean and Mexico, the Spanish planted permanent settlements on the Atlantic coast of Florida and the banks of the Rio Grande, on the coastal plain of Texas and the Gila Valley of southern Arizona, and, by the late eighteenth century, along the coast of California. The French founded their core area along the St. Lawrence and then, moving south and west, built a series of commercial-military centers, trading towns, and villages in an arc from the Great Lakes to the mouth of the Mississippi. At the same moment, in the early seventeenth century, English, Dutch, and Swedish colonists established settlements along the Atlantic coast from

91

which several European ethnic groups, including Germans and the Protestant Irish, spread through the coastal plain, into the piedmont, and eventually over the Appalachian barrier to the great inland valleys. Extending their Siberian fur trade operations across the Aleutian Islands, the Russians founded trading posts on the Alaska coast in the second half of the eighteenth century and finally pushed as far south as northern California. In the nineteenth century the final colonization of the trans-Mississippi West included not only descendants from many of these frontiers but thousands of Japanese and Chinese, northern and eastern Europeans, and other ethnic groups.[3]

Constructing these indigenous and intrusive societies with their own unique cultures and histories, placing them in radically different environments, and acknowledging the resulting cross-cultural frontier encounters, as well as the intense territorial rivalries between imperial powers, one begins to grasp the remarkable complexity and diversity of North American history. But developing a new narrative of the frontier requires even more: an analysis of the relationship of these many parts one to the other and each to the continental whole. The project before us is nothing less than the comparative history of North America societies.[4]

Scholars have been looking into the comparative history of frontiers for more than fifty years, and their studies have notably advanced our understanding. Work that sets the frontiers of North America in relationship to one another, however, has been less common. Such a project calls for concepts and questions that are explicitly cross-cultural, allowing us to examine common phenomena in distinct societies, noting their similarities and differences, in order to generalize about their meaning. Only on such a systematic foundation can a new narrative of North America's history articulate the ways in which various societies collaborated and contested each other for hegemony, for self-determination and self-definition, for survival. One might select any number of fascinating topics for study. James Axtell, for instance, examines acculturation on the frontiers of New France and New England; Joan Jensen and Darlis Miller review gender relations across cultures; Howard Lamar focuses on ethnic labor systems; Jerome Steffens compares resource extraction. Here I wish to suggest the ways in which the study of frontier communities may advance this comparative project.[5]

A community focus has much to recommend it. As a concept, community meets the prime test for comparative history because every complete society requires small-scale groups to carry out the process of social reproduction. As sociologist Conrad Arensberg observes, a community is "the minimal group capable of reenacting in the present and transmitting to the future the cultural and institutional inventory" of a "distinctive and historical tradition." A community focus, then, is applicable to all frontier societies, including native inhabitants and people of mixed ancestry. It allows historians to develop more fully the notion of the frontier as a zone of cultural interpenetration.[6]

Excellent ethnohistorical monographs of groups undergoing the process of cultural revitalization, for example, provide community accounts of Senecas in western New York and Cherokees in upcountry Georgia during the early nineteenth century and Sioux on the upper Missouri some seventy-five years later. There is much to recommend extending this ethnohistorical view of the colonist's side of the frontier as well. Nineteenth-century American frontier communities, deep in the throes of camp meeting revivalism, might also be interpreted as a species of revitalization. Comparisons become possible in all directions, across time, space, and cultures. Virginians established decentralized, log construction fort communities in Kentucky, based on farming, livestock grazing, and hunting. One can explicitly contrast them with their Shawnee enemies north of the Ohio, who some decades earlier had also founded decentralized, log construction council house communities based on farming, livestock grazing, and hunting. Such community studies would allow us to assess more precisely what these combatants of the middle ground shared and how they differed. The first American pioneers on the fringe of the Great Plains should be contrasted with community histories of Cherokees or Wyandots, who upon their removal fifty years before had become the first settlers west of the Mississippi to plant composite Indian-European cultures that included commercial agriculture, slaveholding, schools, churches, and constitutional government. Mixed-ancestry métis communities of the Great Lakes and northern plains had counterparts in the Russian Creole communities of the northern Pacific coast, the mestizo settlements of Spain and Mexico's northern frontier, and the numerous Indian communities along the American frontier where so-called mixed-bloods constituted large pluralities. Studies of their respective communities could reveal a great deal about the structures of these contrasting frontiers.[7]

A community approach also has the advantage of focusing on groups that encompass within their manageably small spheres a critical mass of interrelating social and cultural parts that reflect their larger societies. Pat formulas cannot short-circuit the task of selecting significant and researchable parts for study, assembling evidence about them, assessing their connections, and relating them to larger wholes. For the comparative treatment of diversity, however, it is important that historians ask the same general questions of different frontier communities. To what extent can we explain the trajectories of North America's frontiers by their distinctive environmental relationships, social structures, patterns of collective action, values, and beliefs?

I am proposing a "relational" model of community. A community is, first, a system of ecological relations. Historians must ask about community patterns of land and water use, distinctive modes of production, and the process of creating a local landscape as the setting for community life. Second, a community is a system of reproductive relations. There are important historical questions to ask concerning the age, gender, and ethnic composition of communities, their social stratification, the relations among what might be called community *members* (men, citizens, landlords) and community *subjects* (women, minorities, the landless or impoverished), as well as the struggles among these groups over the definition and control of public culture. Third, a community is a field for collective action. Historians of communities must discover the particular dialectic between collective and individual action, the alternating force of cooperation and competition in economic life, the centrifugal and centripetal forces of neighboring, the role of kinship, religion, and other local institutions in creating social networks. Finally, a community is a set of affective bonds. We need to know about the role of shared communal sentiment in cementing social relations, about the creation of local and regional identity, about the use of the community as a base of support for individuals and families. Focusing on communities in these ways allows us to link the details that make a place and time unique with the broader social phenomena about which historians would like to generalize.[8]

This relational model contrasts with a more familiar "essentialist" model, laden with prescriptive assumptions about what an "ideal" community should be. In a time-honored protocol of western social thought, the prescriptive "good community" is located in some past time, is seen to have suffered irretrievable declension, and is imaginatively reconstructed in order to critique the dislocation and anomie of contemporary life. In his influential history of eighteenth-century Dedham, Massachusetts, for example, Kenneth Lockridge asserts that American communalism atrophied when New Englanders "abandoned the web of relationships created by residence in the villages" for settlement in the open country, thereby surrendering to "the incoherence of individual opportunism." His perspective is part of a powerful interpretation, first promoted by the Puritans themselves, that reads American history as decline, from *Gemeinschaft* to *Gesellschaft*, community to individualism, meaning to "incoherence." The appeal of the essentialist conception, sociologist Kenneth P. Wilkinson suggests, "rests on a vaguely articulated but passionately held belief that community somehow is a good thing, a beloved entity or quality to be promoted, defended, and restored in social life." It seems to me that historians have frequently confused the ideal of *communitas* with the analytical concept needed to reconstruct the ways social groups operated. In so doing, they have narrowed the history of community to a search for *essences*. This strategy has little to offer a comparative historical analysis. As Wilkinson argues, most social groups, past and present, have fallen considerably short of the ideal of "pervasive, all-embracing solidarity," yet have still functioned as communities.[9]

The comparative study of frontier settlements should begin with the first European attempts to plant reproducing communities in North America. Charting their parallel development through several generations is important, for these nascent efforts profoundly influenced subsequent community formation. Historians should then compare the founding communities of the Atlantic coast with Spanish communities like St. Augustine or Santa Fe, French ones like Montreal or Detroit, and Russian ones like Sitka in southern Alaska or Fort Ross in northern California. Choosing communities with similar functions would assist in a more rigorous comparison of frontier settlement. How, for example, did eighteenth-century agropastoral communities of the Rio Grande Valley compare with their contemporary herding settlements in the backcountry of the Carolinas? How did irrigation villages of Hispanic New Mexico compare with those of Mormon Utah? How did mining camps of nineteenth-century California compare with those of northern Mexico a century or two before?

Not all colonial outposts were communities. Most mining camps and other resource extraction sites, such as lumber camps, fishing stations, fur trade posts, and military forts, were populated exclusively by men, not families, and thus were incapable of reproducing themselves. Unlike indigenous or settlement communities, these bivouac frontiers were often transitory, dependent upon direct lines of supply to a metropolitan base, and maladapted to frontier conditions. On the other hand, these camplike settlements often tried to forge some form of community, sometimes by importing women or families, sometimes by interethnic marriage and family formation that led to new ethnic groupings within frontier society. The development of what Sylvia Van Kirk calls fur trade society was a particularly successful example of this process. In either case, a relational approach to settlement, sensitive to the distinction between camps and communities, helps clarify the social history of North America's frontiers. Studies that compare communal and noncommunal patterns of frontier societies over time can help us rethink our history.[10]

One topic that badly needs rethinking is the social history of the American farming frontier. A canard of the old frontier narrative presented frontier and community as antipodes. Timothy Flint, a Yankee transplanted to the Old Northwest, wrote in 1822 that on the frontier "everything shifts under your eye; the present occupants sell, pack, depart. Strangers replace them. Before they have gained the confidence of their neighbors, they hear of a better place, pack up, and follow their precursors. This circumstance adds to the instability of connexions." Seventy years later Frederick Jackson Turner similarly argued, though in tones more celebratory than cautionary, that "the frontier is productive of individualism." For "these slashers of the forest, these self-sufficing pioneers, raising the corn and live stock for their own need, living scattered and apart," he concluded, "individualism was more pronounced than community life." How well do these assessments hold up when a relational approach to community is used to reexamine frontier farming settlements?[11]

Illinois was the setting for one such typically "Turnerian" frontier. After the War of 1812 broke the ability of the Kickapoos to defend their towns, and they removed across the Mississippi, Kentuckians and emigrants from farther east began pouring north across the Ohio, in what contemporaries called the Great Migration. By 1820 the Sangamon River drainage in the center of the state was dotted with farming families. About fifty of them lived along the banks of one local stream, Sugar Creek. Population there increased dramatically over the next forty years, and by 1860 some two thousand persons lived in over 350 households. These men and women dispersed themselves on homesteads, their cabins separated at intervals of a mile or so. The millers, craftsmen, and tavernkeepers serving the settlement were similarly scattered. Although service towns later developed along the rail line that pushed through the area in the 1850s, for most of its early history Sugar Creek had no central village. It was an open country settlement, a pattern typical of American farming frontiers since the early eighteenth century. This pattern provided Flint and Turner, and indeed Lockridge, with important evidence for their beliefs about the weakness of community on the frontier.[12]

Within the first years of settlement, however, important relationships had already bound these separate families into a community. People dispersed their farmsteads, but mostly in the margin between creekside timber and open prairie, where they had easy access to water, fuel, and grazing land for their livestock. Thus several distinct neighborhoods developed where soil, water, and flora combined to form particularly attractive sites: Drennan's Prairie, Harlan's Grove, Rauch's Mill, and Pulliam's Sugar Camp among them. Cart paths linked cabins and neighborhoods, and some of these eventually became public roads, tying Sugar Creek to settlements along other nearby watercourses. Roads were maintained by the collective labor of the road gang, on which men worked in lieu of paying road taxes. Roads required that local residents reach consensus about the best routes. Churches, cemeteries, schools, and other assembly sites sprang up at convenient crossroad locations. The boundary lines of political life—road, militia, and election districts—recognized and reinforced these patterns. A clear sense of place that would help underpin community identity was in the process of creation.[13]

Labor on the roads was one example of the collective action from which communities take form. In this republican society the public rituals of democracy were another example. On election day men and their families gathered at Drennan's Stage Stand, the community polling place and muster ground. Voting for most of this period was conducted viva voce, men stepping forward as their names were read from the roll and publicly announcing their choice. They similarly elected their own militia officers and mustered twice a year at Drennan's, an occasion that usually called for more drinking than discipline. Schools were under local management and were important forums of community life. Even more significant were the several churches in which more than half the heads of household had found spiritual homes by 1840. Camp meetings, a summer perennial at Harlan's Grove, were community affairs that included the unchurched as well as the faithful. Believers congregated about the preacher's stand while the wayward gathered at the fringe, where they passed jugs and shared picnics.

Underlying all such behavior was a frontier economy that demanded a great deal of mutuality. During the first four decades of Sugar Creek's history, key resources such as prairie grazing land and a good deal of the timberland, as well as fish and game, were treated as common property. "All unenclosed lands," Rebecca Burland observed, using her native English terminology, "are considered common pasturage." In American parlance, this was "free range." Not just these lands were common to all. Cabin raisings, logrollings, butchering, haying, husking, harvesting, or threshing all were traditionally communal activities—shared work among neighbors. Personal exchanges outside the market of labor, tools, and products— "the borrowing system" some contemporaries called it—were part of the day-to-day operations of agriculture. To be sure, farms were owned and operated privately. Families succeeded or failed as a consequence of their own initiative and fortune. But the frontier community of Sugar Creek demonstrates the fallacy in what Mody C. Boatright called Turner's "myth of frontier individualism." [14]

This community, like others on the American frontier, formed on the periphery of an expanding capitalist nation-state. By capitalist standards, however, it was relatively egalitarian. Among owner-operators, land was quite evenly distributed. In 1838, the first year for which tax lists are extant, the wealthiest tenth of owners held about 25 percent of the acreage; twenty years later their wealth concentration had increased to only about 35 percent. There are no comparable data available on national patterns of landholding, but in this same period the wealthiest tenth in the country as a whole controlled approximately 60 percent of national wealth. The great divide in Sugar Creek was between those who owned property and those who did not. Throughout this period owner-operators constituted about half the heads of household. In the earliest years the landless staked squatters' claims on unsold land, grazed their livestock on free range, and supported their families within the borrowing system. Later, after common resources had become private property, landless families found places in the community as tenants, renters, or farm laborers.

This stratification, however, did not form the basis for frontier class antagonism. Potential conflict was defused through the mechanism of geographic mobility. Only three in ten heads of household persisted in the community between the federal censuses of 1820 and 1830. About the same proportion stayed over the next decade; then the number fell to only two in ten from 1840 to 1850 and the decade following. Among those who owned their farms, however, persistence rates were much higher: seven or eight out of every ten heads of household. While the remarkable general mobility of the population meant that a great number of families, rich and poor, landed and landless, left the community during its formative generations, the poor and landless contributed disproportionately to the turnover in local population.[15]

The social structure of persisting owners and transient poor was reinforced by patterns of kinship. Most individuals from persistent families found marriage partners within the local community. This pattern of endogamy reflected the localistic nature of social life in which people rarely traveled far from their homes and farmsteads. Moreover, the extensive local practice of what some scholars have called sibling-exchange marriage, in which the children of one family married children from another, facilitated a concentration of real property that might otherwise be divided into small parcels through partible inheritance. Within the persistent population core of the community, family alliances and kinship connections were lodestones in the formation and growth of neighborhoods, churches, and local political factions. Likewise, kinship connections were prominent in the networks of shared labor, contributing further to economic success.[16]

Persistence and transience, then, were the two sides of community formation on the American farming frontier. Two groups coexisted in Sugar Creek. One had high levels of mobility, farming for a time before pushing on. The other was much more permanent. Its members supplied the continuity required for sustaining community institutions. Through their overlapping kin networks they came to control those institutions and much of the community's real property as well.

American open country farm communities represented one of several traditions flourishing in the North American continental interior in the early nineteenth century. Others included Mexican villagers to the south and métis hunter-cultivators to the north. How did these rural settlements contrast with those of the American frontier?[17]

The communities of Mexico's far northern frontier were terra incognita for all but a handful of Americans until the opening of the Santa Fe trade in the 1820s. Josiah Gregg, one of the hundreds of American traders who crossed the plains to the New Mexican capital, became the most important early chronicler of these new and exotic sights. Impressed by Santa Fe's contrast with the open country landscape of his rural Missouri home, he wrote in *Commerce of the Prairies* that "the population of New Mexico is almost exclusively confined to towns and villages, the suburbs of which are generally farms. Even most of the individual *ranchos* and *haciendas* have grown into villages."[18]

The Spanish landscape of clustered settlements had, in fact, been decreed by royal plan and ordinance. As John Reps notes, "to a far greater degree than any other colonizing powers in the New World the Spanish followed a system of land settlement and town planning formalized in written rules and regulations." Settlers were to cluster themselves into villages to ensure good order, with churches and civic institutions at their center. But this pattern, repeated again and again in rural settlements on the northern frontiers of New Spain and Mexico, owed as much to Hispanic folk traditions as to the intentions of imperial authorities. Chimayo, a small community established in the Santa Cruz Valley north of Santa Fe during the seventeenth century, was typical. It survives today largely in its original form: sixty or seventy family dwellings abutted to form a protective enclosure, doors and windows facing the public plaza, all surrounded by individual and common fields. Over the years some residents relocated their homes onto their fields at the fringe of the village bounds, but they maintained their connection with the central community as their primary identity. Settlements along the lower Rio Grande and in Texas were also typically nucleated, though the ranching economy demanded a wide circuit of activity; on ranchos, herdsmen clustered their families in distinct little rancherias. California, too, was characterized by centralized settlements in the missions, presidios, villas, ranchos, and rancherias, although the tendency toward dispersed settlement there was somewhat stronger. Everywhere the pattern was the same: towns for living, countrysides for working.[19]

The village landscape signaled a strong collective sense of community. Under the Spanish, lands not reserved for Indians were initially granted to whole communities. In 1794, for example, fifty-two heads of household from Santa Fe petitioned the New Mexican governor for a large tract to the east on the Rio Pecos, promising to enclose themselves "in a plaza well fortified" and to keep the available land open to an influx of settlers. When granted, the deed specified that much of the land was "to be in common" and that all work for the common welfare "shall be performed by the community with that union which in their government they must preserve." Settlers drew by lot for central homesites and outlying fields, holding other resources in common for the community as a whole. Other grants were made to individuals, especially during the Mexican period, but their terms usually required the patron to settle about a plaza several dozen families with individual rights to dwelling and garden lots.[20]

These communities exercised a great deal of self-management. In arid environments, the regulation of scarce timber, grazing land, and water rights compromised individual property rights and emphasized community obligations instead. After independence, Mexico permitted these communities even greater self-regulation, so that by the 1830s nearly every village and every town of the northern frontier were guided by a local council. These were frequently controlled by wealthy local landlords, but there were other sources of authority as well. Rural justices of the peace, chosen by farmers, were responsible for the protection of common grazing and watering sites. The operation of *acequias* (water districts), and the selection of the *mayordomo de acequia*, rested in the hands of users. Settlers were also required to muster into militia to protect the community against Apache or Comanche attack, thus constituting the people themselves as an armed force of the community. Men frequently tried to avoid service, but historian David Weber believes that "the sense of community in small frontier settlements probably encouraged people to volunteer." Hispanic villagers, Robert Rosenbaum concludes, enjoyed a "tradition of autonomous control over local matters."[21]

A thousand and more miles north, from Michigan to Montana and from St. Louis to Great Slave Lake, the settlement landscape of the métis contrasted with both the Mexican and American patterns. Surveying the métis settlements at the confluence of the Assiniboine and the Red River of the North in the 1820s, Governor George Simpson of the Hudson's Bay Company found "no village or collection of houses." Métis dwellings were strung out in ribbonlike patterns fronting river and road, with their fields and meadows "running back into the plain *ad libitum*," Simpson's Latin implying individualistic disorder. His point of reference was the well-ordered English village so dear to nineteenth-century sentiment, but other contrasts were possible. At about the same time the Illinoian John Reynolds contrasted the open country landscape created by his countrymen with that of the mixed-ancestry French along the Mississippi near St. Louis. The French, he said, would "not reside on farms, each family to itself, like the Americans," but "always live in villages where they may enjoy their social pleasure." Many of these métis settlements were what are called line villages. In the early nineteenth century, at the fur trade settlement of Prairie du Chien, three hundred miles north of St. Louis, four hundred French and métis lived in cabins stretching several miles along the Mississippi. Catholic mission priests, who held mass, taught school, and operated infirmaries and hospitals, were invariably present in these communities. There was a spirit of conviviality in the closely spaced dwellings, yet freedom from the ever-present collectivity of the Mexican clustered village. This riverine pattern of settlement had first been established by French habitants along the St. Lawrence. Then, following the waterways of the northern transportation system, it was transplanted to the rivers, bays, lakeshores, and portage points of the West.[22]

The proximity of the homes of Red River métis to river and road was also suggestive of their distinctive way of life, which was a form of transhumance. Having planted their crops in the spring and leaving them in the care of elders, families set out by the hundreds to follow the buffalo herds. Along the way they made meat, pemmican, and robes, which they then sold to the Hudson's Bay Company when they returned to their settlements for the winter. While on a tour of the northern plains in 1854, Governor Isaac Stevens of Washington Territory encountered the métis of Pembina, a community on the Red River just south of the international boundary. They were in the midst of their summer hunt, and he counted over eight hundred Red River carts, twelve hundred horses and oxen, and thirteen hundred men, women, and children living in more than one hundred lodges. With them was their parish priest. Rarely did the wagon trains of western lore reach such proportions, yet somehow the métis never became part of the standard frontier chronicle.[23]

These hunts were extremely important. Agriculture in this northern country was only marginally productive, and buffalo hunting supplied food enough to sustain the entire community, as well as exchange enough to keep up substantial commercial relations with the company. Indeed, Governor Simpson's criticisms notwithstanding, as long as the fur trade promised sufficient profits, the company did much to encourage this métis pattern of settlement. In the 1840s the métis forced the company to loosen its restrictions on outside trading and expanded their sphere of operations to include towns like St. Paul, Minnesota, well south of the forty-ninth parallel. Moving south along a series of trails, they pioneered a northern equivalent of the Santa Fe Trail. Hundreds of carts carried meat, robes, and furs to market, their wooden axles screeching, as one observer put it, like "the scraping of a thousand finger nails on a thousand panes of glass." So tied were these people to their distinctive carts that in the sign language of the plains "métis" was indicated by circling the fingers of each hand about the other, then drawing a finger down the center: half wagon, half man.[24]

The collective organization of the march, derived from Plains

Indian tradition and infused with the military practices of the great fur companies, provided the métis with the most important institutions of self-governance. The Pembina hunters, Stevens noted, were led by four elected captains, one of whom was designated the "governor" of the hunt. Captains, lieutenants, and councils of officers typically supplied leadership; in their communities along the rivers, company-appointed councils and local officials invariably included these same men. But the métis were never as much at home as when they were on the march, for then they were completely under their own authority. "The organization of the hunt," concludes historian A. S. Morton, "became the framework of Métis society, the mode of their corporate life."[25]

Like the Americans, then, the Mexicans and the métis formed their own distinctive communities, possessed with the technical, social, and cultural skills necessary to colonize the arable grasslands. Their relationships to expansion, however, were in marked contrast with those of the American frontier. In New Spain, authorities responded to the chronic labor shortages that resulted from the collapse of the indigenous population—reduced from an estimated twenty-five million on the eve of contact to about one million a century later—with a series of restrictions on movement that became embedded in the structure of Mexican society. Combined with a reluctance to emigrate to the dangerous northern frontiers, these policies resulted in extremely low rates of in migration after initial government-sponsored settlement. By 1820 nine of every ten New Mexicans were native-born. This suggests a demographic stability in startling contrast with the rapid turnover of American frontier populations; studies of populations in the other northern provinces of Mexico suggest the same pattern. In the métis northland, the westward passage of emigrants from Upper and Lower Canada (Ontario and Quebec) was blocked by the forbidding Canadian Shield—a geologic structure of pre-Cambrian granite, covered with muskeg and pine, surrounding Hudson Bay for a radius of five hundred miles. The shield made agriculture impossible from Ottawa west to the Red River and forced expanding farm communities south into the territories of the Old Northwest. The métis, as they insisted, were native sons and daughters of the country, its very geology shaping their lives.[26]

Community formation in the absence of large in-migrating groups helped shape New Mexican and métis settlements into what geographer Marvin Mikesell calls frontiers of inclusion, in which indigenous peoples were incorporated within the settlement community either as separate but assimilated groups or as intermarrying populations. The métis were the offspring of two centuries of such interethnic mixture between French or English traders and the Athabascan, Cree, or Ojibwa peoples of the northern frontier. Mestizos, of Spanish and Indian ancestry, constituted majorities in most Mexican frontier communities. By contrast, Americans established what Mikesell calls a frontier of exclusion, confining indigenous peoples to separate "reserved" territories or forcing their removal farther west. Settlers came to avoid exchanges with native peoples as "barbaric." Among Mexicans and métis, on the other hand, a rich process of cultural interpenetration was everywhere to be seen. One American observer of the métis—it could have been the Mexicans—spoke of "the curious commingling of civilized garments with barbaric adornments," a phrase that perfectly captures the mixed communities of these frontiers. One saw this commingling from language to subsistence strategies, in the mixture of homespun and calico with beadwork, moccasins, and trade blankets, in the bark-covered houses of the Great Lakes métis and the thatched-roof, mud-plastered shelters of Rio Grande mestizos, both derived from indigenous housing styles.[27]

Despite the lack of immigration, however, both the Mexican and the métis experienced significant demographic growth in the first half of the nineteenth century. Between 1821 and 1846 New Mexico's population grew from thirty-seven thousand to sixty-five thousand, expanding at an average annual rate of better than 2 percent. Annual growth rates for most agricultural societies have been less than 1 percent, and few populations in the developing regions of this century have exceeded 2 percent. In the absence of migration, therefore, the growth in New Mexico must have reflected a dramatic improvement in the quality of life, a lessened impact of epidemic disease, and a fall in general mortality. Population growth strained local resources, and communities began to "hive off," forming new settlements to the east along the Canadian River, to the south down the Pecos, and as far north as the Arkansas in what became Colorado. As D. W. Meinig has commented, this expansion is one of the great untold stories of the North American West. In the 1840s New Mexicans involved in the growing trade with California even planted village communities east of Los Angeles.[28]

In the north the population of the Red River Valley, estimated at only five hundred in 1820, had reached nearly twelve thousand by 1870. Most of this increase resulted from the arrival of large numbers of western fur trade families of mixed ancestry. As their numbers

increased, the Red River métis extended their settlements south
down the river, where Pembina experienced a surge in its population,
west along the Assiniboine, and eventually along the western reaches
of the Saskatchewan, as well as the Missouri and Milk rivers south of
the international boundary in Montana Territory. At the same time
the métis stepped up their collective hunts, pushing farther south of
the border, engaging in aggressive warfare with the Sioux over hunting territory, and worrying American officials, who viewed them as
potential rivals for the upper Missouri country. In the 1840s groups
of métis families moved as far west as the Oregon country, where they
established farming communities.[29]

In the 1840s, then, all three agropastoral societies could be described
as expansive. But the dynamo of Anglo-America was propelled by
forces considerably more powerful than those of Mexican and métis
societies. There was, first, the unprecedented growth of American
population. The United States experienced an average annual growth
of about 3 percent from 1790 to 1840. Growth was even more remarkable on the western border: The population of the Old Southwest
expanded from 17,000 in 1770 to 2.6 million in 1840, the Old Northwest from a few thousand to 2.9 million in the same period. By 1840
these regions had "hived off" two trans-Mississippi territories, Iowa
and Arkansas, whose populations stood at 43,000 and 98,000 respectively. Such growth in part continued the eighteenth-century pattern
of high rates of natural increase among rural and frontier populations.
Increasingly, however, it resulted from rising standards of living, fall-
ing death rates, and growing levels of foreign immigration, all following from the rapid commercialization and industrialization taking place
throughout the economy. Finally, the United States had assembled
and tested a strong central state system. It may have had significant
internal conflicts, but it included a colonial framework for encouraging its people to expand into border regions and incorporating those
regions into the purview of the nation state. In this, it was quite different from the elite factions and weak federalism of Mexico or the
weak nationalism of the Hudson's Bay Company's commercial suzer-
ainty.[30]

American expansion, in other words, was linked to the development of a national capitalist society. The prevailing ethic of American
communities was progress. Indeed, the genius of community formation on the American frontier was the way groups of persistent and
mobile people shared a common belief in the values of improvement

and expansion—the twin ideological expressions of persistence and mobility. To men and women actively engaged in settling the land, "improvements" meant acres cleared, plowed, and enclosed, barns and cabins built. Logs gave way to clapboards or were replaced altogether with frame houses; cart paths gave way to roads, and roads to rails, all linking the community with the development of the nation. Evangelical Christianity and the certainty of white supremacy convinced settlers of their status as a "chosen people," in contrast with the barbarians on the other side of the frontier.

All agreed on the goal of improvement, although by the very definition of capitalism, not all could participate in its ultimate triumph. But for those who could not, expansion beckoned. As new lands had attracted the aspiring poor from developing Pennsylvania to frontier Virginia or Carolina, and from there to trans-Appalachia, so American farmers set out for Iowa and Arkansas. Americans would eventually set their sights on former Mexican territories, and Ontarians would focus on former métis lands in Manitoba. The historic pattern of mobility and persistence, unique to the Anglo-American frontier, kept alive the hope of future landownership for the mobile poor while reproducing landed communities that in themselves acted as powerful symbols of what persistence could accomplish.

By contrast, Mexican and métis community formation was a folk process. Driven by the force of population growth rather than by a vision of economic development, expansion was not intended to improve but simply to preserve the character of the established communal order. This preservationist perspective appears in the conflicts that took place between such communities and Anglo-Americans in the second half of the century. At the conclusion of the Mexican War in 1848, the villages of Mexico's far northern frontier suddenly found themselves colonies on the far southwestern periphery of the United States. After the conquest, when interethnic struggles over land and labor took center stage, the underlying agenda was to integrate these borderlands into the political economy of the capitalist state. In those difficult times Mexican communities, many with histories extending back many generations, became a refuge and a base of support for native inhabitants. Indeed, according to Rosenbaum, areas with the strongest communal traditions were most successful in mounting resistance to American domination.

One important example took place along the Rio Grande in 1859. There the mistreatment of Mexican workers by Anglo ranchers and sheriffs set off a regional war between American authorities and Mexican locals, who were led by Juan Cortina, a charismatic leader from a prominent border family. Riding at the head of a small army of vaqueros, Cortina freed Mexicans from local jails, besieged the Anglo town of Brownsville, and controlled the countryside for several months. Attacked north and south of the border by both American and Mexican armed forces, Cortina acted in the interest of locals, among whom his actions found widespread approval and support.

Twenty years later, in San Miguel County, New Mexico, arriviste ranchers and railroad men tried to claim traditional communal lands for their own private or corporate use. They were opposed by community groups called Las Gorras Blancas (White Caps), who cut fences, organized Mexican workers, and eventually allied themselves with the Knights of Labor. Their struggle to maintain common rights guaranteed in their original Spanish grants was vindicated by a finding of the Court of Private Land Claims in 1894, although that decision was later gutted by a U.S. Supreme Court ruling that claimed common rights applied only to the small cultivated strips bordering irrigation canals. Similar community-based struggles took place from east Texas to California, illustrating the powerful ties Mexicans felt to their localities.[31]

As David Weber suggests, however, the supremacy of *patria chica* over *patria*, of local over national loyalty, made it difficult to construct from these local strengths a pan-local political unity. It was nearly impossible to forge a progressive political program that transcended village traditionalism. Ethnic consciousness with a progressive orientation developed slowly among Mexican-Americans and did not take political form until after the mass emigration from Mexico, when the revolution of the 1910s pushed individuals out of their traditional communities and into the twentieth-century labor market.[32]

Community preservation was also at stake in the conflict, from the mid-1860s to the mid-1880s, between the métis and Ontarians over the creation of a Canadian confederation. Here métis consciousness took an ethnic rather than localist dimension. Gradually taking form in the eighteenth century, métis ethnic identity burst into life in a violent struggle with the Hudson's Bay Company over its plan in the 1810s to settle European farm colonies along the Red River, territory the métis considered uniquely their own. This confrontation, concluded satisfactorily from the métis point of view, set the terms for relations with the company for the next half century and gave the métis the social and geographic space to develop their semisedentary communities. In the 1860s, however, looking ahead to a radical decline in fur trade profits, the company developed plans to introduce the American system of township survey to Rupert's Land in order to open the country to large-scale farm settlement. When the Red River métis stopped the surveyors to protect their riverine landscape, the company transferred its colonial holdings to the newly formed Canadian confederation. The métis leadership, headed by the brilliant Red River leader Louis Riel, thereupon declared the independence of "the métis nation." They established a provisional government and insisted that any union with Canada was impossible without specific protections for their way of life.[33]

The Canadian government wrote into the Manitoba Act of 1870 most of the protections demanded by métis communities. But there is a pathos about the story, for by then that way of life, tied as it was to the traffic in furs and the extensive use of the grasslands, was already in terminal decline. As imperial troops headed for the Red River to take possession of the province for Canada, they sang:

> If the girls of Manitoba are as kind as they are charming,
> The half of us will stay behind, and settle down to farming!

They were harbingers of thousands of Ontarian farming families that emigrated to Manitoba over the next few decades. As this happened, and as the métis were abused and treated as barbaric vestiges of the past, communities began to leave Red River. By 1880 the métis population of Red River had been cut in half. Some joined their Indian kin in mixed communities, others moved to communities of compatriots in the United States, but most emigrated west into Saskatchewan. There, in 1885, another métis rebellion broke out over many of the same issues but was crushed by a combination of troops and farmers. Louis Riel was arrested, tried, and hanged, and other leaders fled into exile. Again many of the métis dispersed. A few landed métis communities remained after this disaster, but they were increasingly overtaken by open country farming. By 1890 the protections of métis traditions built into the Manitoba Act had been legislatively removed, and the provinces of Saskatchewan and Alberta had shown themselves equally unfriendly. Many métis moved to northern Alberta; others, to the Mackenzie River area. Those who remained frequently lived on the fringe of Anglo communities, in ghettos along railroads and highways. Others became migrants with no established residences. It was common in the late-nineteenth-century northern plains to see métis families wandering the countryside in their carts, searching for seasonal work. Ethnic consciousness among the métis was strong, but because of their transhumant lifeways, their attachments to locality were weak. The paramount issue of the dispersed métis in the twentieth century would be the struggle for a land base.[34]

In his presidential address to the American Historical Association in 1932 Herbert E. Bolton urged historians to write what he called "the epic of greater America." The heartland of the continent, he reminded his audience, lay in the pathway of several expanding peoples. "It was," he declared, "an affair of all North America, not of any single nation. The outcome no one could predict, patriotic historians to the contrary notwithstanding."[35] The triumph of Anglo-American patterns of agrarian settlement in North America must not cause us to neglect the earlier forms of community that preceded that outcome. We can better understand the contingencies of this story by appreciating the historic priority on the land of other communities, each with its own unique relationships to environment, its own social structures, its own patterns of action, and its own cultural values. The similarities and differences they share with the Anglo-Americans will clarify the process of conquest, destruction, survival, and adaptation. To command attention comparable to the old frontier history, a new narrative must also connect with timely cultural and political concerns. Ours is a society of many cultures in search of common purpose, a search to which frontier history can speak directly. At its core, frontier history is the story of the contact of cultures, their competition, and their continuing relations. It cannot be the story of any one side.

109

Landscape of Enclaves

Race Relations in the West, 1865–1990

SARAH DEUTSCH

About two miles from the center of Greeley, Colorado, on the dry, flat plains, children play in the streets of a neighborhood that bears little resemblance to the rest of town. Founded by eastern utopians, Greeley has remained in appearance an Anglo community. Here, on the other hand, adobe walls austerely line the narrow, dusty streets.

The *colonia* is about sixty years old, and a few of the more than one hundred inhabitants have lived in it almost that long. They came as sugar beet workers in the 1920s, stayed through Communist party meetings in the 1930s, and watched fellow Spanish Americans from southern Colorado and northern New Mexico and Mexican immigrants come and go and sometimes stay. They have cousins among their neighbors. They mind their churches and businesses. The Spanish Americans tend to keep their distance from the Mexicans, looking down on them, and both groups keep a wary eye on Anglos. Anglos, they say, come only to vandalize or to collect bills.

Despite the solid feel of its adobe bricks the community simply does not exist in the eyes of outsiders. In the early 1980s the Greeley planners' office, trying to aid a flood control consultant, had trouble finding the colony. It was not on the map. Where it should have been, there was only the green belt, an uncomplicated swath of green, with no intruders.[1]

In many ways the *colonia* in Greeley epitomizes both the historical process and, in its very invisibility to Anglos, the continuing salience of race as an issue in the twentieth-century West. The colony's roots lie in the nineteenth-century U.S. conquest of Mexican territory. After the conquest Hispanic farmers' land grants became eroding islands in a stormy legal sea. The farmers, who needed ever greater cash supplements to shore up their home villages, sought wage labor in the Anglo economy. When they began to settle in Anglo areas, they were shown to the margins of towns, ideally across the tracks. Often they found only colonies. The Great Western Sugar Company had built the isolated colony at Greeley to save money on annual labor recruiting and still retain good relations with Anglo sugar beet farmers.

Spanish Americans slipped across the line from more permeable ethnic group to race. Recalling their earliest memories, colony residents spoke of watching through their windows as the burning crosses of the Ku Klux Klan, so powerful in 1920s Colorado, marked the boundaries of the Greeley colony. Signs such as NO MEXICANS ALLOWED kept colony residents from getting even a hamburger in town. By 1930 the federal government had also redefined "Mexican" from a nationality to a race, one that included Hispanic citizens born in Colorado and New Mexico.

Racial tensions emerged in sexual fantasies. Anglo residents depicted drunken revelries with dancing girls as a regular colony feature and, unannounced, sent in a team of experts to conduct tests for syphilis on Greeley colony residents. At the same time Anglo reformers sent in Anglo female social workers to teach Hispanic women how to cook "properly." One elderly resident recalled, "We already knew how to cook," and commented with bitter irony on the subsequent proliferation of Taco Bell restaurants in Greeley.

The Greeley colony offers tantalizing glimpses of new fields for research on the post–Civil War West. Its invisibility was achieved through language and behavior, as definitions of race, ethnicity, and "otherness" changed. Such shifts not only occurred in relations between majority and minority groups but affected relations among minority groups. Spanish Americans and Mexicans also constructed definitions of "otherness." All the groups called the intimate connections among race, sex, and gender systems into play in this process of reshaping cultural and social boundaries. They embedded this constellation of issues in a particularly western heritage of conquest and territoriality. New methods of textual and cultural analysis that explore how language and behavior affect each other shed new light on the centrality of race to the history of class formation, politics, economics, and culture in the West.[2]

Despite its salience, the history of race relations in the West presents intractable problems of periodization. Each group and each subgroup have their own histories and their own historical dynamics, responding to internal as well as external impulses. The lens we use to view the actions of and reactions to the dominant group can distort the lives and motives of every other group and magnify the significance of the dominant group. Those historians who call for a new synthesis would do well to call also for a new narrative form more appropriate to a pluralistic concept of history. This essay does not pretend to solve the narrative dilemma. It focuses on race relations, on the interaction itself, rather than the histories of particular groups. It relies on shifts in federal policy to mark watersheds and provide an element of coherence. The disproportionate role of the federal government in the West relative to other regions has meant that shifts at the federal level changed the rules and sometimes even the players of the game. The dynamic between community and region, between region and nation can overcome a tendency toward fragmentation almost irresistible in the study of race and ethnicity in the West and give us four overlapping periods of study: 1870s–1890s, 1890s–1930s, 1930s–1950s, and 1960s–1980s. Within these periods people's languages, spaces, sexes and genders, and economic systems wove a uniquely western pattern of race relations that historians are only beginning to discern.

The violence of racial confrontation from the 1870s to the 1890s signified a desperate struggle for control in the West. Massacres littered the landscape with corpses. In 1876 a fair-haired glory boy disobeyed orders and led his relatively small force to death against the largest encampment of Plains Indians in memory. For this the much-loved General George Armstrong Custer, though dead, or perhaps because dead, became even more loved and more heroic in the popular imagination. The fascination with this battle, which has inspired more literature than any other battle, demonstrates the centrality of western race relations to national as well as regional history.[3] But the violence was not limited to mutual massacres of Indians and whites. White workers rioted against Chinese laborers in California, Washington, Wyoming, and elsewhere. Hispanic vigilantes cut fences and destroyed railroad ties in the names of the people. The United States flag fluttered over the entire trans-Mississippi West by 1865, but dependence and order by no means followed conquest.[4]

It was the railroad—symbolized by the completion of the transcontinental line in 1869—rather than the military that tipped the balance of power. It prefigured the outcome of the confrontation. The railroad, linking city to city, coast to coast, countryside to markets, symbolized national capitalism's triumph over local autonomy. The railroad also revolutionized the demography and altered the pattern of opportunity in the West. And the two changes were entwined. In part as a result of the new technology, blacks and European immigrants searching for a better life and Mexican and Chinese laborers responding to the higher wages of the West could do so in unprecedented numbers and reach the farthest corners of the region. The plains were no longer remote.

Since the railroads legally owned the land in the eyes of the United States government, and because they enjoyed government subsidy and support, they had the power to impose their vision on the West, to shape the environment to meet their needs. In 1865 ten million buffalo roamed the plains. By 1890 the remaining thousand or so were all in private hands. The railroad brought into the contest all the resources of the West, eroding the refuge of time and distance that had allowed diverse peoples to make their forays into the market on their own terms. Territories became enclaves. Indians and Chicanos became minorities.

In a sense the violent western conflicts over resources were "race wars," in which "race" connoted more than biological composition.[5] The victory of the industrial North in the Civil War cemented the belief by the victors that a certain set of attributes, including race, constituted virtue and civilization. These attributes included Protestant individualism, female domesticity, and male enterprise, all of which fed the large-scale capitalism and commercial development that were considered the source of future opportunities. Sexuality and private property were intimately related in this Anglo pantheon. Manliness itself depended on landownership and dominion. "Otherness" lay in the gender and labor structures of Chinese immigrants, the communalism of Hispanic villages, the power and autonomy of Indian women and their hunting men. "Otherness" lay in the insistence of these peo-

113

ple on slipping, at will, in and out of the capitalist economy and all it stood for and in remaining, as one government investigator put it, "outside of American civilization."[6]

In the imperative of Anglo capitalist expansion, there was no concept of equality that was not "same," no concept of difference that was not threatening. The role of the West in eastern eyes was to save the United States from European-style class conflict while still allowing industrial development. The West was meant to provide opportunities for refugees from the industrial East, not a safe haven for Asians, Mexicans, or Indians. In 1874, two years before his fatal meeting with Sitting Bull, Custer ignored orders to keep whites off the Sioux reservation and to keep his mission a secret. Instead, he took an enormous entourage of reporters with him when he went to investigate rumors of gold in the Black Hills. To Custer, land containing gold belonged in the hands of whites. In the prevailing view, Sitting Bull's triumph over Custer at Little Bighorn in 1876 marked savagery's triumph over civilization. Sitting Bull, a Sioux traditionalist, threatened to impede white development and therefore endangered the fragile framework of the new society Americans believed themselves to be building.[7]

Naturally, the struggle looked different to other eyes. To Sitting Bull, it resembled more a rampage of greed and selfishness, of exploitation and rigid hierarchies, whether based on race or sex or both. Resisters of this onslaught from the 1870s to the 1890s did not necessarily resist progress but the form they saw progress taking. Many adopted, when they could, new technology and manufactured goods—iron bedsteads, cookstoves, guns, and plows began showing up in remote Hispanic villages—but for their own ends.

Other groups exploited aspects of the new Anglo West to fulfill dreams impossible elsewhere. Chinese farmers bought and leased land from Anglo corporations in amounts inconceivable to them at home. Black Exodusters, fleeing the night riders of the post-Reconstruction South, found security of tenure in Kansas and Oklahoma.[8] The lives and strategies of Indians, Hispanics, Chinese, and others did not spring only from resistance to outside aggression. They were also driven by their own past patterns and aspirations. And they struggled against loss of opportunities, self-definition, and control. Though some were new possessors and others newly dispossessed, they had this in common: None participated fully in the Anglo mythology of the West.

These groups called all elements of their social life—food, gender structures, sexual relations, labor relations, house forms, religion, values regarding land and profit making and accumulation—into the struggle. Considering the all-encompassing nature of the contest, the ability to claim physical territory on a scale unimagined in the East was central to the ability to resist total accommodation and dependency. Territorial control provided a key card in negotiating status. Not only Chicanos and Indians but Exodusters and Asians sought safe space for development according to their own lights. Lieutenant Colonel Allensworth had escaped slavery, joined the navy in the Civil War, turned clergyman in Kentucky, and finally served as an army chaplain for the black Twenty-fourth Infantry before retiring and founding Allensworth, California, to be a black "city on a hill." Its promoters touted it as the place where "your exertions are appreciated."[9] Too few histories have compared racial and ethnic minority settlements in the West with those in the East, but the territorial dimension of race in the West seems more deeply rooted than in the East. Indian reservations simply provide the most obvious example of the persistently territorial nature of race relations, which, like the colony at Greeley, will not disappear.

It is problematic, on the other hand, to create a history that shows Anglos united, pressing forward usually swiftly and always surely toward their aims, maximizing order and domination as though they always knew how and where to find each. Anglos from the 1870s to the 1890s were also adjusting to the new force and vigor of large-scale industrial capitalism. They, too, had trouble adapting and often resisted. And then there were the other immigrants: the ones from Europe.[10] Irish and German, Cornish and Welsh laborers, who tried to drive the Chinese into the sea in the West, could be both engines and victims of change. Chinese exclusion and western racism from the 1870s to the 1890s emerged in the context of shrinking economic opportunity, of frightening conflict and disillusionment across the country. Philadelphia, New York, Baltimore, and St. Louis went up in flames during the railroad strike of 1877. And Big Bill Haywood made a prototypically western drift from cowboy to miner to farmer to radical labor organizer for the Industrial Workers of the World. If the West was the last great hope the United States had of avoiding industrial strife and a permanent working class, then amid that strife it seemed only sensible to preserve that haven for the chosen. The myth of western opportunity had a shaping impact on the region not only because it molded federal policy but also because newcomers brought those fears and mythic expectations with them to the West.[11]

Members of ethnic and racial groups under fire were hardly in a position to provide a united resistance. There is a recurring theme of minority groups gaining opportunities or resisting repression at the expense of other minority groups. Black Exodusters, for example, moved onto what had been Kaw Indian land, and the government placed its black troops in the frontier as Indian fighters. Moreover, in Dodge City, blacks complained of Chinese competition in service-sector jobs. Oklahoma Indians who had owned many slaves before the Civil War did not seem universally disposed to welcome black tribal members.[12]

Through intermarriage and interracial sex, different races did make common cause of a sort. Our understanding of the sexual dynamics of race relations in the West, however, is still primitive. In Butte, Montana, labor organizations boycotted Chinese services and employers of Chinese immigrants. They claimed the action "protected" white women endangered not by sexual advances but by labor competition from Chinese men. Yet women's sexuality was at issue. In Butte, as in most of the West, the local labor market options for Chinese men and for women of all races had long been limited to the service sector, and organized labor in the 1890s claimed white women were drifting into prostitution because Chinese competition undermined their wages. True (white) womanhood apparently lay not in the home but in the shop. Yet white women were not party to the movement, and the boycott forced out of business several white female lodging house keepers who employed Chinese male servants. When these white women asked the police for the much-vaunted "protection," the police refused. Similarly ambiguous, whites condemned the Chinese for immoral practices yet supported the total control tongs exercised over their prostitutes; police returned escapees and turned the other way at murders.[13] Clearly these constructions of feminized men (men in so-called women's jobs) and women unworthy of protection (Chinese prostitutes and independent female lodging house keepers) were related to the legitimation of larger structures of economic, racial, and sexual subordination. Definitions of proper womanhood were used to accord or withdraw protection. Similarly, manhood was bound up in providing protection for proper women against "others." It is in this light that William Curtis's statement, reporting from Custer's camp in 1874 for the *Chicago Inter-Ocean*, should be read: "If Susan B. Anthony wants to vote . . . let her take a scalp."[14]

In the business of boundary maintenance, of ensuring "otherness" on a racial frontier, sex itself is hardly beside the point. In the West, sexuality and gender played a crucial role not simply in fantasy

116

and fear of captivity by Indians but in ideology, law, and behavior. Fur trappers and traders had married Indian women. Anglo entrepreneurs had married daughters of Hispanic elites. As Anglo settlement and economic dominance increased, however, intermarriage at elite levels declined and sexual alliance gave way to (sexual) conquest. Rumors abounded that General Custer, with lordly liberality, distributed captive female Indians among his men.[15] It was not simply the sex ratio that led white men to be more active in interracial sex than white women. It is women, after all, who are the repository of racial purity, and the rape of women has been a traditional part of a conquering army's celebration. Such sex could exhibit hegemony concretely as well as symbolically.

In miscegenation laws, which remained in force through much of the twentieth century, as well as in the more studied landowning and school segregation acts, western Anglos institutionalized racial-sexual frontiers not just with Indians but with blacks, Mexicans, Chinese, Japanese, and other groups. Gender, sexual, and race systems reinforced each other in the West as in the South.[16] A systematic comparison of southern and western attitudes toward miscegenation and other forms of race mixing is desperately needed and should be built on an as yet unwritten account of the subject for the West.

While there has been little serious attention paid to sexuality and sexual rhetoric in the West beyond prostitution, there has been increasing attention paid to the gender differences in racial contact.[17] But historians should be more sensitive to the power relations involved. Women creating careers for themselves as interracial mediators, for example, may not have enjoyed the freedom to question the larger framework within which they worked. In 1881, five years after Little Bighorn, Alice Fletcher sat in a tent on the Great Plains, conversing with Sitting Bull. According to her, Sitting Bull looked at his wives and then implored Fletcher, "You are a woman, take pity on my women for they have no future. The young men can be like the white men, can till the soil, supply the food and clothing. They will take the work out of the hands of the women. And the women, to whom we have owed everything in the past, they will be stripped of all which gave them power. Give my women a future!"[18] Six years later Fletcher was administering the Dawes Act, allotting land only to men. Working with the United States government, she could not control the structure within which she operated. Women of both sides, it is crucial to remember, were constantly negotiating their status within their own groups and families while negotiating their status vis-à-vis other groups.

117

A woman's position in one group could supply her with leverage in others or, conversely, could undermine her influence.[19]

The framework in which Fletcher operated prevailed by the 1890s. Under the weight of eastern expectations and resources, resistance by minority groups had had limited impact. Subordinate groups did retain some measure of control over their communities and choices, but the parameters of the larger world in which they found themselves were increasingly codified and fixed by the 1890s.[20] Land claims courts determined Hispanic land grant ownership based on Anglo, not Hispanic, law, and the Dawes Severalty Act provided for the individual allotment of Indian lands only to adult males. Both were symbols and realities of the primacy (though not totality) of Anglo conceptions of property and manliness by 1900.

With wider hegemony clearly established by the late 1890s, the decades up to the 1930s were years of boundary setting, of jostling within the framework. In this period local dynamics more than federal actions governed racial and cultural relations. The theoretical unity that joined Protestantism to capitalism, civilization to particular gender roles, foods, and other social forms began to give way to a more "scientific" compartmentalized approach. Even in the dominant view, the world seemed to require less coherence. It is possible to see the retreat from mission-governed Indian reservations in this light. After the Civil War it had seemed logical to turn the troubled administration of Indian affairs over to the churches. The rhetoric of the North, after all, had wedded evangelical Protestantism to evangelical industrial capitalism. Abolitionist activists had made the shift easily and filled the ranks and leadership of Indian reform organizations.[21] With the twentieth century's increasing compartmentalization, often loosely labeled "secularism," their influence began to wane. The trend culminated in the 1930s with the advent of John Collier and his social scientists in the Bureau of Indian Affairs.

With Washington no longer backing a holistic cultural evangelism, the federal role in this era, even during the New Deal, paled in relation to the role it had played in race relations during the military exercises and court battles of the previous century. With statehood, western inhabitants could lay claim to more authority in governing their own affairs. On some occasions they even overstepped the line of legality. In 1935 and 1936 the Colorado governor called out the National Guard and closed the border with New Mexico to keep out Hispanic citizens and Mexican immigrants.

In other ways, too, the local majority population chipped away at enclaves as semiautonomous refuges. Homesteading policies encouraged Anglo settlement in heavily Hispanic and Indian areas. Anglos gerrymandered counties to achieve Anglo domination in southwest Texas. Alien land laws swept western states in the 1910s, forcing back the number and reducing the enclaves of Asian farmers. In 1899 it had still seemed possible to dream of a black empire in the West. Sutton Griggs, a black novelist born in Texas who later joined W. E. B. Du Bois's Niagara movement, in 1899 produced *Imperium in Imperio*, the fictional story of a secret black organization that united with America's enemies to take Texas and Louisiana with the aim of retaining Texas as a black empire. The early twentieth century found all-black community settlers petitioning for the admission of Oklahoma as a black state.[22] Yet despite the pleas of black residents, grandfather clauses in Oklahoma had disenfranchised black citizens by the 1910s and dashed their hopes of achieving elective office.[23]

The efforts of minority groups in the West in this era often centered on the attempt to reserve a place apart where they could exercise control over their lives, society, and surroundings. They sought to rescue their enclaves from encroaching domination and dependency. New forms of racial confrontation had already begun to emerge in the 1890s. The short-lived Ghost Dance was an early sign of a pan-Indian identity. La Alianza Hispano Americana, launched in 1894, provided independent institutional means to fight increasingly intrusive racism.[24] With the passing decades, migrant labor in and out of enclaves, chiefly a strategy of retreat, increasingly gave way to more assertive strategies. Indeed, the era saw an avalanche of ethnic institution building. The Japanese American Citizens League fought for neighborhood improvement and an end to racist legislation. The League of United Latin American Citizens originated in Texas and spread through the Southwest. And conflict over Indian land led in 1922 to the first all-pueblo organization since the 1680 revolt.[25]

Yet more diffuse strategies also continued to emerge from these groups' own traditions and values, and sexual divisions of labor continued to play a crucial role.[26] New strategies built on but also changed relations between men and women in the group, without necessarily assimilating to Anglo roles or expectations. Hispanics in northern New Mexico developed a culture of village women and migrant men in order to keep alive distinctly Hispanic villages on a dwindling subsistence base. By taking over the men's fields when the men left for the coal mines, Hispanic women shared actively in restructuring economies and societies without leaving home. In doing so, they not only helped the group survive in a slightly altered form but transformed their own roles.[27]

It was not simply different races that converged on this frontier but different ways of life—systems of economy, politics, family, society. All these systems were organized fundamentally by gender. Federal Indian policy foundered in the late nineteenth and twentieth centuries in large part because its administrators never understood the family systems they confronted.[28] Economic development policies based on assumptions about private ownership or autonomous male actors ran into stubborn communal systems of responsibility and female property control. The point is not just that women gained or lost power but that a whole system built on one method of sexual division could be undermined, not simply altered. Resistance to off-reservation mission schools for girls, mission rescue homes for Chinese prostitutes, and agencies charged with getting men, not women, to farm, signified that conflicts over gender lay at the heart of a larger cultural and racial contest.

On the other hand, historians should avoid the temptation to posit a static and golden past, to reify culture and gender roles. Autobiographical accounts, such as Maxine Hong Kingston's *Woman Warrior*, can help us recognize tensions in gender and other roles already extant in the "traditional" culture. Kingston's mother, a doctor in China with a husband "sojourning" in the United States, had been a "woman warrior," a strong and independent woman, in China. Once in America, however, she prescribed demure obedience for her daughter. Simply reuniting the woman warrior and the sojourner as husband and wife, reconstituting the Chinese family, was problematic enough, but reunion on hostile foreign soil drew suspicion and called forth caution. Like other women and men, Kingston had to create a new identity for herself that suited the new world.[29]

Ethnic identities, in part the fruit of the interaction between minority and majority systems, emerged clearly in the West's highly segmented labor market. Work opportunities tended to be determined by ethnicity or race. Even when specific opportunities varied, job categories rarely crossed racial lines in this era and often did not cross sexual ones. Given their limited opportunities, men and women moved in and out of the labor force and shifted from one economic sector to another from year to year or even from season to season. Ethnic labor studies by western historians need to make the same links between different industries and economies. Any attempt to locate ethnic or racial groups in the economy, to identify them with the work culture of a particular industry, and to explain their behavior in labor conflicts needs to take such variation into account.[30]

Labor organizations born in this era usually fed on mixtures of ethnic consciousness and even more recently emergent class consciousness, a combination appropriate to the nature of the labor market. In some ethnic colonies, labor organizations drew the enmity of middle-class coethnics. Class triumphed over race when Anglo farmers rallied to the aid of Japanese-American farmers they had formerly tried to eradicate and fought with them against Japanese-American farm labor unions. On the other hand, beet workers in Greeley, in the colony and outside it, had the backing of local Hispanic businessmen when they joined beet workers across the state to form a coalition of union locals. The locals themselves ranged from the IWW and AFL to those independent of affiliation and from Hispanic to Anglo or Mexican or mixed. Such new strategies and alliances provided evidence of changes in self-definitions of "Hispanic" or "Chinese" or "Japanese." These redefinitions altered the equation as well as the style of race relations in the West.[31]

Though the enclaves that fostered ethnic consciousness and labor organizations became less and less a refuge and more a measure of confinement and loss of autonomy, they retained many of their positive features. Here a Chicana, like Dolores Huerta's mother, could launch a successful, if small-scale, business and achieve a class and status unavailable to her in the larger community.[32] And despite their vulnerability, enclaves fended off complete control from the outside. Indeed, enclavement spurred political mobilization. Concentrated settlement and access to the polls raised the possibility of voting coethnics into office for other groups as it had for blacks.

The increasing permanence and assertiveness of racial and ethnic enclaves forced Anglos to abandon the illusion that Mexicans disappeared each year below some imaginary border, that Indians were dying out, and that Asians had been excluded. The persistently territorial nature of ethnic and racial difference in the West reinforced an enduring xenophobia. Recurrent fears of a Hispanic or Indian fifth column in the West surfaced with a vengeance during World War I with the Zimmermann telegram. Similar fears reemerged with even more heat in the early years of World War II and led to Japanese-American internment.[33] As the West's majority population came to grips with the reality of a multiracial West, its boundary setting became more aggressive and institutionalized. It attempted to deny the franchise to blacks, Chicanos, and Asians. It burned crosses and placed signs of exclusion in shopwindows. It tightened local residential restrictions. In short, a multitude of words and deeds proclaimed that it was still a "white man's West."[34]

The demarcating of land as off limits to certain races demonstrated a connection between space and power also clearly evident in the era's racial violence. Race riots broke out in Brownsville, Texas, between black troops and white residents in 1906 and in Houston in 1917. More work needs to be done on the different functions of race riots (eradication) and lynching (discipline of an essential but uneasily dominated group). Comparisons of race riots by region and comparisons of lynching incidents across races in the West would take us beyond current generalizations and deepen our understanding of the construction and abuse of "otherness" in the West.[35]

Certainly some "other" remained essential to the Anglo vision of the West as the land of opportunity, the "white man's country." The history of minorities in the West and the history of development are a single story. It is evident throughout this era in the demand for unlimited Mexican immigration. Anglo small farmers, whose own status on the roller coaster of western climate and international commodities prices was hardly secure, wanted to live an American Dream: freedom from dirt and manual labor, "a little automobile for the farmer . . . running water in the house and victrola for the wife." It was, as the president of the National Sugar Company put it, "an expensive proposition." Only the low-paid labor of some group defined as outside that dream made it possible.[36]

Yet after four decades of struggle between local players, the conquest of that "other" was still incomplete. Moreover, the framework in place in 1900 was cracking. Farm laborers, garment workers, and coal miners crossed racial and ethnic lines and pursued their common interests in labor protests.[37] In this context of increasing cross-ethnic unity, the New Deal government adopted a new pluralistic policy toward Hispanics and Indians that reinforced ethnic distinctions. From the 1890s to the 1930s the dominant group had striven to establish a clear racial and cultural ordering; other groups had resisted such ordering in favor of their own visions. By the 1930s, however, residents of enclaves had become thoroughly aware of an enclave's double edge: refuge and confinement. With the new weapons a war economy brought them, minority groups ultimately formed new strategies.

The impact of World War II on race relations was immediate, immense, and immensely varied. The depression had brought federal spending in the West to unprecedented heights. Yet from 1941 to 1945 the federal government spent four times as much in the West as it had during the entire preceding decade. A minimum of forty billion dollars was channeled into the West, inducing massive demographic shifts.

With the desperation of war, the relative shortage of white men, and the aid of the Fair Employment Practices Commission, Chicanos, blacks, and other groups entered urban factories in large numbers for the first time. The black population of the West exploded. In 1940, 3,000 blacks lived in Los Angeles. Then, in mid-1942, black men and women took to the streets, marching through Los Angeles to protest their exclusion from war opportunities. As a result, wartime training courses in black and Chicano neighborhoods opened. Word got out, and blacks across the nation flocked to the West Coast. By the end of 1942 Los Angeles contained 131,000 black residents. The black community of Boulder, Colorado, vanished and reappeared in California, where its members could make more money in a month than they had in the previous year.

Enclavement outside the workplace remained the rule. Blacks and Chicanos made little headway against segregation in housing and recreational facilities. Even so, such tumult in the racial order, suchmassive shifts in demography and opportunity did not occur peacefully. By 1943 approximately five hundred thousand Chicanos lived in Los Angeles County. They formed about 10 percent of the total population and over half the population in substandard housing. Their barrios had youth gangs like those of other lower-income neighborhoods, and the youths had their own distinctive style: zoot suits and longish, slicked-back hair. The suits, with their exaggerated shoulders, wasp waists, and baggy trousers tapered to tight-fitting ankles, marked off both an ethnic group and a generation caught between their parents and their peers. Ethnic enclavement fostered their gangs and their distinctive style. Growing up in the massively segregated city, however, these youths also knew ethnic enclavement as confinement. In early June 1943, with the war going badly in the Pacific, sailors on leave rampaged through Los Angeles and into the barrios, dragging zoot-suiters out of theaters and beating them up, following them into their neighborhoods and attacking them, linking arms and taking over the city's streets. The intervention of the Mexican government played a key role in finally pushing the United States to end the violence.

Throughout the country World War II was marked by violent race riots similar to the zoot suit riots. In the riots of other regions, however, a foreign government and nonresident sailors were not players. Just how different were the zoot suit riots from those that occurred elsewhere? It is significant that this riot, unlike the riots in Detroit and New York, did not involve blacks despite Los Angeles's recently augmented black population? Though such questions are central to our ability to understand the late-twentieth-century West, we know far too little of what characterized Chicano and black relations and almost nothing of regional factors in urban race riots.

Chicanos, like African-Americans, faced demographic changes. With more lucrative opportunities available in war work, Chicanos fled the fields for the city, and the government replaced them with Mexican nationals. While the destructive effect of the availability of bracero labor on incipient agricultural labor unions is clear, more work needs to be done on the relations between braceros and Mexican-Americans during the war.

In another racial displacement black migrants had moved into a section of Los Angeles made vacant by the internment of Japanese-Americans. The destruction of the Pacific fleet, the sense of vulnerability, the long tradition of anti-Japanese sentiment, the image of a mighty Japan, and absurd rumors about radios in garden hoses, everything, in fact, except evidence of Japanese-American complicity with Japan, contributed to the government's decision to place Japanese-Americans, both first-generation aliens ineligible for citizenship and second-generation citizens, in what Franklin Roosevelt himself called concentration camps.

The impact on Japanese-American communities was wide-ranging. In a period when other groups accumulated savings from high-wage war work, their livelihood had been destroyed. The structure of the camps and the policies of the War Relocation Authority enhanced trends toward a peer culture among Nisei (American-born) youth. Issei (immigrant) women daily faced a humiliating lack of privacy. But they also shared more opportunities to develop relations with women of similar backgrounds, to learn English, and to form women's associations. It would be impossible to retreat from some of the consequences of this dispersal and new "freedom."[38] Little, if any, of the literature on internment addresses the issue in its regional context. Was there anything peculiarly western about the internment decision? Hawaii, with a much larger Japanese population and much more at risk, did not indulge in mass internment. New York did not intern its

Italian and German citizens. Beyond Japanese dominance of the Pacific and American racism, did an American mythology of the West and a western regional culture place Japanese-Americans particularly at risk?

The postwar period witnessed a resurgence of individualism and conformity logically flowing from the patriotic rhetoric and propaganda of the war. No loyalty to any group but the dominant group was acceptable. The pluralism and big-spending government of the 1930s now seemed an aberration. The rapid polarization between the United States and the USSR made "difference" seem a threat to national security, and Indian reservations seem both Communistic and confining. Dillon Myer, who had served as director of the War Relocation Authority, saw Indian reservations as concentration camps. Appointed Indian commissioner in 1950, Myer wanted the federal government out of the personal lives of Indians. He also promoted that perennial policy goal of self-reliance in a capitalist market economy. To him, the new policy of "termination" was not Dawes-style allotment revisited; rather, it would permit true tribal self-rule, ending not the tribe but the Bureau of Indian Affairs. Together with the slow-moving Indian Claims Commission, established in 1948, it would, theoretically, resolve the Indian "problem" once and for all.

But for those Indians who fell prey to termination, it removed federal programs at a time when demand for Indian labor had plummeted from its wartime high; simultaneously it made Indian land, which had never generated sufficient income, liable for property taxes for the first time. Similarly, land claims were intended by the government to result in cash settlements, not land restoration, and hefty fees went to tribal lawyers.[39] Clearly the federal government still played a key role in defining not simply the region's race relations but its racial and ethnic groups.

Territoriality could not always be so easily erased, however, nor would dispersal necessarily submerge ethnic identity. The "terminated" Menominees were restored to their previous status in 1973 by law. Nor did other ethnic and racial groups dissolve into individual identities. Even had internal cohesion diminished, discrimination provided a continual reminder of ethnic and racial identity. Anti-Japanese referenda still appeared in California, and it took a United States Supreme Court case to permit a black ex-serviceman to enter his Los Angeles home in a white suburb. World War II left the large new populations of blacks and Chicanos in western cities with raised expectations and de facto segregation. The GI Bill added to the small middle class of minority groups. The war and the Indian Reorganization Act had given minority groups experience in organizing.[40]

The tremendous demographic and policy shifts in the West from the 1930s to the 1950s need more exploration. The perception of national emergencies throughout the period—the 1930s depression, the war, and the cold war—returned the federal government as a major player in the region's racial dynamics. At the same time the massive population movements altered the teams at the local level. We know far too little about the shifting language of race in the era, the roots of coalitions that emerged more effectively in the 1960s, relations among groups, and the impact of new industrial workers—women and men of color—on dynamics within minority groups.

From the vantage point of the mid-1980s, it looked as though the period from 1960 to the 1980s witnessed minority groups ascendant in the West. Tom Bradley became Los Angeles's first black mayor, Federico Pena became Denver's first Chicano mayor, and Henry Cisneros became the first Chicano mayor of San Antonio since the 1840s. Japanese-Americans finally got an additional token reparation for the damage done to them during World War II, and Indians began to win substantial settlements in the courts. Certainly a central theme in the history of race and ethnicity in the West from the 1960s to the 1980s was the transformation of ethnic politics. But by the decade's end the victories looked more problematic.

The increasing activism on all fronts after World War II exploded in the 1960s. Although nonwhites had become majorities or near majorities in western cities, segregation in housing and occupation had remained constant. Nationwide race rioting began in 1965 in the black Los Angeles neighborhood of Watts. With its single-family houses, rampant unemployment, segregated schools, and absentee landlords, Watts became a national symbol. Just as the labor unrest of the late nineteenth century had shown Americans that perhaps they were not exceptional, so the Watts riot exploded the myth of western or California exceptionalism.

The full meaning of Watts has yet to be explored in terms of the growing assertiveness of other minority groups. Why did Mexican-Americans not join in the rioting to the same extent that blacks did? Did the zoot suit riots have a legacy? In 1967, when Reies Lopez Tijerina raided the courthouse of Tierra Amarilla, a county seat in northern New Mexico, and destroyed land deeds and other documents, observers claimed to see the influence of the black civil rights movement.[41] But such vague "contagion" needs more specific cross-racial analysis by historians. Certainly the context of student activism, Vietnam War protests, the black civil rights movement, and shifting coalitions in the Democratic party altered consciousness and possibilities, but Indian and Chicano civil rights groups, like black ones, had predated the 1960s. Was there evidence of a new cross-racial solidarity?

Change was interactive and fast. It depended not only on a receptive climate but on the internal dynamics of the group. For example, the United Farm Workers succeeded in part because the union was shaped by the changing gender structure of the group concerned. When Dolores Huerta became the most visible woman in the United Farm Workers movement, she tore apart Anglo notions of Chicano migrant workers as irresponsible vagrant men and of Chicanas as passive and cloistered. She also transformed the United Farm Workers into an enlarged family, redefining family and family roles.[42] Later, when the union sent families, not single men, to publicize the boycott in the East, the UFW used the convergence between that familial style and middle-class values to gain middle-class support. In such moments of convergence the entwined relationships among culture, race, class, and gender show themselves most clearly and have the most to offer historians.

By the mid-1970s the arena in which protest occurred had altered almost beyond recognition. Now when Dolores Huerta lobbied for the California farm workers, she worked out of the office of a Chicano member of the state assembly.[43] Yet there were already signs that the resurgence was in trouble. After all, Ronald Reagan, elected as an antifarm union, procorporation governor of California in 1967 and as president of the United States in 1980, still stands as a more common symbol of the West than does Cesar Chavez or Dolores Huerta. The mid-1970s witnessed increasing abuse of illegal immigrants who took the place of braceros in the labor market, but with greater vulnerability. Dual unionism plagued the UFW, and class tensions within groups as well as external harassment helped fragment and weaken minority rights organizations. The number of Chicano state representatives in Arizona, Texas, Colorado, California, and New Mexico had risen from thirty-two in 1960 to seventy-three in 1974, but the next ten years showed no further gains.[44]

The increasing mobilization of minorities in the Southwest had been more than matched by the increasing power of economic elites in business and national politics. Recruits to the new West augmented the ranks of the elite and legitimated their claim to conservative leadership for the nation. The successful minority mayoral officials could not ignore this power configuration. Bradley's task forces were dominated by the same corporations and banks that had exercised power in previous administrations. Pena insisted, "I am not an Hispanic candidate. I just happen to be Hispanic."[45]

Yet the contest continues between the developers' lingering gold rush mentality and the persistent territoriality and shifting strategies of minorities. The history of minorities and the history of development are still tightly entwined. Access to inexhaustible supplies of low-paid labor and low-cost resources remains central to the success of western booms. Federal policy has fostered both of these through immigration laws and subsidies for highways, water, and oil. The secretary of the interior let oil leases on Indian lands go undervalued. Indian groups continue to fight for the restoration of land rather than money payments, and the government strives to secure title to open the way to development. Immigration policy was driven by the needs of consumers of labor: deporting Chicanos in the 1930s; importing them in the 1940s; rounding up illegals in the 1950s; looking the other way at the use of illegals to break strikes in the early 1960s; rounding up illegals participating in strikes in the 1980s. And the story continues with the border factories or *maquiladores* in Mexico and agricultural exemptions to new immigration legislation. The labor pool is not divided by the international boundary, but that boundary nonetheless affects the way workers can bargain. The western economy has continued to rely on groups that could be labeled sufficiently "other" to justify lower wages and poor working conditions, to justify exclusion from the "gold rush" benefits.[46]

Activism has often taken the form of symbolic physical reconquest: Tijerina's courthouse raid at Tierra Amarilla and his occupation of Carson National Forest, formerly a Hispanic communal land grant; the takeover of Alcatraz, Wounded Knee, and even the Bureau of Indian Affairs headquarters in Washington in 1972 by Indian activists. At the 1976 centennial commemoration of the Battle of the Little Bighorn, Indians, having warned planners that any attempted symbolic reenactment of the battle would have more realism than the National Park Service desired, circled the much-reduced, predominantly white ceremony while holding the American flag upside down and chanting, "Custer died for your sins." To an extent the Indians did manage to redefine the monument, as texts displayed by the park service shifted from the glory of civilization's ultimate triumph to, as one participant put it, "groping toward mutual understanding."[47]

Yet territory alone is not the answer. Indian youth in the early 1980s committed suicide at a rate one hundred times that of all youth. The 1970 census showed 45 percent of Native Americans living in urban areas, where they showed up in disproportionate numbers on police blotters and with high rates of alcoholism, job instability, and poverty. Moreover, despite all the rhetoric about increased self-determination, Indians are not the final arbiters even of the fate of their own reservations. States, rebelling against the tax-exempt status of reservation lands, have been able to impose restrictions against income-producing use of enlarged reservations. Tribal autonomy over tribal land is only fitfully upheld. In a classic demonstration of the conjunction of gender, race, and culture and of the selective validation of tribal will by the federal government, the United States courts in 1978 upheld the Santa Clara Pueblo's decision to bestow tribal membership only on children of male tribal members on the ground that it was an issue of civil law and so of tribal autonomy. The courts so ruled despite accusations of sexual discrimination that might have prevented a similar ruling for a group defined as less "other" and autonomous. On the other hand, in the mid-1980s the federal government refused to permit Indians to run a brothel on reservation land in Nevada, though in Nevada brothels are legal. This time the court ruled on the ground that prostitution, in federal law, is a criminal offense and so falls under federal, not tribal, jurisdiction.[48] The defining of "civil" and "criminal" here reflects a certain configuration of race, gender, and sex relations in the dominant culture that the courts have brought to bear on others.

It is not yet certain whether the activism of the 1960s and its legacy have brought the West closer to true pluralism or simply a more cosmetic pluralism, a reconquest or a reconquest forestalled. In 1982 the Commission on Wartime Relocation and Internment of Civilians submitted its report, *Personal Justice Denied*, condemning in every respect the internment of the Japanese, and in 1988 the federal government finally paid an additional token settlement to survivors. Yet the same years witnessed renewed anti-Asian agitation in California, from arson and protests against plans for a Buddhist temple in Los Angeles to marches protesting the rising numbers of Asian students admitted to Berkeley. Only two years earlier, in response to an increasing Chicano population, California passed Proposition 63,

"English Is the Official Language."[49] The tensions inherent in a mythological white man's West dependent on the labor of "others" are far from resolved. The West remains not a frontier but a continuous series of frontiers formed and re-formed from all sides, characterized by change, interchange, and mutual dependence.

Racial confrontation lay at the root of western history, and it never went away.[50] Central to the discourse of any succeeding era were the language of race and a struggle between races for territory, for hegemony, for boundary setting, for definition. "Otherness" itself had a fluid definition. In Anglo eyes, Mexican-Americans were sometimes a race and sometimes a more permeable ethnic or cultural group, depending on the demands of the local economy. Ethnicity and race were constructs specific to time, place, and persons.[51]

Historians have had a crucial role in such redefinitions. Chief Justice William Rehnquist placed the blame for a 1980 judicial reversal squarely on "revisionist historians." In 1877, in the aftermath of the Black Hills gold rush and Custer's last stand, the United States government abrogated an earlier treaty with the Sioux and took the Black Hills for white development. In 1942 the courts upheld the government's action. In 1980, however, the Supreme Court acknowledged possible treaty violations. Rehnquist, in a scathing minority dissent, claimed that the law had not changed since 1942 but that the interpretation of events had.[52]

Rehnquist was right; no longer can the West be seen as a place where whites fled to work out their destiny in splendid isolation. To write the history of race and ethnicity in the West, to make the invisible visible, is to re-create the West's history. Historians had a strong hand in creating a picture of the post-Civil War West as an empty West, ignoring the international frontier that preceded it.[53] Though they now recognize that conquest internalized the borderlands and did not erase them, there is still a long way to go in achieving coherence as well as color for the new portrait.

My aim here is not simply to create one possible framework for a more comprehensive, coherent picture of race and ethnicity in the West. It is also to transform our understanding of other aspects of western history, such as sexuality and gender systems and national political and ideological shifts whose relation to issues of race and ethnicity has never been clear. The West is a messy place. The experiences of both majority and minority groups occurred in the context of multiracial or multicultural dynamics. Any larger historical narrative of the region must partake of an interactive multifaceted model. It must allow the constant interaction and diversity within and between groups itself to become the story. By doing so, it builds a framework within which we can understand the continual tensions created by forces that simultaneously erode boundaries and re-create them.

Engendering the West

KATHERINE G. MORRISSEY

After reaching the age of seventy, a retired English professor from the University of Chicago started to write stories about his youth, about growing up in the West. Norman Maclean, previously known as an award-winning teacher and Shakespearean scholar, is celebrated today as the author of *A River Runs through It*—a novella and two short stories published in 1976. Although his oeuvre is small, including various essays along with the book, it has gathered numerous admirers and critical acclaim.[1]

The pure and evocative prose of Maclean's engaging stories draws his readers into gradually unfolding narratives set in an early twentieth-century West. They tell of fly fishing and families, logging and literature, fighting and faith, as they circle gently around a particular place and time: Montana during the 1910s and 1920s. It is a world peopled by family members—his Presbyterian minister father; Scottish mother; brother, Paul; wife, Jessie—and by friends and acquaintances. The men are tough—or trying to be. The women are understanding—or trying to be.

Writing from Chicago in the 1970s, Maclean nostalgically recalls his earlier life in Montana. Although wistful, his is neither a naive nor an innocent recollection; he identifies ambiguities and illuminates complexities of the people and the place. He remains "haunted by waters," haunted by the West of his younger years. The popularity of his work suggests that it contains familiar echoes for his readers. At times gently mocking an earlier incarnation of himself, at other times celebrating a lost certainty with rueful regret, Maclean captures not only the way individuals remember their pasts but also the way Americans tend to think about the West. His Montana, his American West, reflects the cultural myths to which many of us subscribe.

What is this West? For Maclean, it is a beautiful place where skilled men work with their hands. Young, sometimes rough, and always heroic, his main characters—Big Bill Ben, the toughest Forest Service ranger, his pal Jim Griesson, the "best lumberjack in camp," or his brother, Paul, the master fly fisherman—epitomize imagined masculine virtues. They excel in fighting, drinking, and gambling. Their mastery over the environment as well as their inability to articulate their emotions occur against a backdrop of the powerful Blackfoot River or the wild Bitterroot Mountains.

Maclean's equation of masculinity and the West is not, of course, his alone. In popular culture as well as scholarship the American West is most often associated with masculine images. Cowboys and soldiers, gold miners and fur traders—the cast of characters that peoples the stereotypical West is male-dominated. Many of the activities celebrated as central to the western experience—conquering a "virgin" land, subduing Indians, building railroads, ranching, farming, logging, establishing governments—are those perceived as "men's work." Imbued with these masculine images, the ideology of the West celebrates a particular, and gendered, form of American identity.[2]

Individual stories help maintain cultural ideology. We all tell each other and ourselves stories about our lives and about the past. Although these stories contain much truth, they present a highly stylized version of that past and change over time as we reinterpret our histories. Likewise, Maclean's stories mark the moments when "life turns into literature," when "real-life" experience comes closest to cultural myth. The West, a powerful ideological place, is an especially appropriate setting for this endeavor. Here, in this larger-than-life land, "tough men" and "understanding women" are part of the "natural order of things." Sharply defined gender roles fit comfortably into this dialectic cultural landscape. While Maclean, a westerner with "real-life" experiences, participated in the continuing creation of the cultural myth of the West, he was also a writer who recognized, in some ways, the artificial nature of that creation. Reality was never so tidy. Although his writings tell of real people and transpired events, he called them "stories." Both within these stories and in interviews, he notes the fictionalizing nature of memory. For Maclean, the "waters of memory" mold the past through erosion, obscuring its rocks and rough patches behind fast-moving rapids.[3]

Just as Maclean shaped his experiences into stories reflecting ideologies of the West and of gender, so, too, do western historians. While scholars try to interpret western mysteries, to order and organize the region's history, they also participate in the ongoing construction of a West that lives in mainstream cultural ideology. Ideology—the set of beliefs, situated in time, that reflects, imposes, and reinforces the needs and aspirations of society—shapes our understanding of the present and the past. It is worth taking a closer look at the role of experience and ideology in shaping western history and, in particular, at the ways in which the West is gendered. How have cultural ideas about the social roles of men and women influenced western experiences? How do historians themselves participate in this process of gendering the West?[4]

My specific focus is on gender, defined here as an ongoing cultural construction that shapes identities and the social practices of women and men over time. While I will not specifically address the complex interrelationship of gender, race, class, and ethnicity, these cultural constructs clearly all play a critical role in formulating the western past. For the purposes of this analysis I will artificially isolate gender from this intricate web to identify some of the patterns formed by its ideological and experiential strands. Exploring the relationship between the ideological and the experiential Wests will reveal both the necessity of, and the complexities inherent in, engendering the West.

In recent years scholars have identified the pervasive influence of the masculine image of the West not only in literature and popular culture but also in historical writing. The western drama as told by Frederick Jackson Turner, Frederick Merk, and Ray Allen Billington did not cast women as central characters.[5] Early corrective studies focused on the "missing" women and worked to incorporate their stories into the narrative of western history. Some historians described women as instrumental in changing the masculine "frontier" past. In the 1950s Dee Brown, for example, identified women as the "gentle tamers" of the "old wild west." For Brown, these "practical creatures," whether army wives, overland emigrants, "stage darlings," or schoolmarms, worked with "quiet force" to civilize and feminize the region.[6] Other scholars studied individual women who participated in activities central to the western story; their works celebrated such "exceptional" women as the guide Sacajawea, the missionary Narcissa Whitman, or Judge Esther Morris.[7] Whether portraying gentle tamers or exceptional women, these studies retained the traditional framework of western history.

Later studies challenged that framework. Fueled by new feminist scholarship in a variety of disciplines, western women's history emerged as a distinct field during the 1970s. Feminist historians went beyond simply incorporating women into the western story. By identifying women's perspectives as distinct from those of men and by recognizing that history had largely been confined to the latter, feminists revealed the narrowness and inadequacies of conventional historical narratives.[8]

From the vantage point of women's studies, feminist scholars measured western women with yardsticks provided by women historians from other fields. Were western women constricted by the "cult of domesticity"? Was the frontier liberating for women? Why was the struggle for women's suffrage first successful in the West? Although this effort expanded the story of the western past, it had limitations of its own. The questions tended to arise from concerns identified in studies of eastern, rather than western, women; they also tended to give primacy to the experiences of middle-class, Euroamerican women with eastern roots.[9]

Whether working to expose the stereotypical portrayals of women and men that pervade the story of the West or to interpret women's western experiences, historians have relied on the words of western women.[10] As part of the "new social history," which emphasized the everyday experiences of everyday people, western women's historians uncovered the memoirs, letters, diaries, and other personal accounts of women moving to or living in the West. Looking at the West "from the inside out," John Faragher, Janice Monk, and others have analyzed community life, family structure, work inside and outside the home, and perceptions of the western landscape.[11] Historians have found that the experiences of these western women were fundamentally different from those of men. Glenda Riley, for example, defines a distinct "female frontier." In her study of the prairie and plains, Riley argues that "women's words demonstrate that their experiences exhibited a remarkable similarity as a result of being shaped by the prevailing concepts of the female gender and associated ideas of 'women's work.' " The focus on gender differences has characterized much of the work of western women's historians.[12]

More recently the acknowledgment of other differences, defined by racial, ethnic, regional, or class affiliations, has enriched our understanding of women's lives. A "multicultural" western women's history that recognizes these differences is the aim of an active group of scholars. Moving away from the words of prolific white, middle-class diary keepers, some historians have worked to identify the muted voices of non-English speakers, the illiterate, and anonymous authors, through the creative use of nonliterary documents. Comparing the experiences, and gender systems, of Native American, eastern-born, métis, Hispanic, or Asian westerners, scholars have also called attention to the diversity of western women's lives.[13]

All these works in western women's history have opened the way for a more comprehensive approach to the study of the western past.[14] The inclusion of women in the new western history has called into question our understanding of men as well; raising questions of gender brings male and female identities into joint consideration. Patricia Nelson Limerick sums it up in *Legacy of Conquest*: "Exclude women from western history, and unreality sets in. Restore them, and the Western drama gains a fully human cast of characters—males and females whose urges, needs, failings, and conflicts we can recognize and even share."[15] By exploring the roles of women, western women's historians have done more than simply add women to the western drama. Identifying the ways in which women have been included as well as excluded reveals the influence of ideology upon historical analysis.

Even as recent publications in western women's history note the influence of gender ideology on the way historians have told the story of the West, the new scholarship is influenced, too, by historically specific gender constructions. Like other scholars, western women's historians reflect the concerns of their times. Dee Brown, writing in 1958, for example, finds it ironic that western Americans, "the descendants of miner, cowboy and Indian fighter, [are] . . . reduced to a routine of freeway commuting, do-it-yourself gadgetry, tract-development living, dishwashing, baby-sitting, neighborhood committee meetings, and television viewing."[16] Writing in 1976, Julie Roy Jeffrey explains that "my original perspective was feminist. I hoped to find that pioneer women used the frontier as a means of liberating themselves from stereotypes and behaviors which I found constricting and sexist. I discovered that they did not."[17] Today, as well, writers—whether historians, novelists, or autobiographers—ask questions of the past that are influenced by the ideology and experience of the present.

Norman Maclean's reminiscences of his experiences in the Montana forests offer another illustration of this point. In his autobiographical fiction, Maclean writes of his emerging sense of masculinity while working for the Forest Service among "tough" men. Measuring himself against both the heroes and the land, the young Maclean sought an identity in the world. But the older Maclean, the writer, reflects on that quest with disillusionment. Working two summers "for one of the toughest and most legendary old-time rangers in the Forest Service," Maclean recalls, "was a shock." The young Maclean emerged from the experience "forever leaving all childish things behind me and forever, so I thought for a while, making a man of me."[18] In retrospect, what working in the woods taught the Montana boy was the skill to control the natural world and a love of technology. Maclean's attraction to the power of these activities is a particularly gendered one. As he explains in an interview, urban construction work shares these attributes with logging:

> That's one reason why I like logging so much. It's a gigantic thing. But a lot of this big urban work and industry is just as gigantic and fabulous. Fabulous what men can move and do. Every time they dig a goddamned basement over at the University for a new building, I can't keep my eyes off that son of a bitch running the crane. He does things with that crane a woman can't do with a sewing machine, they're so delicate.

In his comparison of men who build and women who sew, Maclean emphasizes gender differences in scale and skill. He defines women, even those who, like men, operate machines, according to traditional feminine virtues. In Maclean's western world, the ideal caring, supportive women handled men, not machines. "My mother," he explains, "handled a man's world all about her. It was a tough world for her. She and three men—and they trying hard to be men, too. She handled us with great power, and in part by just not concerning herself with our efforts to be men." Clara Maclean's power, according to her son, came from recognizing her place. An interloper in the "man's world all about her," she is contained in and defined by her relation to that world.[19]

As a writer Maclean controls the past through his words; women appear in his fictional world in carefully defined spaces. Yet his power and control over that fictional world, like that over his past, are illusory. Readers with different concepts about the proper social roles of women and men will question his construction of distinct gender identities.

Still, Maclean is not alone in the way he defines the world of the woods. Rare, indeed, are historical studies of western logging and forestry that raise questions of gender.[20] Even western women's history, which has explored the role of women in many traditionally male-identified spheres of activities, has little to say on the topic. While Elizabeth Jameson, Susan Johnson, Ralph Mann, Paula Petrik, and Marion Goldman, among others, have started to reveal the gendered aspects of the western mining world, life in the woods remains essentially the story of men.[21]

Why does the story of western logging and forestry remain the story of men? The answer lies partly in the demographics of these activities and in the sexual divisions of labor. As Stewart Holbrook explains in an introduction to one logger's wife's account, "It is only natural that most of the literature about logging camps has been about males. . . . [N]o place on earth was more thoroughly male."[22] But the answer lies as well in the perspective from which historians have looked at the timber industry.

What might a revised, gender-conscious history of logging look like? Implicit in that question is the need to include women in the story, to identify the women who worked in the woods. Doing so provides a more contextualized view of a traditional economic activity, one that is explicitly gendered, one in which women and men played distinct roles according to the gender expectations of the time, one in which men and women were crucial to the ongoing enterprise.[23] Women have long been involved in various aspects of forestry and lumber production. Western deed and timber culture records indicate that both women and men established timber culture claims and owned timber rights and timber lands. Barbara Vatter notes in her study of Douglas County, Oregon, that despite certain census omissions, there is evidence that "women, single and married, worked in the logging camps of the 1890's." Local organizations, such as the Umpqua Circle of the Foresters and the Knights and Ladies of Security, included or were limited to female members.[24] During the World War I era of the Industrial Workers of the World (IWW) unrest in the

Pacific Northwest and again during World War II, the timber industry actively recruited women to work in logging camps, shingle factories, and sawmills. In the twentieth century women also worked as Forest Service lookouts and as logging camp service workers—cooks, waitresses, laundresses, or prostitutes. Even where these workplaces remained essentially single-sexed, male loggers and foresters were always part of a world of men and women through kinship networks that extended beyond the boundaries of their immediate workplaces.[25]

Furthermore, a gender-conscious history of logging would not only include "missing" women but also examine men *as men* in the world of the woods. Why was logging celebrated as a masculine profession? Why has this particular economic activity been so closely identified with one gender? How did the single-sexed bias of the industry influence relations among men as well as between men and women? How did the changing social construction of gender during the nineteenth and twentieth centuries affect the industry? What were the socioeconomic underpinnings of the sexual divisions of labor in the forest? Bringing a gender-conscious perspective to the study of the logging world will help answer some of these questions.

Listen, for example, to the voices of women and men writing during the 1950s about their experiences in western forestry and logging. In their memoirs they use the language and ideology of the decade to describe and explain their early-twentieth-century experiences. The reminiscences define a particular western past; they share a nostalgia for the "Old West," a lost "frontier" populated by men, where women were notable by their absence or rarity. "Following the last frontier from the time I could earn my own living," comments logger Emil Engstrom, "women have ever been strange creatures." The women who ventured into this masculine realm must be initiated into its peculiar language and customs. Cook's assistant Irma Lee Emmerson describes "the curious system of manners and morals in logging camps":

> These loggers operated right back in the golden days of the Old
> West. At least as far as women were concerned; floozies could have
> a whale of a time dancing on barroom tables in long black stockings
> but the little woman at home kept her golden curls hidden behind
> a sun bonnet and forded rivers with her skirts pinned modestly
> down to her shoe tops. If you worked at the Ticoma logging camp,
> in the eyes of the loggers, you represented the little woman at
> home and you had better act like it.[26]

Along with regret for the passage of the frontier life, the writers comment, both explicitly and implicitly, on changing gender roles. Although, according to these memoirs, life in the woods retained its sexual division of labor in the 1950s, it also reflected different gender expectations. The idealized rangers and loggers were now practical and professional "organization men." The author of a 1955 *American Forests* article, "The Forest Ranger: Yesterday and Today," for example, suggests that the view of rangers as "real men's men—outdoor men, men who fight fires against big odds; men who are never without a sidearm; men who fight evil and greed in every form . . ." should be tempered by consideration of their role as hardworking land managers, a "job fully as exciting in its own way." Acknowledgment of changing gender ideology is also evident in women's writings. "Ranger's wife" Dorothy Gray Gluck, for example, regrets that "Times are changing. I'm afraid that rangers' wives must eventually be content with less of the actual participation in the work plan of their husbands' districts and put their conservation fervor into Girl Scouts, PTA, Women's Clubs. . . ."[27]

Although I have chosen to illustrate my point here with this example from logging and forestry, other popular and historical accounts of the American West share similar ideological constraints. A gender-conscious version of western history that recognizes the powerful influence of ideology can open up our understanding of both the past and the present.

It is always easier for scholars to recognize the ways in which ideology operated in the past than it is to analyze the ideological influences of their own circumstances. For many of today's scholars, feminism and other contemporary theoretical critiques present serious challenges to the ways in which they think about the past. Let me offer two examples from my own work.

A few years ago I was doing some research in a local western historical society when one of the volunteers cataloging the collection called my attention to a new acquisition. It was an incomplete set of letters recently found in the attic of an old building in town. As I read the letters of Abbie Widner, I found myself asking a number of unanswerable questions about this young woman of turn-of-the-century Spokane. She spoke of picnics and the weather but also of two men who had been paying her attention. "*I hate them both like snaks,*" she wrote in her phonetic prose, underlining her words for emphasis. "But I get good money out off them both. I am so tirred of this damed life

I could die but I see no other way before me but to live it disgrace and shame as it is."[28]

As the volunteer, an older woman from the community, looked over the letters, she wondered aloud which of the two men Abbie had decided to marry. My questions were different. Was Abbie Widner by occupation a prostitute? Or was she a woman relying on her sex, trading sexual favors for economic support in a less definable way?[29] The questions that the letters provoked in us reflected generational, professional, and personal differences. We each brought our own frames of reference to the task of interpreting Abbie Widner's life and letters. Widner's own view of her situation was similarly defined by her historical moment. The economic realities of limited employment opportunities for women in the West, along with the changing definitions of "proper" roles for women (that is, contemporary gender ideology), influenced her experience and perspective.

Constrained by her situation, Widner was also constrained by language. As she struggled to express her feelings, she employed the words and structures of meaning available to her. It is unclear just what she intended by her comparison of men and snakes or by her suggestive prepositions. Among the meanings her words suggest to a late-twentieth-century reader are biblical references to lost innocence, euphemistic references to sexual organs, or literal references to ensnaring reptiles. Just as western images offer caricatures of western types and encode primacy to a masculine West, so, too, do the images Widner employs shape her perspective.

In the ideological masculine West, feminine images do exist—the sunbonneted pioneer wife who brings civilization to the frontier or the dance hall girl with a heart of gold, for example. The latter image is a far cry from Abbie Widner's experience. These images, and their relationship with personal experience, also differ from the masculine images. In fact, their existence depends on their male counterparts. Rather than reflect women's experience, these images serve principally to cast male images in relief. Without the cowboy saloon drinkers, the dance hall girl loses much of her definition. Similarly, the full meaning of the sunbonneted pioneer woman emerges only when juxtaposed with her fearless protector.

It is difficult to imagine an individual whose life and activities fit less into the stock images of the female pioneer than Catharine Burgess Carr. As a hosiery and undergarments saleswoman Carr traveled by herself through the industrial mining towns of turn-of-the-century northern Idaho. Her account of her experiences on the road reveals the difficulties female saleswomen faced in the masculine West and illustrates her own acceptance of the contemporary gender ideology even as her very life represented something of a deviation from the norm.

Catharine Carr was a woman who identified with the critical gender-related issues of her day. An ardent suffragist, she subscribed to the *Woman's Journal* and patronized women-owned businesses. On the road she made numerous informal connections with other women she met along the way in boardinghouses or on doorsteps; "I met a woman in St. M[arie, Idaho] yesterday from near Plummer. She canvasses for hair and makes switches. She advises me to canvass Tekoa that she did so well there."[30] But Carr did not listen to everyone's advice; she was less than welcoming toward a saloonkeeper's wife, whom she perceived as implicated by her husband's trade. A member of the Woman's Christian Temperance Union, Carr found it hard to condone the proliferation of saloons in the mining camps she visited.

A saleswoman in the West faced difficulties not experienced by her male counterparts. Identifying safe lodging and dealing with male hostility were unusual concerns in the cost-benefit world of sales, but women had to address them. Catharine Carr clearly calculated both her financial expenses and her physical needs as she planned her itinerary: "I am going to remain in Harrison over First day, my menses are due, they may not come for a day or two but after tonight my room will be 25 cts, first night 50 cts I do not think it wise to start to Burke before my menses come, for I do not know how much room rent I will have to pay and I may have to stay abed one day."[31] Translating her biological necessities into economic terms, whether those necessities were defined by her sex or by gender expectations, Carr negotiated with accepted terms. As she sold female undergarments to mold women's bodies to cultural expectations, the saleswoman molded herself, at least on one level, to ideological expectations. While her words reveal the contradictions implicit in her life, they also work to smooth over differences.

In some ways Catharine Carr fits uneasily into expected roles for western women. Yet in other ways the image of a pioneer wife is not too far afield. For how do we gain our glimpse into the world of such a woman? Her words are those composed for letters to her husband, William. Reporting to him from almost every stop, Catharine turns to William for guidance, advice, and approval, rarely, it would seem, making a move without his comments. She keeps an eye out for potential economic opportunities for him, from raising poultry to growing hops. His presence shelters and shadows her activities even while she is away from home.

As I read the documents left by Abbie Widner and Catharine Burgess Carr, women living in the same region of the West within the same historical period, I considered the messages they communicated in the past and those they communicate now. Certainly the experiences of these western women as revealed in their letters are infused with contemporary ideology. The letters present an intriguing view of the mixture of public and private spheres as they deal with economic realities and record social relationships. But as objects of interpretation they also suggest something about the ways in which historians create stories of the past.

The primary texts historians use to reveal the western past, such as the letters of Abbie Widner and Catharine Carr, are constructions shaped by a variety of visible and invisible constraints. As part of the letter-writing genre, for example, they are governed by their own representational demands. As documents created in the past, they reflect a reality different from our own. Just as people in the past create their own reality, so, too, do we as historians participate in cultural structuring.

The historical narratives we create to explain the past are also constructions shaped by visible and invisible ideological constraints. My understanding of the letters of Abbie Widner and Catharine Carr, like Norman Maclean's presentation of his Montana and western women's historians' interpretations of the West, is shaped by my own experience and education. The work of feminist scholars, for example, directs my attention to gendered concerns. Literary studies lead to questions about the historically specific use of words, the culturally specific structures of meaning, and the contemporary interpretation of these writings. My questions are also influenced by the work of postmodernists, especially their emphasis on the relative and partial character of reality, language, and narrative. For a recently trained scholar interested in western American history and equipped with the theoretical tools of an interdisciplinary education, these letters reveal a particular story of the West.[32]

When examined together, ideology and experience open questions about the complex social world of the West and about western history. It was, and is, a world of diversity. Women and men of different races, ethnic identities, and class affiliations confronted themselves and each other in the western space. Their various stories, created amid different experiences and ideologies, now confront historians involved in their own representational concerns. Just as conceptual categories, such as gender, race, ethnicity, and class, contain both ideological and experiential components so do the stories, the memoirs, the letters, and the histories created by and about the American West.

Let me return to the Abbie Widner letters one more time. The attic in which those letters were found—that American repository of outmoded possessions that continue to have meaning for their owners—might serve as a metaphor for cultural memory. American culture tenaciously retains ideas and images about the West and about gender that continue to shape our understandings. My own juxtaposition of two sets of letters, even as it calls such ideas into question and privileges contemporary concerns, is a part of the process of meaning making. Recognizing the pervasive power of ideology and its impact on our own experience is the first step toward engendering the West.

Religion
in the American West

D. MICHAEL QUINN*

Imagine a gathering of past and present: Wovoka of the Ghost Dance; Werner Erhard of est; Junípero Serra, the Catholic missionary; the actress Shirley MacLaine, of New Age "channeling"; Brigham Young, the Mormon colonizer; Maharaj Ji of the Divine Light Mission; Aimee Semple McPherson of radio evangelism; Anton LaVey of the Church of Satan; Don Pedrito Jaramillo, a *curandero* for thousands; Jim Jones of the People's Temple; Dr. John Elsner, the circuit-riding *mobel* (circumciser) in four states; L. Ron Hubbard of Scientology; Cleng Peerson, the "Peer Gynt of the Prairies"; Troy Perry, founder of the gay Metropolitan Community Church; Marcus and Narcissa Whitman, the Protestant missionaries; Bhagwan Rajneesh of Rajneeshpuram; John Fife of the sanctuary movement; Manly Hall of the Philosophical Research Society. What could these people have in common? Religious experience in the American West is the answer.

In 1893, the same year that Frederick Jackson Turner proposed his frontier thesis, the director for the census of religion observed,

*Mr. Quinn completed this essay as a fellow of the National Endowment for the Humanities at the Henry E. Huntington Library, San Marino, California.

145

"The first impression one gets in studying the results of the [1890] census is that there is an infinite variety of religions in the United States." He went on to note that two western territories had the highest rates of church participation in the nation, and one western state the lowest.[1] Clearly there was something unusual about the American West's religious experience, something that might require considerable effort to understand. In 1890 there was a future for writing the history of religion in the West.

A century later the religious character of the West remains as complex and intriguing as it was in Turner's day, and a full history of religion in the West remains to be written. A comprehensive account of western religious history might begin by considering the manner in which particular regions in the West have developed distinctive religious characteristics. In 1961 the historical geographer Wilbur Zelinsky identified seven religious regions in the United States; four of them lay west of the Mississippi River. In Zelinsky's model the *upper middle religious region* of the northern plains is dominated by Lutherans and Catholics, with significant Congregational influence. In the *western religious region* beyond the mountain states to Southern California, there are no dominant churches, and many unchurched. Between those religious border zones, Zelinsky identified two regions of intense religious influence: the *Spanish Catholic region* of New Mexico, borderland Texas, Arizona, and California and the *Mormon region* extending from Utah outward.[2]

Additional subcategories might sharpen Zelinsky's regional scheme, but overrefinements can be counterproductive. For example, one revision of Zelinsky's classification urged abandonment of any denominational designations in favor of four categories: intense, conservative Protestants; diverse, liberal Protestants; Catholics; and super Catholics. The misgivings one might have about identifying geographic distinctions between Catholics and "super Catholics" are only intensified when this revisionist approach also identifies the traditionally anti-Protestant Mormons as "intense, conservative Protestants."[3] Zelinsky's approach seems more useful.

Zelinsky's great contribution to scholarship is his recognition of the role of religion in defining American regionalism. As a recent interpreter observed, Zelinsky's geographic model suggests that "the persistence of Mormons in Utah, Baptists in the South, Lutherans in the Dakotas, and Catholics in New Mexico, for example, results in the ongoing divergence of those places from other areas or regions of the country. Regionalism is not dying out in the United States, and the religious factor is one main reason."[4]

Historically religion helped balkanize the trans-Mississippi West and will continue to be a factor in distinguishing the West as a whole from the rest of the nation. The religious balkanization of the West, like its Old World referent, is often linked to the existence of ethnic enclaves, and its interpretation therefore requires some additions to Zelinsky's mainstream, European religious categories. The West has, for instance, become the dominant location for such groups as Indian Sikhs, Arab Sunni Muslims, Iranian Shi'a Muslims, Armenian Christians, Oriental Buddhists, Shintoists, Confucianists, and Taoists, and followers of the Native American Church. In addition, the West has higher proportions of Reform Jews than the rest of the nation. Although often lost in the demographic big picture, the American history of these religious-ethnic groups is primarily a western history.

The emergence of Asian and Middle Eastern religious communities in the West is, for the most part, a twentieth-century story. The U.S. Census of religious bodies made no reference to Sikhs through 1936, even though this religion had a foothold in the American West two decades earlier.[5] Sikhs from India established their first American organization and oldest gurdwara (Sikh temple) in 1906 at Stockton, California. The largest Sikh community (five thousand people) in the United States and the largest Sikh temple in the world are in the Yuba City-Marysville area of California. The majority of Sikh gurdwaras are also in California.[6] The American experience of this world religion and its ethnic Sikhs are part of the West's history.

That is also true of another Indian subcontinent religion, Jainism, which has its second-largest state population in California.[7] The immigrant Jains of America have been largely ignored, but during the 1980s national attention focused on Bhagwan Shree Rajneesh, a Jain who moved from India in 1981 to establish Rajneeshpuram, his sectarian commune near Antelope, Oregon. The controversies about Rajneeshpuram in the 1980s echoed conflicts in the West involving Mormon Utah a century earlier. These Jain communalists in Oregon should be understood in the contexts of Indian religions in America as well as of the congeniality of the Far West to Eastern religions.[8]

Although America's first mosque was built in Cedar Rapids, Iowa, in 1934, the Census Bureau report of 1936 deemed the various Muslim groups in America too insignificant to note.[9] New York State now leads the nation with sixty-one mosques or Islamic information cen-

147

ters, followed by California with thirty-two.[10] Since World War II (especially during the past decade), Muslims have immigrated to the United States in a hundred different subgroups from sixty different countries, and the Muslim population of 2.7 million in the United States outnumbers the Chinese, Japanese, or American Indians. Although America's Muslim population now resides primarily in New York City and Chicago, Los Angeles and Houston have the next largest concentrations of Muslims.[11]

Future historical work on the Muslim experience in America will have to focus on the American West. Even though the Muslim population as a whole is not distinctively a trans-Mississippi phenomenon, Arab Sunni Muslims and Iranian Shi'a Muslims have settled predominantly in the West, especially in the Los Angeles area.[12] Since the Arab oil embargo of 1973 and the Iranian Revolution of 1979, American hostility toward Arabs and Iranians has been prominent in the gas-guzzling West, where these groups have primarily settled. This ethnic-religious hostility has brought the desecration of mosques in the American West.[13]

The religious identity of Arab immigrants to the United States is certainly not restricted to Sunni or Shi'a Islam. Arab-Americans also are adherents of the Druze Muslim sect, the Antiochian Orthodox Christian Church, the Coptic Christian Church, the Maronite Christian Church, the Byzantine Rite Catholic Church, the Syrian Orthodox Christian Church, and the Chaldean Christian Church. Indeed, four of nine Chaldean parishes are in Southern California.[14]

The Near Eastern and Turkic region is also the source of Armenian migration to the United States and increasingly to the American West. Nineteenth-century Armenian immigrants settled primarily in Massachusetts, where the first Armenian Christian church was established in 1891, but by World War I California was becoming the second-largest population center of Armenian Christians in America.[15]

More recently Armenian immigration, especially from Soviet Armenia, has focused in the Los Angeles area, where thousands of Christian Armenians have settled in sections of Hollywood and Glendale. Seventy percent are members of one of the two Apostolic Armenian churches, but church attendance is low.[16] With the devastating earthquake of 1988 in Soviet Armenia, Americans who had never thought about Armenians before began donating to Armenian church organizations in Southern California and elsewhere. Incidentally, San Francisco had been the headquarters of the Russian Orthodox Church in America until 1905.[17]

The "Shintoist Temple—Los Angeles" was among the "Small Sects" about which the Census Bureau did not gather information in 1936, and the bureau also ignored the "Buddhist Mission of North America" until 1936.[18] This benign neglect in the religious census is reflected more remarkably in general histories of the Chinese in America published during the past twenty-five years. Even scholarly studies totally omit discussion of religious experience or give only passing reference to the fact that the Chinese in America followed Confucianism, Buddhism, and Taoism and were proselytized by Christians.[19]

Religion has fared better in major studies of Japanese-Americans. Christian missionary societies were wont to emphasize that by 1924 California had forty Japanese-Christian churches, Washington State seven, Oregon one, Utah and Colorado two each, and New York State four.[20] Although the baptism of the first Japanese converts in San Francisco in 1877 was unplanned, by 1888, when Japan's consul to Hawaii was baptized, a program of Christian proselytizing of the Japanese was beginning there and in California. This gave the Christian missionaries a fifteen-year lead on Buddhist missionaries in the New World. Yet the Issei remained primarily Buddhist (four hundred Christians out of twenty-five thousand Japanese immigrants in Hawaii as of 1894, for example).[21]

The next generation of Japanese-Americans, the Nisei, was more receptive to Christianity. In 1932 a Nisei professor at Stanford University described the persistence of Buddhism as an "unfortunate" obstacle to Americanization, which came through membership in Christian churches. The next year Stanford University surveyed 10 percent of California's Japanese and showed that the Issei were 77 percent Buddhist and 18 percent Christian, compared with 39 percent Buddhist and more than 50 percent Christian for Nisei.[22] In 1936 a survey in Seattle indicated the extent of that Christian assimilation of the Nisei: Out of two thousand Japanese-American residents, twelve hundred were members of Christian churches.[23]

Still, Buddhism remained significant for some Nisei and most Issei in America. With no reference to the territory of Hawaii, the 1936 census of religions listed America's Buddhist population as 10,732 in California, 1,486 in Washington, and 1,253 in Utah. Twenty-two years later a Nisei became bishop of the Jodo Shinshu sect of the Buddhist Church in America.[24]

The religious activity of both Chinese and Japanese immigrants and their American-born children deserves more attention. For the same period extolled by the Christian missionary boards, a Stanford

University study observed during the 1920s that the ethnic Chinese and Japanese in California were largely indifferent to Buddhist, Shintoist, and Christian participation. Regarding Los Angeles as typical, the report noted that "not more than 30 per cent of the Japanese are in the habit of going to church (Christian, Buddhist, or Shintoist)," and Christian mission boards were reaching only 20 percent of the Chinese and less than 8 percent of the Japanese on the Pacific Coast.[25] Interviews with 6,550 Nisei of Honolulu in 1923 likewise demonstrated that more than 60 percent "are not touched at all by any religious agency."[26] Only 7.5 percent of Chinese-Americans were Christian (mainly Presbyterian) as of 1962.[27] Current scholarship confirms the general nonaffiliation of both Japanese-Americans and Chinese-Americans, and in the 1980s the Chinese Coordination Centre of World Evangelism estimated that only 6.4 percent of the Christian Chinese in America were actually "committed Christians."[28] The lapse of religiosity in Asian immigrants and their children is worthy of exploration with respect to the larger phenomenon (to be discussed later) of the "unchurched" in the American West.

Koreans in the West exhibit a different religious pattern. Beginning with the first arrivals in America in the early 1900s, many Korean immigrants were already Christian. Today in Los Angeles (which has the highest concentration of Korean-Americans of any major American city) 70 percent of Koreans are Christian. That is a higher percentage of Christians than in any other American city's Korean population and double the percentage in Washington, D.C. So whereas the religious history of Korean immigrants outside Los Angeles shows their continued devotion to shamanism, Buddhism, Confucianism, or the Korean syncretic religion Chondokyo, Koreans in California have a primarily Christian religious history. Thirty percent of America's Korean Christian churches are located in Los Angeles.[29] And the greater church participation by Korean-Americans in the American West "gave new life to declining Protestant churches."[30]

Rivaling Korean immigration since World War II has been the flood of Southeast Asian immigrants to the United States. From 1961 to 1988 (primarily in two different waves) Southeast Asian immigration has included more than 499,200 Vietnamese, 145,500 Laotians, 114,900 Cambodians, and 95,200 Thais.[31] Most have settled in California, especially in the Los Angeles area, which Southeast Asians call "the refugees' capital."[32]

Even though Catholics accounted for only 10 percent of South Vietnam's population, the first wave of highly educated and westernized refugees to come to the United States from South Vietnam in 1975 was predominantly Roman Catholic. For example, whereas 40 percent of Vietnamese refugees in Thai camps were Catholic, more than 75 percent of the Vietnamese immigrants who passed through the Fort Indiantown Gap processing center in 1975 were Catholic. A major part of the history of the Vietnamese immigrant in the American West will involve the role of the Roman Catholic Church as a direct agent for resettlement.[33] The religious acculturation of these Roman Catholic Vietnamese is a part of their history in America.

The second wave of Vietnamese immigration, which began in 1978, was rural, less educated, less westernized. The majority of these Vietnamese-Americans adhere to traditional Buddhism, Confucianism, Taoism, and the veneration of ancestors, as well as the Vietnamese religions Hoa Hao and the syncretic Caodaism, which combines Oriental religions with Christianity.[34]

Adherence to Christianity has less significance among the other Southeast Asian refugees living primarily in California: the Hmong, the Laotians, and the Cambodians. Because of their close association with U.S. forces, the Hmong (mountain peoples of Laos) suffered dramatically with America's loss of the Vietnam War. Although they have not been resettled significantly in Los Angeles, more than two-thirds of the Hmong immigrants have located in Fresno, Merced, Sacramento, Stockton, and Orange County, California. Half of the Hmong immigrants claim Christianity, but they have merged it with their traditional animist beliefs and with Buddhism, Confucianism, and Taoism.[35] Buddhism is the primary religion of the overwhelmingly rural Laotian and Cambodian refugees, the latter having settled mainly in Long Beach, California.[36]

To summarize, Southeast Asian immigrants have settled mainly in the trans-Mississippi area bounded by Los Angeles, Seattle, St. Paul, and Houston. Their religious history features themes of continuity and adaptation, as well as the importance of Christian and Buddhist organizations in resettlement and acculturation. Although even the most detailed studies of Indochinese refugee acculturation virtually ignore the challenge of worshiping in a strange land,[37] a recent study of the Laotian Hmong indicates widespread abandonment of traditional beliefs and rituals.[38] Indochinese immigrants are passing through Genesis, Exodus, and Numbers—without much outside notice.

The opportunity to explore the relationships among migration, social transformation, and religion in the West is not limited to Asian-Americans. Although Jewish history in the West has been explored from a number of perspectives, the *Western States Jewish Historical Quarterly* has never in its more than twenty-year history specifically addressed the question of whether there are distinctive features to the American Jewish experience in the West. One article in the *Quarterly* did note, however, that "almost every pioneer Jewish man [in San Bernardino] was ready to serve as [a lay] marriage performer."[39] In Tucson, Sam Drachman served as lay leader of the city's Jewish community from 1867 to his death in 1911, and Dr. John Elsner performed ritual circumcisions in Colorado, New Mexico, Wyoming, and Nebraska during the same period.[40]

Lay participation is common in the American Jewish community generally but appears to have been greater in the West because of the scattered Jewish population and lack of rabbis. Apparently for at least some Jews there was a Turnerian religious frontier. Was this true for Jews throughout the West? What settlement patterns encouraged this, and what urban processes discouraged or minimized rabbinic service by laymen? To what extent did Jewish communities in the West experience tensions between familiar lay officiants and newly arrived rabbis?

Secularization also seems to have influenced American Jews more in the West than in the East. For example, the 1980 data for Jewish classification as either Conservative or Reform indicate that throughout the American West the proportion of Reform Jews tends to be 15 percent higher than it is east of the Mississippi.[41] This fact appears to be a continuation of the secularized, nonobservant, and Reform character of the Jews in early California.[42] This trend toward secularization in the West may have been a consequence of greater social mobility available to Jews in San Francisco and Los Angeles in the 1880s than to Jews who lived in the urban centers of the Northeast, Midwest, and South.[43] Only added research can confirm whether the California pattern of Jewish social mobility was typical of the smaller Jewish populations elsewhere in the West during the period.

Since the 1950s America's second-largest Jewish community has been Los Angeles,[44] where 55 percent of ethnic Jews do not affiliate with the Jewish religious community.[45] The sources of this division deserve historical analysis. Yet a 1970 history of Jews in Los Angeles, sponsored by the Jewish Theological Seminary of America and published by the Huntington Library, barely mentioned nonaffiliation and dismissed it as a result of "the year round sunshine."[46] But Jewish assimilation in the West is not just a Los Angeles phenomenon. In the 1950s more than 40 percent of Iowa's Jews were marrying non-Jews, while a decade later the intermarriage rates in Washington, D.C., still varied from 1 to 18 percent. Rabbis have estimated that in the 1980s more than 50 percent of Jews in the American West were marrying non-Jews, compared with intermarriage rates of 20 to 35 percent in the East.[47] Current synagogue membership of 38 percent in the West is the lowest in the nation, compared with 66 percent in the north-central states.[48] In a comment about nonaffiliation, an organizer of a national Jewish leadership conference in Los Angeles expressed the perspective of 1989: "We have to reach these people before we lose them."[49] Historians need to explore the development of present trends of Jewish religious participation in the American West, necessary as well with many of the West's other ethnoreligious groups.[50]

Another example of the complex interaction between religious traditions and social developments in the West may be found in the Lutheran experience. Like the Jews, Lutherans have significant numbers throughout the United States, but Lutherans became dominant in the plains as mid-nineteenth-century immigrants from Scandinavia. Unlike religions of the Orient, the Lutheran state churches of Scandinavia condemned emigration and virtually abandoned emigrants in America.[51]

Immigrant Swedish clergymen were religious renegades not only in their journey to America but also in their temperance attitudes and pietistic reactions against the conservative Swedish church.[52] These Augustana Lutherans promoted a social cohesiveness that diminished the fragmentation of the Swedish synods in America, but they also produced the clannishness demonstrated by the 1869 charter of Lindsborg, Kansas, which allowed only practicing Lutherans to be part of the community.[53]

Norwegian-American immigrants had a similar background as religious outsiders within European Lutheranism, but their religious and social experience was somewhat different from the Swedish-American experience on the plains. Cleng Peerson, known as the Father of Norwegian Immigration and the Peer Gynt of the Prairies, was a religious nonconformist in touch with communitarian thought and practice.[54] Although Norwegian-Americans shared a pietistic emphasis with the Swedes, the Norwegian immigrant laity was far less responsive to authority than the Swedes, more commonly practiced lay ministry, and engaged in frequent outbursts of congregational insults, harassment, and physical assaults against their Norwegian-American clergymen.[55] In fact, one author argued that because their church tolerated this religious turbulence, a far greater proportion of

Norwegian-Americans remained Lutheran than was true of the more stringent Swedes.[56] Nevertheless, by the 1940s less than a third of the Pacific Coast's Norwegian-Americans remained Lutheran.[57]

Even more than their fellow Scandinavians, Danish and Finnish immigrants underwent religious fragmentation. In the West they became "Happy Danes," "Holy Danes," or Mormon Danes. Only 9 percent of the immigrants from Denmark remained Lutheran, and Danish-Americans were less inclined to participate in organized religion than other Scandinavians.[58] Finnish immigrants were the fewest in numbers, the last to arrive and to Americanize religiously. Their greatest religious challenge was the competition of Lutheranism with socialism for the adherence of Finnish-Americans.[59]

Unfortunately studies of Scandinavian immigrants tend to isolate religion from social dynamics. The need for integrated studies of religion and society may be more apparent with other groups and regions, but it is no less important on the plains. Religion and community intersect, for instance, in the degree to which religious participation correlates with economic status. In Scandinavian communities with detailed church records, it should be possible to link adult membership lists with tax assessment rolls. At the least this allows comparisons of the economic status of the affiliated with that of the unaffiliated. More detailed church records will also allow economic differentiation for degrees of church participation. A corollary would be to link church membership records with residence identifiers (census, town and city directories, deed records) in order to test to what extent religious affiliation or participation created residential segregation in these tightly knit settlements. Scandinavian authors will be able to avoid the danger of "dry bones" social history if they note the flair in one denominational history's chapter on the Social Gospel: "Lutherans Discover the Human Race."[60]

The potential benefits of integrating the study of religion with the history of settlement patterns are well demonstrated in Terry Jordan's study of German-Americans in Texas. Like Scandinavians in the northern plains, Germans created rural ethnic enclaves by settling the hill country in south-central Texas along religious lines: ascetic Methodists in Llano Valley, Catholics and Lutherans in Pedernales Valley, and freethinkers and agnostics in Guadalupe Valley.[61] Like the Mormons of Utah, these Germans used western environment and topography to reinforce religious boundaries and promote devout observance of their sectarian creeds. By 1870 immigration trends and geographic insularity had combined to create a Bible Belt that helped distinguish Texas from the rest of the country.[62]

The history of religion in the borderlands from Texas to California demonstrates still another dimension of the interaction between religious belief and social movements. Out of compassion for refugees from repressive Central American regimes, southwestern clergy and laity have led a religious challenge to the federal government, the sanctuary movement. The movement was ecumenical at its inception in Tucson, where the Presbyterian minister John Fife, the Quaker Jim Corbett, and the Catholic parish priest Ricardo Elford joined forces in urging a religious embrace of illegal refugees and a religious rejection of current immigration restrictions. On March 24, 1982, the anniversary of Archbishop Oscar Romero's murder in El Salvador, Reverend Fife was the first minister in the nation publicly to declare his church a sanctuary against the U.S. Immigration and Naturalization Service. This new "Underground Railroad" for Central American refugees has spread from the Southwest throughout the nation in defiance of Congress, the INS, the FBI, and local law enforcement.[63]

As the sanctuary movement unfolds, it reminds us of an earlier and continuing tension between church and state in the West: the conflict over religious use of peyote by Native Americans. In the centennial year of the Wounded Knee massacre, the U.S. Supreme Court reignited what had been a largely dormant matter by reversing the Oregon Supreme Court's decision to exempt sacramental use of peyote from illegal drug laws.[64]

Much remains to be learned about the origins and spread of peyotism, but in general Native Americans are one ethnic group whose religious history has been a consistent topic for analysis. Because of the diversity of Native Americans (most of whom reside in the trans-Mississippi West),[65] twentieth-century authors have published massive numbers of books and articles about their indigenous beliefs and practices, about Christian proselytizing efforts, and about Indian responses to the Christian culture of Euroamericans. Scholars such as Edward Spicer, Robert Berkhofer, Anthony F. C. Wallace, Francis Paul Prucha, Joseph Jorgensen, and James Axtell, to name only a few, have published some of the most sophisticated work in western and frontier religious history. Nevertheless, decades of intensive research and writing about Christian missions among the western Indians have not exhausted the field of inquiry.[66] Moreover, that interest is not simply the domain of scholars, as demonstrated by the controversy over the papal beatification of Father Junípero Serra, whose work among California's Indians was saintly from one perspective and genocidal from another.

In fact, the continued Native American adaptation and resistance to Christian churches call for more study. Alvin Josephy has observed that government assimilationists sensed that "the Native Americans' religion, whatever it was, was the force that held Indian societies together" and became dedicated to eradicating it.[67] An assimilationist government was joined by competing Christian churches united only by their equal determination to destroy native religious culture in America. For example, 449 Christian churches now actively compete for Navajo converts.[68] Yet "the insight has slowly dawned on the scholarly world that American Indian religions are not just a thing of the past . . . [that] they continue to flourish, sometimes in traditional forms, and sometimes in new appearances."[69] Zuñis merge tribalism with Christianity, 75 percent of the Shoshonis follow peyote religion, and traditional religion remains the practice for 30 percent of the Cherokees, widely regarded as the most assimilated of all Indian societies.[70]

Resistance to Euroamerican churches is a continuing part of Indian history and a central part of Navajo George P. Lee's accusation that Mormon church leaders are racists, committing "silent, subtle, scriptural and spiritual slaughter" of the Native Americans. Not an outsider to the Latter-day saint (LDS) Church, Lee was a general authority with life tenure until the public announcement of his excommunication for "apostasy" in September 1989.[71]

Despite a century of anthropological and historical study, the religions of Native American Indians are still open for reassessment. Sam Gill protests: "We remain deaf to their insistence that we have not understood them [religiously], that we have not seen them, that our studies radically transform, even violate them."[72] That invitation for a revitalized religious history applies to many of the West's peoples.

Perhaps no other western region better demonstrates the need for and difficulty of achieving the integration of social, cultural, and religious history than the Spanish Southwest. Although scholars such as Sarah Deutsch and Arnoldo De León have addressed at length the role of religion in the Chicano experience,[73] much of the best recent Chicano scholarship virtually ignores religion.[74] The historiographic vacuum is well described by Leo Grebler, John W. Moore, and Ralph C. Guzman in their *Mexican-American People:* "How they [the churches] operate within a distinctive minority reflects the societal milieu as well as religious or ethical norms . . . [but] . . . [t]his kind of institutional analysis is rare either in the standard literature on religion or, for that matter, in the writings about Mexican Americans."[75]

One of the most serious challenges for the history of the Southwest is the need to address the complex, emotional response of the region's people to Catholicism. Alfredo Mirande identifies deeply rooted anti-Catholic, anti-Chicano, and American imperialistic biases that run through the work of many scholars, including Chicano authors.[76] In the context of Rodolfo Acuña's critique, for example, to speak favorably of the dedication of early Catholic priests in the Southwest or of Catholic institutional efforts to "Americanize" the region after the Mexican War blames "Mexicans for their own oppression" and praises a religious instrument of capitalist oppression.[77] Such a perspective would indict even David J. Weber's study of the Catholic Church's failure in the borderlands because of his empathetic approach to the clergy's problems.[78]

One possible response to these criticisms would be for future histories to continue a pattern of us-them emphasis, in which the "us" are Hispanics and the "them" everyone else. This is the self-declared approach of Acuña's history.[79] It is also the approach of a recent sociological analysis of "California's Newest Immigrants," which features charts with categories for Mexican immigrants and "all others."[80] Although there are always benefits to focusing closely on a subject, an isolated emphasis on the Chicano or Hispanic experience can inadvertently draw biased conclusions from nonbiased data.

Consider, for example, the issue of religious noncompliance or indifference among southwestern Hispanics.[81] One recent history of the Californios states that Mexican-Americans were "out of touch religiously with the American [Catholic] Church." A recent Chicano dictionary also briefly observes: "As a result of historical background, large numbers of Mexican Americans today who call themselves Catholic conform minimally to the accepted norms of the church. As a group their Sunday mass attendance is appreciably lower than the national average for Catholics. . . ."[82] A third author seeks to put the matter in positive terms by explaining that the "Mexican reluctance to participate in parish life stemmed in part from the strength of the Mexican extended family,"[83] but this implies that lack of religious devotion is limited to Hispanics. Ultimately, however, any arguments that try to explain nonparticipation among Chicanos solely in ethnic terms seem dubious, for they fail to consider that poor church attendance is characteristic of westerners generally, not merely Hispanics.

Zelinsky identified this historical trend defining the West as a distinct religious region partly because of its many unchurched people. In the 1890 census of religions only 7.58 percent of Oklahoma's population (excluding Indian Territory) belonged to any church, with Nevada next at 12.84 percent, the lowest rates in the nation. Of eleven states or territories whose rates of church membership fell below 25 percent in 1890, ten were in the trans-Mississippi West.[84] There is little reason to question these data[85] since they are supported by contemporary observations as well as subsequent trends for the nation.

Colorado, Nebraska, Nevada, Oklahoma, Oregon, Washington, and Wyoming all had lower rates of church membership in the 1890 census than California's 23.23 percent. A California minister remarked in 1893 that "there is a tacit conviction cherished by many that religion is not so important but that one can get along very well without it in California"; he added nonetheless that among these late-nineteenth-century unchurched westerners, "God is acknowledged and believed in."[86] Less than ten years later 2,566 Montana leaders wrote their own biographical sketches, and 81.4 percent listed no religious affiliation.[87]

The trend of religious disaffiliation has continued in the West, America's "Unchurched Belt."[88] The Pacific West has the lowest membership (33.8 percent), and the West as a region has the lowest attendance (36 percent) in church or synagogue.[89] The state with the lowest rate of church membership during the 1980s was again Nevada (29.3 percent), followed by Alaska (30.8 percent), Washington (31.0 percent), Hawaii (33.2 percent), California (34.5 percent), and Oregon (36.1 percent). Moreover, there were a number of western counties with less than 20 percent church membership: Alaska (five counties), California (eight), Colorado (twelve), Idaho (two), Montana (one), Nevada (two), Washington (three).[90] Of 215 U.S. metropolitan areas, the Far West accounts for 21 of the bottom 25 in church membership, as well as the highest rate of those who never attend church and the highest rate of atheism. A religious survey of 113,000 adults in 1989–90 reflected similar trends, with Oregon, Washington, Wyoming, and California at double the national rate of Americans who claim no religious affiliation.[91]

The Unchurched Belt of the American West is the inverted image of the Protestant mainstream. The Protestant clergy in the West had to confront religious diversity a generation before the clergy in the eastern states faced the religious challenges posed by new immigrants from eastern and southern Europe.[92] By the 1880s Protestant evangelicals in California saw themselves as both isolated and different from Protestants "back East."[93]

The embattled character of mainline Protestantism in the West has not changed. The American West still accounts for the smallest proportion of national membership for Episcopalians, Methodists, Lutherans, Baptists, Church of Christ, and Presbyterians.[94] Furthermore, membership support is extremely weak: Only 7 percent of professed Methodists in the West attend church weekly, compared with three to four times that rate for Methodists elsewhere. In addition, 39 percent of western clergymen have considered leaving their religious vocations, the highest rate in the nation.[95] There is no exaggeration in a recent assessment of the West Coast as "a kind of continental shelf in which conventional churches seem unable to put down healthy roots."[96]

Despite its claims to the contrary, televangelism has not reversed these trends, even for fundamentalists. Although Arbitron ratings showed Jerry Falwell's largest listening market in the early 1980s to be Los Angeles, which itself almost equaled the total audience of his next two cities, Falwell's sixty-three thousand listeners in Los Angeles were a very small percentage of its population, compared with his twenty-five thousand listeners in fifth-ranked Knoxville. Likewise, Robert Schuller and Oral Roberts had smaller percentages of their listeners in the West than the western percentage of the potential national audience.[97] Somewhat different A. C. Nielsen ratings confirm that televangelism has a significant audience in the Midwest but shares mainline Protestantism's difficulty in the Unchurched Belt.[98]

The consistency and longevity of unchurched behavior patterns in the American West require far more historical attention, and current data can provide a starting point. What can we discover about the 65 to 80 percent of the West's adult population that has historically shunned formal religion? One approach would be to examine through literary sources the extent to which recent Gallup polls also describe the unchurched of the past: "The unchurched are believers. . . . In fact, with a few variations, the unchurched claim the same turf as the churched—except they are not attending, supporting, or belonging to a congregation of the visible church."[99]

Literary sources indicate that the unchurched of the past read the Bible and may have attended religiously oriented meetings without formal affiliation. Particularly in the nineteenth century, the West's unchurched masses may have participated extensively in noninstitutional alternative expressions, such as spiritualistic séances or ritual healings. Census data on denominations will not reveal these patterns; their analysis will require us to read the literary sources with the new history's emphasis on the everyday.

Another line of inquiry into the phenomenon of nonparticipation would be to examine black religious experience in the West, a topic given little or no attention in monographs on western blacks.[100] Recent data indicate that nonmigrating blacks show higher church attendance in the West than nonmigrating blacks of other regions. Furthermore, blacks who migrate to the West demonstrate increased church attendance rates, compared with decreased attendance by Catholic and Protestant whites who migrate to the West.[101] This is an unexplored part of the black experience and of western migration.

What is it about the West's milieu that has historically encouraged Caucasians and most Orientals to be unchurched or nonattending yet also encouraged blacks to have higher rates of religious participation in the West than elsewhere in the nation? Historians should consider to what extent the churched and unchurched division may have influenced (or been influenced by) the political, economic, and social life of the West.

The greatest exception to the unchurched character of the West is Zelinsky's Mormon region, centered in Utah. As one geographer of religion noted, "Nothing else in the nation compares with the dominance of the Latter-day Saints in the intermountain area."[102] In 1890, the year the LDS Church officially abandoned polygamy, the census of religions showed that the Territory of Utah had the second-highest rate of church affiliation in the nation (61.2 percent), second only to New Mexico Territory's 68.9 percent church affiliation.[103] As of 1980, 72.2 percent of Utah's population belonged to a church (primarily LDS), second only to Rhode Island's 75.5 percent. By 1990 Utah's religious affiliation reached 92.2 percent, the highest west of the Great Plains.[104] Out of 215 metropolitan areas in the United States, the Provo-Orem area of Utah has the highest rate of church membership.[105]

Mormon membership has been doubling every fifteen years or less. The LDS Church has become the largest religious organization in Utah and Idaho, the second-largest in Arizona, California, Hawaii, Nevada, Oregon, Washington, and Wyoming, the third-largest in Alaska and Montana, the fourth-largest in New Mexico, the fifth-largest in Colorado, and the fifth-largest separate religious organization in the United States as a whole.[106] In 1984 the sociologist Rodney Stark projected that world membership of the LDS Church (now more than

8 million) will reach 265 million by the year 2080 on the basis of consistent trends for 50 percent growth per decade. Five years later Stark found LDS membership growth actually ahead of his projection, which suggests that non-Mormons in the American West will become increasingly isolated religiously.[107]

Mormon-Utah social dynamics offer tremendously rich potential for study. Following hundreds of earlier books on Mormon polygyny, Lawrence Foster's comparative study of the early Mormon practice stands as a landmark and has been complemented by a recent study of polygynous and monogamous dynamics based on oral histories with children from hundreds of families.[108] With its almost unparalleled trove of records, Utah Mormonism is a historical demographer's dream.[109] Nevertheless, the flowering of interpretative Mormon history over the past twenty years has been achieved despite atavistic efforts by LDS leaders to restrict Mormon archives and intimidate historians.[110]

Just as the Mormon West defined itself as God's alternative to traditional Christianity, so it seems no coincidence that the West's Unchurched Belt is also a region of alternative religious movements. Two analysts of America's religious future have observed that "cults abound in the West precisely because the conventional churches are so weak."[111] A recent study of literary sources found a religious "patchwork" of diversity and heterodoxy among California's Protestants from 1850 to 1910.[112] Religious census data for America's 122 largest cities (25,000 plus population) show that Oakland had the highest statistical score for religious diversity in 1890 and that Sacramento and Los Angeles had the highest levels of religious diversity in 1906.[113] This supports religious historian Sydney E. Ahlstrom's observation that "quantitatively speaking, California leads the nation in the proliferation of diverse religious movements."[114]

Others narrow the focus of the West's exotic religious experience to Los Angeles alone. According to one Southern California historian, "Whereas San Francisco is a city of churches—Catholic, Presbyterian, Episcopal—and thus is religiously similar to other great American cities, Los Angeles is a City of Sects."[115] By the 1920s Los Angeles had a national reputation as the new "burned-over district" of sects and cults.[116] Yet an urban historian has recently pointed out that in the 1920s Chicago (in proportion to population) and New York City (in actual numbers) had more small sects and cults than Los Angeles. Religious historians have suggested that Southern California's reputation for unusual religions may be overstated.[117] Still that same urban

161

history shows that in Los Angeles small sects and cults grew by 381 percent from 1920 to 1930, compared with a Protestant increase of 64 percent and Catholic of 102 percent. Today California hosts the national headquarters of 234 religious groups, while New York State is second with only 128.[118]

Addressing the question of California's religious polarities, a theology journal noted that "there are more accredited Christian theological seminaries in California than in any other state. But no religious mainstream appeared . . . [and] California gives the impression of a religious circus in the tents of secularity."[119] Concerning alternative religious groups, each of which appeals to only a "minute fraction" of the population, one sociologist concludes that "taken all together, however, these movements [in the American West] are clearly a noteworthy new force in American religion."[120] With that perspective, the *Lutheran Quarterly* seemed almost enthusiastic in proclaiming a decade ago, "California is the laboratory—'the great crucible,' so to speak, where these new religious forms are being forged, where the revival of traditional Christianity, the importation of the ancient religious beliefs of the Far East and the psychological insights of the 'new consciousness' are blending to create a new form of religious experience."[121]

Despite their small numbers, western American cults can attract international attention with sensational claims or actions. After moving from its base in California to Guyana, the People's Temple stunned the world with its murder-suicides of more than nine hundred people in 1978, led by a former ordained minister.[122] As one historian recently wrote, "Overlooked in almost all explanations of Jim Jones, the People's Temple, and Jonestown is their religious character. The People's Temple was a religious movement, animated by a particular religious world view, that can be interpreted in the larger context of the history of religions."[123] Thousands of religious "cults" or "new consciousness" groups may attract no more than a few hundred adherents each, yet their aggregate numbers and their very proliferation are impressive. In a 1982 national resource directory for such groups, California had 306 entries; the next largest was New York State with only 83 entries.[124]

The Golden State is also home to the religious occult, both Christian and anti-Christian. In 1918 the Ancient and Mystical Order of Rosae Crucis, the largest Rosicrucian organization in America, moved to San Francisco and later to San Jose. Santa Clara, California, is headquarters to the spiritualist Universal Church of the Master with its three hundred congregations, thirteen hundred mediums, and ten

thousand ministers. Throughout the twentieth century the Theo-
sophical Society has been headquartered in Southern California, which
also hosts such occult groups as Manly Hall's Philosophical Research
Society, the Builders of the Adytum, and the Ordo Templi Astartes.[125]
On the dark side, Anton LaVey organized the Church of Satan in San
Francisco in 1966 and claims seven thousand contributing members.
Across the bay Berkeley has been home since 1975 to America's sec-
ond-largest witchcraft group, the Covenant of the Goddess, and the
Susan B. Anthony Coven No. 1 functions in Oakland, California.[126]
And throughout the Southwest are individual Indian and Hispanic
shamans whose practices are "occult" to outsiders but benignly reli-
gious to their participants.[127]

Most of these groups are known only to followers and research-
ers. On the other hand, some alternative altars in the American West
have too many devotees to ignore. During the first decade of what is
called the Human Potential Movement, est trained more than three
hundred thousand people, a quarter of them from California. One out
of every nine college-educated young adults in the San Francisco Bay
area was a graduate of est but with virtually no conventional religious
affiliation.[128] This is only one of scores of groups in the continuing
Human Potential Movement, which often serves as an alternative religious outlet for participants.[129]

There have also been significant conversions of young Americans
to Asian religious practices, particularly in the Far West. Perfect Liberty Kyodan-Shintoism is headquartered in Glendale, California, and
half of its five thousand members are Caucasians, blacks, or Hispanics.[130] A decade ago two thousand students enrolled each summer in
Tibetan Buddhist instruction at Boulder, Colorado, and the largest
Tibetan Buddhist group reports two thousand American members.
Of approximately three hundred thousand American converts to the
militant Buddhist sect Soka Gakkai, 95 percent are non-Orientals.
Estimates are that half a million Caucasian Americans have participated regularly in some form of Buddhist instruction, with 90 percent
of the participants on the West Coast.[131] Currently, non-Asians constitute the clear majority of Buddhist Americans.[132]

Various Hindu exports have also gained significance in the West.
Oldest in this group, the Vedanta Society began in New York City
in 1894 but soon added centers in California. The Vedantic Center of
Agora, California, has the distinction of being led by a female Afro-
American who has proselytized predominantly among blacks.[133] The
International Society for Krishna Consciousness (ISKON) located its

headquarters in Southern California during the late 1960s, and presently more than a third of its North American centers are in the trans-Mississippi West. Saffron-robbed Hare Krishnas number about 2,500 in America, with 250,000 lay temple attenders.[134] In addition, there are 5,000 to 10,000 "white-American Sikhs" in the Sikh Dharma Brotherhood headquartered in Los Angeles, where it was founded as the "Healthy, Happy, Holy Organization" (3HO) in 1968.[135] In 1971 Guru Maharaj Ji established the headquarters of his Divine Light Mission in Denver, Colorado, from which his 50,000 followers were assigned to ashrams throughout the nation. After internal dissension split the American group from its mission in India, Guru Maharaj Ji took the simplified name Maharaj, renamed his movement Elan Vital, and transferred its headquarters to Malibu, California.[136] The most popular export Hindu movement is the World Plan Executive Council, popularly known as transcendental meditation. TM has trained more than a million Americans, purchased an Iowa college campus in 1974, and has nearly half of its U.S. "World Plan Centers" located in the West.[137]

A decade ago estimates were that eight thousand groups and techniques of "new consciousness" existed in the United States, and this essay has undoubtedly left out someone's favorite.[138] In February 1989 thirty thousand people attended a three-day New Age convention at Los Angles.[139] Although Martin E. Marty argues that the existence of all of these alternative religious groups did not displace and "seldom crowded" the mainstream religions of the nation, it seems clear that alternative religious traditions have indeed crowded the Far West's weaker mainstream churches.[140]

In religious experience the West has been neither desert nor Eden. The American West has never been a religious monolith, a melting pot, or a battlefield between two adversaries. Its diversity defies comparison with India's religious multitudes and is more benign than Lebanon's. If any symbol captures the religious West, it's the symbol of a giant aquarium—God's aquarium. Throughout the wide spaces in God's western aquarium, there are schools of familiar (but easily startled) denominational species, there are slow-moving crustaceans, there are religious exotics from the depths and an occasional shark, there's the Mormon leviathan, and unchurched plankton are floating everywhere.

The aptness of this bizarre metaphor may help explain why "there has been no definitive overall study of religion in the American West."[141] It would be no easy task to encompass all the diversity of the West's religious experience, including the impact of each religious group on the region and vice versa. Lacking such a resource at present, I propose that the relationship of region and religion in the American West is sometimes symbiotic and sometimes parasitic and usually transforms imported religions. The generalization holds true with Native American religions, as well as all the imports: Catholicism, mainline Protestantism, Mormonism, Judaism, Eastern religions, and alternative religious expressions in the American West. The frontier was only a temporary influence on religions, which continue a multifaceted dynamic with the western region. The acknowledged distinctiveness of religion in the area is both an evidence of and a factor in the character of the American West.

But the daunting complexity of the West's religious life does not wholly explain why "the story of religion in the American West, however, has seldom received the attention it deserves."[142] Church missionaries, Native Americans, and Mormons are virtually the only groups for which the West is not "a trackless wilderness in the realm of religious historiography."[143] As we have seen, scholars often ignore (or give only passing reference) to religion when writing about the *social and community* experience in the West of Chinese, Hispanics, Indochinese, blacks, and Anglos.

If "objective" history is a goal, then something is wrong in ignoring or denigrating religious dimensions at play even in secular communities and unchurched lives. This is especially true for the recent "new history" of the American West, which examines common people's devotion to family and community but often excludes their responses to religion and church. Despite this gap in historical writings, religion was an important part of the social world of the West, even for its unchurched majorities, and scholars must acknowledge that it influenced the preceptions and experiences of westerners, not just Mormons, Native Americans, and various missionaries. The work of Grebler, Moore and Guzman, Deutsch, and De León—as well as most scholarship on Indians and Mormons—points the way for integrating religion with secular history.

My own work on popular religion in early America convinces me that when scholars set aside secular biases, they will find religiosity (often foreign to that of the historian) in the West's diverse population.[144] Both churched and unchurched, westerners have reacted to or against religion in ways that have shaped their social world. Much of their religious experience has, in fact, been private, distant from clergy and churches. Diaries, correspondence, folklore, newspapers, county histories, institutional records, and material culture give historical evidence of this, and opinion polls demonstrate it currently.

The frontier West and the postmodern West have nurtured various religious communities that have attempted to maintain homogeneous or communal social orders. Because this has balkanized the West religiously, historical study has often also focused on groups in isolation. Still, western religious communities call for comparative study across space and time. This obviously includes such examples as Amana, Orderville, Theosophist Point Loma, Rajneeshpuram, various communes and ashrams, and the West's ethnic enclaves from Chinatown and Koreatown to rural enclaves of European immigrants. But often ignored are "religious neighborhoods" developed informally by otherwise assimilated groups like Seventh-day Adventists and Latter-day Saints who have residential networks in metropolitan areas.

A century of urbanization and secularization has not ended efforts to maintain some form of religious communalism in the West. Why did the ideal of a "city on a hill" die in the East with the Puritans and transcendentalists, whereas the ideal of "a commune in a valley" lives on in the West? To write of this western religious experience, historians will need to employ oral history interviews and the tools of family history, comparative history, and social history.

There is much to be done in understanding and writing the history of religion in the West. A revitalized history of western religion must be interdisciplinary because religious issues cut across the traditional concerns of psychologists, sociologists, anthropologists, economists, demographers, and political scientists.[145] The attention to religion in any general history, social history, economic history, political history, community history, or demographic history will vary, but western religions deserve more than footnotes and isolated remarks in major studies. Correspondingly, any denominational history or western religious study must devote attention to social, economic, demographic, political, and other disciplinary concerns. So much of the American West's religious history has been neglected that historians should be anxious to get on with the task.

Making the Most of Words

Verbal Activity and Western America[1]

PATRICIA NELSON LIMERICK

In 1849 Kit Carson set out to rescue a white woman, providentially named Mrs. White, who had been taken captive by the Jicarilla Apaches. When the search party caught up with the Indians, it was too late; Mrs. White had just been killed. But Kit Carson came upon a surprising souvenir. "We found a book in the camp," he reported, "the first of the kind I had ever seen, in which I was represented as a great hero, slaying Indians by the hundreds."[2]

It could pass as a moment in postmodernist fiction: Kit Carson, in the midst of an adventure, comes upon a printed and bound history of the adventures of Kit Carson. In experimental fiction Carson's course of action would be clear: Look up "White, Mrs., failed rescue of" in the index, and check to see what happened next. Surreal options aside, this incident highlights the complicated connection between words and actions in western American history. Much of western expansion had, of necessity, a kind of heightened self-consciousness about it, as written words framed and shaped experiences, sometimes even before the experience had occurred. In 1849 the universe did indeed seem to be asking Kit Carson to reflect on the relationship between printed words and western actuality. Carson took a stab at the question: "I have often thought that Mrs. White must have read it [the book], and knowing that I lived nearby, must have prayed for my appearance in order that she might be saved."[3] But Carson, in life, was not the omnipotent, individualistic hero of the printed text. If Mrs. White did indeed read it, the book would only have given her false hopes. And in that case she would then represent a widespread pattern in the relationship between printed words about the West and their readers. That pattern is one of betrayal, and the critical question in any individual instance is this: Did the reader, unlike Mrs. White, live long enough to discover how much he or she had been deceived?

Writing and thinking about western history today, we have by no means escaped the treachery of words. We do not, to put it in the simplest terms, want to be suckers. Yet we know that western history is virtually the P. T. Barnum of historical fields, providing opportunities galore for suckers to confuse literal fact with literary fact. Simply quoting from Kit Carson's ostensible autobiography raises one aspect of the problem. While Carson clearly did not write the autobiography, he did, apparently, dictate it. But whose words, exactly, appear on the page? How reliable was the transcriber? How reliable was Carson's own memory? These are questions we more often associate with the problems of Indian history: fitting oral traditions into written history; appraising and filtering written records of spoken words. But even a society devoted to recording the world in written words relies on oral transactions in the vast majority of its daily activities.[4] In dealing with print or speech, the words of the nonliterate or the words of the overliterate, one simply must learn to live with uncertainty, applying measured doses of skepticism and trust, incredulity and confidence, as circumstances warrant.

The obligation to read words critically rests heavily on historians in any field, but it lands with particular weight on western American historians for three principal reasons. First, western historians inherit a long and sometimes embarrassing legacy from predecessors who did not keep a critical distance between themselves and the written words of the pioneers; this earlier breed of western historians adopted the terms, the point of view, and the assumptions of the people they studied. Their dependence on words like "civilization," "savagery," "frontier," and "progress" left western scholars echoing, not analyzing, the thinking of Anglo-American colonizers.

Second, the process of invasion, conquest, and colonization was the kind of activity that provoked shiftiness in verbal behavior. Filled with people using written words to justify, promote, sell, entice, cover up, evade, defend, deny, congratulate, persuade, and reassure, western history puts a premium on the critical evaluation of written words. In most settings, colonization was preceded by a torrent of words exaggerating the future and was followed by a torrent of words exaggerating the past, leaving western actuality sandwiched between romances of prospect and retrospect.

Third, the slipperiness of the essential term "West" leaves the field of western American history in a constant crisis of definition. If "the West" is sometimes in Massachusetts, sometimes in Florida, sometimes in Kentucky, sometimes in Illinois, sometimes in California, sometimes in Colorado, then what on earth is a "western American historian"? However one solves this conundrum, a western American historian had better be the sort of person who can comfortably cope with the shifting meanings of key words, the sort of person who is more challenged than irritated by questions of terminology, such as that endless refrain "What is the West?"

In this essay that question receives a simple answer: "the trans-Mississippi West." While I am, here and elsewhere, committed to a regional definition, I recognize that Anglo-Americans once thought of other regions of the United States as the West. It is, of course, essential to compare the history of conquest and colonization in the trans-Mississippi West with parallel events in other parts of the nation and the planet. Although I will not focus here on the colonial West, the trans-Appalachian West, the Old Southwest, or the Old Northwest, my examination of verbal behavior in the trans-Mississippi West may well be of some comparative interest to specialists in those other regions that briefly wore the label "West."

More important than a regional definition of "the West," this essay rests on an expansion and exploration of that phrase "verbal activity."[5] Most readers easing into an essay on words and the West might well expect reflections on the image of the West in literature, especially in fiction. I myself first took on the topic with a resigned feeling that I was off to the literary wars, off to the trenches to reread Cooper's *Leatherstocking Tales* and to keep track of the plots of dime novels. This topic seemed to me, in other words, to give marching orders that directed me to the periphery, away from the daylight zone of political, economic, and social behavior and off to the twilight zone of myth and symbol. The phrase "verbal activity" proved to be my ticket out of this methodological despair. It is my hope that it can provide a similar service for other western historians, providing a category of analysis that permits cross-cultural comparisons, bridges the gap between oral and literate cultures, and squarely addresses the significance of the human relationship to words.

In substituting the study of verbal activity for the usual categories of "myth and symbol interpretation," or "literary history," one looks directly at what westerners have done to and with words and what words have done to and with westerners.[6] Just as one writes the history of the western environment by looking at what westerners have done to nature and what nature has done to westerners, so one approaches the history of verbal activity with an eye out for concrete and visible consequences. One looks, especially, for behavior that has become repeated, ritualized, and formulaic. This often entails returning to the turf of what used to be "myth and symbol" studies, but now one asks, much more concretely and literally, "What are the functions and consequences of this patterned human behavior toward particular words?" This approach does not simply recast the old territory of myths and symbols; it adds new subject matter that in turn refreshes our interpretation of the old material.

I will begin with an exploration of the founding text of the myth and symbol school, Henry Nash Smith's *Virgin Land*. I will then explore some of the topics that fit under the more inclusive category of verbal activity: the convergence in western America of people who spoke diverse languages, sometimes understanding each other and sometimes not; the Anglo-American penchant for newspapers and printing presses and the related compulsion for literacy, as they showed themselves in western settings; and the status of laws, statutes, executive orders, instructions, and treaties as a kind of literature, with legislators, lawyers, judges, and bureaucrats acting as authors and literary critics, improvising, interpreting, and amending this most consequential body of western literature. I will then return to the intellectual offspring of *Virgin Land* and explore the ways in which the study of verbal activity can give those inquiries a more reliable anchor in actuality.

"On a Different Plane": How the Study of Words Lost Consequence

More than most fields, western history has suffered from the segregation of fact from significance. On one side sit narrowly factual studies of mining towns, railroad lines, Indian wars, cattle trails, and agricultural settlements; on the other side—at some considerable distance—sit highbrow studies of the meaning, significance, imagery, myth, and symbolism of the West. Those who deal in ideas and those who deal in facts have set up their booths at opposite sides of the bazaar, and more often than not, those booths face away from each other. The two camps have not approached each other's enterprises with sympathetic understanding, much less enthusiasm. The only idea that has brought them together—for brief and curt exchanges—was the concept of the frontier, especially the Turner thesis variety. But then the inclusion of minorities as a subject in western history made the Turner thesis an untenable meeting ground for both idea people and fact people. In so doing, the breakdown of a racially defined segregation ironically hardened the segregation between those who studied western myth and those who studied western fact.

In these matters all roads lead back to *Virgin Land*, and the American Studies approach it represented. Indeed *Virgin Land* may well be the essential founding book for American Studies. It is, therefore, a fact full of consequence for the whole field of American Studies and cultural interpretation that *Virgin Land* is about the American West. If Smith had brought his methods of interpretation to bear on automobiles or streetcars or factories or schools or cemeteries, then he would have been investigating the ways in which human minds responded to and shaped ideas of undeniable actuality. But when he chose, instead, the American West, he launched himself—and American Studies—into the mysteries intrinsic to a study of abstractions about an abstraction. To Frederick Jackson Turner and his followers in conventional western history, the frontier (and, by extension, the West) was a process, not a place; a concept, not an actual geographical location. In this way of thinking, the West is wherever the American mind puts it—a pretty vague and ephemeral target for "image" analysis.

Throughout the twentieth century both western American history and American Studies suffered persistent aches and pains around the joint that connects idea to actuality, a joint that always seemed close to separating. When, in *Virgin Land*, American Studies teamed up with western American history, that weakness was compounded. One brief line in the introduction to *Virgin Land* came to encapsulate the problem. Defining myth and symbol, Henry Nash Smith said further: "I do not mean to raise the question whether such products of the imagination accurately depict empirical fact. They exist on a different plane."[7] Since the book's publication in 1950, critics and commentators have devoted themselves to that perplexing phrase. The world of events and the world of words and ideas, Smith's phrasing seems to say, were separate worlds. He, for one, would not plunge into "the question of whether such products of the imagination accurately depict empirical fact." Consistent with that determination, discussing Frederick Jackson Turner's allegiance to the Myth of the Garden, Smith declared: "To determine whether Turner's hypothesis is or is not a valid interpretation of American history forms no part of the intention of this book."[8] "Well, why not?" one wonders now. Having shown that the Myth of the Garden misrepresented the reality of plains farming, and having then shown that this myth held considerable power over Turner, Smith stood on the verge of responding to the question of "whether Turner's hypothesis is or is not a valid interpretation of American history." Since he had gone two-thirds of the way, why would he not complete the journey?

This question does bewilder me, but I would imagine that Smith thought in 1950 that it would cheapen the richness of meaning to put his myths to a shallow test of accuracy, to sell them out for a simple "relevance." Certainly no one could accuse the second part of the book on the western hero of grabbing for a reductively practical significance. For critics determined to find the American Studies method inconclusive and insubstantial, a futile tracking and tracing of pointless images, then Part Two is the book's weakest link. It is easy for *Virgin Land*'s fans to identify and defend the point and consequences of the Passage to India and the Myth of the Garden, but it is considerably harder to justify the endless details of "The Sons of Leatherstocking," the plots and proper names of novels that evidently stood in some relation to some audience and revealed something of substance about that audience and its attitudes. But what relationship? What audience? What substance? In the meantime, one trudges along through that second section, noting, for instance, that Charles Webber "introduces a brother of Emilie who kills Albert when he discovers that the Count [Albert] has deceived his sister by the familiar device of a spurious marriage ceremony."[9] If the Count, Emilie, her brother, and all their fictional siblings and suitors did indeed stand in some dynamic relationship to the actual course of western history, one would not like to be put on the spot and asked to give a name to that relationship.

Justifiably or not, many western historians came away from their encounter with *Virgin Land* convinced that the investigation of fictions for their content in myth and symbol was an inconsequential word game. My own initial encounter with this way of thinking came at Yale in 1973, in a class on "'Theories of American Literature." When *Virgin Land* came up in the discussion, the graduate student seated next to me took the occasion to pass along an agitated note. "*Virgin Land*," he had written, evidently unaware that I had myself recently sent a fan letter to Henry Nash Smith, "is the most pernicious book ever written in American Studies."

"Pernicious"? The charge seemed to be that Smith, like a perverse museum guide, had directed us away from the important exhibits of actuality and sent us off, instead, to a colorful gallery of trinkets, bric-a-brac, and knickknacks. Once settled into the myth and symbol gallery, we frittered our time away, disputing and analyzing the meaning of cultural artifacts that carried nearly as much authentic significance as the Taiwan-made tomahawks for sale in southwestern "Indian trading posts." Meanwhile, we evaded the serious challenge of determining what had happened in the West.

This was by no means my only encounter with this charge. Indeed, to be a western American historian suspected by some of being "too literary" is to have frequent encounters with this particular legacy of *Virgin Land*. I will admit that after several encounters with scholars certain that my American Studies dissertation on deserts must be devoted to the "myth and symbol of deserts," I came close to blaming Henry Nash Smith for my troubles. He was the one, I could start to believe, who firmly, persuasively, charmingly took scissors in hand and cut the ties, letting the balloon of myth and symbol drift far up and away from the actual West. But then one must reread *Virgin Land* and rediscover that Smith is not, in fact, the culprit. The idea that America promised a passage to India, he clearly showed, led to wagon roads and railroads, to the acquisition of the Pacific Coast and its ports. He went to even more trouble to compare and contrast that agrarian myth with the real world of agriculture and to show the agrarian myth at work in shaping and sometimes distorting legislation, party politics, and sectional rivalry. Thomas Hart Benton, Asa Whitney, John Charles Frémont, the Homestead Act, sectional and party politics, John Wesley Powell—there is plenty of ballast in *Virgin Land*, plenty of weight to offset any helium in the abstractions. Why then did we draft Smith for the undeserved position of scapegoat for the conceptual problems of the American Studies approach to western history?

Beyond the misleading signals of the "different plane" claims, a great deal of the problem can be traced to a tiny, seemingly insignificant phenomenon. The verb tenses in *Virgin Land* are haywire. The temporal location of the book swerves from past to present to past, sometimes in the same paragraph. In the book, the world of ideas—especially ideas expressed in written prose—may well appear separate from the world of actuality because those two worlds occur, more often than not, in separate verb tenses. Speaking and writing generally appear in the present tense, while other kinds of actions appear in the past tense.

We can assume that Smith did this on purpose; he was too good a writer to do it by accident. He might have wanted to invite the reader to enter texts, to move into the eternal present of a novel or even into the eternal present of a Thomas Hart Benton speech. The end may have been immersion and immediacy, but the means to the end carried unfortunate side effects. Instead of *blending* history and literature, the verb tenses *separate* them, leaving Thomas Hart Benton the politician firmly settled back in 1840 and Thomas Hart Benton the writer and speaker floating weirdly around in 1950 or, for that matter, in any year in which *Virgin Land* gets read. Although myth and actuality are not necessarily on "different planes" in the book, they are in different time zones, and this, I believe, has undermined the force of the literary commentary, opening the door to all the various critiques on the lack of connection between idea and fact.

The verb tenses, the unwillingness to be consistent in connecting myth to actuality, the refusal to take Turner on directly, the unchallenged abstractness of the West—these, I think are the weaknesses of *Virgin Land*, weaknesses passed on to both American Studies and western American history. But Henry Nash Smith steered us toward the right goals, toward topics of lasting significance. The theme of the Passage to India and the role of the West as the connecting link to Asia continue to grow in significance as Asian immigration increases and trade shifts from the Atlantic to the Pacific. The recent farm crisis has revived a whole set of questions about the relations between the strong American sentiment for farming and the actuality of a rough commercial world. His chapter on the evolution of the female western hero placed Smith far ahead of his time in raising the question of gender in western experience, and he was the pacesetter in locating social class in the wilderness that Turner and others had assumed to be egalitarian. Despite the ethnocentricity of the term "virgin land" and a general lack of attention to Indians, Smith included in his last chapter this surprisingly contemporary line: "[T]he conception of civilization had been invoked to justify a number of dubious undertakings in the course of the nineteenth century, including European

174

exploitation of native peoples all over the world."[10]

In our time, with the resurrection of "frontier" metaphors in celebrations of modern technology and the "conquest" of space, with the continued prominence of the cowboy—who retains ten times the appeal of any other category of American wageworker—with the persistent nationalistic pride in a noble pioneer past, with the popularity of Ronald Reagan and the apparent public ratification of his fondness for western imagery, there is every reason, and urgent reason, to press on with the kind of inquiry Smith began. The presumption of different planes aside, these ways of thinking clearly shape behavior, and a failure to understand their origins leaves us still at their mercy.

Smith knew these matters were of national significance and not limited to a parochial, antiquarian western history. Both the West and the nation were and are actual places where beliefs have played a powerful role in shaping events. The connection is complicated, but much of it is within the grasp of common sense, a grasp not necessarily strengthened by academic obscurity and methodological self-consciousness. On that count, Smith's straightforward, down-to-earth method is more of an inspiration than the conceptually sophisticated and obscurely written offerings of some of his followers and critics. What Henry Nash Smith needed in *Virgin Land* was more faith in the powers of his own plain thinking, aimed directly at the point of intersection between language and events.

On the Beach:
"Babel" in California

If Henry Nash Smith represented one kind of interpreter of western words, Richard Henry Dana represented another, even more significant kind. Curing hides in Southern California in the 1830s, Dana took a great leap forward in the analysis of western history. What he saw taking shape on the San Diego beach was no Turnerian wave of Anglo-Americans relentlessly pushing a frontier line westward. Instead, Dana observed an amiable, haphazard colony of men from "almost every nation under the sun." Convivial evenings bridged the cultural gaps. "[A]mid the Babel of English, Spanish, French, Indian, and Kanaka," Dana remembered, "we found some words that we could understand in common."[11]

In this passage Dana captured a central fact of western American life that many later writers on the West barely noticed. As one of the great meeting grounds of the planet the trans-Mississippi West played host to a remarkable convergence of languages. Dana's list is, of course, only the beginning. Add the whole array of Indian languages, the range of European languages beyond Dana's "English, Spanish, [and] French," and Asian languages from Chinese and Japanese through Vietnamese and Hmong, and "Babel" becomes a mild term for the flurry of words echoing through western America.

In episode after episode of cultural conflict, when different groups acted "as if" they were speaking different languages, they sometimes were. Conflicts over property, trade, or social behavior were often compounded by the failure to find a common language. When one speaks to people with a limited command of one's own native language, it is all too easy to slip into speaking as if the audience were childlike or stupid, an impression apparently confirmed by their struggles to speak in what is to them an alien language. Novitiates fumbling with new languages have a way of sounding simpleminded. Might it be that much of the Anglo-American belief in the inferiority of Indian, Hispanic, or Asian people emerged from this dynamic—from English speakers meeting non-English speakers and constructing judgments of the intrinsic character of "others" based on this mismatch in speech? Surely the English speakers would not have come out of these encounters looking much more impressive themselves. Apache people now have a standard set of teasing rituals concluding with the punch line "White men are stupid." Some of the inspiration for these jokes and others like them must have come from white people's fumblings with non-European languages.[12] Nonetheless, in studies of cultural contact and conflict the role played by language has gotten short shrift.

Despite the variety of speech and culture on the San Diego beach, Dana remembered, "we found some words that we could understand in common." That memorable sentence fixes our attention on the remarkable peacefulness of the nineteenth-century West, encapsulated in the fact that western people talked with each other far more than they shot at each other. And with the challenge of these linguistic differences, to talk with each other often required spirited intellectual effort. Sometimes that effort was anonymous and collective, as in the creation of the Pacific Northwest's Chinook jargon, combining Indian, English, and French words into a trading patois.[13] Sometimes it involved individuals working together in the quietest setting, as in Washington Territory during the 1850s when an old Indian man would join Phoebe Judson's family on social evenings and try "to instruct us in his lan-

176

guage, by giving the names of different objects, while we, in turn, gave him the 'Boston' names." Judson realized that this exchange only scratched the surface: "As I listened to the legends and superstitions told in the limited Chinook jargon, of which I could understand only enough to make me long to know more, how I wished I could understand [the Indians] in their native tongue, as it flowed so fluently and softly from their lips; but the jargon and signs were our only method of communication."[14] She was quite right; communication by Chinook jargon was always limited. But it was also a considerable advance over silence and an even greater advance over hostile misunderstanding. Like Dana and his fellow hide curers, Judson and her Indian acquaintance "found some words that we could understand in common."

The professionals at providing these words were the interpreters who played essential roles in transaction after transaction—in trade, land acquisition, labor negotiation, and the acceleration and resolution of conflicts. The diversity of languages in use in the West made the translator a crucial mediator. Of necessity, the broad stream of relations between groups contracted to fit the narrow channel of the interpreters' words. The serious consequences of the interpreters' role appear in the records of every treaty-negotiating session. They appear more dramatically in instances like the Grattan Massacre of 1854, when an inept interpreter bungled the exchange between Lieutenant John L. Grattan and a group of Sioux, triggering the killing of Grattan's party and opening the Plains Wars. Interpreters were crucial players in western history, yet, in a misallocation of energy symbolic of the problems of the field, we ended up with hundreds of studies of miners, cattlemen, cowboys, and farmers and with no systematic, book-length studies of interpreters and translators.[15]

Dana's passage raises one final issue: the relationship of power, dominance, and language. Neither temperament nor status inclined Dana to see the diversity of western languages as a problem in need of correction. As a common sailor he did not have the authority to make others meet him on his linguistic homeground. Moreover, as a man who had already studied classical languages he evidently found more pleasure than injury in the necessity of learning new words. But in his delight in languages, Dana did not represent all Anglo-Americans. The counterpoint to the intellectual curiosity and flexibility of Dana and Judson was the intolerance of Indian school officials who forbade the use of native languages or the irritability of more recent campaigners in the cause of making English the official language of various western states. In the midst of "all manner of languages," Richard Henry Dana wrote, "Spanish was the common ground upon which we all met; for everyone knew more or less of that."[16] One cannot help wishing that California historical preservation officials could secure a special provision, exempting the plot of land that housed Dana's beach "Babel" from the current "official English" law and establishing a museum on the site to explore both historical patterns: the celebration as well as the condemnation of western linguistic diversity.

Off the Press:
The Necessity for Newspapers

In newly created western towns, where one expects every ounce of energy would have gone to more practical concerns, newspapers were an almost immediate crop. It was, indeed, peculiar that Anglo-Americans would leap with such urgency into the production of paper with printed words. But it was another example of the compulsion to write and to read demonstrated in many episodes of Anglo-American colonization. With dutifully recorded diary entries, anxious trips to check the mail, and carefully packed editions of the Bible or of Frémont's reports, westerners showed their dependence on the written word as a device to hold things together when the process of expansion threatened to pull them apart. Yet for all the centrality of literacy as a mechanism of cultural (and personal) cohesion, we do not yet have studies of western literacy that are in any degree comparable with the studies of literacy in the colonies and early republic.

Newspapers are, of course, prime sources for the study of verbal activity in the American West.[17] They embody the community's compulsion to put words to immediate and permanent use. They show editors and writers as active and practical wordsmiths, trying to hold the town together and to advance its fortunes (and their own) with their words. They record the self-consciousness and, often enough, self-dramatization of western settlements, targeting audiences at home and elsewhere with the message of the town's possible prosperity. Newspapers give us an excellent opportunity to study the booster mind at work, hovering between knowing misrepresentation and sincere self-deception and exhibiting a remarkable uniformity of expression, regardless of era, location, or local enterprise. Consider, for instance, the archetypal (if also unusually frank) thinking of a Southern California booster in the 1880s: "In fact, we may say that San Diego has a population of 150,000, only they are not all here yet."[18] Using a ritualized language, boosters constructed what they hoped would be self-fulfilling prophecies, spinning virtual incantations to bewitch the future into following their hopes.[19]

Newspapers reveal patterns of social change. When, if ever, did western newspapers go beyond boosterism, and what changes in their surroundings made that possible? The historian Charles Rankin points out one unfortunate symptom of a locale's "maturation": Newly founded western newspapers had more room for humor, whether in the play of the editor's personality or in the inclusion of hoaxes and spoofs, a trait that faded with the passage of time.[20] Newspapers provide case studies in cultural replication and regional distinctiveness: How did western newspapers resemble or differ from eastern newspapers? Newspapers reveal, as well, the workings of power. "Ruling elites," as Rankin puts it, made "the press a filter, rather than a conveyor of information," a case made dramatic by the Anaconda Copper Company's control of "almost three-fourths of the newspaper circulation" in Montana for "more than half a century."[21] Finally, newspapers provide us with opportunities for cross-cultural comparisons, returning us to an awareness of the West's language diversity. The region ended up stocked with newspapers in a variety of languages, serving various ethnic communities, American Indian, Chinese, Japanese, German, Norwegian, Swedish, Spanish, and Basque, to name a few.

Western history shows us repeatedly that we make a mistake when we take for granted any people's behavior toward written words. As compulsively literate sorts ourselves, historians have an obligation to step back in astonishment from a demonstration of white people's compulsive literacy like the one provided by the overlander William Swain. On the Humboldt River in 1849, preparing for the last, difficult crossing of desert and mountains, Swain made this diary entry:

> This forenoon the committee on which I am chosen and whose business is to report to the company upon the reports of the Agents and Directors met and spent the forenoon in examining its papers and making out its report. We recommend a reception of J. D. Potts', James Pratt's, H. Ladd's and F. Cook's reports, and a rejection of Thomas Rawson's and R. Hobart's reports and of the report of the Directors, for reasons set forth in our report.[22]

Here and elsewhere Swain and his people seemed to be one step short of calling a halt to the journey while they ordered in a printing press to assure all these reports their necessary permanence. Compulsive literacy and ritualized language, shown in the struggles that produced thousands of western reports and newspapers, demand an ethnohistorical analysis. What did the use of words mean to these people, and why did their need for written language sometimes take precedence over what might have seemed to be more urgent matters of life and death?

In the Courts:
The Law as Literature

Mark Twain led the way in recognizing the West's rich potential as a site for literary mining. He knew how central newspapers were to boomtown life and saw in legal language another variety of literature that could outdo James Fenimore Cooper in romantic expectations of an ideal West and Mark Twain himself in comedy. Taking office as the Nevada territorial secretary, Twain's brother had "sworn to obey his volume of written 'instructions.' " It quickly became clear, however, how utterly inappropriate those words were for the Nevada setting. Putting his brother's "instructions" to their proper use, Twain reported, "We used to read a chapter from them every morning, as intellectual gymnastics, and a couple of chapters in Sunday school every Sabbath, for they treated of all subjects under the sun and had much valuable religious material in them along with the other statistics."[23]

Along with metal pots and firearms, Bibles and plows, Euroamericans imported into the West cartloads of legal words—from territorial instructions to lawbooks. Western expansion produced its own flood of legal words: treaties; town, county, territorial, and state laws and regulations; judicial decisions and precedents. Along with the words, and quite in line with Twain's allusion to religion, came the priesthood—a subpopulation of lawyers and judges and officials devoted to interpreting those words. Indeed, most of the central struggles over power, property, and profit in the West came to a focus in legislatures and courtrooms, with much of western history hinging on the question, Who could most effectively cite, interpret, or rewrite legal words to support their (or their clients') interests? The practicality of the outcome may have caused us to forget that litigation, in both written and oral argument, is finally a literary exercise.

Probably the most effective way to add solidity and consequence to the study of western words is to add words with legal status to the usual list of items that qualify as literature.[24] To poems, novels, autobiographies, letters, diaries, and speeches, add "laws, treaties, executive orders and instructions." And to the more conventional interpreters of words, add legislators, lawyers, judges, and officials charged with applying and enforcing statutes. With these additions, no one can claim to be mystified by the proposition that words and their interpretation carry consequence.[25]

To drive this point home, consider a set of words that have been more puzzled and pored over than anything ever written by a poet. According to the treaties of the 1850s, the Indians of the Pacific Northwest have the right "to fish at all their usual and accustomed places in common with the settlers." "Usual and accustomed places"? Do those words take precedence over any drawing of official reservation boundaries? Does "in common with" mean "some part of the catch"? If it does, then *which* part of the catch? A third of the catch? Half the catch? "Usual and accustomed," "in common with"—the words are evocative, maybe even poetic. They are certainly susceptible to multiple interpretations, as that unacknowledged literary critic Judge George H. Boldt surely knew when he handed down his controversial ruling in the 1970s, restoring fishing rights to Indian peoples in the Northwest.[26]

Western history is full of other examples of words consulted and puzzled over as if they were Scripture. When mining law awarded ownership of all the "angles, dips, spurs, and variations" of a vein to the person who claimed the "apex" of that vein, lawyers took on the trying task of translating a verbal construction into a geological reality. The keepers of the national parks are charged with providing for the "enjoyment" of the parks "in such manner and by such means as will leave them unimpaired for the enjoyment of future generations," adding "enjoyment" and "unimpaired" to the list of words to be puzzled over and weighed, defended and contested. Perhaps the culmination of the literary history we have more conventionally known as the law came with recent environmentalism, when forests and rivers, antelope and coyotes, found themselves well represented by lawyers. When inarticulate nature found a voice in legal proceedings, the world of words had reached its peak of inclusiveness.[27]

As do newspapers, legal words provide abundant opportunities for cross-cultural comparisons. The prevailing trend in western legal history leads naturally in that direction; following John Phillip Reid and David Langum, western legal historians have been looking at "legal culture," at the whole complex of behavior by which people of different groups reveal their legal assumptions.[28] Written or oral, legal tradition is transmitted in words, by which power and influence flow toward the appointed custodians and interpreters of those words. The study of law and verbal behavior also provides important information on intergroup relations in the West.[29] Anglo-American efforts to prohibit Indians, blacks, or Asians from testifying in court give the most concrete demonstration possible that the key to keeping a group powerless is to keep it speechless, to deny it access to the formal record of conflict. By the same token, the training of Indian lawyers and the emergence of groups such as the Native American Rights Fund show the proposition in reverse, as Indian-initiated litigation revives the words of forgotten treaties and restores the voices of Indian tribes.[30] Once again, in the study of behavior toward words the divide between oral cultures and print cultures dissolves. With its combination of oral argument and written briefs and decisions, legal behavior itself falls right on the border.

Toward a New Way with Words: The Cultural Study of Verbal Activity in the American West

Following the lead of Henry Nash Smith, a significant group of scholars has undertaken to study words about the West as artifacts, products, even symptoms of American culture, not simply as records of the "facts" of Western history.[31] But this approach has carried certain risks. It has, for instance, been unable to push beyond a preoccupation with the "Anglo-American mind," in part because the most accessible written sources lead the investigator in that direction, in part because of a persistent habit in western historiography of awarding more significance to the thinking of the winners than to the thinking of the losers. How, after all, could the business of analyzing words to discover what "the West" meant to Anglo-Americans translate into comparable studies of what "the West" meant to the Pawnees, to the Cayuses, to the Hopis, or to Hispanic New Mexicans? Getting the proper training to understand nuance and implication in those other languages would only be part of the problem. More important, the Anglo-American idea of "the meaning of the West" dissolves when applied to the thinking of people who saw the region not as a direction but as home. The myth and symbol approach had the added disadvantage of restricting Indians and Hispanics to the status of object of Anglo-American perceptions; they were only the interestingly shaped blots to which the colonizers had revealing cognitive reactions. Moreover, this approach ran the risk of contributing to that traditional Anglo-American habit of conflating Indians and nature, making trees, soil, wolves, deer, and Indians simply the pieces and parts of the "wilderness" Anglo-Americans perceived.[32]

The myth and symbol approach ran into similarly rough waters on the question of sincerity and deception. Henry Nash Smith more or less skipped over the question of sincerity, apparently assuming that scholars should analyze the meanings of what Americans said rather than their intentions in saying it. A decade or two later the study of words in the context of Anglo-American conquest took a leap to the other side of the ring, as the subtitle to a book by Francis Jennings suggests: *The Invasion of America: Indians, Colonialism, and the Cant of Conquest*. With "cant" as the concept of preference, the scholarly agenda shifted from deciphering mythic meanings to debunking self-serving, cynical cover-ups and justifications for conquest.[33]

Empathizing with the losses of Indian people and responding with anger to the misbehavior of whites, the debunkers made a peculiar allocation of methodologies, applying cultural tolerance to Indian peoples and harsh judgment to whites. When Indian people said one thing and did another, this was a culturally shaped behavior, revealing a strain on traditional leadership patterns or a tension within a cultural ideal. When white people said one thing and did another, however, this was more often hypocrisy and deception. The refusal to apply cultural understanding to white people's words caused the debunkers to miss the most intriguing question about the self-righteous words so steadily employed by Anglo-Americans: Why were these people driven to put so much time and energy into justifying and rationalizing their actions? Why not simply invade, conquer, exterminate, and have done with it? What does it tell us about the power of words to intoxicate, console, or relieve consciences to see so much attention devoted to the creation of a considerably happier version of the story of western expansion than the one now taught in up-to-date college courses?

These questions bring us back squarely to the cultural study of verbal activity, a study that can encompass Indians, Hispanics, Asians, blacks, and Euroamericans of all backgrounds. It can, for instance, compare and contrast "origin stories" and the ways in which different groups have invoked divine influence and sponsorship to explain their presence in the West. It can encompass Mormon history; it was, after all, a quarrel over a printing press and a newspaper that broke up Nauvoo and triggered the western migration. Moreover, it has been, most recently, a scandal over forged historical documents that has propelled Mormon life back into national attention. The cultural study of words can encompass the study of expectation and anticipation—what William Goetzmann called programming[34]—in the shaping of western experience, as easily as it can encompass the study of nostalgia and nationalistic pride in the shaping of western historiography. Grounded in matters as practical and consequential as language diversity, newspaper production, and laws and litigation, it can bring the ethereal musings of the myth and symbol school down to earth. Perhaps most important, it can remind western historians that we are ourselves fundamentally interpreters, standing at an intersection where many groups—racial, ethnic, religious, national—have met and will meet. At that crossing our mission is to find order, pattern, and meaning in a swirl of perplexing events and perspectives, and it is no violation of scholarly objectivity to hope that a better understanding among these various groups might be one result of our inquiry. This is a challenge that requires us to offer our interpretations with a full respect for the power and complexity of words.

Views and Reviews

Western Art and Western History

——— ·••· ———

MARTHA A. SANDWEISS

On a late summer day in 1873 photographer Timothy O'Sullivan set up his cameras on a scubby piece of land near the abandoned military fort at Fort Defiance, New Mexico, and photographed a group of Navajo Indians clustered around an outdoor loom. In his second season of fieldwork for Lieutenant George M. Wheeler's survey of the lands west of the one hundredth meridian, O'Sullivan had already made numerous landscape views in the region. Now, using both a stereoscopic camera and a larger view camera, he was photographing the region's native people. With his small double-image negatives he could produce inexpensive stereographs for the mass market; from the larger negatives he could make six-and-one-half-by-twelve inch prints for the more expensive albums that chronicled the survey team's discoveries.

O'Sullivan left no literary record of his thoughts during his four seasons of work with the Wheeler survey, so for a contemporary interpretation of his pictures we must turn to Wheeler, an ambitious promoter of a westward expansion. In 1876 Wheeler published an album of twenty-five photographs made during the 1871–74 survey seasons by O'Sullivan and William Bell. Here O'Sullivan's large-format photograph of Navajo Indians working at a loom is offered as evidence that the Navajos are "an intelligent and fierce people by nature" who have made "good progress towards civilization" since their subjugation by U.S. troops. They are presented as good farmers and fine weavers, the sort of neighbors any American settler might welcome.[1]

A lithograph based on a variant of this image appears in the formal report that Wheeler issued thirteen years later in 1889. Here O'Sullivan's image is transformed, both visually and conceptually. Two Indian figures pose in a landscape that seems swept clean; the tangle of twigs and debris that littered the ground in the photograph have been removed by a lithographer. The gritty realness of O'Sullivan's image is gone. The text completes this transformation, changing the industrious Navajo farmers into exotic anachronisms. "The head and lord of the family looks on with phlegmatic equanimity at the patient industry of the squaw and indulges in day dreams, undoubtedly of victories of war or excitement of the chase, performed by him or his ancestors."[2]

As the West changed between 1876 and 1889, Wheeler's narrative for O'Sullivan's pictures changed accordingly. In the mid-1870s Wheeler's audience needed to be reassured that the western Indians had, indeed, been subdued, making most areas of the West and Southwest safe for settlement. By 1889 his audience assumed this. No longer a potential threat, Indians had become a romantic symbol of an old West that was fast becoming more a legend than a place. Mirroring the changes made by the lithographer, Wheeler used language to transform O'Sullivan's pictures from descriptive images of a changing present to imaginative illustrations of a bounded past. The transformation offers compelling evidence about one of the fundamental shifts in western history, the point at which a frontier of boundless possibilities became in the American imagination a more mundane region whose uniqueness lay in its past.

Our western past is emphatically visual as well as literary. And visual images—like literary texts—have histories of their own: complex pasts that involve artists and patrons, changing audiences, and assigned meanings that mutate and evolve over time. Focusing on the static content rather than the dynamic context of these images, western historians have generally used visual documents as illustrations rather than as sources of primary meaning themselves. There has been little recognition that visual documents can yield information of central importance to broader historical questions about western culture and the westering experience. Yet as this brief discussion of O'Sullivan's work suggests, visual imagery can inform our understanding of some of the most basic issues of western historiography, in this case the periodization of western history and the shifting notions of frontier and region.

The O'Sullivan case study is also a wonderfully rich example that introduces many of the major themes and characteristics of what is generally termed western art. First, it suggests the functional role of much nineteenth-century art, which was designed to provide descriptive information for a distant audience. Artists were concerned from the start with the marketing, exhibition, and publication of their work. O'Sullivan certainly had his public in mind when he used two cameras of different formats to photograph his Navajo subjects. Second, the O'Sullivan episode suggests the central role of patronage in the creation and presentation of the descriptive western imagery produced by nineteenth-century artists. Third, it conveys the importance of mediators, in this case both a lithographer and a writer, in bringing images to broad public attention. Set in a narrative literary text that ascribed to it a particular meaning, O'Sullivan's image took on a public meaning that may or may not have been intended by the photographer himself. Such reappropriation of imagery was a common occurrence in the nineteenth century, as indeed it is now, and it points to the final lesson suggested by the story of Wheeler and O'Sullivan. For the historian's purpose, the most interesting aspect of a visual object is often not the object alone but the object as it is embedded in a complex web that involves artists and patrons, publishers and audiences, images and words. Visual objects provide us a way of looking at a vast interlocking network of cultural forces. And over time, as these visual images acquire new contexts and meanings, they supply us with a way of studying changing cultural beliefs and practices. The challenge to historians who would use visual imagery as a source of primary evidence is to uncover these fragile and constantly shifting associations of meaning.

The very term "western art" conjures up a particular association with highly realistic imagery that depicts archetypal western landscapes, scenes, or figures. This has been true since European and American artists first pictured the Far West in the early nineteenth century. The early artists in colonial New England lived and worked among settled communities of people who provided a local market for portraiture and other sorts of documentary and decorative painting. But the earliest Anglo-American artists to work in the West ventured

Timothy H. O'Sullivan's 1873 photograph of Navajo weavers. *Courtesy Yale Collection of Western Americana, Beinecke Rare Book and Manuscript Library.*

A print published in 1889 derived from O'Sullivan's photograph. *Courtesy Yale Collection of Western Americana, Beinecke Rare Book and Manuscript Library.*

westward ahead of the line of American settlement and thus served a distant audience. In 1819–20 Samuel Seymour and Titian Ramsay Peale accompanied Major Stephen H. Long's government-sponsored expedition to the Rockies and became the first Anglo-American artists to depict the Far West. The chief audience for their pictures was in Philadelphia and Washington. To satisfy this distant public, they and subsequent expeditionary artists created instructive and realistic visual reports of the distant western landscape and the West's native peoples.

Alternative artistic traditions flourished within the Native American communities and scattered European settlements of the Far West. In the Catholic communities of northern New Mexico, for example, Hispanic *santeros* had created a tradition of religious art by the eighteenth century. Indian artisans also worked within a culture that valued decorative items for purposes other than their informative or narrative value. These traditions, however, had little influence on the initial evolution of Anglo-American images of the western landscape.

Anglo-American western art was characterized by a didactic tone and realistic style until about 1890. As Wheeler's 1889 recontextualization of O'Sullivan's image suggests, the function of art then began to change. Wheeler's romantic reinterpretation of the Navajo picture heralds a great change in graphic imagery even as it seems to anticipate the findings of the 1890 census and the subsequent pronouncements of Frederick Jackson Turner about the closing of the American frontier. For while most of the images made before this time were created to transmit factual information about an actual place, those done in subsequent decades were more concerned with imagined or reconstructed visions of a frontier West that had already faded into history. Although many nineteenth-century paintings, prints, and even photographs suggested a romantic view of the land and its native inhabitants, even these images described the physical and cultural landscape of the West in a way that acknowledged the public's curiosity about an exotic place. Sometime around 1890 the West ceased to be so strange. Its "savage charms," Francis Parkman wrote in 1892, had been subdued by the "irresistible commonplace."[3]

From this point on traditional western art—that is, images of western subjects rendered in a realistic style—becomes less concerned with reportage than with the evocative re-creation of a historical period. Nostalgic sentimentality becomes the thematic link between the turn-of-the-century cowboy paintings of Charley Russell, the Indian photographs of Edward S. Curtis, and the studied primitivism of Texan chairs newly fashioned out of longhorn cattle horns to evoke the mythic days of the great cattle drives. Suddenly the West was less real than ideal. The Cowboy Artists of America, a small but influential organization devoted to contemporary western painting, continues to give voice to this idea, defining the American West not as a place but as a particular "phase of American culture."[4]

The insistent realism and particular subject matter of nineteenth-century western painting and the lingering allure of these qualities in the popular imagination have proved a great hindrance to the scholarly study of this material. Historians have felt entitled to use nineteenth-century graphic material as illustrations without examining the cultural context or accuracy of the imagery. But as anthropologist John Ewers suggests in his systematic analysis of nineteenth-century paintings of Indians, neither artistic skill nor firsthand experience ensured an accurate portrayal of a subject. Many talented American artists of the mid-nineteenth century, for example, inaccurately depicted the sparse ground cover of the Great Plains as waist-high stands of wheat-like stems. By contrast, the more conscientious French painter Rosa Bonheur created a highly accurate image of the plains after having plant specimens shipped from the Botanic Society of Colorado to her Paris home. No picture is worth a thousand words, Ewers reminds us, unless it is truthful.[5]

The widely held supposition that western art must somehow be truthful in its depiction of a particular scene has also hindered the investigation of western art by art historians. On the one hand, countless coffee table books and catalogs have eschewed scholarly criticism in favor of arguments over whether a particular artist really "knew the horse" (or the Indian, or the cowboy).[6] On the other hand, serious scholars have scorned western art because the subject matter somehow seems inimical to "high" art. Even the organizers of a major 1988 retrospective exhibition of the work of painter Frederic Remington played into this trap. Trying to command serious attention for their subject by emphasizing his academic skills, they downplayed the content of his paintings of cowboys, Indians, and military expeditions. Like their more traditional scholarly colleagues, they glossed over subject matter that seemed closely allied to popular culture. "But," as critic Elizabeth Johns asks in a review of the exhibition, "can we understand Remington as an artist if we refuse to consider the implications for him and his audience, as well as for us, of the experience he referred to in his work and the very ways he interpreted that experience through representation?"[7] The problems presented by the conventional subject matter of western art have so marginalized this work within the canon of American art history that a recent article proudly proclaiming the coming of age of American art history ignores western art and artists altogether.[8]

The phrase "western art history" is problematic largely because the descriptive tradition established by nineteenth-century painting has defined and limited the field. Yet modernism has a rich tradition in the West, beginning, most notably, in the 1910s, when painters in New Mexico began to treat western subjects in a nonrealistic manner. Only recently have their images been embraced in general histories of western art.[9] This suggests the need for a broader working definition of western art, one that discards particular stylistic requirements and a narrowly defined list of approved subjects. If we define western art as art that deals in some way with the West as a place—whether a place with a specific history, a particular physical appearance, or even a certain quality of light—or with the experience of living in the West, we can overcome the stylistic and conceptual gulf that seems to divide nineteenth-century realism from turn-of-the-century romanticism and early-twentieth-century modernism. We can also begin to explore whether a regional tradition can persist in an age when television, art magazines, and air travel make a variety of experiences, places, and styles easily accessible to artists everywhere.

In addition to expanding the traditional definition of western art, we need to expand the traditional focus of art historical inquiry to include the changing social context in which this art has been created and used. After all, the forms of western art have been as dependent on changing business practices as on stylistic trends. During the nineteenth century few western artists had the luxury to express their personal visions without regard for the marketplace or the interests of their patrons. O'Sullivan, for example, traveled under the protection of Wheeler and his military entourage, photographing specific scenes to meet Wheeler's requirements. Critics intent upon making O'Sullivan and his fellow expeditionary artists cultural spokesmen for post-Civil War America have generally failed to acknowledge the very specific, directed focus of their work. The end result has been confusion about how to read their work. While one critic may claim that O'Sullivan portrays the West as an "unforgiving" land in which "man is not embraced by nature but engulfed in it," another may claim that O'Sullivan's West is a place where man and nature join in a "sympathetic relationship."[10] Wrenched from its original context and subjected to a close iconographic reading, the photographer's work becomes more like a mirror reflecting the interests of modern critics than a source of primary evidence. To discuss the artist as a point man for a culture is to ignore the influence of patronage and the direct impact of the marketplace on the business of art.

In the nineteenth-century West artistic patronage came from many sources. In the middle two decades of the century a wide variety of patrons competed to create western images that would serve their own notions of what the West was and could be. The United States Army, state and federal exploring expeditions, well-to-do European gentle-men-adventurers, railroad entrepreneurs, land speculators, and the newly emerging social elites and business organizations within the West's growing cities all sought to present their own images of the West to the American people. Still later, money continued to flow from eastern as well as western sources. New York financier J. P. Morgan supported Edward S. Curtis's monumental effort to document the western Indian tribes. Former New York socialite Mabel Dodge Luhan created an artists' colony in New Mexico after World War I and lent her Taos Indian husband, Tony, to artists who needed a native model. Government money flowed to artists during the 1930s under the aegis of the Works Progress Administration and became available once again after the creation of the National Endowment for the Arts in 1965. In the West large business interests, especially the railroads and the Fred Harvey Company, continued to shape popular imagery of the region well into the twentieth century. Western art is not a homespun, homegrown phenomenon; western artists have always been the beneficiary of eastern training, eastern ideas, and eastern money.

To counter the fashion of writing about Remington's West or Bierstadt's West, we need a study that reenvisions the artists' West as the patrons' West. We need to survey the different visual Wests created by the railroad, by European interests, by government patronage, and by local commercial concerns and examine how the resulting art served their various interests. The majority of significant nineteenth-century western painters worked for commercial, private, or government sponsors at some stage in their careers. The influence of these collaborative ventures on the artist might extend beyond the bounds of a particular assignment to have a significant impact on later work. Likewise, a patron might continue to exercise influence over an image long after his working relationship with an artist had ended, by controlling the exhibition and reproduction of the picture.[11]

During the nineteenth century western images reached audiences in a limited number of ways: sometimes through exhibition, more often through reproductions. Although patrons, like Wheeler, often facilitated the reproduction of western images, another group generally determined what the reproductions would look like. Until the advent of photolithography and photomechanical reproduction techniques late in the century, all artists had to rely on draftsmen to transfer their paintings, sketches, or photographs to engraving plates and lithographic stones. By the time an original work had been reproduced for public consumption it thus reflected the vision of the original artist, the biases of his patron, and the interpretive license of the graphic artist who re-created it for wider distribution. The visual West presented to the public was in large part the work of little-known technicians rather than the better-known artists usually given credit for the views.

To understand the potential importance of these technicians, we might consider the extraordinary photographs made by the Canadian photographer Humphrey Lloyd Hime, who accompanied a Canadian surveying party into that nation's western interior in 1858. The forty-nine surviving images form the earliest body of survey photography from either north or south of the forty-ninth parallel and suggest the photographer's extraordinary confusion. The images convey every stereotyped notion about the western frontier, from fearsome hell to Edenic garden. One photograph of a young half-breed woman lounging against a tree evokes the romantic, idyllic spirit of the scenes that Alfred Jacob Miller had painted in the Rocky Mountain West some twenty years before. But another image innocently titled *The Prairie Looking West* is as horrific as any landscape ever made in the American or Canadian West. A flat, grassless prairie, decimated by a recent grasshopper infestation, stretches across the print beneath a razor-straight horizon. Under a pale, featureless sky lies a bleached white bone—perhaps a human femur, perhaps an animal bone. In the foreground is the unmistakable form of a human skull. Major Stephen H. Long popularized the idea of a "great American desert" in the 1821 report of his expedition to the Rocky Mountains. But neither he nor Samuel Seymour, the sketch artist who accompanied him, provided such a vivid image of the harsh, terrifying emptiness that awaited the western adventurer.[12]

Hime's photograph never found a public audience. The "chromoxylograph" reproduction of the photograph that appeared in the final expedition report was altered and sanitized. The sky was tinted blue, the decimated prairie made to bloom with green, and a flock of white geese added to the sky to bring life to this stark image of death.

It is unclear who initiated this transformation. It might have been Hime, the expedition leader, or a government functionary intent upon conveying a more positive image of the prairies. Likewise, it could have been the publisher or simply the printmaker who wanted to make his own mark on Hime's bleak photograph. In any case, the image presented to the public undercuts the power of Hime's original vision. The example reminds us that the original artist often could not control the associations that adhered to his picture by the time it reached a public audience.[13]

Whether nineteenth-century audiences viewed printed reproductions or original works of art, they rarely saw western images without some sort of accompanying didactic material that made explicit the intended function of the pictures. Printed texts explicated the significance of images reproduced in books, the popular press, or government reports. Narrative texts were likewise an important part of art exhibitions and other carefully staged presentations of visual images. George Catlin, who traveled and painted extensively among the western and midwestern Indian tribes in the mid-1830s, presented his "Indian Gallery" to eastern audiences by lecturing on his canvases, one by one. Less elaborate Indian galleries were displayed by New York-born painter John Mix Stanley in 1845 and by the Canadian artist Paul Kane in 1848.[14]

Even more popular than these exhibitions were painted panoramas: long, detailed canvases unrolled from one reel to another in highly theatrical productions that included spoken narratives and music. During the 1840s these panoramas favored western themes: the Mexican War, John C. Frémont's exploring expeditions, travel on the Mississippi, and, after 1849, California and the gold rush. They were part newsreel and part political oration with flamboyant rhetoric that echoed the patriotic tone of more literary narratives. But like the more highbrow Indian galleries, they were aimed at a public that expected information from art.[15]

Ironically, even early western photographers—whose images were implicitly accurate, precise, and informative—looked to the narrative structure of the Indian galleries and the panoramas as models for the public presentation of their work. The San Francisco photographer Robert Vance took his collection of three hundred California daguerreotypes east to New York in the fall of 1851 and presented them in sequential order on the walls of a gallery. Not trusting his audience to understand the import of his work, Vance published a descriptive catalog and, like George Catlin, stationed himself in the gallery to describe individual images to visitors. His fellow Daguerrean artist J. Wesley Jones photographed the entire overland route from California back to St. Louis in 1851, then took his daguerreotypes back to Boston and transformed them into a painted panorama that he presented with an elaborate narrative text. The daguerreotypes themselves were never exhibited. They seemed insufficiently instructive or entertaining.[16]

With the passing of the Daguerrean era and the advent of paper prints in the 1850s, photographers developed another way to make their images instructive. Printed texts affixed to the photograph or its mount could serve the same narrative function that the photographers' personal presence and narration had once done. From this point on, most nineteenth-century western photographs—aside from portraits—were published and marketed as series; individual images and their accompanying texts were conceived as part of longer, more complex narratives. Many of these narratives have been lost as albums, and collections of prints have been broken up over the years, making it difficult to understand the intent of the photographer, the motives of his publisher, or the way the images were received by contemporary audiences. The photographic narratives mirrored popular literary tracts; they dealt with the settlement of the West, the beneficence of the railroad, the marginalization and then romanticization of Native American communities, the emergence of the cowboy myth. Their contribution to popular American attitudes toward the West has been overlooked mainly because the haphazard circumstances of historical collecting have made them so hard to reassemble.

The magic lantern slide show—a way of presenting images that reinstated the primary role of an artist- or producer-narrator—was another popular form that blended art and literary narrative. As early as 1859 an enterprising lecturer in Colorado was using hand-tinted slides to promote the Pikes Peak goldfield. In 1870 the New York lecturer Stephen Sedgwick began giving illustrated lectures with slides made from Andrew J. Russell's photographs of the Union Pacific Railroad. In the early twentieth century lantern slide lectures on Indian subjects proved appealing to such disparate photographers as the Norwegian anthropologist Frederick Monsen, the Yale graduate Walter McClintock, and the Coloradan Laura Gilpin, a successful fine arts photographer. Cultural historians who study the impact of films on the popular image of the West might also examine these ephemeral productions, viewed by tens of thousands, which shaped public perceptions of the West for more than half a century.[17]

The nineteenth-century public's taste for informative, instructive art depicting the West may be loosely correlated to its general lack of knowledge about the physical and social landscape of the West. As eastern communities grew increasingly familiar with the West, and the West itself grew more and more like the rest of the United States, public expectations for western imagery began to change. Once eager to accept western images as reportage, the American public began to demand that the art take on a more symbolic role, as evocative re-creations of a faded past. William Henry Jackson, whose 1871 photographs of Yellowstone were accepted by Congress as persuasive evidence in favor of preserving the site as a national park, spent his old age making paintings of western sites and events he had never seen to meet the demands of history buffs.[18] His early audience passively accepted his photographs as facts; his later audience wished to play an active role in shaping his imagery. If his art had once informed the public, it was now informed by public taste.

Instead of looking to artists as reporters, the increasingly demanding audiences of the late nineteenth century began to look to them as masters of stagecraft who could summon up images of a mythic West with their art. These changing expectations affected all media. The invention of the Kodak camera in 1888 meant that amateur photographers could secure their own descriptive views of sites. What they then demanded from professional photographers were romantic evocations of western history rather than the grand descriptive views that had previously been popular. History-conscious patrons also influenced painting. Cowboy artist Charley Russell took his cues during the formative period of his career (1896–1900) from a public that wanted vivid images of the old Wild West. It seems fitting that he and many other western painters later gravitated to Los Angeles during the 1920s and, befriending many of the cowboy stars, stayed on the periphery of the burgeoning Hollywood film industry, which even then catered to a public demand for mythic narratives of the American West. If the old frontier West of mythic proportions could be depicted in a relatively straightforward style, the new, more commonplace West had to be remythicized through artistic invention.[19]

Native American artists were also enlisted in the effort to create a mythic visual image of an old West. During the 1930s instructors at the Santa Fe Indian School introduced to the curriculum their own preconceptions of what authentic Indian art should be. White artists and collectors had influenced Indian arts in the past. George Catlin and Karl Bodmer, for example, had had some effect on the painting style of the Mandan chiefs they met on the upper Missouri in the 1830s. Anglo collectors and explorers had influenced the design of Northwest Coast native art since the early nineteenth century. But no previous encounters between white patrons and native artists had resulted in such a widespread and pervasive refiguring of traditional art or had contributed so much to the creation of a myth about the true nature of Indian art and the Indian past. The flat, decorative style of painting introduced at the Santa Fe Indian School in the 1930s has, like Russell's paintings, acquired a false aura of truthfulness, accuracy, and authenticity.[20]

Because art is often a business as well as a form of expression, it seems only logical that artists should be sensitive to the changing tastes and demands of their clients. But when we examine the connections between art and an audience's expectations and tastes, we must also consider how different audiences can influence subsequent readings of a particular image.

After it has been created, an art object is continually reinvented, as new viewers or users approach it with different questions or interests. These new interpretations are beyond the original artist's control and may well be beyond his or her intent. Even if a painter or photographer can control the exhibition and reproduction of his work, he can successfully communicate his ideas to an audience only if that audience shares his cultural assumptions. Thus, early-twentieth-century Salish Indians, who used commercial studio portraits as effigies in traditional ceremonies, could find meaning in the photographs that neither the white photographers nor their tourist customers could perceive. And young Northwest Coast Indians—oblivious of the theatrical role their ancestors played—can find in the carefully staged and deliberately nostalgic turn-of-the-century images of their forefathers politically potent pictures of a traditional past to which they should return. Such unintended uses of images are important not because they stress the imprecision of visual communication but because they suggest the rich interpretative possibilities implicit in a study of art that make the changing responses of an audience an inextricable part of an object's cultural meaning.[21]

The reinvention or reinterpretation of imagery occurs not only across cultural boundaries but across time. Historians have transformed George Trager's grim photographs of Sioux warriors lying frozen in death after the battle at Wounded Knee into rich symbols of the death of traditional Native American culture and the failure of federal Indian policy. But Trager was not a political critic, and neither

George Trager's photograph of the dead at Wounded Knee, 1890. *Courtesy Yale Collection of Western Americana, Beinecke Rare Book and Manuscript Library.*

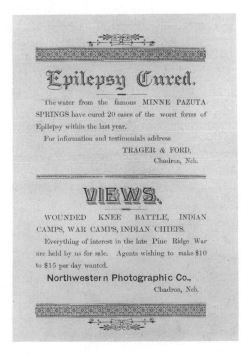

Advertisements for patent medicine and for additional photographs of scenes at Wounded Knee that appeared on the backs of Trager's photographs. *Courtesy Yale Collection of Western Americana, Beinecke Rare Book and Manuscript Library.*

199

he nor his audience read much symbolic import into the pictures when they were first made and marketed in January 1891. Trager was an entrepreneur eager to capitalize on the passing public interest in the events at Wounded Knee. Only a few weeks after the battle, when the market for his views was gone, he was on to a new career in patent medicine. The dusting of snow in Trager's photographs of the Sioux dead seems to lend a chilling sense of finality to the events depicted in the images. But it was only Trager's good fortune that it snowed between the time of the battle and the burial of the dead. Attuned though he was to market demand, Trager could not have orchestrated that himself.[22]

This process of investing art with new meanings is not a destructive one; rather, it is part of the process by which art lives on from one age to the next. Historians using visual materials as primary source evidence thus can approach a work in two ways. First, they can unravel the tangle of meanings that an object might have had at the time it was created. To do this, they must examine the interests of the artist and any patron he may have had; the needs of the subject; the purposes of any publishers, writers, or printmakers who brought the work to a wide public audience; and the desires and responses of the various contemporary audiences for the work. Then historians can trace these clusters of interests forward in time, tracking the shifting associations that adhered to a particular image. Second, they can become part of the process of reinventing art by bringing their own questions to an object or group of images.

Consider, for example, the issue of how different groups of people have responded to the westering experience and the physical presence of the western landscape throughout the nineteenth and twentieth centuries. Just as historians have long sought answers in literary documents, so they can also look to bodies of visual material for rich evidence. In the many thousands of landscape photographs made between 1916 and 1979 by Laura Gilpin, the first woman to photograph the western landscape with any sustained interest, we might seek evidence for a distinctive gender-based response to the land. While her male contemporaries, such as Ansel Adams or Eliot Porter, photographed a pristine natural world that betrayed no trace of human contact, Gilpin photographed a "historical landscape" that was constantly modifying and being modified by human settlement. While the men portrayed a heroic landscape, she depicted a vernacular one that stands in marked contrast with the tradition of grand landscape views pioneered by the male photographer-explorers of the nineteenth century. Her approach continues to find resonance in the work of younger women photographing the West today.[23]

But we might also consider the possibility that Gilpin's work was influenced less by gender than by her western upbringing. Unlike any of her nineteenth-century predecessors, Gilpin was born and reared in the West. Landscape, argues Donald Meinig, is what lies before our eyes as well as what "lies within our heads."[24] It is reasonable to suppose, then, that an artist might depict the familiar landscape of home differently from unfamiliar terrain. We might raise similar questions about differing generational responses to the West and even consider whether the more romantic vision of the region created in the late nineteenth century can be attributed more to true westerners like Montanan Charley Russell who knew what they had lost or to outsiders like Frederic Remington who came to regret what they had missed.

Such queries suggest broader questions about the formation of western identities. Photography provided the quickest and least expensive way for western immigrants of the mid-nineteenth century to document their new western selves. Photography studios quickly became ubiquitous features of California's gold rush communities. In 1857 a photographic journal reported that in San Francisco "it is quite a novelty in all the Photographic Galleries on the day previous to the departure of a steamer, to witness the strife and anxiety to procure these portraits for transshipment to the East."[25] These pictures—like the pictures immigrants brought with them from the East—formed a powerful bond between early western emigrants and the communities they left behind. They were powerful reminders of the ties of family, the continuity of history, and the meaning of geographical dislocation. In these portraits—as rustic garb gives way to Victorian dress and working miners shed their tools for the material symbols of the middle class—we can read the creation and re-creation of the new western self. We can also perceive the emergence of a kind of parodic self-image in the self-consciously staged images of subjects dressed as cowboys, mountain men, or freewheeling gamblers—images that seemed to gain in popularity as the real-life prototypes disappeared. But even as we approach these images with new questions of our own, we must keep in mind that the images are deeply rooted in a particular historical time. Our inquiry takes on more significance—not less—when we can determine whether the subject of a picture had been in the West for one year or ten, whether the picture was made for a local buddy or a business partner back East, whether the photographer's fees put the process within the reach of all or a few.

Visual images can matter. When they are used only to illustrate ideas gleaned from other, more traditional historical sources, their real meaning is trivialized. The sanitized lithographic version of Timothy O'Sullivan's photograph of Navajo weavers that appears in Lieutenant Wheeler's expedition report is interesting not because it documents native dress but because it shows how art could be subverted to other ends, how images acquired new meanings from new contexts, how craftsmen employing new printing technologies could bring art to vast audiences even as they altered its meaning with their own imprimatur.

I do not suggest that we can write a new history of the American West purely from visual documents. People, places, events, and ideas are visually documented in selective and quirky ways, and any history written solely from visual documents would be incomplete and misleading. But we should learn to write history with the aid of visual materials. When we acknowledge that images may have imprecise messages and culturally determined meanings and accept that the audiences for these images—who have an almost infinite capacity to reenvision them—are as worthy of study as the objects themselves, we can begin to understand visual images as important bearers of social meaning. Then, instead of turning to a graphic image because we need it to illustrate what we already know, we will turn to it because it can teach us what we want to learn.

The View from Wisdom

Four Layers of History and Regional Identity[1]

CLYDE A. MILNER II

Where is the West? Who are westerners? Imagine the many possible answers. But as you think of answers, consider who may be asking these questions and where they are asked. To those outside the West, the region is one of vast indistinct contours with grand landscapes of mountain and plain and lone heroic figures—the mountain man, the woman homesteader, the daring cowboy, and the doomed Indian. From inside the West, on the other hand, the answers to these questions constitute a gritty and endlessly varied range of local contexts, in which region and identity acquire their most enduring connections with the complex history of the West through the lives and memories of self-proclaimed westerners.

Sit down with some friendly folks at the Antler Bar in the wonderfully named town of Wisdom, Montana. Ask the ultimate dude's questions. "Is this the real West? Are you real westerners?" Expect a few strange looks, but don't expect a Neoplatonist response about the nature of reality. Instead, if the mood remains friendly, expect answers that dwell on local history. After praising the spectacular scenery of southwestern Montana, one patron might explain that the present-day

Big Hole River had been named the Wisdom by the explorers Lewis and Clark after one of President Thomas Jefferson's principal virtues. Of course, the origin of place-names is only one aspect of history and identity. Another barroom narrator might go on to recount the Battle of the Big Hole, the 1877 fight between the U.S. Army and the Nez Percé Indians that is marked by a national monument twelve miles west of the present town. Rambling on, he might describe the arrival in 1882 of the first white settlers, who took up farming and ranching in the Big Hole Basin, a place locals still call the land of ten thousand haystacks.[2] Explorers, Indians, soldiers, ranchers, and farmers—these historical figures certify that Wisdom and its residents are part of the West by more than geographic location. These ancestors live in the memories of the town's modern residents, for whom the question "Are you real westerners?" will always have an affirmative, personal reply.

A visit to Wisdom might produce an answer to our original, larger questions, Where is the West and who are westerners? But it would be only one answer among many to be found in the West. The regional identity of a people is not monolithic; it is expressed in a complex multiplicity of memories shared by communities and individuals. Like a geological stratification, it builds up over time, expanding the definition of westerners and their region. A visit to Wisdom suggests at least two layers that cohere in any regional identity: region as the locale of personal life—revealed in the individual memories of those who live in a place—and region as the terrain of collective history—revealed in memories shared across generations. These two layers of personal locale and shared memory constitute the bedrock upon which many people construct their westernness.

At least two more significant strata appear in the rocky formation of western identity. A third layer exposes region as national epic, suggesting that events in Montana represent not just the West but American history generally. Adhering to this is a fourth layer: regional identity as reaction to other peoples, other regions, and even the nation as a whole. These additional two layers reveal the work of external forces, which like water on rock, shape and channel the formation of regional identity. Finally, as with the sand and gravel that are transported across space and time to produce a clastic, sedimentary rock,[3] historical perceptions are part of all four strata. These fragments of perception vary from clearly remembered personal insights to popularly shared social stereotypes. Many other layers and fragments may adhere to this bedrock, and like the people in the West, they may be diverse and multitudinous.

Region as Personal Locale

The first layer of regional identity emerges from personal experience and the retelling of that experience in later years. Memories colored by the passage of time focus on events that explain a coming of age in a distinct location. Through the process of retrospection, this West—as personal locale—often becomes a nostalgic landscape of youth.

As an adult wage earner Si Gray constructed a landscape crossed by high-voltage power lines, but he did not let it define his life. In 1889, Gray began work for the Helena Light Company at $2.50 a day. For forty-five years he helped wire western Montana with electricity and long-distance telephone service. But in 1935, at age seventy-nine, he produced a reminiscence that devotes only four of forty typescript pages to his life's work. More than thirty pages recount two years, 1880 and 1881, when Gray worked with sheep and cattle and rode with Charley Russell, the cowboy artist.[4]

Although born in 1856 near Lake Geneva, Wisconsin, Si Gray started his memoir in 1879, when his older brother Dal came to visit the family's new farm near Hastings, Nebraska. Dal came from Helena, Montana, and convinced Si by February 1880 "to go with him and try my luck in Mont." The Grays had arrived in Nebraska only a year earlier, but Si's account does not bother to mention how recently his family moved west. That was his parents' story, not his own. In the first two sentences of his reminiscence, Si leaves the farm in the care of his father and "youngest brother," Gene. He does not mention his mother or his other seven siblings. Si chose to begin his life story with the decision to go to Montana.

The brothers worked briefly in a sawmill at Jefferson City, south of Helena. By the spring of 1880 they were off to "the new and uninhabited place called Judith Basin [.] [O]f course I was the Pilgrim, or tenderfoot, of the bunch[,] a name I detested, but took it without regret, though being a pilgrim I found that when it was time to have meat Si Gray the Pilgrim baged the first Deer, Antelope, Elk, Buffalo & Bear. . . ." Many of Gray's stories emphasize how he outgrew his tenderfoot years through action and bravery. Whether he was breaking a spirited pinto pony or killing rattlesnakes "till I was played out," what Gray remembered was proving his manhood. In one account, having forgotten his claim to have killed a buffalo on the trip to the Judith Basin, Gray dramatically dispatches "My First Buffalo" from horseback and brings proof of his triumph to his fellow hayhands.

". . . I managed to open him and take out his insides and heart and liver. Those I tied to my saddle and made for home, and was I swelled up[.] I thought it about time to disregard that old name 'tenderfoot.' "

Written in 1935, Si Gray's story seemed influenced by pulp westerns as well as personal memory. He encountered harsh weather, threatening Indians, and vicious outlaws. He especially remembered "Kid" Russell, who placed Gray in at least two of his drawings. After recounting another dramatic buffalo killing, a "Humdinger," Gray casually mentions, "Kid Russell drew a picture of the happening[,] which I lost with others of his work[.] I was mighty sorry that I lost them[,] for Charlie & I were good chums." With the practiced restraint of an experienced storyteller, Gray recounts a few more stories from his days with Charley Russell. Each of these anecdotes asserts a special association that Gray did not need to exaggerate for an audience of fellow Montanans. They would have been impressed simply to hear that Si Gray had known Charley Russell and that one episode in Gray's passage to manhood had been sketched by one of the West's most revered artists.

Gray produced a memoir that explained, on his own terms, the formation of his personal identity. If asked directly, he would have called himself a westerner and probably would have supported that designation with more tales of his days hunting wild animals and riding the range in the Judith Basin. State and local historical societies throughout the West, and, indeed, throughout the United States, contain many thousands of unpublished memoirs comparable to Si Gray's account. Few are complete autobiographies. They tell only part of a larger story, but they capture at least one special aspect of the individual life. Si Gray's memoir celebrates his passage into adulthood upon his embracing a new life in the West.

What led Si Gray, at age seventy-nine, to tell his selective life story? We cannot know for certain. Advanced in age, Gray may have wished to record his formative days before his life ended. With his talent for telling stories, he chose personal narrative as the expression of his life review. He might have expressed his life's summation in other ways—in craftsmanship, through wood carving or saddlemaking, for example. His choice of personal narrative not only depended on the skills and knowledge he had acquired earlier in life but also depended on the expectations of his chosen audience.[5]

Who was his audience? His memoir mentions no marriage, no children, and only one niece. Nonetheless, his family, nuclear and extended, may have been the main audience. His obituary in the *Hel-*

Cattle roundup in Judith Basin in 1880. Silas Gray is the second standing figure from the right. Charley Russell, with light mustache, is seated in the foreground, third from the left. *Courtesy Montana Historical Society.*

Silas Gray with
his grandson Norman,
November 10, 1938.
*Courtesy Montana
Historical Society.*

ena Independent in 1940 states that his wife, one son, two daughters, and five grandchildren, all of Helena, survived him, as well as "several nephews and nieces." Si Gray's reminiscence dwells on the years when his wife, children, nieces, and nephews did not know him. Perhaps he felt free to rush through the remaining, nearly fifty years of his life in the final pages because those were the years his family had shared with him.

Gray may have had a second audience in mind for his memoirs: the men and women of the community in which he had become a well-known figure. Si Gray won election to Helena's City Council in 1912 and afterward served as city electrician for nineteen years. In addition, he participated in the Fraternal Order of Eagles, serving one term as president of the Helena chapter. Just one week before his death he attended the meeting of the Montana Cowboys Association in Great Falls, "where he recalled experiences he enjoyed when he first came to Montana and settled in the Judith Basin in 1880." As his obituary reports, "Mr. Gray" was "widely known not only for his interesting anecdotes of early-day life on the plains, but for the relics he had saved from the old days. They include guns, bullets, arrows, arrowheads, beads and Indian clothing."[6] Si Gray had told his tales of adventure many times to many people. At age seventy-nine, he may have decided that the time had finally come to record them, so that when his voice became silent, the memories of his early manhood and his encounters with Kid Russell would not be forgotten.

Silas B. Gray's reminiscence reveals what he considered the formative period of his life, before he married and established his career. His memoir explains how he became the adult known by his family and recognized in his community. His rite of passage to manhood involved hard work, violent acts, and exciting adventures. Had he never come west, the motivation to focus on his formative years in another location would no doubt have remained. The layerings that produce a regional identity can apply to other people, places, and times. But in the early 1880s Si Gray began to form a strong personal identification with a distinctly *western* locale and with a decidedly *western* figure. His two years in the Judith Basin with Charley Russell made Si Gray a westerner.

Still, his reminiscence displays only one of a multitude of personal stories with the power to establish a western, or any other regional, identity. Riding the range with Charley Russell is not the only way to lay claim to being a westerner. Yet any claim gains greater legitimacy if other people recognize and accept it. Si Gray's stories could have been rejected by his family and community as personal delusions. He might have stopped telling them if that had been their response. But Gray understood the expectations of his audience, and his audience understood him. His stories of his young manhood capture familiar themes of western action. Audiences in his day recognized and accepted his accounts, whether they happened or not. Such is the power of personal narrative when it taps a shared identity.[7]

How is a collective identity created and retained? The sociologist Robert Bellah and his colleagues suggest that in a "community of memory," the sharing of "group histories" explains who we are.[8] Si Gray participated in such a "community of memory," and we should consider his memoir within the second, as well as the first, layer of history and regional identity. Region as personal locale and region as shared memory are two laminated strata within the clastic rock of Gray's western identity. Had he written in later years and seen himself as a man of the new twentieth-century West, Gray might have emphasized how he helped bring electrical power and telephone service to Montana's capital city. But cables and wires were not part of the personal locale that formed Si Gray's identity. His West began on an earlier landscape, peopled with cowboys and hunters at home on the open range.

Region as Shared Memory

Si Gray's personal locale represented a landscape and time that were equally vivid to many of his peers. Over and over again other westerners reminisced about similar pasts. In some cases they sought to capture a time when the community they remembered had itself come of age through the exertions of one generation.

Cornelius Hedges grew up in Westfield, Massachusetts, and graduated from Yale College in the class of 1853. But he did not spend the remainder of his life in New England. In 1856 Hedges completed his law degree at Harvard and married Edna Layette Smith of Southington, Connecticut. That same summer the two moved west to Independence, Iowa, where an older sister already had settled with her husband. Hedges practiced law but did not prosper. He returned to New England in late 1860, taught at an academy in Southington until 1863, and then went back to Independence, where he took up journalism and reestablished his law practice. As editor of the *Independence Civilian* he supported the Union and remained thoroughly Republican but did not march off to war. Instead, with financial difficulties increasing and with two sons as well as a wife to support, he left in April 1864 for a few seasons of panning for gold in Montana. Three years later he brought his wife and sons to Montana by steamboat along the Missouri River. Helena had become his home and remained so for the rest of his life.[9]

As a lawyer, probate judge, state senator, and federal district attorney Cornelius Hedges became a distinguished citizen in Montana. Beginning in 1872, he served four terms as the territory's first superintendent of public instruction. He also wrote a series of articles published in the *Helena Herald* advocating the creation of Yellowstone National Park. In 1884 he served in the convention that wrote a state constitution. That attempt at statehood failed, but some of his ideas on education carried over to the successful 1889 convention. By the mid-1890s Hedges had played so prominent a role in Montana's brief history that fellow citizens asked him to speak about his early days in Helena.[10] So he, too, became a public teller of tales about his own life on a past landscape.

Like Si Gray, Hedges chose a special period in his earlier life for the main portion of his narrative. He recounted events from April 1864, when he began his overland journey, to the late fall of 1866, when he returned east to bring his family out to Montana. Over the succeeding years Hedges may have developed a repertoire of these same stories that he first told to his wife and their five surviving children, since those were years that they were not with him. Like Si Gray, Hedges may have honed his reminiscences over time through presentations to, and responses from, two audiences: his family and his community. As did Si Gray, Cornelius Hedges highlighted his western rite of passage to manhood. But his talk also fitted what his audiences expected in a pioneer's memoir in the 1890s, whether that audience gathered for a public address or for an informal session of storytelling.

Setting out from Independence with two male friends, Hedges made the entire journey by foot and claimed that before the trip "I had never fired a rifle in my life." Nonetheless, he took three rifles and a revolver for hunting and for "a fancied sense of security among Indians and many strangers." His small party traveled up the North Platte to Fort Laramie, where an army officer insisted that they join a larger company of 150 wagons for protection against Indians. Fear of "being killed or captured by Indians" did not prevent Hedges from hunting. Success in shooting an antelope "almost the first time I had ever fired a rifle" created "an ovation for the time being as the best hunter in the train." Danger and the hunter's rite of passage lay near the heart of this remembered landscape as well.

Hedges told of only one meeting with Indians. After he and two or three men had walked some four miles ahead of the train, the party rested among boulders. During their conversation Hedges "heard some rustling overhead and looking up an Indian was looking down in my face not three feet away." Jumping to his feet with pistol in hand, Hedges allowed the visitor to put up his hands and proclaim, " 'good injun.' " This Indian quickly left to rejoin his own party, which soon rode away. Hedges claimed, "The night following some horses were stolen from our train by these 'good Injuns.' " It may not have been an especially dramatic encounter, but this meeting provided one episode with Indians and thus fulfilled at least the minimum that his audience expected for a pioneer's narrative of the western crossing.

Severe weather and a nearly disastrous crossing of the Yellowstone River did not prevent Hedges from arriving in the gold camp of Virginia City a few days after the Fourth of July. He found his greenback dollars useless; everyone insisted on payment in gold dust. With no well-paying jobs available for "pilgrims," Hedges moved upslope to the camp of Summit. "Here I soon struck a job of shovelling tailings at $6 a day." With cold weather came less work and rumors of more gold at Last Chance Gulch in the new camp of Helena. Arriving on January 16, 1865, Hedges discovered a town of several hundred people living mostly in tents. He soon found that he could make better wages practicing law than he could mining.

Yet the courts remained so weak and informal that in response to a dramatic murder a vigilance committee took to the streets. It was in the early summer of 1865 that "one gambler named Keene shot another named Slater for an old grudge, in a very ungentlemanly way." A crowd of bystanders pursued Keene, who tried to take refuge with the sheriff, but he was delivered to the crowd. A trial by jury followed immediately. The jury ruled him guilty, the crowd voted for a hanging, and a wagon took Keene to a pine tree in Dry Gulch. After consuming a final drink of whiskey, Keene "handed back the glass, and said 'Let her rip.' " The wagon moved forward, and Keene met his end. "He was left hanging for some hours till everybody who cared to see the sure and swift execution of justice was satisfied."

After this episode a vigilance committee became active in Helena. It voted to reject the territorial governor's pardon of a man named Daniels, who had been convicted of manslaughter in the regular courts

211

but served very little of his four-year sentence. Daniels brazenly returned to Helena, only to be met at the stage by the vigilantes. Having been escorted to the same pine tree, Daniels met the same fate as Keene. His body, left hanging from the tree, bore "the Governor's pardon pinned on his back with an intimation that it would be imprudent for the Governor to repeat such contempt of justice." A "terrible excitement" followed. The governor threatened to send the militia and declare martial law, "but it all ended in a prolonged drunk. The case had gone to a higher court beyond recall."

Cornelius Hedges may not have been a vigilante, but in retrospect he approved of such actions.[11] So did most Montanans of his generation, especially those who claimed some connection with the more famous vigilantism in Virginia City and Bannack that destroyed Henry Plummer's gang of road agents. In Helena Hedges numbered the vigilantes at "several hundred strong" and claimed that they drove off the community's "desperadoes" within two weeks. "It was rude, rough justice, only to be defended on the plea of necessity and the right of self-defence and self preservation. . . . Helena never has forgotten what it owes to the vigilantes, and the law has no more loyal supporters."

Cornelius Hedges recalled more stories from "those pleasant, busy, exciting days," but his account of the overland journey and of Helena's vigilantism certified his participation in the shared memory of Montana's first generation of pioneers. Beginning in the 1890s, the same decade as Hedges's retrospections, these self-identified pioneers authored a series of memoirs and reminiscences. Their writings focused on certain incidents from the 1860s, especially threats from Indians on the overland journey and hangings by vigilantes in the mining camps.[12] As in the reminiscences of other overland pioneers, exaggerated fears and fictional accounts of Indian attacks abound.[13] In comparison, the "good injun" story of Hedges seems restrained.

Over time, pioneer accounts inflated the threats and killings. In 1928 Wyllys A. Hedges, Cornelius's second-oldest son, addressed the Kiwanis Club of Lewistown, Montana. He reported on the most recent annual meeting in Butte of the Society of Montana Pioneers, where the members, "in response to repeated calls for 'Indian stories,' told of their experiences." Wyllys Hedges wryly noted, "If all the Indians killed and supposed to have been killed by pioneers could all be brought to life, there would be a lot of them."[14]

The inaccuracies and fictions in the Montana memoirs are easily documented. These accounts nevertheless demonstrate the sharing of collective memories—even false memories—and the expression of group values that merged to become "living history." Stories of Indians and outlaws emphasized the wildness of the early days and the role of the pioneers in establishing their own ordered world in the midst of what seemed to them a lawless, violent chaos.

As an expression of the second layer of regional identity, each memoir recounted a personal history through a set of stories that had been told many times before. The pioneer's immediate family—grown children and grandchildren—constituted the primary audience for both the oral and written memoir. But they reached a broader audience, too: fellow pioneers and residents of the local community. For story-teller and audience alike, the memoir forged a backward link to a collectively remembered past.

Examining the context of these shared memories, folklorists would consider not only the content of the stories and their performance but also the response of the audience, for in that response lies the broader meaning of the tale. As the folklorist William Wilson explains, "If the story is to live, [the storytellers] cannot, in the telling of it, depart too far from the value center of the audience whose approval they seek." That center reveals what Barre Toelken calls the ideational core of the community:

> There is a something being done, performed, by someone who has done it before, for an audience of people who already know it. Their reason for doing and experiencing the performance time and time again is of course that—beyond the pleasure of entertain-ment—such familiar performances help to reinforce and maintain the central ideas of the group (their value centers), help to induct newcomers (children, greenhorns), into the group, and help to define outsiders and strangers. [15]

In this manner the ideational core of memoirs and reminiscences not only created an "idealized" pioneer history but also attempted to define the values of the first "true" Montanans—and, just possibly, the values of "true" westerners.

In Montana, as in many other western states, organizations of "first settlers" promoted the informal transmission of shared memories among pioneers. In addition, these associations formally defined those who could claim the status of pioneer. The rules for membership were precise. For example, the Oregon Pioneer Society limited its membership in 1894 to all those who had arrived before statehood. The

Society of California Pioneers established a dual membership. All residents, prior to January 1, 1849, were recognized as senior members, and all residents who arrived during the gold rush—that is, prior to January 1, 1850—became junior members. When the last senior died, the surviving juniors dropped their label and became members only.[16]

The Society of Montana Pioneers, established in 1884, tried to set the latest time that an individual could have arrived in the gold camps and still be called a pioneer. The initial deadline was May 26, 1864, before the legal creation of Montana Territory. But the inherent trouble with such a date was that it progressively excluded more and more people who believed that they had arrived early enough to be "pioneers." Minutes of the society's annual meetings in the 1890s are filled with debates about the appropriateness of the 1864 date. Eventually, in 1901, the deadline for membership was advanced to December 31, 1868. This change meant that Wyllys Hedges could join the society and, in 1928, serve as its president, a post his father had held in 1905.

But even within Montana a unified definition of the "pioneer" could not be maintained because other organizations insisted on recognizing pioneer status on a local basis. For example, the Pioneers of Eastern Montana, founded in 1903, chose 1884 as its cutoff date (i.e., the year of the founding of the statewide pioneer society). It also allowed anyone who arrived in Montana before 1884 to join so long as the "pioneer" eventually lived in one of the nine counties of the state's eastern section.[17]

Organizations founded later in the twentieth century would abandon cutoff dates for a stated period of residence, as with the self-explanatory Twenty-Five Year Pioneers Club of Lewis and Clark County, established in 1933. Such organizations made "pioneer" synonymous with "old-timer." The emphasis on period of residence meant that a community could maintain a supply of living pioneers because the cutoff date would move forward automatically each year. Other groups preferring to retain the idea of "pioneers" as original founding families counted descendants. This was the policy of the Sons and Daughters of Montana Pioneers, founded in 1892.

Such formal associations are part of a much broader effort to keep the shared memories of a region alive. Throughout the West museums, libraries, and historical societies have collected oral interviews and personal memoirs. Pageants and celebrations reenact earlier times, and numerous clubs exist whose members occasionally dress and live like fur trappers or frontier soldiers. Similar public expressions of historical heritage may be found in every other region of the United States and in countries around the world. All convey special status to specific settings and historical characters, although they often do so without regard to historical inaccuracy and in an arbitrarily selective way. Certain peoples are elevated as heroes, whereas others are ignored as "outsiders."

In their shared memory of life on the overland trail and in the mining camps, Montana's self-defined generation of pioneers excluded Indians and outlaws from its membership. These groups had threatened the pioneer enterprise of the 1860s. They also ignored other groups, such as cattlemen, sheep raisers, homesteaders, and copper miners, to which many of the "original" pioneers may later have belonged but that arrived too "late" to be among Montana's founders. So these latecomers created their own ideational core of shared memories. Like fragments in sedimentation, their retrospective stories hardened over time within the clastic rock of regional identity. Writing in the 1890s and early 1900s, original pioneers such as Cornelius Hedges identified with a different generation, locale, and time from Si Gray, who wrote his reminiscence in the mid-1930s. Si Gray may have considered himself a pioneer as well as a westerner, but he belonged to a later stratum within the second layer of regional identity. He could not have joined the Society of Montana Pioneers.

The definition of a pioneer remains subject to endless variation within Montana and across the West. But the exclusion of certain groups entirely from these formal definitions amplifies the larger question of who is a westerner. Most problematic is the pioneers' effort to exclude native peoples. The pioneers, who clearly were not the first people to settle in the region, considered themselves the West's founding generation. They recognized the existence of American Indians but saw native peoples in ethnocentric terms as "others"—obstacles to the creation of a new society. The pioneers defined themselves in opposition to these natives, who were really the first westerners by virtue of their earliest arrival and longest residence in the region.[18] Native peoples thus became a distinct substrate upon which the bedrock of western identity formed, although they themselves were never fully incorporated into that identity. It is almost as if Indians formed a part of the regional landscape, quintessentially "West" without ever becoming "western."

Region as National Epic

By the 1920s one observer could describe the regard of Montanans for the state's pioneers as "a form of ancestor worship of which hardly less is heard than in Massachusetts Bay itself."[19] Like the first families of New England, the pioneers of the West and their worshipers celebrated American nationalism as a story of migration and settlement. In so doing, they produced a third layer of regional identity. Formed out of the epic of national expansion, it also partook of economic and cultural imperialism.

Montana's pioneers fitted what the geographer Wilbur Zelinsky has called the "Doctrine of First Effective Settlement." In his *Cultural Geography of the United States* (1973), Zelinsky maintained that the first Euroamerican population established the economic and social foundation for an area and thereby determined later settlement patterns.[20] The pioneers of the West fashioned a regional identity based on early arrival and long-term residence. Ironically, this apparently stable group identity underplayed the constant mobility of individuals that has characterized much of the population of both the nineteenth- and the twentieth-century Wests. The pioneers moved west, but they also stayed west, typically in one particular area. Later immigrants followed this pattern as they laid claim to a western identity. This growing population of self-identified "westerners" repeated the layerings of earlier generations through personal locale, shared memory, and national epic.

Consider the reminiscence of Bertha Josephson Anderson, which she wrote in the late 1930s.[21] As a young girl in Denmark Bertha learned about cows when her mother taught her to milk. In 1880, when she was eighteen, her father sent her to a large farm to work as a milkmaid. There she met a gardener, Peter Anderson; their engagement lasted twenty months; their marriage, fifty-five years. The two fathers-in-law helped the couple purchase a peat farm on poor land. A brother, Carl, wrote of good land in eastern Montana, with logs that he would use to build a house. With their three children, Peter and Bertha traveled in steerage to Castle Garden, New York. The same night as their arrival in the United States, they took the train to St. Paul, Minnesota, and stayed over with another brother, John. "Stunned" to see how well "working people" lived in the United States, Bertha soon learned that milking cows was not exclusively "women's work." Pondering the "strange country we had come to," Bertha

Anderson and her family reached Glendive, Montana, near midnight. The next day, taken by wagon fifty-five miles for a fee of thirty dollars, they arrived in Sidney, near the present-day Montana-North Dakota border. On April 12, 1889, they ate their first meal in their new home, a two-room log "shack," only a few "rods" from the Yellowstone River. The entire trip had taken less than three weeks.

A look at a map had made the Andersons believe that the climate of Montana would resemble that of France. They stored little food for their first winter, and although they nearly starved, they never considered slaughtering a calf from their small dairy herd. "We had but one aim," Bertha wrote, "to struggle along as best we could, planning in five years to have enough money made so we could go back home to Denmark and buy back the little home we sold to come over here." It was an immigrant's dream destined to be eroded by prosperity and a new American identity. Raising sheep and milking cows, the Andersons improved their situation, and soon the children had started school. They insisted that their parents speak English at home. "We could by that time both read and write it fairly well. In fact, we learned to be good Americans."

By the summer of 1892 Bertha and Peter thought less about returning to Denmark. "We liked most of the settlers we saw, and they showed us that we were not outsiders anymore." In 1895 they made the final filing on their land and took out citizenship papers. Three years later, in the fall of 1898, they helped organize the first Dawson County Fair in Sidney. "We had been here only nine years," Bertha wrote, "but we were a real part of the community. Peter was the secretary of the first fair, and we had helped to put Sidney on the map." Shortly after this time fourteen members of Bertha's extended family moved to Montana from Denmark.

The arrival of so many family members may have revitalized the Anderson's Danish identity, but it also may have strengthened their identification with their home in the West. A visit to Denmark helped clarify matters. To celebrate the eighty-third birthday of Peter's father, three of the Andersons—Peter, Bertha, and their youngest daughter—returned to Denmark in the summer of 1902. The father found it hard to accept stories about life in Montana—one hundred head of cattle with no barn or a log house with a dirt roof. To him, they seemed just yarns. Bertha noticed that in Montana people walked "half a mile to catch a horse to ride or drive one mile." In Denmark she had never owned a horse. There people expected to walk, especially if the weather was bad and a horse might get wet. "Everything [in Denmark] seemed so small compared to what we were used to. Even our rough and leaky loghouse seemed much better than the swell looking houses which they had. . . ." She concluded that she and Peter had gained "a wider outlook."

Bertha Anderson now identified more positively with life in Montana than with life in Denmark. A land rush to the northern plains began in the early 1900s, and many new homesteaders arrived from Europe. Bertha complained that the Danish settlers would not go to the English-speaking church "as we did" and seemed to visit only among themselves. In her eyes they were refusing to embrace the new identity that had become her own. "I suppose," she opined, "there was not that inner urge, that they must learn the language of the land."

As with Si Gray's memoir and Cornelius Hedges's reminiscence, Bertha Anderson's retrospections dwelt on the formative years in Montana up until 1907, only three years after the birth of her last child. The Andersons became well established as American citizens in Montana. They assisted other Danes searching for suitable lands. Peter helped plan an irrigation project for their valley, and Bertha organized the first telephone company. Together they raised eight children in the state. But Bertha's memoir jumps over the family era and lands twenty-five years later at the Andersons' golden wedding anniversary. A large crowd, including twenty-five grandchildren and three great-grandchildren, attended the event. Peter died five years later in 1937, but Bertha ended her reminiscence with a proud report of her "baby girl," Camilla May Anderson. Born in 1904, she had become a medical doctor, taught at two universities, wrote a "good book," and was listed in *Who's Who in America*.

From milkmaid to medical doctor in one generation, the saga of the two Anderson women is astonishing. It not only captures some of the success of immigrant families in the West but also raises a question: Did Bertha Anderson consider herself a westerner? Her memoir reflects the greater story of Americanization, the national epic of immigrants making a new home in the United States. Yet the setting and style of her Americanization are distinctively western. In comparison, both Si Gray and Cornelius Hedges underwent a process of "westernization." These Americans from Wisconsin and Massachusetts became westerners in Montana. This did not preclude their retention of other identifications. Cornelius Hedges organized a New England Association in Helena, Montana; Si Gray became an Elk. Were she alive today, Bertha Anderson would undoubtedly call herself a Danish-American. All of them, however, had established new homes in a new land. All were Montanans and westerners.[22]

Gray, Hedges, and Anderson represented the first generation in their families to come west. Their memoirs reveal a process of identification with the region in a local context. They explained the formative years of their adulthood for their children and their communities. In this personal locale Hedges and Anderson rationalized the significance of their lives in positive, nationalistic terms—Hedges as a founding pioneer establishing order in a new land and Anderson as the immigrant mother becoming an American in a western place.[23] In other western locales other newcomers also underwent this process of creating a new identity; for some though, this was a profoundly divisive process in which groups became cut off from larger communities. For example, what identity did non-Mormons create in the areas of the intermountain West dominated by the Latter-day Saints? What cultural interconnections and separate identities did Hispanos, Mexicanos, and Anglos produce in their memoirs of life in the Southwest? What reactions did native peoples have to newcomers who defined Indians as "outsiders" in a "West" that for centuries had been their homeland? Regional identity produced inclusion for some peoples and exclusion for others. This contested terrain will repay greater attention in the study of western history.

Region as Reaction

The tensions within a far from singular regional identity suggest a fourth stratum to be excavated, one in which other cleavages suddenly become visible. Here regional identity manifests itself as a sense of separation from other peoples and places. Such cleavages may apply within a region to distinguish subregions from each other, as in the differences between the Pacific Northwest, the arid Southwest, and the Great Plains. They may separate people within a region, as in the Euroamerican view of Native Americans or Asian immigrants as "others." But they may also apply *trans*regionally, as when westerners have rallied to oppose "outside" forces. Especially in the twentieth century, western opposition to economic exploitation and federal domination has colored the regional identity.

One of the angriest twentieth-century attacks on eastern exploitation of the West came from a westerner who moved east. Writing in 1934 for *Harper's* magazine, Bernard De Voto entitled his article "The West: A Plundered Province." Raised in Ogden, Utah, by a Mormon mother and Catholic father, the independent-minded De Voto had moved to Massachusetts and taught at Harvard University. But he had not become an easterner. If anything, his eastern sojourn had intensified his identification with the region of his birth and energized his polemic. De Voto claimed that the financing of western development had benefited eastern capital. Wall Street banks and corporations had exploited the resources of the West for staggering profits, leaving the region an economic colony of eastern interests.[24]

De Voto's argument tapped an old vein of resentment. His ideas hearkened back to those of the western Populists in the 1890s who had stressed the threat to silver mining from eastern capitalists and government policies. Later Progressive leaders, such as Governor Joseph M. Dixon in Montana, tried to curb the predatory exploits of eastern corporations. Dixon's efforts to tax fairly the profits of Montana's metal mining industry brought down the wrath of the Anaconda Copper Mining Company, which controlled more than half the newspapers in the state. Anaconda's money and power limited the reform governor to one four-year term. He lost his bid for reelection in 1924.[25]

Nineteen years after Dixon's defeat, another Montanan wrote about the exploitation of his state. This time the idea had greater popular appeal. Joseph Kinsey Howard's *Montana: High, Wide, and Handsome* appeared in 1943. By July 1944 the publisher, Yale University Press, had brought out a fifth printing, and the book continued to sell. In 1959 Yale produced a special illustrated edition; a paperback version is still in print. In 1982 nearly eight hundred subscribers to *Montana— The Magazine of Western History* indicated their five choices for the best books on Montana. Howard's book finished first out of 531 different titles. Such continued recognition of one eloquently angry book suggests how important cleavages and opposition can be in sustaining a regional identity.[26]

In 1919 Joe Howard moved to Great Falls, Montana, with his family. Four years later, at the age of seventeen, he began his career as a writer and newsman with the *Great Falls Leader*. So began his long love affair with the state he was to capture in his famous book. As its title indicates, *Montana: High, Wide, and Handsome* bespoke a passionate appreciation of Montana's landscape. Historian Richard Roeder has seen Howard's effort as "an early example of ecological history" with a biology "more romantic than scientific."[27]

Howard's love of the land led him to rearrange the heroes and villains of Montana's past. He denounced the outsiders who, in his view, had exploited the state, but he also criticized people who moved to Montana. The promotion of a land rush by railroad tycoon James J. Hill received special condemnation. It was a "witless nightmare" that encouraged speculators to build "starved towns" for the new European homesteaders.[28] Other corporate powers plundered the state, especially the Anaconda Company, which controlled copper mining, ran the legislature, and turned Butte into Montana's "black heart." Howard's hostility was directed not just at corporations but at all exploiters. Groups that came west to get rich and get out—such as placer miners and buffalo hunters—earned Howard's wrath. He favored cattlemen, mainly because he saw them as stewards of the land who devoted their lives to working on the range.

Joe Howard liked those whom the writer Wallace Stegner has called "stickers."[29] People with a sense of place and connection to community won his praise. "Grass-roots planning" by ordinary folk could work, in Howard's view, if only academic scientists with their "morass of pedagogical jargon" and federal agencies with their innumerable bureaucratic conflicts did not get in the way.[30] In short, Joe Howard admired people like himself. His heroes protected their place in the West against destructive attacks whether from inside or outside the region. The long-lived affection Montanans continue to feel for Howard's book indicates that even present-day readers appreciate his impassioned love of the land and his highly charged interpretation of history. Howard expressed basic challenges to which westerners still react. He gave voice to the question of what forces and whose values should control the West.

In the last half century the question of control has continued to be central for westerners. As historians Michael Malone and Rodman Paul have stated, "the 'colonial exploitation' of the West by the East, the 'rape' of its natural resources, and a distrust of easterners in business suits have received spasmodic bursts of angry attention."[31] At times, as in the late 1970s, inflamed western opposition has denounced the control of public lands by federal agencies, even though the bureaucrats who staffed these agencies in the West were often themselves westerners. And the "outside" economic powers that exploited the interior West were based in Los Angeles or San Francisco, not in New York.[32] The values and identities of westerners remain divided, even among themselves.

To what extent do westerners have the power to shape their own region? How much are their actions explained by a shared identity? These questions look beyond the formative four layers of western identity and set an agenda for future scholarship. But the fragments and strata of this clastic identity, and the process that continues to form it, remain vital legacies from the past.

The West is neither a separate nation nor an autonomous region. It is disunited—crosscut with various subregions, distinct states, and diverse peoples. A unified western region is no more likely than a monolithic western identity. But westerners do share a territory, a history, and a future. They are affected by others both within the region and without. Newcomers keep arriving. They will share in the process of creating and re-creating a regional identity, within generations and across generations. This ongoing process gives the future of the western past a great prospect. Like Stegner's stickers and Howard's grass-roots communities, the best-sustained understanding of western selfhood will start at bedrock, in a local context. New generations within the West will add layers of personal perceptions, shared values, and living histories to their regional identity. Future travelers will learn that the view from Wisdom is always changing.

History for the Masses

Commercializing the Western Past

ANN FABIAN

Presenting the Past

On July 12, 1893, Frederick Jackson Turner read his paper on "The Significance of the Frontier in American History" to members of the American Historical Association who had come to Chicago for their annual meeting. Chicago, the upstart city of the West, had won the bidding war for the American celebration of the 400th anniversary of Columbus's landfall in the New World. The historians who visited the World's Columbian Exposition on the shores of Lake Michigan had much to amuse them after they had listened to their colleagues' scholarly papers. Along with thousands of other fairgoers, they could gaze with wonder on the splendors of the White City, thrill to the heights of the Ferris wheel, or dance on the Midway Plaisance to the ragtime music of Scott Joplin. Some perhaps ventured outside the fairgrounds and joined the pleasure seekers who thronged to Buffalo Bill Cody's Wild West Show. There they would have found a version of the western past every bit as compelling as Turner's.[1]

The events that summer in Chicago have stayed with American

223

western history. There is no reason for me to rehearse the significance of "The Significance of the Frontier" other than to acknowledge that it stands as a foundation document for the serious study of frontier processes that characterized the white settlement of successive American Wests. It is also a cultural artifact quite unlike the usually ephemeral papers delivered at gatherings of historians. Like the staging of the fair at Chicago, Turner's scholarship marked the coming of age of things western, and he offered American historians a distinctly New World explanation for the evolution of democracy. By turning to the environment, by writing in poetic cadences, and by basing poetry on an inspired reading of freshly minted statistics, Turner transformed the very recent past into something recognized as history. He appealed with particular force to the first generation of professional historians, and their descendants have passed on to posterity a continuing debate about the frontier and its role in the American past, granting Turner a measure of fame rare among American academics.[2]

If Turner has stayed around to haunt successive generations of historians, so has Buffalo Bill. It was no coincidence that both Turner and Cody were in Chicago. Both staked a claim to the perpetuation of the frontier just as the distinctive social and economic relations characteristic of frontier settlement ceased to exist. Both made careers exploring imagined versions of the past, and both profited personally and professionally from the production of images of a world transformed from vital present to rich and mysterious past. Scholars like Turner explained the past and claimed for their explanations the virtues of accuracy, veracity, and authenticity. They supported their versions of the past with the well-constructed archives that attested to their professional competence. But the scholarly pursuit of the western past was joined immediately by an impish popular double. In contrast with their scholarly kin, popular purveyors of the western past disrupted studious contemplation in the archives and turned to new tools of mass culture to offer the thrills of dramatic spectacles and the pleasures of good stories. They mocked the labors of professional historians by picking and choosing the pieces of the past best suited to dramatic needs.

In few other scholarly fields has popular culture played so prominent a part; in few other realms of popular culture has history been so central. If the historians who traveled to Chicago bought a ticket and watched Buffalo Bill perform with his horses, his cowboys, and his Indians, they also watched their very subject—the past—turned to commerce and marketed to audiences with minimal interest in what professional historians valued as scholarly, literary, and scientific.

In terms of longevity, Cody's appropriation of the past has proved as powerful as Turner's, and since the 1890s competing Wests have staked claims to territories of the popular imagination. In western American history, teachers meet students schooled from early childhood in a vast array of popular images derived specifically from questionable readings of the past.[3] Movies, stories, pictures, rodeos, Wild West Shows, and even advertisements have challenged the controlled textuality of serious scholarship and the careful interpretations of serious scholars. Historians have never been entirely sure how to handle the competing interpreters who have kept versions of the past before mass audiences, and they have often been embarrassed by the fertile proliferation of popular Wests. To our occasional disgust, the audience for the popular always seems to extend far beyond the serious readers we historians try to cultivate.[4]

The great popularity of the western past has meant that competition over western materials has generally involved money—often quite a lot of money. Buffalo Bill and Professor Turner both made their livings as showmen, presenting Wests they each marked with a distinctive signature. Although we have come to see them both as imaginative interpreters, related in their follies and expressive excesses, their fashions of displaying the West were almost guaranteed to produce mutual suspicion. Buffalo Bill catered to popular tastes, creating a mass audience for the very materials Turner and his fellow professional historians, recently established in the universities, would have reserved to the literate and educated. At the same time, popular novelists and moviemakers joined showmen like Buffalo Bill and tried to profit from the spectacular display of an imagined past that was not scientific, analytic, or archival.[5]

Contests between the scholarly and the popular, between elite interpreters and mass audiences, between the intellectual and the anti-intellectual continue to trouble historians of the American West. As recently as the fall of 1985 Gene Gressley complained in an address to members of the Western History Association that western history still had an "image problem." He then offered a "potpourri" of theoretical postulates that he argued could be used to organize the history of the West. He suggested that historians avoid the horrors of anti-intellectualism by studying such serious topics as "federalism, pluralism, regionalism, colonialism, and classical and neoclassical liberalism."[6]

But why reject the popular as suspect, as dangerously anti-intellectual, when the field remains wide open for investigation of the troublesome twin births of western pasts, for exploration of the constant doubling of the Wests of scholars by the Wests of mass culture? The story of the West has always been contradictory and contentious, at once high-minded and venal, adventurous and silly, noble and base. And it has been told numerous times and in numerous styles. With this cacophony of voices in mind, even serious historians can explore the history of popular representations of the West. They can ask not only why stories about the West have had such appeal but also how western materials have been marketed, to whom and why. Who has told the story of the West? Have professional historians really differed so much from the popular image makers they have shunned? How has the West as popular frontier played to those who have called regions of the West home?

The contradictory content of western stories is only part of the problem. Whatever their content, the various versions of the imagined past have altered and continue to alter the reality of the present. Time and again historians have found traces of erroneous readings of the past shaping and reshaping the economics and culture of the present. Bearing in mind the particular presence of the popular and the commercial in the pasts of the American West, I will argue that western history (both the history that has been written by scholars and the history that has been lived by western peoples) cannot be set up as pure, scientific, and free of the artful distortions of the popular imagination. The twin versions of the West are Siamese, and the scholarly and the popular, the factual and the legendary are so thoroughly entwined that they cannot be separated.

"Print the Legend"

John Ford, the consummate architect of popular Wests, understood the competition over western pasts. In his extended meditation on the western genre, the 1962 movie *The Man Who Shot Liberty Valance*, he portrayed legendary figures of a frontier past who return to the thriving town of Shinbone to bury one of their dead. Jimmy Stewart's Senator Ransom Stoddard, the man who brought literacy and law to the frontier, has built a political career on the story that he once killed the notorious gunfighter Liberty Valance (Lee Marvin), a sociopath with a particular hatred for law, order, and the printed word. Valance, it turns out, was killed by the one man tougher than he was,

John Wayne's illiterate Tom Doniphon. The graying senator has returned for Tom's funeral, and a bumptious reporter, sensing a good story, asks him for an interview. The press follows the senator to the undertaker's. In the present of the film Stoddard tells the story of the past. He is, he says, the one who "can tell it true." As the legend of Stoddard's bravery dissolves, the poor young reporter watches the solid past he thought he knew disappear: The senator's legend is a lie. His wiser editor nevertheless counsels, "This is the West, sir. When the legend becomes fact, print the legend."

The editor's advice captures more than the dilemma facing the journalist in the film; for our purposes it points toward useful ways of understanding the troubled relations between the scholarly study of the western past and the legendary versions Americans have often preferred to hear. The editorial caution is ambiguous. It suggests a rejection of the revealed truth that a more dutiful investigator might have published, a choice of the good story over the hard facts. But it also suggests that in a peculiar way in the West, legend actually *becomes* fact. The town and territory thrive because of the legendary past, and the present makes sense only when acknowledged as legend becomes fact. The editor has wrapped the revealed lie in the more immediate truth of Shinbone's present prosperity.

Historians working in today's scholarly West still labor to demystify the past, to print the facts and dispel the legend, but the process of demystification can never be complete. Throughout the twentieth century politicians, fashion designers, and producers of mass culture have kept right on turning popular legend into the social and economic facts of the living present. In so doing, they keep the legendary past vibrantly alive, promising future historians a West made and remade by the constant interplay of fact and fiction.

The popular history of the West has become an industry in its own right, an industry with an economics and history of its own. Before the popular West reached full expression in Buffalo Bill's traveling Wild West Shows, in Beadle and Adams's dime novels, and in Hollywood westerns, the popular and the commercial graced many of the earliest writings on white life on the western frontiers. Seventeenth-century white captives returned from lives among the Indians shaped sensational stories that they told, and then profitably sold, to friends, neighbors, and tavern acquaintances. Ministers and moralists discovered useful lessons in tales of redeemed captives and frequently framed them with introductions designed to guide readers to their correct interpretation. By the early nineteenth century western publishers also exploited a market for tales of frontier adventure. The tales circulating freely through an oral culture were printed, bound, and sold to readers who were left free to interpret as they chose. Readers had been turned into customers. This commercial side of western tale telling—tale selling—has been an abiding characteristic of representations of the West.[7]

At the end of the eighteenth century, when John Filson constructed his famous pamphlet *The Discovery, Settlement, and Present State of Kentucke* to lure settlers into Kentucky, he was careful to include with his descriptions of soil and mineral resources a version of Daniel Boone's captivity—"transcribed," like a good tavern tale of an oral culture, from Boone's "own mouth." Boone's adventure served two purposes in a pamphlet designed as much for real estate promotion as to satisfy "human curiosity." It suggested the violent past of a territory now tamed and made ready for settlement, and it painted that past in precisely the legendary terms that enhanced the present value of Kentucky real estate. Kentucky was a famous place, and Boone had made it so.[8]

Commercial pandering may have disquieted those who were devoted to moral lessons, but since tales of violence and bloodshed continued to serve the commercial ends of western boosters, these gaudy stories continued to ornament printed versions of the western past. Popular texts rendered the violence of territorial expansion as benign sensationalism and so served the ends of conquest and commerce. One finds a particularly lucid instance of the connections among commerce, storytelling, and destruction in the pamphlets on steamboat explosions and railroad accidents that the cartographer James T. Lloyd sold to travelers venturing West in the 1850s. Lloyd fancied himself an accurate mapmaker but did not shy away from the commercial aspects of his trade. He shamelessly promoted himself on his maps and his books and pamphlets. He took over the western guidebook style first made popular by Zadok Cramer in the early nineteenth century, but he added lurid descriptions of wrecks and accidents and lists of the dead and wounded to Cramer's careful maps. Floyd also sold advertising space to companies hoping to profit from the commercial development of the West. With accurate maps, horrifying descriptions, and advertisements all neatly packaged together, Lloyd then sold his pamphlets to travelers who not only might patronize the advertised businesses but also risked the very accidents and gruesome deaths the pamphlets so carefully documented.

Lloyd's little books seem particularly restless compilations. As

Lloyd and his reporters searched for metaphors to describe the destructive force of steam boiler explosions, they kept confronting what they acknowledged as "scenes too horrible for description." But with recourse to a stock of references to scenes of war and torture, however inappropriate to the mid-century Mississippi Valley, they managed the task. To a late-twentieth-century reader horrible descriptions of scalded flesh and mangled bodies rest uneasily beside advertisements for companies that stand to profit from developments assured by steam navigation. We have grown used to reports of catastrophic devastation appearing near the sunny promises of advertising, but even our most sensational press holds disaster at a distance, creating a safe contrast with the lulling intimacies of advertising. Lloyd's readers perused pamphlets about the very dangers they faced. But Lloyd's intent was to promote commerce, not to discourage it. By adding names of the known dead to his accounts of accidents, Lloyd erected small memorials to victims of commerce, and as memorials his compilations may well have helped assure the commercial future of the West. Unlike Filson, Lloyd could not confine risk to the past, but this hardly mattered. His little books served the future as monuments, justifying catastrophic loss of life with proof of the commercial property such sacrifice had made possible.[9]

When Lloyd could call on no witnesses schooled in the vocabulary of commerce, sensation, sacrifice, and sentiment, his stories of steamboat disasters took a different turn, and his search for language to convey destruction yielded different results. In October 1837 the steamboat *Monmouth*, which had been commissioned by the United States government to remove the Creeks to lands west of the Mississippi, collided with another boat, killing between three and four hundred Creeks. Without a sentimental witness, Lloyd was quick to label the accident a "massacre, a wholesale assassination." He faulted the journalists and news gatherers who had deemed the accident of "too little importance to deserve any particular attention."[10]

Behind Lloyd's analysis of the news lay a realization that audiences for the events he described were racially constructed. For Lloyd's readers, the Creek victims were mute witnesses to their own destruction. To take the more familiar example of *Moby-Dick*, it was as though Queequeg, Daggoo, or Tashtego—cannibal, illiterate, and savage—were those who survived to recount the voyage of the *Pequod*. If versions of the adventure circulated through archipelagoes, the Dark Continent, or desert wastes, they were not necessarily shaped by the trained sentiments of white witnesses and not necessarily preserved in archives of written reports. The Indians who witnessed the frenzies of white commerce had stories to tell, but they are hard for historians to find, for they told them mainly among themselves. In bits and fragments, however, one finds shadows of such stories in the actions of nonwhite witnesses. During the early 1830s, years before the wreck of the *Monmouth*, government agents were already reporting the great Indian "aversion to steamboats arising entirely from the exaggerated stories they have been told of their danger." In a letter to Secretary of War Lewis Cass, the Indian agent James Gardiner described the worries of Indians he knew in Ohio. "[T]hey were fearful," he wrote, "some of their children might be drowned, and that all, young and old, would be in danger of being scalded to death, *'like the white man cleans his hog.'* " The aptness of the Indian simile for deaths by boiler explosion suggests that they well understood the risks of mechanical innovation. Moreover, because they did not stand to benefit from the white man's commerce, their images of pain and torture were free of white circumlocutions. Nothing in their rhetoric seeks to justify the destructive risks of steam. For them, death by explosion was neither sensational nor sentimental; to be scalded like a hog was anything but banal.[11] Placing their language beside Lloyd's suggests some of the ways popular relics of the western past can raise larger intellectual and material questions.

Nothing but the Facts

Like John Ford, Lloyd was happy to tell many versions of the West at the same time. The clever mapmaker bound his stories together and marketed them to a captive audience on Mississippi steamboats. Professional historians have been more conscientious about reconciling contradictory and competing stories, directing history, sometimes with great zeal, to accuracy and authenticity. For the last two decades historians working on the West have labored to correct the misrepresentations in both Turner and the popular conception of the western past. The scholarly past, like the popular, had deceived its audiences on many fronts, and we can now hope for a more accurate and inclusive sense of western history.

In a brief essay published in 1977, *The Trader on the American Frontier: Myth's Victim*, Howard Lamar argued that a lingering Turnerian emphasis on the mythic figures of "explorers, pioneers, and settlers" had led historians to neglect "a dual tradition of trade and mercantile capitalism" that better explained the social world of inter-racial and intercultural frontiers. Social historians have elaborated that project and washed the mud off the mythic past with a cold shower of sober fact. The facts of the real West gave us cowboys who were overworked drovers, prosaic ranch hands, and active union members confronting the power and wealth of agribusiness. Social historians described miners who worked not on the frontiers of individual liberty but in urban islands constructed as economic frontiers of capitalism by greedy financiers and industrialists pushing the search for raw materials into rural hinterlands. And they returned women to the pioneer communities where they lived and worked. A single heroic trajectory of development was broken into episodes of greed and failure. An American story was retold as part of a long history of the migrations of European peoples. The worlds of the West became complex, authentically gendered, interracial, and multiethnic; violence became bloody, not heroic; and expansion stood exposed as conquest.[12]

Even the minor figures of western drama were redrawn. Prostitutes became hardworking purveyors of commercial sex—women (often women of color) who worked where men outnumbered them and whose dull, miserable lives frequently ended in despair and suicide. Gamblers became ephemeral figures who, like prostitutes, found themselves banished when settlers, seeking eastern investment, remade western towns in the image of eastern propriety and stability. Gamblers had taken advantage of the frontier economies where money appeared in sudden windfalls. They had a harder time winning the careful wages of a commercial economy and surviving in moralized marketplaces built around such virtues as industry, sobriety, and frugality.[13]

Like Ford's Liberty Valance, Billy the Kid may have been a gritty little sociopath, but social historians have shied away from psychologizing about solitary gunfights and notorious outlaws, studying instead far more pervasive patterns of ethnic, racial, and labor violence. They have changed our understanding of the West by integrating outlaws into ethnic communities and by exploring the ways bandits embodied local traditions. Western violence could be best understood as a response to local conditions, not as some timeless expression of American psychpathology.[14]

While social historians have cleared away clutter from the realm of fact, literary critics and historians of popular culture have devised ways to understand better the realm of legend. Rather than reenact the disjunction between the highbrow pursuits of intellectuals and the lowbrow pleasures of the masses, they have instead pursued those pleasures, trying to understand just what popular culture can tell us about life in the past. I see no reason to indulge in a "bright-eyed boosterism" of the popular, but some of the recent literary debates about relations between popular culture and high culture, between "great novels" and popular fiction, teach us about the competing pasts of the West.[15]

Historians have long understood that Americans, particularly white literate middle-class easterners, embraced a version of the western past just as it ceased to be reality. Easterners turned to nature just as they unleashed the patterns of corporate development, urban growth, and industrial expansion that threatened to overwhelm the wilderness. Intellectuals turned to ethnography just when the last battles had apparently eliminated the possibility of reconstructing independent Native American cultures. Anthropologists and photographers joined historians in documenting a vanishing world, and they turned knowledge of western people, things, and landscapes into new forms of professional expertise and artistic expression.[16]

Tales of the American West often exemplified what the anthropologist Renato Rosaldo has called imperialist nostalgia, a yearning for what one has destroyed. Rosaldo acknowledges the work of historians who have tried to demystify the conquest of the West, to unmask the "class interests" and "social strains" that underlie mythic descriptions of western adventure. But he would turn their work in a slightly different direction, asking how ideological forms can be compelling or convincing as well as contradictory and pernicious. Rather than searching for the guilt, greed, venality, destruction, and conquest that mythic tales might conceal, Rosaldo urges scholars to explore the strength of myths and the power of mythic appeal. Rather than seek to reveal a "truth" hidden behind ideological formations, he would find cultural truths in the tales themselves. "This mode of analysis attempts not so much to overpower an ideology, by grabbing hold and demystifying it, as to evoke it and thereby make it more and more fully present until it gradually crumbles under the weight of its own inconsistencies."[17] He turns the insight to ethnographic ends, but his formulation might prove useful for historians seeking to understand relations between popular formulations and their historic audiences. If popular western materials have performed ideological work, we need to know how and for whom they have performed it. How do we account

232

for the appeal of the West? More important for historians, how has that appeal changed over time?

Popular fictions offer some evidence. Along with historians and showmen, dime novelists and popular publishers rushed into the West of the imagination. Just as photographers took advantage of technological developments in their equipment, so purveyors of popular fiction took advantage of innovations in printing technology that made books less costly to produce. They marketed cheap adventure stories, hoping to exploit working-class leisure that might be turned to reading. But readers of popular fiction were not just an empty territory waiting to be colonized; they brought their own complicated concerns and interpretations to the fictions they read. In the hands of dime novelists, fictions provided what Michael Denning has called allegories for eastern working-class readers. He argues that one can read popular texts as the dialectical productions of writers and readers together. He suggests that if one reads the tales of Jesse James and Deadwood Dick that appeared between 1877 and 1883 through the lens of the railroad strikes then rocking the eastern United States, the tales become allegories for battles between labor and capital. In western fictions robbers stopped treasure-bearing trains, and battles against the railroad ended with laborers reappropriating the wealth they had created in the first place. Western outlaws were not delinquent sons of Leatherstocking; rather, they were contemporary heroes cheered on for their daring defiance of mine bosses and railroad barons. According to Denning, readers found in dime novels not a senseless escape to fantasy frontier adventures but imaginative expressions of the economic and cultural battles they faced at home.[18]

Here once again the popular West meets Professor Turner. In his successive Wests Turner had found pragmatic schools of democracy. In settling a continent, white people had acquired "that practical, inventive turn of mind, quick to find expedients," that assured them a democratic culture.[19] The chaos of settlement retold in dime novels may well have offered democratic opportunities to a massive number of working-class readers. Popular fictions carried political and economic battles into the realm of culture and let working-class readers re-create a frontier world that was open, democratic, and just.

233

Popular Culture, Regional Cultures

Historians of the twentieth-century West are fond of pointing out the persistence of frontier imagery in the construction of western regional consciousness. They recognize that evocations of the past serve economies of the present. In his last book, *The Mythic Frontier*, the historian Robert Athearn described in great detail the ways pioneer celebrations, however far from historic fact, have brought tourists and their money into the West. Westerners, Athearn argued, performed pageants of the past for easteners and for tourists while simultaneously embracing development for themselves. A mild schizophrenia was built into western character. Without pageants of false pasts, more than one major western industry would surely suffer.[20]

Athearn's descriptions of frontier pageants suggest a larger pattern. Mythic constructions seem to defy time and development, but they have had a distinct bearing on the history of the West, where real people have lived and died. The legends of the past have become the facts of the present, illustrating, like Senator Stoddard's career, that there is no "real" history of the West, no history that can neatly excise its popular or legendary representations. Popular images have always been played out in actual western landscapes, and there they have had real material consequences. As Richard Slotkin has often argued, mythic constructions of the frontier have been used to explain the glories of white expansion—to justify conquest, genocide, and environmental destruction. Even if myths have been patently false, their consequences have been all too real.[21]

The production of western images to extract wealth from audiences stands behind the Hollywood film industry. In the early years of the twentieth century the movie industry remade the economy and culture of Southern California as surely as the discovery of gold had remade Northern California half a century before. Whether the pioneers of moviemaking arrived fleeing patent battles in New York and New Jersey or simply searching for good weather for outdoor filming, they found a landscape well suited to the production of generic westerns. In *The Birth of a Nation* D. W. Griffith presented a history of the South that might have inspired another regional cinematic genre—the southern, one might call it. But the special pathos and racialism of the South could not match the appeal of the open West. Like any good genre, the western proved capacious enough to contain many human stories, its symbols sufficiently polysemic to survive changes in culture and cultural production. Men on horses (like car chases) also filmed well, and the physical features of Southern California landscapes could easily mark any movie as a western.[22]

Westerns did not suddenly appear full-grown in a cultural vacuum. Richard Brodhead has argued that fictions of regional life were the "dominant form of literary production and literary-cultural consumption in the post-Civil War decades." If we follow his formulation, we can understand the popularity of western images as an extension of literary commodities produced for a marketplace that both public and publishers already understood. The settings of generic westerns grew out of regional stories in which the West was simply one region among many. Regional stories, Brodhead has written, served to fix ideas of the local just as an entrepreneurial and industrial culture was eroding regional difference. Regional fictions became the "registrant and articulator" of the regional pasts overriden by a nationalizing economy and of the racial and ethnic pasts effaced in a uniform entrepreneurial culture. According to Brodhead, the cosmopolitan middle class used regional fictions as textual ground to imagine the inscription of work and leisure onto a local landscape. Regional authors helped designate certain territories as vacation destinations for tourists, and they articulated the varied dialects that characterized a country not only divided by regional dialects, but transformed as well by waves of new immigrants. For historians interested in the popular culture of the West, Brodhead offers a way of reconstructing a middle-class audience for western texts and for understanding the regional fictions that were widely read before the great proliferation of generic western fiction and film in the early twentieth century.[23]

Dressing for the West

The popular West has not been confined to texts and images; it has had its moments in advertising and in fashion. And in this vein the most skilled recent exponent of popular western imagery has not been a historian, a filmmaker, or a novelist but a clothing designer— Ralph Lauren. The popular West successively has represented ideologies of expansion, conquest, manhood, progress, virtue, independence, possibility, prosperity, and democracy, and Lauren has built upon them all. He has made a fashion empire out of a magnificent pastiche, out of materials culled from British imperialism, native American aesthetics, and working westerners' rugged wear. Rather

than the history of the West Lauren has used the long history of representations of the West, choosing freely from the art of Frederic
Remington and from the devices of Madison Avenue and Hollywood.
His adept manipulation of a repertoire of mixed images makes him a
great figure of the postmodern West. In the late 1970s Lauren adopted
all the white male cowboy paraphernalia filmmakers had recently
abandoned, added a whiff of the trail, and mixed them all to market a
men's perfume he called Chaps. Lauren knew he had a ready audience
well schooled in the vocabulary of the West, and he pitched his particular vision to customers shaped by the special combinations of greed
and nostalgia that characterized America in the 1980s. Lauren has
been very successful.[24]

Lauren is the latest in a long line of entrepreneurs who have been
able to turn a profit with metaphoric evocations of a frontier past.
Several things about his career suggest that western history and its
popular representation still have much to offer both scholars and
entrepreneurs. Lauren began by elaborating on the Marlboro Man. In
the 1950s the R. J. Reynolds Tobacco Company appropriated images
of western manliness to sell effeminate filter cigarettes to male smok-
ers. When Lauren launched his western ventures, he built on the long
labor not of white western settlement but of Marlboro advertising. He
gave the man on horseback a well-dressed female companion and a
well-furnished interior.

Lauren's play with western images has a biographical side. He
says he was inspired to create a line of western clothes when he had
trouble finding a snap-button cowboy shirt in Denver. Like so many
other tourists, Lauren had been deceived by what he thought he knew
of the western past. He had seen himself, perhaps, traveling to a Denver that was a nineteenth-century cow town, not the financial center
of the mountain West. Since that first disappointing excursion Lauren
has more than compensated for our lack of western wear. But he did
not stop with the production of perfume, fashion, and images. In the
grand style of his western predecessors he turned to a western landscape to refashion himself. Like pioneers before him and like the pioneer
entrepreneurs of western images—Theodore Roosevelt, Owen Wister, and Frederic Remington—Lauren used the West to market himself. In so doing, he made a fortune, and transformed himself from
eastern entrepreneur to rugged westerner.[25]

Lauren, a native New Yorker, first made himself into his own
best western model. Not content to wear his western clothes in the
city, he and his wife created a ranch on thirteen thousand acres in

southwestern Colorado. The ranch, redecorated to his exacting standards, has become the setting for his collection of the "real" antiques that have inspired his clothes and furniture. Lauren has been able to design and build the structures of the western past on his own land, he has been able to hire cowboys whose rugged good looks complement his dramatic landscapes, and he has begun to produce steaks, a mythic food of the western diet, to feed his well-dressed customers. If he succeeds with his meat line, Lauren will have extended his empire from his own imagination to the outsides of bodies, from the bodies to the Colorado landscape, and from the landscape back to the insides of the bodies he has clothed. Just as professional historians began to turn western legend into fact, Lauren resurrected the legend for hungry customers. Moreover, he has had the wherewithal to try to turn the facts of the Colorado present back into carefully elaborated fictions. Along the way he has sharpened the tools of taste and style that in an aesthetic universe serve to enhance the cultural power of the moneyed.[26]

Lauren has sometimes found the real twentieth-century West a bit truculent. Considering the town of Ridgway, Colorado, to fall below his aesthetic standards, he offered to redesign it at his own expense. And when *Vanity Fair* sent Brooke Hayward to interview Lauren, she succumbed to his vision and gushed over the beauty of his ranch, describing him as a "real godsend to Ouray County. He set the tone for the new look of it—really beautiful, well-kept land."[27] Coloradans may have had their doubts about the tone he set. Yet in his very failure to consult the locals, Ralph Lauren once again proved himself a fit heir to traditions of the West. With Lauren in charge, decisions about the economic and aesthetic future of Ouray County would be made, as they had been in the past, in New York. Lauren resurrected an older version of western colonialism to go with his clothes. Decades ago John D. Rockefeller pocketed profits from iron and coal mined in southern Colorado, soothing restive locals with the promise of welfare capitalism. We perhaps assumed that Rockefeller's smooth pattern of profit taking belonged to an era long past, but we were wrong. Lauren found the profits in a reinvented past, and he has been busy retelling in fashions and home decorations a story of white male migration, imperial conquest, and American development. At the close of the twentieth century, he leaves to the cultural historian the task of understanding the appeal of his new version of a very old story.

Lauren reopened old channels in the commerce of western history, and his career helps us understand how the same search for profits that lured men and women to the West could be extended to the presentation of western pasts. Like prospectors who took over abandoned claims, the entrepreneurs of western imagery continue to eke wealth from well-mined sites. Representations of the West, drawn from the past, continue to reshape the present, to alter the economy, ecology, and demography of communities where westerners live and work. In the West the legend continues to become fact.

Lauren envisioned a future for the western past, but his labors in the fields of fashion have also produced materials historians will be able to mine far into the twenty-first century. But Lauren, like all his fellow entrepreneurs of western images, will also pursue the historians, doubling, mocking, and distorting their labor as Buffalo Bill did Turner's and reminding another generation of scholars just how often interest in their interpretations depends on the entrepreneurs of mass culture.

Is There a
Twentieth-Century West?

MICHAEL E. McGERR

The question has been asked before, and it still needs to be asked. Is the West a coherent region that has played—and continues to play—a distinctive social, economic, political, and cultural role in the United States? The issue is not whether the twentieth-century West is worth studying; obviously there are a host of important western topics we ought to explore. But does the West, as region, exert a significant and identifiable influence on its people and institutions and on the nation? Must the historiography of the modern United States take the region into account? Is the West, as the social scientists would put it, an "independent variable" in the equation of the twentieth century?

Such questions are not unreasonable. In fact, western historians have worried for some time whether the modern phase of their subject will ever thrive.[1] It is not hard to understand their concern. The notion of a twentieth-century West runs up against powerful obstacles. In a way American historiography has conspired against the modern region. The development of United States history leaves the existence of the twentieth-century West in doubt. Ultimately we can make a strong

239

case for the existence and importance of the region, but it is a near thing.

The nineteenth century, of course, is the chief culprit. The sectional crisis, the Civil War, and Reconstruction have given us our sense of what regions or sections are all about. First, there is that clear tripartite sectional geography. In the mid-nineteenth century, an antislavery (or at least antisouthern) North confronted a proslavery and antinorthern South, the two regions at odds over the right way to settle a third, the West. Sections, we believe, rest on deep economic differences that lead in turn to differences in culture and ideology— differences serious enough to fracture the nation, start a bloody four-year conflict, and change American life forever. Such notions exert a not-too-subtle tyranny over the study of the twentieth century. As we look at the West, the South, and the East, we have certain unspoken expectations. Any region worthy of the name should be aggressively self-conscious; if dominant, it should be smugly imperious; if oppressed, it should be angrily rebellious. But the modern equivalent of the Civil War is just not there. While the People's party was a good start, the Populist attempt at a western and southern alliance failed before the twentieth century had even begun.

Not only do we have rather firm preconceptions about what a region ought to be, but we also have a strong notion of what the twentieth century is all about. To oversimplify, but not by much, the predominant interpretation describes the emergence of a bureaucratized, corporatized, and centralized notion. This organizational synthesis of modern America, focused on the power centers of Washington, D.C., and New York City, has no need to look westward. Emphasizing the homogenity of a society bound together by economic, professional, political, and communications networks, the organizational approach has room for contending interest groups but no place for regions.[2]

To be sure, the twentieth-century South still somehow manages to eke out a historiographical living. Historians seem to agree that the region plays a distinctive role in the twentieth century. The persisting sense of a southern region rests on two critical facts, both consequences of the past. First, the modern South has faced enduring problems of race relations, rooted in slavery and emancipation. Second, the white majority shares a regional self-consciousness, the legacy of slavery, the Lost Cause, and segregation. Underneath these reasons lies the tacit conviction that southern history has meant something, that the past still has an impact on the present.[3]

For hopeful students of the modern American West, the comparison with the South is sobering. Over the centuries the West has seen different modes of production, including slavery, but there has been no single, distinctive labor process that marked the region and set it apart from the rest of the country.[4] Western racial and ethnic relations, for all their complexity and tragedy, have not decisively influenced national life in this century. The internment of the Japanese, the mistreatment of Mexicans, the continuing abuse of Native Americans are certainly significant and revealing events, but they have not exerted the persistent force of black-white relations in shaping the course of modern America. Finally, there is the matter of regional consciousness, grounded in the past. As we will see, modern westerners, in some ways share a distinctive sense of identity, but they do not have the heritage of southerners, shaped by slavery, rebellion, defeat, and the civil rights struggle.

If all that is not enough to depress the historian of the modern West, then there is the impact of western historiography itself. The chief developments of historical writing about the West make it even harder to imagine a coherent, distinctive, significant region in the twentieth century.

Above all, the modern West has to contend with the heritage of the frontier. For most of the western past, the frontier was always there—forbidding for the settler but reassuring for the historian following along behind. From Frederick Jackson Turner on down, the frontier was a safe concept, the means of building a literature about a vast region. Even historians unpersuaded by the frontier thesis have been able to make a good living by criticizing Turner and his disciples. But historians of the twentieth-century West have not been able to use the frontier to lay the foundation for their own period. Of course, the demise of the frontier in the 1890s was greatly exaggerated, but most students of the modern era seem to agree that the frontier was relatively unimportant for most of the twentieth century. If anything, the frontier thesis has thrown them into the arms of organizational history.

The archetypical example is Walter Prescott Webb, whose account of the relationships among American regions, published in 1937, lamented "The Crisis of a Frontierless Democracy." Historians, Webb observed, "have told us that [the frontier] promoted individualism, stimulated self-reliance, fostered equality and political democracy; they have not told us, at least not emphatically, that the absence of the frontier tends as surely through undernourishment to destroy those things that its existence stimulated." In fact, Webb insisted, the absence of the frontier helped promote corporate America, the antithesis of individualism, liberty, and democracy. American history, he argued, had two "great peaks": the frontier and the corporation. With the frontier gone, the corporation dominated, and the West, by implication, might even disappear. This was a depressing prospect for a man who believed deeply in regionalism and in the need for the South and West to rebel against the corporate lords of the East. "For nearly three centuries America drank deep the potent wine of the frontier, a wine which produced exhilarating experiences of freedom, adventure, and boundless opportunity," Webb concluded. "It was a long, gay evening, but now America must face the morning after with its headache, moody introspection, and pathetic glance at an empty bottle wherein only the tantalizing odor of the wine remains." We can sympathize with Webb's morose flirtation with organizational history; indeed, half a century later the historian trying to assess the study of the modern West is tempted to borrow from him and describe "The Crisis of a Frontierless Historiography."[5]

Before we join Webb in depressed contemplation of the empty bottle, there is still one more outrage. Ironically, the history of the modern West suffers because the last twenty-five years have been so fruitful a period in western historical writing. Influenced by the rise of social history in all its varieties, western historians opened up new topics and reworked old ones in the 1960s, 1970s, and 1980s. A host of books and articles studied communities, women, racial and ethnic minorities, and private life as well as politics. As a result, we now have a more pluralistic West, fascinating in its variety. But along with this gift comes the difficulty of summing up all these parts in one "West." The pieces of the region, we suspect, may never be put back together again.[6]

Despite all these historiographical obstacles, there are still hardy pioneers willing to bear the hardships on the real frontier of western history. These writers have tried to raise one sort of regional structure or another on three different foundations: the relationship of the West to the East, the western environment itself, and the western past. In each case the results are true frontier architecture—simple, even a little crude, and vulnerable to the elements.

The first historical pioneers on the frontier of the modern West attempted to define the region by its allegedly subordinate relationship to the East. Beginning in the 1930s, amid the Great Depression, Bernard De Voto and Walter Prescott Webb laid out this colonial approach to the twentieth-century West. De Voto considered westerners "the fall guys of the United States . . . victimized by every-body." Webb spun a tale of economic imperialism, the story of "an American feudalism" imposed on western serfs by the eastern barons of finance capitalism. All the standard injustices were there: discrim-inatory freight rates, confiscatory tariffs, exclusive patents, expensive pensions, and rapacious corporations. "Wherever I turn in the South and the West," Webb lamented, "I find people busily engaged in pay-ing tribute to someone in the North." Others took up the colonial lament. In 1946, for instance, A. G. Mezerik described the East as a "financial dictatorship"; the rest of the country, he charged, was under the thumb of "the Eastern corporate aristocracy." Under the circum-stances, Webb, Mezerik, and the others demanded and expected some kind of sectional rebellion. Webb bravely compared the situation of the twentieth-century West and South with the sectional crisis that produced the Civil War; he even borrowed from Lincoln and called his most important statement on the subject *Divided We Stand*. Mez-erik anticipated *The Revolt of the South and West*. "In the making, across and down the United States," he insisted, "is a new and strange indus-trial civil war."[7]

Of course, the war never came—and that is the main obstacle to a colonial interpretation of the modern West. No one doubts the infe-rior economic position of the West through much of the twentieth century; there is little reason to drop the litany of freight rates, tariffs, and corporate rapacity. But the problem is that these structural inequalities have never been translated into a strong ideology of regional rebellion. Webb himself gave the game away early on. "Unfortu-nately, the South and the West have not been able to unite on a com-mon program and, therefore, have not exercised a political influence in proportion to their strength. The difficulty has come from the West, which has not always been able to formulate a definite program, even of opposition, or to see that its cause is the same as that of the South." The historian John Caughey bluntly summed up the situation shortly after World War II. "Curiously," he wrote, "westerners have shown relatively little awareness that they are cast in this subordinate role." Caughey attributed the lack of sectional consciousness to the con-cealed nature of eastern exploitation, to the distractions of western scenery, to the absence of a unifying western metropolis—and to the consequences of western history. "The West has never been organized as a political unit, much less as an independent confederacy," Caughey observed. "It has no flag, no shibboleth such as states' rights, no feel-ing of cultural and intellectual mission like that of New England. It has never gone to war on its own account, much less had a great defeat to cherish as a lost cause." Some parts of this argument make sense; others (those scenic distractions) do not. The weakness of colonial consciousness is an intriguing question, not easily resolved, but its consequences are apparent: It will be hard to build the colonial interpretation without rebellious colonists.[8]

Lately, of course, historians have made less use of the angry language of colonialism. Major regional trends—the relative decline of the Northeast and the industrial heartland, the boom of the Southwest—make it difficult to talk of a subjugated West offering feudal homage to the North. Too, the rising western cities—Houston, Phoenix, San Francisco, Los Angeles, Seattle—make it difficult to talk of a homogeneous West, united by the experience of exploitation. As Bernard De Voto realized as early as the end of World War II, there would be plenty of westerners ready to take the place of the eastern barons. "The West," De Voto observed, "does not want to be liberated from the system of exploitation that it has always violently resented. It only wants to buy into it, cumulative preference stock if possible." Most western men and women may still be paying economic tribute today, but now they are paying more of it to other westerners; the West of the 1960s, 1970s, and 1980s, like the East, has its own corporate citadels of concrete and glass, its own portfolios of "cumulative preference stock." The old colonialism, it seems, will not explain the latter part of the twentieth century.[9]

While the regional transformations of the last few decades obviously weaken the colonial approach, they also suggest another interpretation based on the relationship of the West and the East. In the 1970s, some writers, among them Kevin Phillips, Kirkpatrick Sale, and Carl Oglesby, began to describe a "power shift" taking place in the United States. The booming states of the "Sun Belt" or "Southern Rim" or "Pacific Rim" seemed to be seizing control of the nation from the declining "Rust Belt" of the East and Middle West. To Sale and Oglesby, the political phenomenon of Watergate reflected the new regional struggle for power: Richard Nixon was one of the western "cowboys" fighting to take control of America; his opponents were eastern "Yankees" launching a regional counterattack.[10]

At worst, such notions are fanciful amusements; at best they are as yet largely unexamined. But the concept of a "power shift," however unsubstantiated by historical inquiry, presents serious problems for the western historian. First of all, this interpretation threatens the whole idea of the West as a region. The Sun Belt, the Southern Rim and the Pacific Rim disassemble the traditional regions of the United States. According to the Sun Belt and Southern Rim models, the Southwest—California, Arizona, New Mexico, and Nevada—should be torn away from the rest of the West and joined to the lower South. According to the Pacific Rim model, California should be joined to Oregon and Washington, and the three states separated from the rest of the West. All this should give pause to western historians eager to pile articles and monographs atop the power shift; the East may not be the only region to suffer a decline in modern America.

Second, the power shift is essentially the old colonial drama with the roles reversed, and like that drama, it has a hard time getting enough regional actors and actresses to play the key parts. At the popular level there is no compelling evidence that westerners see themselves as members of a new regional imperium or that Californians feel they belong to the Pacific Rim or the Southern Rim. The kinship of Floridians and Arizonians is undemonstrated; the alienation of Oregonians and North Dakotans, undetermined. At the elite level it is hard to think of Richard Nixon, New York lawyer and New Jersey resident as well as California native, as the representative of any western region, belt, or rim in particular. And what do we make of George Bush, an ersatz Texan with Connecticut roots and patrician values? If Bush symbolizes anything, it is not the power shift or the irreconcilable conflict between "Yankees" and "cowboys" but rather the relatively easy merging of the upper classes of the East and the Sun Belt. That comfortable regional settlement suggests a final problem: The West, at least in its class structure, may be resembling the East more and more. That is only speculation, of course. We still know too little about the development of western society since the Second World War. But what we do know makes it seem unlikely that either the colonial or the power shift approach by itself can serve as the foundation for twentieth-century western history.

If regional power relationships do not fully define a modern West, then perhaps the land itself can save the historian. At first glance the western environment, so striking, so distinctive, offers a hopeful basis for arguing the special significance of the region. Already we have had some impressive attempts to build a western historiography on an environmental foundation.

Once again Walter Prescott Webb played the pioneering role. "The heart of the West is," he insisted in 1957, "a desert, unqualified and absolute." Webb pointed to the band of relatively arid states running south from Montana, Idaho, and Wyoming, through Nevada,

Utah, and Colorado, down to Arizona and New Mexico. This desert, he argued, was "the dominating force" of the West, "a gigantic fire" within the region. The remainder of the West, those less arid places on either side of the desert, was tempered by the flame; Webb dismissed California and Texas, Washington and North Dakota, with the label "Desert-rim States." From these insights Webb spun out an intriguing tale of limits. "Granted the prevailing influence of the desert," he wrote, "it is obvious that the West is in comparison to the East a land of deficiencies. It is full of negatives and short on positives." Webb offered a series of arresting notions: The desert West has served as a kind of national dumping ground, a place for such supposedly undesirable peoples as Native Americans and Asians; the desert West has been the one part of America where the federal government could own so much, because so much was unwanted; the desert West has been a refuge for the "bizarre," for Mormonism and gambling.[11]

In the thirty years since Webb staked out the desert, more pioneers have followed along behind him. Donald Worster, clearly influenced by Webb, described a West defined by the unequal control over the scarce water needed to exploit the desert. "This American West," Worster argued, "can best be described as a modern *hydraulic society*, which is to say, a social order based on the intensive, large-scale manipulation of water and its products in an arid setting." Gerald Nash noted another consequence of the desert: So much arid land has remained empty that the region is relatively less rural and more urban than the rest of the nation. For Nash, the twentieth-century West was notable for its populous towns and cities. He was so struck by the importance of these communities that he gave his textbook on the twentieth-century West, the first work of its kind, the subtitle *A Short History of an Urban Oasis*.[12]

Taken together, the work of Webb, Worster, and Nash suggests the possibilities of a regional interpretation that begins with the consequences of the land, that charts the ways the environment has shaped distinctive regional life. Of course, there are difficulties with each of these approaches. Although Webb's picture of the "gigantic fire" is captivating, obviously all the West is not a desert. Texas, California, the rest of the lush Pacific Coast, and the fertile Great Plains are defined by something more than their location along the edges of the desert states. The "hydraulic society" is another arresting vision, but Worster exaggerates the importance of water and the distinctiveness of the exploitation it has produced. Critical as the control of water may have been to much of the West, the region's economy has also been decisively shaped by other resources, such as minerals and federal defense dollars. The West is too complex an entity to encapsulate in the term "hydraulic society." Finally, it is hard to conclude that the West's distinctive contribution to modern America is its "urban oases." Nash is probably correct about the relative urbanization of the country's different regions, but somehow the Northeast seems to have embodied the city more than the West.

Still, Webb, Worster, and Nash are suggestive: The land and its consequences appear to set the West apart. But like the colonial and power shift interpretations, this approach to the modern West is still undeveloped. While we have important studies on aridity, irrigation, conservation, and urbanization, historians are only beginning to figure out the lay of the twentieth-century land.[13] Among other things, we need to know more about how the landscape has affected westerners' consciousness. What has it meant to live in a desert or an urban oasis or a hydraulic society?

Historians working on this frontier will have to deal with some dangers. When the western landscape becomes more than desert, waterways, or cities, when it becomes more variegated and complex, the region can crumble in our hands. Historians and social scientists have long been offering all sorts of subregional schemes for the West.[14] There is nothing wrong with that, but we have to decide whether the West is a unified entity or simply a collection of different areas, each distinctive in its way. Do lush Seattle and desert Utah inhabit the same region?

Historians also have to confront the possibility that a distinctive environment may not translate into a distinctive regional society. That possibility is especially evident in the work of Nash and Worster. Each historian began with the most clearly unusual characteristic of the West: its arid land. Yet the regional edifices Nash and Worster built on that land look very much like the architecture of the rest of the United States. Nash's urban West seems to resemble urban society elsewhere. Worster, following Karl Wittfogel, argues the peculiar character of "hydraulic society." But Worster's tale of corporate exploitation in the West resembles tales of exploitation in the cotton fields of the South, the sweatshops of New York, and the factories of New England; capitalism is capitalism. The desert West is unique, but is the urban West or the capitalist West different enough from the rest of the country? At this point it is not at all obvious that the land alone can save the region.

A third basis for a twentieth-century West lies in the past. Like the modern South, the region can be defined by its history. There is some irony to this since most historians of the modern region have tended to dismiss the major element of earlier western history, the frontier. But the past—including the unfashionable frontier—has shaped the twentieth-century West in critical ways.

A historical approach does present us with a certain paradox. We might almost say that while the modern South is defined by its history, the modern West is defined by its lack of history. Walter Prescott Webb was the first to grasp the point. "Historically, the West has no depth, no long background of slow development," he realized. "Its story is told in current events. It came on the scene too late to participate in the founding of the nation or to prevent its dissolution in the Civil War."[15] Of course, this is an exaggeration, and of course, it is an insult to the Native Americans, who had lived in the West for thousands of years before the whites arrived. But there is a kernel of truth to Webb's observation. The West entered the Union late and last; that accident of timing has had considerable impact on the region.

For one thing, it meant that the political structures of the East and West would be markedly different. Mass political parties appeared in the East in the first half of the nineteenth century, a heady period of democracy when "universal" suffrage and partisanship were glorified. But when the territorial West began to develop its own politics in the Gilded Age and the Progressive Era, parties, partisanship, and even the suffrage were under attack. Westerners did not necessarily deplore party politics any more than did easterners. In the East, though, the Republican and Democratic parties—long-established organizations—had the institutional strength to resist their attackers; in the West, the parties had not had the chance to develop such organizational strength. The consequences were felt for decades. At the turn of the century state and even local party machines were far more prevalent in the Northeast and the Midwest. More strikingly, traditional party organizations endured well into the 1960s in these regions—but not in the West. While we do not fully understand the reasons for this situation, it does seem clear that the West's late entrance into American electoral politics had a profound impact on its party structure.[16]

That structure, in turn, affected the course of western politics in the twentieth century. Largely without traditional party machines, the West has been more open than the East and South to the less partisan innovations of twentieth-century politics. It comes as no surprise that such antiparty reforms of the Progressive Era as the initiative, referendum, and recall flourished, and even originated, in the

West. Nor is it surprising that the woman suffrage movement, with its strongly antiparty and sometimes antidemocratic roots, found early success in the West. And we should not be surprised to find that the modern, advertised style of political campaigns took quick hold in the West, home of the first political consulting firm. These developments had ironic consequences for western democracy. Weakly socialized by parties, only sporadically engaged by advertised campaigns, westerners were less likely than easterners to exercise that fundamental democratic right—the right to vote—for most of the twentieth century.[17]

The timing of western history has also affected the enduring role of the federal government in the region. The territories of the East— Indiana, Ohio, and the others—came under Washington's control in the early nineteenth century, when Americans had a more limited conception of the responsibilities and powers of government. But much of the West retained territorial status in the late nineteenth century and even the early twentieth century, when the reach and pretensions of government had increased considerably. Washington was far more ready to intervene in the life of the West than in the East. And because the West was essentially the last part of America to be "settled," the federal government had special incentives to remain; there was nowhere else to go—nowhere else to put the Indians and the military bases, nowhere else to set up the national parks and forests, nowhere else to claim millions of acres of land. As a result, the twentieth-century West maintains a unique relationship with Washington. The federal government has pumped an extraordinary amount of money—three hundred billion dollars from 1850 to 1970—into the West; in some western states it is the largest employer.[18]

We do not want to exaggerate the impact of history, or the accident of timing, on modern western politics. These structural differences between the West and the rest of the country—the weakness of political parties, the strong presence of the federal government—did not make westerners into a lasting political bloc. Political scientists have long since conceded the numerous divisions within the western electorate.[19] But it does seem that the pattern of political development in the West has given the region a special role in national politics. Because of the weakness of the major parties, the West has been vulnerable to insurgency from the left and right. Unusual ideas seem to have a greater chance to find the light of day—think of the Wobblies, or Upton Sinclair's EPIC (Campaign to End Poverty in California) or Francis Townsend's old-age revolving pension plan or Barry Goldwater's conservatism. Radicalism never seized the West, of course.

For one thing, the region's political structure let new ideas emerge but also acted to limit their impact. Because political apathy was so prevalent in the West, particularly among the poor, more radical movements had difficulty mobilizing a constituency.

The region's relationship with the federal government had similarly contradictory implications. Westerners had strong reasons to embrace the federal government—and strong reasons to loathe it. Not unexpectedly, therefore, the West has never been consistent in its thinking about Washington. More important, that sort of ambivalence pushes the region toward extremes. In the 1930s westerners looked more favorably on active government than did easterners or southerners.[20] After World War II westerners led the rejection of the activist state.

The influence of history on the twentieth-century region is apparent in yet another way. As we have seen, historians of the modern West consider the frontier essentially irrelevant to their subject. Frederick Jackson Turner himself announced that the frontier was gone; western historians have not been about to disagree. Good liberals, they are uncomfortable with the violence and exploitation of the frontier. Good scholars, they are understandably eager to reveal an older interpretation's shortcomings. But perhaps they have written off the frontier too quickly.

For one thing, it has not disappeared completely. As commentators have long recognized, pace Turner, the frontier did not come to a close in 1890. While most historians of the twentieth-century West were abandoning Turner, Howard Lamar has argued that the region features a "persistent frontier." He notes, for instance, the movement of population into the Great Plains until 1919 and 1920 and into the Pacific Northwest during World War II. Moreover, much of the West remains relatively undeveloped even today. Lamar believes that the persistent frontier continues to shape the western consciousness. "[The] fact is that the trans-Mississippi West, or certainly large parts of it, are now more regionally self-conscious than they have been since Populist days," he contends. "Aided by the immutable presence of distinct physiographic regions and a modern-day states' rights movement, this self-consciousness has been made the more significant by the fact that today's national debate over ecology, pollution, and the quality of life tends to center in the West and mainly concerns the future of the West."[21] Historians have hardly begun to pursue Lamar's provocative ideas, but his central contention seems unassailable: The frontier continues to form the modern West. More broadly, the region's past shapes its present.

All that is well enough, but it would be idle to pretend that a historical foundation for the modern West is any more stable than are the environment, colonialism, or the power shift. Single-cause explanations have a compelling, seductive power; it would be satisfying to find the one factor that determines the course of the twentieth-century West and sets the region apart from the rest of the nation. But we are not going to find that magic variable. The truth is that no single factor—history, environment, interregional relationships—is enough to define a distinctive modern West. But taken together, these factors can create a powerful historical equation. Their role in the development of modern conservatism indicates the possibilities.

The West has played a crucial part in the rise of the New Right since the Second World War. Of course, the region is not the only birthplace of modern conservatism. New England produced William F. Buckley and Robert Welch; the South, George Wallace and Jerry Falwell; the Midwest, M. Stanton Evans and Phil Crane.[22] But the great leaders of conservatism, Barry Goldwater and Ronald Reagan, are westerners. That is no accident, because the West powerfully shaped the outlook and career of each man.

Goldwater, the John the Baptist of the New Right, is a synthesis of the modern West. A native of Arizona, Goldwater bears the mark of the diverse western environment—desert, "hydraulic society," and "urban oasis." In his autobiography he movingly recounts his days spent variously in Arizona's desert canyons, along the Colorado River ("part of my chemistry"), and on the streets of the bustling latter-day Phoenix. Goldwater also sees himself as a product of the frontier and its mythology. He spent his formative years, he recalls, on "the American frontier . . . my native Arizona when it was still a territory." There he absorbed the Turnerian vision: "My mother spoke a lot about our country when we were kids—our heritage of freedom, the history of Arizona, how individual initiative had made the desert bloom." Not surprisingly Goldwater, though a businessman, did not turn into some western variant of the "organization man"; he would never see his life and his country in terms of corporations, bureaucratic order, and limited opportunity. "My life," he writes, "parallels that of twentieth-century America—raw energy amid boundless land and unlimited horizons."[23]

At the same time, Goldwater has absorbed and responded to the peculiar constraints of western life. He experienced federal power firsthand: Washington owns thirty-two million acres—44 percent—of his home state; add in the land belonging to the state and the Indians, Goldwater notes, and only 17 percent of Arizona is "in private hands." It is no shock, then, to learn that Goldwater ran for the United States Senate in 1952 by attacking "America's new super state—burgeoning federal spending and a bloated bureaucracy."[24] Goldwater also experienced—and resented—the colonial dependence of the West on the East. He sees his struggle against Nelson Rockefeller and the other eastern powers of the Republican party as one more phase of the old colonial drama. "From the historical perspective of an Arizonan and Westerner. . . ," he writes, "I had no qualms about taking on the Eastern establishment, whether it was Rockefeller, the banks, or the large corporations, because we had long been dominated by these interests. For a century, the West had been a colony of big Eastern money—a boom when they had invested and a bust when they had pulled out of various mining and other operations. We had been left with ghost towns and holes in the ground where gold, silver, and large mineral deposits had been discovered." Drawing on the colonial past, Goldwater can even see modern conservatism as a new phase of western rebellion, "our new populist movement."[25]

Goldwater's crusade against Rockefeller and the eastern establishment was also shaped by the West's political structure and rising sense of power. Raised in the less partisan politics of the modern West, Goldwater has been a Republican but not a traditional party man. He began his political career shortly after World War II as a leader of a nonpartisan businessmen's campaign for municipal reform in Phoenix. Later, as a candidate for the presidency, he relied on conservatives outside the party mainstream. Goldwater has always felt free to see himself as a member of both the Republican party and the conservative movement. That movement, he believes, was fueled by the flow of population and wealth into the West and South after World War II. His conservatism represents not only the anger of western colonialism but also the building self-confidence of the power shift. Reaching for the leadership of the Republican party in the early 1960s, he wanted the organization to embrace "an emerging new America— the Sunbelt, the South, the West, the Middle West, and some of the East. . . ." More specifically, he saw his crusade as part of an "effort to move the party from the dominance of less than a dozen families and others in the East to hundreds of thousands of small businessmen and others in the South, West, and elsewhere."[26]

Goldwater took over the Republican party but missed his ultimate goal, the presidency, in 1964. That defeat did not force him to reconsider his fundamental outlook. His western experiences—the frontier, the land, colonialism, politics, the power shift—still converge in a conservatism that emphasizes freedom and individualism above all else. "Freedom has been the watchword of my political life," he insists. "I rose from a dusty little frontier town and preached freedom across this land all my days." Over his entire public career Goldwater has condemned "political and social engineers" and called for "greater self-reliance across the spectrum of American life."[27]

Goldwater's successor, Ronald Reagan, shares essentially the same viewpoint. A transplanted son of Illinois, Reagan nonetheless embraces the frontier mythology. Like Goldwater, Reagan loves the western environment, and like Goldwater, he resents federal power. Like Goldwater, he embodies both the anger of the colonial West and the rising strength of the power shift. Even more than Goldwater, he is the product of the less partisan politics of the West: the Democrat who could turn into a Republican; the charismatic great communicator who can be sold by the political consultants but who cannot carry his own Republican allies to power in Congress. Like Goldwater, Reagan has preached the western gospel of individualism and opportunity. But unlike Goldwater, he has been elected president. Reagan embodies the success of modern conservatism; he also embodies the continuing impact of the West on American life.[28]

Of course, we do not want to reduce the modern West to two privileged white male politicians. But their examples underscore some useful points. First, the lives of Goldwater and Reagan suggest the explanatory power of a western historiography built on the land, the past, and interregional relationships. Second, the role of the West in modern conservatism indicates the region's importance for twentieth-century American history. Historians of the region may want to put their claim modestly; regions will never dominate the historiography of the twentieth century as they do the nineteenth. Yet the West is clearly a factor in modern America. This is an era of Chinese-menu historiography, when scholars define topics by choosing and mixing two or three items from a list of categories: culture, class, race, ethnicity, gender, family, organization, and so on. At the least the West and the idea of regionalism belong on the menu.

But we can make a still more aggressive case for the West. Here again Goldwater and Reagan provide the ammunition. Notions of individualism—personal autonomy, mobility, and aspiration—run all through their stories. For historians of modern America, so sure of the dominance of centralization, organization, and bureaucracy, that should be an unsettling fact. Major American politicians are supposed to reflect the organizational society; they are supposed to be "corporate liberals," organization men who have absorbed the cardinal lessons of twentieth-century life—interdependence, the supremacy of the corporation and corporate culture, the usefulness of the activist state.[29] They are not supposed to take notions of individualism so seriously. But Goldwater and Reagan do—and they are not exactly corporate liberals either. Hardly hostile to the fundamental interests of corporations, these conservatives have found their ideological inspiration elsewhere—in a region, of all places. It takes western history, not organizational history, to account for these men and their ideology.

To be fair, western historians were as unprepared as organizational historians for individualistic modern conservatism. Since Turner, students of the West have been writing off individualism as a factor in regional life. Turner himself considered individualism one of the most important products of the frontier, but in the 1890s he feared that the disappearance of free land would spell its demise. In his later writings Turner suggested that Americans would trade individual autonomy for a powerful, activist state in order to preserve democracy, another frontier product.[30]

Yet individualism endured. Long after the nineteenth century the frontier experience continued to shape western and American life. Even if popular notions of the frontier have been a fantasy, that fantasy has affected the region and America as a whole. "The western myth. . . ," the historian Gene Gressley notes, "lives on." And not only in modern conservatism. A number of observers of twentieth-century America mark the persistence of frontier values, especially the emphasis on individualism, mobility, and freedom, in the face of corporatization, centralization, and bureaucratization. The men and women of the organizational society have a remarkably stubborn sense of the self, its possibilities, and its prerogatives. It is that individualist sensibility, not the corporations and the bureaucracy, that distinguishes the United States from other industrial nations. Why this should have been so, why individualism persisted and perhaps outlasted democracy, should be a central question of American historical writing.[31]

Students of the twentieth-century West ought to be in a particularly good position to provide some of the answers to that question. But to address the implications of individualism fully and accurately, western historians cannot let their aversion to the frontier and its consequences cloud their vision. Even the best works on the twentieth-century West have tended to explain many of those consequences away. Donald Worster disapprovingly notes the persistence of the frontier creed among westerners. "Again and again," he writes, "they told themselves and others that they were the earth's last free, wild, untrammeled people. Wearing no man's yoke, they were eternal cowboys on an open range." But Worster cannot accept these people's experience; this was not, he insists, the "real West." The "real West" was a place where people "ran along in straight, fixed lines: organized, regimented, incorporated men and women, the true denizens of the emergent West." Anything to the contrary, Worster maintains, was just "myth and rhetoric."[32] That "myth and rhetoric" were often unlovely, but they were just as real as the desert, the irrigation canals, and the glass towers. To accept and explore the individualist legacy of the frontier does not mean winking at exploitation in the West. Quite the opposite. We cannot understand inequality and domination across the region without understanding the character and functions of individualism. Instead of getting irritated with these self-deluded westerners, we ought to be asking how it was that they could maintain such beliefs. We can begin to see how Goldwater and Reagan could cling to individualism, but we need to know much more. "Individualism" is an extraordinarily capacious term; it has had many meanings for many people. What has it meant for different westerners? What has it done to their lives?[33]

To address the problem of individualism properly, western historians also have to abandon their own case of the colonial mentality. The region may have escaped dependence, but its historians have not. Insecure about their subject, western historians have rushed to follow historiographical fashion. They have been eager to fit the West into the mainstream of historical writing, to insist that, yes, the region shares in corporate exploitation or urban growth. They emphasize how much the region is like the rest of the country or, if they are feeling the surge of the power shift, how much the region leads the rest of the country into the future. So much of the writing about the twentieth-century West stresses how modern a place it is; Nash, for instance, calls the region the pacesetting society.[34] Ironically, western historians are undercutting their own enterprise. The very insistence that everything is up-to-date in western history serves largely to persuade other scholars that the region's historiography must be a colonial backwater. Modern American historians look at the writing on the West, find confirmation of what they already believe about the country as a whole, and, not surprisingly, dismiss western history.

Under the circumstances, students of the West ought to be emphasizing how much their region differs from the rest of the United States. Surely the twentieth-century West is modern. But it is also strikingly unmodern. It is a place where an ideology as outmoded as individualism could survive long years in the desert and then re-emerge dramatically in the politics of the 1960s, 1970s, and 1980s. Rather than just a pacesetting society, the twentieth-century West is a strange amalgam of new and old—a modern political and economic structure wedded to nineteenth-century ideas.

The region is more than that, of course. We have much to learn about the character of the twentieth-century West. But we can certainly proceed with the assurance that the region exists, that it shapes its people, that it significantly influences the course of the modern United States. Naturally there is a great deal to do before we can build the structure of the twentieth-century West with any aplomb. Western historians need to get on with the foundation. The organizational interpretation of modern America, with its drab corporate monoliths, badly needs some idiosyncratic western architecture.

Westering in the Twenty-first Century

Speculations on the Future of the Western Past

HOWARD R. LAMAR

The following passage from John Steinbeck's story *The Red Pony* should explain my use of the fourteenth-century Middle English word "westering" as part of the title of this essay. Steinbeck writes:

> It wasn't Indians that were important, nor adventures, nor even getting out of here. It was a whole bunch of people made into one crawling beast. And I was the head. It was westering and westering. Every man wanted something for himself, but the big beast that was all of them wanted only westering. I was the leader, but if I hadn't been there, someone else would have been the head. The thing had to have a head. . . .
>
> When we saw the mountains at last, we cried—all of us. But it wasn't getting there that mattered, it was movement and westering.[1]

Here Steinbeck captures in a few words the whole story of westward expansion, of pioneering, of what Frederick Jackson Turner called the frontier process, and Bernard De Voto dubbed the continental lure.

Steinbeck even embraces the much-quoted sentiment expressed by Henry David Thoreau: "Eastward I go only by force; but westward I go free."[2]

As useful and even occasionally accurate as the themes voiced by Steinbeck may have been in the past, every American, whether professional historian or educated layperson, knows that frontier days and westering in the historic sense of expansion and settlement have long been gone. Indeed, this is the first eloquent message of the editors' thoughtful opening essay to this volume and of the twelve original and challenging essays that follow.

The second eloquent message is that we must find new ways to rewrite the history of older Wests and a first way to write a coherent, intelligent history of the West in the twentieth century, a task that will stretch well into the twenty-first century. The disquieting effects of having to adopt newer, more complex explanations of American history have been brilliantly captured in some lines of Constantine Cavafy's poem "Waiting for the Barbarians":

Why should this uneasiness begin all of a sudden,
And confusion. How serious people's faces have become.
Why are all the streets and squares emptying so quickly,
And everybody turning home again so full of thought?
Because night has fallen and the Barbarians have not come.
And some people have arrived from the frontier;
They said there are no Barbarians any more.

And now what will become of us without Barbarians?—
Those people were some sort of a solution.[3]

Cavafy uses two words—frontiers and barbarians—that evoke two of the most mystical and mythical words in our national vocabulary: frontier and savage, which immediately call up images of pioneers and Indians and the conquest of the wilderness. These terms have come to be associated with a traditional set of such political words as liberty, freedom, democracy, and independence or with their caricatures: rugged individualism, lawlessness, violence, and popular sovereignty. Both Native Americans and white frontiersmen (one should say frontierspersons) or pioneers, as Cavafy might say, have served as a kind of solution to the dilemmas of American nationalism, for they and their confrontations provided Frederick Jackson Turner and his generation an explanation of American development and what then seemed an attractive key to our national character. However, for later generations, including our own, they provided a much less attractive explanation of the American character. These less complimentary interpretations of the frontier's meaning have been the main burden of Richard Slotkin's *Regeneration through Violence* and the major theme of Patricia Nelson Limerick's *The Legacy of Conquest*.[4]

The United States has been an urban, industrial, settled nation for well over a century, and it has been nearly a century since Frederick Jackson Turner stated his frontier hypothesis, yet we continue to discuss our national character in the now-atavistic terms he coined. One of the challenges the future historian of the West faces is how to interpret the American character in newer and more sophisticated terms while explaining why the myth of the frontier continues alive and well. Ann Fabian, in her "History for the Masses: Commercializing the Western Past," goes a long way to explain the persistence of the myth because of its emotional and therefore market value, while suggesting means by which we can study myth as a major force in American history.

As we approach the year 2000, we historians find that we have not yet put together a coherent history of the twentieth-century West. There have been some fine early textbook attempts, but what is most heartening is that new overall strategies are beginning to emerge, as evidenced by the three-day conference at Yale University in 1989 out of which came the twelve essays that make up this volume.[5]

That conference on "The Future of the Western Past" and this essay have also been inspired by the scores of centennials and bicentennials, both national and western, that have recently been observed or will take place in the last quarter of this century—and centennials are wonderful excuses for reinterpretations. Among those forthcoming will be the 100th anniversary in 1993 of Frederick Jackson Turner's famous address, "The Significance of the Frontier in American History," itself given at the Chicago world's fair, whose purpose was to celebrate the 400th anniversary of Columbus's discovery of America.[6] The quincentenary of what Alfred W. Crosby calls the Encounter in 1492 will likely produce a saturnalia of new interpretations.[7] At the least it will provide an occasion for the Indian view of the encounter to be heard for the first time.

One of the several centennials we have recently celebrated has been of the founding of the American territorial system, which was created by the passage of the Northwest Ordinance of 1787. That act was voted by a conservative-minded Confederation Congress anxious to bring law and order to frontier areas and to protect property without somehow seeming to impose imperial rule on these western regions. As the editors of this volume have noted in their joint essay, the way the Congress avoided the charge of imperialism was to promise frontier areas that after satisfactory settlement they could become states in the Union on an equal basis with all the other states.[8] As of today thirty-one of the fifty American states have passed through territorial apprenticeship—or "state-forming"—before being admitted to the Union.

That the territorial system was still a major operating feature of our federal system a hundred years after its passage was dramatically demonstrated on February 22, 1889, when Grover Cleveland signed what was called the Omnibus Bill, which admitted four states into the Union at once: North and South Dakota, Montana, and Washington. A year later Idaho and Wyoming territories were admitted, and Oklahoma received territorial status. Six years later Utah was admitted, and in 1907 Oklahoma became the forty-sixth state. Then after a series of politically inspired delays—many of them stemming from Congress's racist and anti-Catholic views of Mexican-Americans in New Mexico—Arizona and New Mexico were admitted to the Union in 1912. That same year Alaska was given a regular territorial government for the first time.[9]

For many observers 1912 marked the formal end of an old territorial system that in practical terms had already been replaced by an imperial one. The new American territorial system began when the United States annexed Hawaii in 1898 and acquired the Philippines, Puerto Rico, and Guam after the Spanish-American War. The federal government ruled these territories more arbitrarily than it had the continental territories and even established the disturbing precedent that citizenship and full rights did not follow the flag.[10]

Even so, when Alaska and Hawaii began to seek admission to the Union as states in the 1950s, political issues as old as the Union itself arose. Southern interests, it turned out, did not care for the multiracial societies of Hawaii and Alaska because giving the population of those states voting rights would affect the status of blacks in the South. In addition, the familiar game of partisanship was replayed when the Republican party began to fear that the two new states might go Democratic, and under the leadership of President Eisenhower the party sought to dampen admission efforts.[11] To complicate the situation even more, local politicians and businessmen used to the territorial system worried about their future status under a state government. Hawaiian

sugar interests actually veered between prostate and antistate positions depending on what seemed best for their business.[12] It does not
seem too farfetched to argue that both William Cronon's study of copper mining in Alaska and Jay Gitlin's analysis of the local dynamics
of trade with native peoples in French Louisiana can help explain both
the colonial status and the politics of statehood of Alaska and Hawaii.

The coexistence of native Hawaiians, persons of Chinese and
Japanese origins, and white Americans on the Islands and the coexistence of Indians, Aleuts, Eskimos, and white Americans in Alaska
also call to mind Sarah Deutsch's plea to study race, class, and gender,
as well as George Miles's insistence that we focus on successful racial
and ethnic interchanges over time rather than on confrontation. In
short, the approaches and models for study proposed in all the preceding essays could be used to inform us better about the history of Alaska
and Hawaii, which are two of the richest and most varied "landscapes
of enclaves" in the United States.[13]

When Alaska and Hawaii were eventually admitted in 1959, it
seemed that the final act of state making had occurred. Yet when George
Bush became president in 1989, he declared his willingness to support
statehood for Puerto Rico. Meanwhile, the citizens of the District of
Columbia had intensified their long-standing campaign for statehood
or, if not that, for full representation in Congress.

These latest admission efforts at least appeared to be a totally
new story, for Puerto Ricans were divided over which of three courses
of action to take: to ask for outright independence, to retain commonwealth status, or to seek admission to the Union as the fifty-first state.
Familiar shibboleths soon appeared, however. American businessmen
in Puerto Rico questioned the wisdom of coming under a regular federal tax system, and some members of Congress had doubts about
assuming the welfare costs of Puerto Rico once it was a state. Other
federal legislators tried to require Puerto Ricans to make English their
official language just as Congress had attempted to do for Mexican-
Americans when New Mexico sought statehood in 1912.[14] Nor should
it be forgotten that the preservation of the French language and laws
had been an issue when the United States acquired Louisiana in 1803.
The status of Spanish was also debated in gold rush California in 1849
and after. In brief, Puerto Rico's campaign for statehood demonstrates
once again the key role new regions, whether western or not, play in
the evolution of a truly democratic and pluralistic United States.

The western territories of post-Civil War America liked to describe
themselves as mere colonies seeking economic independence and political

equality within the federal system. They suffered political abuse, economic fleecing, and local corruption (although, it must be said, the status of white Americans west of the Mississippi was notably free rather than colonial). Yet once they had achieved political equality in the form of statehood, the same states found themselves under the economic control of eastern-owned railroads and mining companies, midwestern milling firms, Chicago meat-packers, and Wall Street. The language of colonialism continued to apply in the new situation.

Ironically, when big-business control of the West appeared to have been broken in the depression-ridden 1930s, and the West came to enjoy unparalleled prosperity during World War II, the federal government, first as a source of relief and reform and later as the bankroller for defense and aerospace industries in the West, became the new arbiter of western destinies. The political and economic language of colonial protest against imperial Washington continues unabated today.[15]

The irony is that what sounds like colonial protest often flows from a true regional culture and sense of place. As Michael E. McGerr has noted in "Is There a Twentieth-Century West?" a local political tradition can grow out of a region's unique experiences and can produce its own heroes, as exemplified by the rise of Sam Rayburn, Barry Goldwater, Ronald Reagan, Lyndon B. Johnson, Richard Lamm, and many others. Confrontations between the federal government and the states or regions, far from disappearing, are likely to increase in the twenty-first century for four compelling reasons: (1) Because of the economic and population resources of California and Texas, their bargaining with the federal government will almost be that of equals. (2) At the other extreme will be states with limited resources that will be forced to depend heavily on government help. (3) The enchanted areas of the West—the national parks, monuments, and forest areas— will continue to be a major concern of the government and the tourist-minded states. (4) As long as vital national resources like oil, timber, and water are associated with the West, they will provoke national and regional confrontations.

Already present in all these operations is a vast federal bureaucracy. Americans are more used to denouncing bureaucracy than to studying it, but its rise to prominence and even centrality in our daily lives, whether at the federal, state, municipal, or local level, is perhaps the most important institutional development in the United States in this century.

Bureaucracy has long been the subject of penetrating studies by historians and social scientists in European countries, especially in France.[16] Without analyzing how a huge and often confused administrative power structure works, we cannot begin to understand the United States in the twentieth century, let alone the western experience now and in the future. Professor Jan Deutsch has argued that if the key to nineteenth-century America was the frontier, the central symbol of this century is bureaucracy.[17] In his *Rivers of Empire* Donald Worster suggests that in certain regions of the world the scarcity of water has always produced a need for regulation and, therefore, a bureaucracy whose size and monopoly power often mean a loss of freedom.[18]

Power shifts within the federal bureaucracy have strongly affected the West. In the past fifty years, for example, control of the Bureau of Indian Affairs has shifted from exclusive white control to increasing Native American control. In the New Deal era Secretary of the Interior Harold Ickes and Secretary of Agriculture Henry A. Wallace assumed enormous personal power over western lands, forest and mineral reserves, and crop production. Although no secretary of the interior or secretary of agriculture has enjoyed such power since, a largely anonymous bureaucracy has in recent decades assumed even greater power in these areas.[19]

During the Second World War, government power brokers like Jesse Jones dealt with big-business leaders such as A. P. Giannini, Henry J. Kaiser, and William E. Boeing to achieve fantastic levels of production of planes, ships, and other wartime matériel. These joint government-industry activities, as everyone knows, brought the West an unprecedented degree of prosperity and a new migration of settlers, which helped turn western towns into major cities.[20] The postwar economies of many western states were characterized by the rise to prominence of the Defense Department and associated agencies.

With the radical changes in Russian-American relations since 1989, the overwhelming defense presence in the West might well give way to federal environmental control policies that are already causing some of the most ferocious federal-state-regional debates in living memory.[21] Historians will have to understand and analyze policy objectively, taking into account the language and mind-set of both the bureaucrat and the westerner. They must, moreover, reveal the faults and virtues of environmental regulation, rather than resort to an older pejorative language of populist distaste for faceless, imperious power.

Bureaucracy thrives on rules. Rules suggest laws, and laws lead to litigation. In the past fifty years both citizens and the state and federal governments have hired armies of lawyers to fight their battles in legislative halls or in courts. The current debate over water needs, pollution, the environment, and development has been cast in legal terms. In addition to studying the history of these endless litigations, we should ask why the debate has taken this form. Are we a legal-minded people, or, as one suspects, have Americans become so accustomed to using the law as a selfish manipulative tool—from the time of the first Indian treaty on through two centuries of abuse of public lands—that it is a fundamental part of our culture? The new bureaucracy itself now seems to be using the law, sometimes callously, to achieve its own ends. The point is not to condemn but to ask how we came to this litigiousness and why we continue it.[22]

Territories, states, and regions may be considered the arenas in which peoples and groups with conflicting interests constantly negotiate for what they consider their due. Their negotiations comprise an intricate combination of what the editors in their essay call *boundary making*, *market making*, and *self-shaping*. In recounting the oldest, most classic frontier negotiation of all—the confrontation of Indian and Euroamerican in war or in treaty making—we have generally told the story with the Indians in retreat, often passive, their various cultures on the way to extinction. But as George Miles reminds us in his essay "To Hear an Old Voice," Indian culture is flexible and innovative, and the Indians themselves more than foils for, or mere antagonists of, whites. Miles argues that because Europeans and Indians jointly made this continent, a history of interchange rather than confrontation is what we should stress. We must find out what new institutions Native Americans and Europeans developed to mediate their interaction. Then, says Miles, we will "begin to develop a historiographic tradition that integrates the Native American experience into the broader story of America." In addition, Jay Gitlin's essay, "On the Boundaries of Empire," notes that local Indian-white interchange, as in French Louisiana, often achieved successful accommodations that eluded or defied royal policies.[23]

To use yet another recent centennial event to illustrate the promise of Miles's and Gitlin's approach, let us look at the famous Oklahoma land rush of April 1889, which, incidentally, was celebrated in April 1989 by a reenactment of the run at Guthrie. The Kansas boomers who successfully lobbied to open up what is now central Oklahoma assumed that Oklahoma Indians were on the decline. Moreover, with the passage of the Dawes Severalty Act of 1887, pioneers were certain that the Indians would have to become small homestead farmers, freeing still more tribal land for white occupation.[24]

But the various Indian groups in Oklahoma—including all members of the Five Civilized Tribes—responded in different ways to the land rushes, and this provides dramatic support for Miles's argument for studies of interchange. The Five Civilized Tribes protested these latest white invasions not with violence and war but through petitions to Congress, the hiring of lawyers, and rational, if reluctant, accommodation. Having dealt with whites since the seventeenth century, first in the Southeast and later in Oklahoma, the Cherokees, for example, had adopted white farming practices, owned black slaves, adopted Christianity, and promulgated a constitution and tried to form a state while still living in Georgia and Tennessee. By the 1880s this particular tribe was as aware of white society and of the American political and legal system and its curious ways as any group of Native Americans in the country. The Cherokees had also developed a Cherokee syllabary, the learning of which made them a literate nation and helped them set up a rather impressive educational system. At the same time they did not believe in individual property ownership and commercial sale of land.[25] Despite the debilitating effects of removal and violent feuds within the tribe, the Cherokees had made a comeback and were doing fairly well when the land rushes began in 1889.[26]

Ironically, one of the first promoters of the sale of Oklahoma Indian lands to whites was Elias Boudinot, Jr., an Indian who was himself a lawyer for a railroad. In 1871 Boudinot had proposed the sale and allotment of Indian lands in a way that anticipated the disposals of 1889 and after. Other Indian leaders disagreed and spoke eloquently of defending their last homeland. They hated Boudinot, and in the early 1880s he and Kansas City railroad promoters were ordered out of the Creek Nation's capital at Muskogee. But the pressure on Indian land persisted. Meanwhile, the Choctaw Nation was already leasing coal mines in its area, and long before 1889 most tribes were leasing lands to Texas and Kansas cattlemen for grazing purposes.[27]

After 1889 white settlers came en masse, some to newly opened tracts, but tens of thousands of southerners and Texans to live among the Five Tribes even before division into individual ownership by severalty had occurred. The Indians alternately resisted and accommodated. In 1899, for example, the Chickasaws petitioned Congress to defeat a new severalty bill that they called a "land shark" bill.[28] Certain Cherokees and Creeks signed the petition as well. Yet only a year

265

later Pleasant Porter, the newly elected principal chief of the Creeks, delivered his first annual address to the Creek Council. The message was mostly about laws, education, land fraud, and the prospect of severalty. Porter, who had been a vigorous, even heroic crusader for tribal political independence and against severalty, said in effect, let us accept the new American system imposed upon us and seek opportunities under it. Porter urged his people, to use present-day slang, "to get in on the act."[29]

Chief Porter also gave his hearers a most important message in a remarkable peroration:

> The vitality of our race still persists. We have not lived for naught. We are the original discoverers of this continent and the conquerors of it from the animal kingdom, and on it first taught the arts of peace and war, and first planted the institutions of virtue, truth and liberty. The European Nations found us here and were made aware that it was possible for them to exist and subsist here. We have given the European People our thought forces, the best blood of our ancestors having been intermingled with [that of] their best statesmen and living citizens. We have made ourselves an indestructible element in their national history.
>
> (October 2, 1900)[30]

What Chief Porter was saying was truly significant. In 1900 white Americans were busy reading Indians—as a declining race and population—out of their history. In a single strong statement Porter put Indians back in, saying not only that his people would survive but that "we are an indestructible element in their national history." Chief Porter was a prophet, for only in the past thirty or forty years have Indian history and American history come to be merged, and that because of the emergent emphasis on social history, minority history, and ethnohistory. It is further the case that Chief Porter expressed himself in terms of historical concepts, an intellectual construct that Euroamericans had sometimes argued that Indian Americans did not possess.

Historians and political scientists have described the early white citizens of central and western Oklahoma as midwesterners interested in organizing towns as much as acquiring land, Republican in affiliation, and in favor of democratic government, development, and reform of abuses. Their protests gave rise to the important Populist party there in the 1890s.[31] On the other hand, historians describe white leaders in Indian Territory as less interested in popular government, more conservative, and largely southern and Texan in origin. These later arrivals were anxious to stay as free of federal controls as possible. Some historians argue that these white leaders in Indian Territory made a living fleecing the Five Tribes of their wealth and property.[32] But many were also married to Indian women. One is reminded of Sarah Deutsch's remark that "The experiences of both majority and minority groups occurred in the context of multiracial or multicultural dynamics. Any larger historical narrative of the region must partake of an interactive multifaceted model. It must allow the constant interaction and diversity within and between groups itself to become the story. By doing so, it builds a framework within which we can understand the continual tensions created by forces that simultaneously erode boundaries and re-create them."

The story of the very different Indian and southern heritage in eastern Oklahoma is not one that can be pursued here, but it is worth noting that Indians and whites held the Sequoyah Convention in 1905 to propose the formation of an Indian state separate from Oklahoma. The leader of that convention was William ("Alfalfa Bill") H. Murray, a white who was a member of the Chickasaw Nation by virtue of having a Chickasaw wife. Murray was steeped in the lore of constitutions, and when the Sequoyah proposal got nowhere, he was elected to the Oklahoma Constitutional Convention in 1906. There he and others from eastern Oklahoma took control and added many of the clauses of the Sequoyah constitution into the Oklahoma one. They also introduced a number of Populist and social reform measures, the latter proposed by Kate Barnard.[33]

In brief, future Governor Murray and his political allies combined Indian, southern, and western heritages in a reform constitution designed to correct the economic, political, and social ills of the day. Although federal officials such as President Theodore Roosevelt, future President William Taft, and Secretary of the Interior Ethan Allen Hitchcock denounced the document, it represented the wishes of many peoples in one place, and it beautifully illustrated Oklahoma's transition from frontier to self-conscious region.[34]

In his provocative, wide-ranging essay "Americans, Mexicans, and Métis," John Mack Faragher suggests a community approach to the comparative study of the North American frontier. Here one finds superb examples of types of early communities and a whole set of analytical models by which to study them. It almost goes without saying that these models could be used to study twentieth-century communities of all ethnic groups and types, for new communities continue to be formed whether they are towns created and sustained by a factory or defense plant, a ghetto for boat people, Mexican communities that grew up on the edges of a western town or city, a highly publicized retirement community, or the building of yet another suburb of Los Angeles, Seattle, or Houston. The communities created by real estate speculators in both this century and the last are especially interesting.

One such community—fascinating for its unique features and for its universality—was founded in 1906 when a group of black businessmen proposed to open a new Oklahoma town, Red Bird.[35] Calling themselves the Red Bird Investment Company, the officers were successful black Americans whose own Horatio Alger-like rise to affluence suggested that others might emulate them. One was a doctor, one a druggist, several were lawyers and businessmen, and one was an editor. They made Red Bird—near Muskogee—seem the wave of the future. They boasted of railroad connections, rich lands, and a possible oil well. They sounded like latter-day boomers and sooners as they declared, "Now comes the great Indian Territory, the last *good country* of the great southwest to be settled." Waxing eloquent about the fertile valley of the Arkansas and Verdigris rivers, they used poetry to make their point, declaring:

You behold a land of blue skies and copious showers,
Clear streams and blooming flowers,
Balmy breezes and leafy bowers

Foods and vegetables were described as growing in semitropical luxuriance. Urging their potential investors to take Horace Greeley's words seriously, they said, "[C]ome west and grow up with the country," adding that Oklahoma would be a state soon and then "the real boom will come." But their main point was that an area favorable to blacks had been found and it was being built in Oklahoma. The brochure was full of ironies. Red Bird was in what was still Creek Nation Lands—but its Americanness was what was stressed. "The time of the painted Indian on the war path, and the desperado has gone away for the income of civilization, culture and refinement. The Indian Territory of today is as free from the taint of wild barbaric life as is the city of Boston. . . ."[36] Here, in effect, were three societies, Indian, black, and white, in Sarah Deutsch's words interacting and responding, eroding and re-creating "all kinds of boundaries."

The western experience is supposed to be a story of action, conquest, and practical achievement, secular in tone and nonintellectual and nonintrospective. Emerson is said to have remarked, "the trouble with the West was that it was all out of doors." Yet Spanish, French, and American missionaries were key figures in the early West, and the Five Civilized Tribes were mostly Protestant Christian by the mid-nineteenth century. White religious beliefs were central in the Ghost Dance movement and in the formation of the Native American Church. Oral Roberts is only one of the many western fundamentalist preachers active today.

In assessing historians' neglect of the role of religion in the West, Dennis Michael Quinn has reminded us in his essay that four of the geographer Wilbur Zelinsky's seven religious regions in the United States are in the West, perhaps the most distinctive of which is that of the Mormons. Although Quinn does not find most contemporary westerners to be churchgoers, he notes that millions listen to radio and television evangelists and that scores of Asian, Sikh, and Muslim sects are beginning to present opportunities for alternate religions in the West. There are, he reports, 306 cults in California alone, whereas New York, the second most populated state, has only 83. In the 1970s a half million Caucasian Americans received some form of Buddhist instruction.

In texts and specialized studies, religion in the West appears as a separate topic, if at all—somewhat like the coverage of the environment and women. This deliberate segregation of what is the central focus of many people's lives seems indefensible. As Quinn rightly notes, naming denominations and counting their numbers will not furnish us with an adequate religious history. Instead, we must study religious groups and their beliefs with the anthropological, sociological, and historical models used to understand race, class, gender, and community. In addition, we must investigate individual value systems that are not necessarily religious but that still provide a clue to a person's ethical code. Professor Laurie Maffly-Kipp's recent study of Protestant missionaries and ministers in gold rush California finds that while the ministers were convinced that their congregations were uninterested and unfaithful (in part because they did not go to church or support the minister), the majority of the miners themselves followed a noninstitutional code of Christian ethics that was, in fact, a kind of public religion.[37] With the rise of new sects, the debate over religious belief and abortion, and the inevitable interchange with Asian religions and cults, the historian studying religion in the West faces a difficult task. But as Quinn himself concludes: "There is much to be done in understanding and writing the history of religion in the West."

In her thoughtful essay "Engendering the West" Katherine G. Morrissey observes that the West is mostly associated with a masculine image, and she then explains how feminist studies and postmodernist approaches can help tell us how women came to grips with the ideology of the times. Each situation was different—some good, some confining, some appalling. Obviously by studying the role of women and families, we can achieve a far richer, fuller, and more balanced history.

Because existing studies of western women have focused largely on the nineteenth-century frontier experience, the opportunities to write accounts of women in the twentieth century seem myriad and golden.[38] We should learn, for example, how women adjusted to work in the marketplace, who entered the professions and why, or how wives and daughters in traditional Indian, Asian, Mexican, and Mormon households dealt with the "outside." The greatest challenge, however, will be to find ways to integrate women's history with the general western narrative and to make certain that in the narrative they speak with their own voices.

One of the new approaches to western history is linguistic. In her delightful essay "Making the Most of Words: Verbal Activity and Western America," Patricia Nelson Limerick claims that in ignoring verbal activity in our histories of the American West, we have failed to escape from the treachery of words that create a fantasy West. "We do not . . . want to be suckers," she writes. "Yet we know that western history is virtually the P. T. Barnum of historical fields, providing opportunities galore for suckers to confuse literal fact with literary fact." Such deliberate confusions of myth or legend with fact are wonderfully illustrated in Ann Fabian's essay "History for the Masses," especially in her account of how hucksters' use romantic western images to sell books or clothes.

In future studies of the West, Limerick suggests that we use the newspaper and the printed word along with laws, orders, treaties, and the actions of judges and the statements of lawyers, for "most of the central struggles over power, property, and profit in the West came to a focus in legislatures and courtrooms. . . ." Finally, she makes a plea that any future history of the western past should include a cultural study of verbal behavior, a study that could "encompass Indians, Hispanics, Asians, blacks, and Euroamericans of all backgrounds."

Historians presuming to write a new history of the West will find that they have a linguistic challenge of their own—that is, to find a new vocabulary that will explain in nontechnical terms this multifaceted new synthesis. Up to now we have borrowed a vocabulary from the social scientists and the social historians to analyze race, class, and gender, and concepts from geographers to explain space and place. In similar fashion we have appropriated ecological and historical terms to convey environmental history, and we have drawn freely from anthropological and ethnological terms to write Indian history. If we add to these the jargons of the legal historian and that of the bureaucrat, the new history will sound like a veritable Tower of Babel. This is undoubtedly one reason the histories of the environment, and of women's history and Indian history, are so often found in separate text chapters and monographs. But there may be a way out. Just as Hawaiians and Pacific Northwest Indians developed a pidgin language to communicate with whites, we should find a historical pidgin, as it were, in order to tell the complex story of the West in an easily understood narrative.[39]

Rather than develop an Esperanto for western historical writing, however, there are other possible alternatives. One has been suggested by Clyde A. Milner II in his thoughtful essay "The View from Wisdom: Four Layers of History and Regional Identity." Drawing on autobiographical accounts by four Montanans, Milner has let them speak for themselves while noting what they chose to remember and to forget. At the same time he connects their account to larger themes in western and national history. One result is that each memoirist defines both himself or herself and comments on the local or regional world in which each lived.

In a sense all the essayists in this volume have attempted to find the right voice for their particular fields or topics, and certainly one way to do this is to let men, women, and children of all races and groups speak for themselves.[40] It is probably impossible to write adequate accounts of Chinese or Japanese life without having the first-person testimony not only of men and women but of what children remembered.[41]

More generally, the vernacular languages of the different western regions still lack their linguistically trained social historians.[42] We need to analyze even the religious language of the fundamentalist preachers whose audiences obviously understand what they are saying. Perhaps most curious of all, there has been little recent historical study of folk-lore and regional literature, two subjects that absolutely fascinated earlier generations of scholars, including the anthropologist Franz Boas of Columbia University and the literary scholar George Lyman Kit-tredge of Harvard, who were constantly interacting with regional folklorists such as J. Frank Dobie and John A. Lomax. The waxing and waning fortunes of the American, Midwestern, and Texas Folk-lore societies provide clues to what past westerners thought was their own traditional nonliterary voice. The incredible popularity in their time of Dobie, Lomax, and, later, Woody Guthrie, suggests both a western form of self-identification of the sort Milner discusses and a way of communicating western identity to the rest of the United States.[43] The national and regional popularity of Charles Wilson's and William Ferris's recent *Encyclopedia of Southern Culture* (1989) indicates that a similar volume is needed for the West.[44] James M. Gregory's *American Exodus: The Dust Bowl Migration and Okie Culture in California* (1989) provides a splendid model of what might be done to find the contemporary popular cultural voice of western groups.[45]

Although later generations have questioned Walter Prescott Webb's regional and global interpretations of history, his popularity will probably endure because he found a Great Plains voice that was itself fashioned as much from regional self-imaging and folklore as from the hard facts about the Great Plains frontier.[46] In similar fashion Robert Athearn has given voice to a High Plains Rocky Mountain regional culture, and Wallace Stegner has captured a Mormon voice.[47] Only by listening to western voices can we find the means to communicate what we want to say both to the westerner and to the general public.

Martha A. Sandweiss's insightful essay "Views and Reviews: Western Art and Western History" analyzes the meanings that adhere to western paintings and photographs quite apart from the landscapes and objects they depict. Further, by tracing how these meanings change over time, she suggests that we can get at the cultural biases or needs of the public viewing this art. Sandweiss has, in effect, identified ways in which the public's images of the West can be read more accurately and themselves be used as a historical source. She has found a visual voice, as it were, that can assist in writing a new history.

But just as Clyde Milner's Montanans—Si Gray and Cornelius Hedges—came to see themselves as westerners and identified with a special set of events and a region, so Sandweiss describes Laura Gil-pin, the photographer, as seeing the western landscape differently—indeed regionally—because she grew up in Colorado. In similar ways

272

artists who grew up in the West mediated between what they saw and felt locally and the orthodox styles of painting the professional art world imposed on them if they were to be recognized as artists.[48] Because of this peer pressure, hundreds of western artists from the 1880s to World War I used impressionist and postimpressionist styles to depict their homelands.

The personal response of the artist to his or her region was often quite moving. Henry Varnum Poor, who grew up in western Kansas, recalled that he loved "every bit of the familiar land and even more its familiar creatures."[49] Swedish-born but Paris-trained Birger Sandzén, who taught art and French at Bethany College in Lindsborg, Kansas, for much of his life, used an impressionist style to depict the Kansas landscape, but Kansans so loved his drawings that he became the focus of an intense local pride.[50] In this century especially, the works of western artists—Asian, Indian, Mexican, and Euroamerican—deserve to be seen as yet another visual resource for the historian.[51]

Just as we have finished laying an elaborate groundwork for a new western history, Michael E. McGerr confronts us with the disturbing question, "Is There a Twentieth-Century West?" Given the evidence presented in the twelve essays and his own conclusion that there are distinctive western political traditions, the answer would seem to be a resounding yes. Even so, two guidelines probably should be followed in writing its history: (1) The regional story should be presented in such a way that without it our national history would be incomplete, and (2) it must move beyond special pleading for certain topics to an objective comprehension of the whole, even to the acknowledgment that many events have ambiguous meanings. This approach would foster more accurate accounts of what George Miles has called Indian-white interchange, or Jay Gitlin's findings about the contradictions in the operation of trade and diplomacy in French imperial borderlands, or the ways in which a modern-day industry such as Kennecott Copper affects and is affected by factors of distance, climate, and environment as well as by business conditions. It would allow the endlessly ambiguous meanings of language and the manipulation of image to become keys to understanding rather than baffling obstacles.

Perhaps the most difficult task facing the new western history is surmounting the fact that the West is so identified with currently controversial issues—the fate of the spotted owl or the oil spills in Alaska—that the historian almost inevitably becomes advocate or adversary. This difficulty is compounded by the persistent American notion that

273

somehow the West is a symbol of the American future, and there is nothing so endlessly controversial as the American future. Still, the goals of accuracy and objectivity in a full history of the complex matrix of western regions are worth striving for, and it is to the honor and credit of the twelve contributors to this volume that they have joined this effort. Our already considerable debt to them will grow as other scholars test their models and their ideas in the years to come.

Notes

———•─⊰⊱─•———

BECOMING WEST
Toward a New Meaning for Western History

    1. More likely Hollywood has simply shifted its western heroes to new locations, so that Rambo conducts his violent struggle against an unsympathetic bureaucracy in the Oregon wilderness, and Luke Skywalker struggles to preserve his republican federation against the power of an evil empire in a distant galaxy long, long ago. But even the traditional western landscape retains its cinematic possibilities. The extraordinary success of *Dances with Wolves* clearly shows that the western genre is not dead yet.

    2. Throughout this essay we will speak of the "European" or "Euroamerican" invasion of North America without usually signaling that the "Euroamericans" included people from Africa, Asia, and other parts of the Old World. No single word for the invading groups has yet offered itself to solve the problems of a Eurocentric vocabulary. To speak of the invaders as "white" only compounds the problem, but to call them Euro-Afro-Asian-Americans goes well beyond the limits of literary taste. In a subtle way this problem reflects the frontier-to-region shift that we describe in this essay. No matter what we call such invaders, one of their most important qualities is their acquisition of "New World" identities by modifying or leaving behind their previous identities in the "Old World."

    3. Frederick Jackson Turner, *The Frontier in American History* (New York: Holt, Rinehart, and Winston, 1920), 1. We take this to be the most general version of Turner's argument, the more famous statement of which occurs in the sentence that follows the one we have quoted: "The existence of an area of free land, its continuous

275

recession, and the advance of American settlement westward, explain American development." One needs to add caveats here about the ideological problems of viewing Indian territory as "free land," about settlement by no means always proceeding from east to west, and about the dangers of portraying "American settlement [and] development" monolithically, but even this much-attacked sentence contains more truth than falsehood.

4. The great historical document describing frontier settlement in medieval Iceland is the *Landnámabok*, the book of the land taking.

5. Frontier conflicts over landed resources were part of the fur trade economy as well, especially where fur-bearing mammals were hunted more quickly than they could reproduce themselves. In the face of such scarcity, conflicts among tribes for control of hunting territory and for access to market centers became endemic to the trade.

6. The Indian empires of Central and South America, on the other hand, bear a much stronger resemblance to their European successors.

7. Indeed, this was the moment when Turner's frontier "closed." The transition from territory to statehood was generally the moment when Turnerian historians saw the frontier coming to an end.

KENNECOTT JOURNEY
The Paths out of Town

1. The anecdote, which may well be apocryphal, is recounted in Merle E. Colby, *A Guide to Alaska: Last American Frontier* (New York: Macmillan Co., 1945), 245–46. For a review of the early prospecting history of the site and of the stories that have been told about it, see Robert A. Stearns, "Alaska'a Kennecott Copper & the Kennecott Copper Corporation," *Alaska Journal* 5 (Summer 1975), 130–39.

2. By way of comparison, copper mined in Chile today is often less than 1 percent pure. The sources for the history of the Kennecott mines are widely scattered in the technical and popular periodicals of the time. They are best summarized in Melody Webb Grauman, *Big Business in Alaska: The Kennecott Mines, 1898–1938*, Occasional Paper #1, Anthropology and Historic Preservation Cooperative Park Studies, University of Alaska, March 1977. See also the useful manuscript by William C. Douglass, "A History of the Kennecott Mines, Kennecott, Alaska" (1964; reprinted, Anchorage: Alaska Division of Parks, 1974), and the history of the Copper River and Northwestern Railroad by Lone E. Janson, *The Copper Spike* (Anchorage: Alaska Northwest Publishing Co., 1975). Note that Kennicott and Kennecott appear as variant spellings throughout this literature; although the site was named for Alaskan explorer Robert Kennicott, the mine and the company it spawned came to be misspelled as Kennecott. The glacier, on the other hand, is Kennicott.

3. The National Park Service in 1985 produced a superb survey of the different structures on the site, including the industrial processes that went on within them; see David C. Anderson and Nanon Adair Anderson, Kennecott Copper Corporation Survey, NPS, Historic American Engineering Record, 1985.

4. Douglass, "Kennecott Mines," 11; Grauman, *Big Business in Alaska*, 15 ff.

5. Grauman, *Big Business in Alaska*, 20–21.

6. Ibid., 53; Douglass, "Kennecott Mines," 11.

7. "Iron Trail Ends 27-Year Career; Last Train In," *Cordova Daily Times*, November 11, 1938, cited by Janson, *Copper Spike*, 159.

8. For recent theoretical essays on environmental history and its methodologies, see Donald Worster, "History as Natural History: An Essay on Theory and Method," *Pacific Historical Review* 53 (1984), 1–19; Richard White, "American Environmental History: The Development of a New Field," *Pacific Historical Review* 54 (August 1985), 297–335; *Theories of Environmental History*, special issue of *Environmental Review* 11 (Winter 1987); Donald Worster, *The Ends of the Earth: Perspectives on Modern Environmental History* (New York: Cambridge University Press, 1989); and the symposium on environmental history in the *Journal of American History* 76 (March 1990), 1087–1147.

9. For Alaska, a convenient place to start in constructing an environmental map of this sort is Charles W. Hartman and Philip R. Johnson, *Environmental Atlas of Alaska* (Fairbanks: University of Alaska Institute of Water Resources, 1984). For general historical background, the most comprehensive volumes include Hubert Howe Bancroft, *History of Alaska, 1730–1885* (San Francisco: H. H. Bancroft, 1886); Ernest Gruening, *The State of Alaska* (New York: Random House, 1954); Claus-M. Naske and Herman E. Slotnick, *Alaska: A History of the 49th State*, 2d ed. (Norman: University of Oklahoma Press, 1987); Melody Webb, *The Last Frontier: A History of the Yukon Basin of Canada and Alaska* (Albuquerque: University of New Mexico Press, 1985). See also the useful anthology Mary Childers Mangusso and Stephen W. Haycox, *Interpreting Alaska's History: An Anthology* (Anchorage: Alaska Pacific University Press, 1989).

10. Frederica de Laguna and Catherine McClellan, "Ahtna," in June Helm, ed. *Subarctic*, vol. 6, *The Handbook of North American Indians*, edited by William C. Sturtevant (Washington, D.C.: Smithsonian Institution, 1981), 661–62. For a useful historical survey of the environmental circumstances of natives in interior Alaska, see Jean S. Aigner et al., eds., *Interior Alaska: A Journey through Time* (Anchorage: Alaska Geographic Society, 1986).

11. Useful collections of native animal narratives from communities neighboring the Ahtnas include John F. C. Johnson, comp., *Eyak Legends of the Copper River Delta, Alaska: Stories and Photographs* (Anchorage: Alaska Geographic Society, n.d.), and *Chugach Legends: Stories and Photographs of the Chugach Region* (Anchorage: Alaska Geographic Society, c. 1984).

12. Frederica de Laguna, "The Atna of the Copper River, Alaska: The World of Men and Animals," *Folk: Dansk Ethnografisk Tidsskrift* 11–12 (1969–70), 19. De Laguna is the chief anthropological chronicler of these people; her ethnographic fieldwork began in 1938.

13. The most powerful evocation of this universe is Richard K. Nelson, *Make Prayers to the Raven: A Koyukon View of the Northern Forest* (Chicago: University of Chicago Press, 1983). See also Richard K. Nelson, *Hunters of the Northern Ice* (Chicago: University of Chicago Press, 1969) and *Hunters of the Northern Forest: Designs for Survival among the Alaska Kutchin* (Chicago: University of Chicago Press, 1973); Adrian Tanner, *Bringing Home Animals: Religious Ideology and Mode of Production of the Mistassini Cree Hunters* (New York: St. Martin's Press, 1979); and Calvin Martin, *Keepers of the Game: Indian-Animal Relationships in the Fur Trade* (Berkeley: University of California Press, 1978); and Martin, ed., *The American Indian and the Problem of History* (New York: Oxford University Press, 1986).

14. De Laguna, "Atna of the Copper River," 24–25.

15. I tried to suggest the importance of this question in the third chapter of William Cronon, *Changes in the Land: Indians, Colonists, and the Ecology of New England* (New York: Hill & Wang, 1983), 34–53. Barry Lopez writes wonderfully about the environmental cycles of the Far Arctic North in his *Arctic Dreams: Imagination and Desire in a Northern Landscape* (New York: Charles Scribner's Sons, 1986).

16. Henry T. Allen, "Report of a Military Reconnoissance in Alaska, Made in 1885 by Lieut. Henry T. Allen, Second United States Cavalry," *Compilation of Narratives of Explorations in Alaska*, Report of the Committee on Military Affairs, U.S. Senate, 56th Congress, 1st Session, Report No. 1023, 1900, 471. The narrative portion of Allen's classic report (but not his ethnographic and geological summary) has been reprinted as *An Expedition to the Copper, Tanana, and Koyukuk Rivers in 1885* (Anchorage: Alaska Northwest Publishing Co., 1985). I will cite the latter, more accessible text when referring to the passages it contains.

17. Ferdinand Petrovich von Wrangell, "The Inhabitants of the Northwest Coast of America" (1839), translated and edited by James W. Van Stone, *Arctic Anthropology* 6:2 (1970), 7.

18. Allen, *Expedition to the Copper, Tanana, and Koyukuk Rivers*, 57. For the general background of Allen's expedition, see Morgan B. Sherwood, *Exploration of Alaska, 1865–1900* (New Haven: Yale University Press, 1965), 106–18.

19. Allen, *Expedition to the Copper, Tanana, and Koyukuk Rivers*, 32.

20. Ibid., 38–39.

21. Ibid., 45.

22. Among these different commodities, the literature on the western fur trade is the best developed and most suggestive. See, for instance, Harold A. Innis's classic *The Fur Trade in Canada* (New Haven: Yale University Press, 1930), which remains one of the few works that places the trade in a truly national and international economic perspective; Paul C. Phillips, *The Fur Trade* (Norman: University of Oklahoma Press, 1961); David J. Wishart, *The Fur Trade of the American West, 1807–1840: A Geographical Synthesis* (Lincoln: University of Nebraska Press, 1979); Robert A. Trennert, *Indian Trade on the Middle Border* (Lincoln: University of Nebraska Press, 1981); and Carolyn Gilman, ed., *Where Two Worlds Meet* (St. Paul: Minnesota Historical Society, 1982). Among the most valuable of the recent studies is Arthur Ray's uniquely quantitative and geographical study of *Indians in the Fur Trade* (Toronto: University of Toronto Press, 1974), along with its companion volume, coauthored by Donald Freeman, *"Give Us Good Measure": An Economic Analysis of Relations between the Indians and the Hudson's Bay Company before 1763* (Toronto: University of Toronto Press, 1978). That the best economic analysis of the trade dates from before 1800 is testimony both to the quality of Hudson's Bay Company records and to Ray's skill as a scholar, but it suggests that comparable studies remain to be written about later periods and other geographic areas as well. It is likewise true that no scholar has yet done justice to the history of fur farming, the twentieth-century industry that emerged as a response to the inadequacy, unreliability, or collapse of wild fur populations. A preliminary survey of this subject is Anne Malin Erling, "The American Silver Fox Farming Industry: A Twentieth-Century Fur Trade," senior essay, Yale University, 1987.

22. For a masterful survey of worldwide trade networks of this sort, see Eric R. Wolf, *Europe and the People without History* (Berkeley: University of California Press, 1982).

24. De Laguna and McClellan, "Ahtna," *Subarctic*, 642–43.

25. Good general works on the Russian presence in Alaska include P. A. Tikhmenev, *A History of the Russian-American Company* (1865), translated and edited by Richard A. Pierce and Alton S. Donnelly (Seattle: University of Washington Press, 1978), and Hector Chevigny, *Russian America: The Great Alaskan Venture, 1741–1867* (Portland, Ore.: Binford & Mort, 1965). James R. Gibson, *Imperial Russia in Frontier America: The Changing Geography of Supply of Russian America, 1784–1867* (New York: Oxford University Press, 1976) is particularly good on Russian America's international trade networks.

26. Wrangell, "Northwest Coast Inhabitants," 8.

27. Tanner, *Bringing Home Animals*.

28. On the destruction of Alaska's marine mammals, see Charles M. Scammon, *The Marine Mammals of the North-western Coast of North America* (San Francisco: John H. Carmany & Co., 1874); Henry W. Elliott, *Our Arctic Province: Alaska and the Seal Islands* (New York: Charles Scribner's Sons, 1897); and John W. Bockstoce, *Whales, Ice, and Men: The History of Whaling in the Western Arctic* (Seattle: University of Washington Press, 1986).

29. Wrangell, "Northwest Coast Inhabitants," 5.

30. Allen, "Report of a Military Reconnoissance," 487.

31. Lieutenant W. R. Abercrombie, "Report of a Supplementary Expedition into the Copper River Valley, 1884," *Compilation of Narratives of Explorations in Alaska*, Report of the Committee on Military Affairs, U.S. Senate, 56th Congress, 1st Session, Report No. 1023, 1900, 579.

32. Morgan Sherwood, *Big Game in Alaska: A History of Wildlife and People* (New Haven: Yale University Press, 1981), 45.

33. "Instructions" of H. Clay Wood, assistant adjutant general at Vancouver Barracks, Washington Territory, to Second Lieutenant Henry T. Allen, January 27, 1885, in Allen, *Expedition to the Copper, Tanana, and Koyukuk Rivers*, 13.

34. Ibid.

35. Ibid.

36. Alfred Hulse Brooks, *Blazing Alaska's Trails* (Fairbanks: University of Alaska and the Arctic Institute of North America, 1953), 488–92.

37. Inger Jensen Ricci, "Childhood Memories of Kennecott," "Wrangell-Saint Elias: International Mountain Wilderness," *Alaska Geographic* 8:1 (1981), 80–89.

38. There is less written about property law and its relation to environmental history than there should be. On mining rights, Robert W. Swenson's "Legal Aspects of Mineral Resources Exploitation," in Paul Wallace Gates, *History of Public Land Law Development* (Washington, D.C.: Government Printing Office, 1968), 699–764, remains an indispensable survey of this topic, as does Gates's treatment of land law in the same book. I discuss different cultural systems of property in New England in my *Changes in the Land: Indians, Colonists, and the Ecology of New England* (New York: Hill & Wang, 1983), 54–81, but necessarily employed only the broadest of brushstrokes in so doing. That the problem is, in fact, far richer and deserves much more extensive and subtler treatment is demonstrated by Arthur F. McEvoy's superb *The Fisherman's Problem: Ecology and Law in the California Fisheries, 1850–1980* (New York: Cambridge University Press, 1986). Donald J. Pisani reviews much of the literature relevant to this subject in his useful "Promotion and Regulation: Constitutionalism and the American Economy," *Journal of American History* 74:3 (December 1987), 740–68, and

"Enterprise and Equity: A Critique of Western Water Law in the Nineteenth Century," *Western Historical Quarterly* 18 (1987), 15–38. John Phillip Reid offers a similarly useful review in "Some Lessons of Western Legal History," *Western Legal History* 1:1 (Spring 1988), 3–21; his own *Law for the Elephant: Property and Social Behavior on the Overland Trail* (San Marino: Huntington Library, 1980) is richly suggestive of the possibilities of this field. The handful of scholars who have worked in western legal history have been too long ignored by their colleagues; one can only hope that the founding of the new journal *Western Legal History* will begin to help remedy that problem. As Lawrence M. Friedman has remarked, "the law of property is still waiting for its prince to come and rouse it from the long sleep of obscurity." Lawrence M. Friedman, *A History of American Law*, 2d ed. (New York: Simon & Schuster, 1985), 703.

39. In this area the work of James Willard Hurst stands as one of the great monuments of twentieth-century scholarship, exploring the ways in which law has shaped the changing relationships among markets, economic growth, and state power. Hurst's extraordinary analysis of the lumber industry in northern Wisconsin suggests just how critical legal institutions were in defining the shape of resource markets and environmental change and is a superb model for other such studies. Yet his work, perhaps because of its sheer daunting bulk, has produced surprisingly few offspring. There are suggestive works on the relations among markets, government regulation, and corporations during the nineteenth century, but these have not by and large pursued Hurst's fortunate interest in natural resources. See James Willard Hurst, *Law and the Conditions of Freedom in the Nineteenth-Century United States* (Madison: University of Wisconsin Press, 1956); *Law and Markets in United States History: Different Modes of Bargaining among Interests* (Madison: University of Wisconsin Press, 1982); and *Law and Economic Growth: The Legal History of the Lumber Industry in Wisconsin, 1836–1915* (Cambridge: Harvard University Press, 1964).

40. This history may be traced in the annual reports of the Kennecott Copper Corporation, 1915–1939; see also Carpel L. Breger, "Story of Kennecott Copper," *Financial World* 35:21–23 (May 23, 30, June 6, 1921).

41. For surveys of the Alaska salmon industry, see Richard A. Cooley, *Politics and Conservation: The Decline of the Alaska Salmon* (New York: Harper & Row, 1963) and Patricia Roppel, *Alaska's Salmon Hatcheries, 1891–1959*, Alaska Historical Commission Studies in History, No. 20, 1982. The most sophisticated study of fishery development on the Pacific coast is McEvoy, *The Fisherman's Problem*.

42. See, for instance, Donald W. Meinig, "The Growth of Agricultural Regions in the Far West, 1850–1910," *Journal of Geography* 54 (1955), 221–32; Donald Meinig, *The Great Columbia Plain, 1805–1910* (Seattle: University of Washington Press, 1968); and Richard White, *Land Use, Environment, and Social Change: The Shaping of Island County, Washington* (Seattle: University of Washington Press, 1980).

43. Carl Ortwin Sauer, *The Early Spanish Main* (Berkeley: University of California Press, 1966); Wolf, *Europe and People without History*; and Sidney W. Mintz, *Caribbean Transformations* (Baltimore: Johns Hopkins University Press, 1984) and *Sweetness and Power: The Place of Sugar in Modern History* (New York: Viking Penguin, 1985).

44. Alfred W. Crosby, Jr., *The Columbian Exchange: The Biological and Cultural Consequences of 1492* (Westport, Conn.: Greenwood Press, 1972) and *Ecological Imperialism: The Biological Expansion of Europe, 900–1900* (New York: Cambridge University Press, 1986).

45. De Laguna and McClellan, "Ahtna," *Subarctic*, 652–57; Tanner, *Bringing Home Animals*.

46. William D. Douglass to Melody Webb Grauman, March 25, 1976, quoted in Grauman, *Big Business in Alaska*, 41.

47. Ricci, "Childhood Memories of Kennecott ," 82–83; Grauman, *Big Business in Alaska*, 46.

48. Ricci, "Childhood Memories of Kennecott," 89.

49. Priscilla Russell Kari, *Tanaina Plantlore Dena'ina K'et'una*, 2d ed. (National Park Service, 1987), 67–68.

50. To compare Kennecott with mining in Alaska today, see "Alaska's Oil / Gas & Minerals Industry," *Alaska Geographic* 9:4 (1982).

TO HEAR AN OLD VOICE
Rediscovering Native Americans in American History

1. Mark Twain, *Roughing It* (Hartford: American Publishing Company, 1872), 146–49.

2. *Buffalo Bill and the Indians, or Sitting Bull's History Lesson*, Dino de Laurentiis Corporation, 1976. Available in videocassette through Key Video, a division of CBS / Fox Video.

3. James Merrell, "Some Thoughts on Colonial Historians and American Indians," *William and Mary Quarterly*, 3d series, XLVI:1 (January 1989), 94–119.

4. Gary Nash, *Red, White and Black* (Englewood Cliffs, N.J.: Prentice-Hall, 1984); Edmund Morgan, *American Slavery, American Freedom* (New York: W. W. Norton, 1975); Bernard Bailyn, *The Peopling of British North America* (New York: Alfred A. Knopf, 1986). See also Bailyn's *Voyagers to the West* (New York: Alfred A. Knopf, 1986).

5. Edward Bruner, "Ethnography as Narrative," in *The Anthropology of Experience*, edited by Victor W. Turner and Edward M. Bruner (Urbana: University of Illinois Press, 1986), 139.

6. Two books that explore at length the theme of the Indian as the necessary "other" are Leslie A. Fiedler, *The Return of the Vanishing American* (New York: Stein and Day, 1968) and Robert F. Berkhofer, Jr., *The White Man's Indian: Images of the American Indian from Columbus to the Present* (New York: Alfred A. Knopf, 1978).

7. Stan Steiner, *The New Indians* (New York: Harper & Row, 1968); Deward Walker, *The Emergent Native Americans* (Boston: Little, Brown, 1972). My observations about the character of these titles ought not be taken as an evaluation of their contents. For a brief but useful discussion of the mistaken idea that the Native American literary tradition is a creation of the twentieth century, see the introduction to Daniel F. Littlefield, Jr., and James W. Parins, *A Biobibliography of Native American Writers, 1772–1924* (Metuchen: Scarecrow Press, 1981), xi–xvii.

8. Ella Deloria's publications include *Dakota Texts* (New York: G. E. Stechert & Co., 1932); *Dakota Grammar, Memoirs of the National Academy of Sciences* 23:2 (1941); *Speaking of Indians* (New York: Friendship Press, 1944); and *Waterlily* (Lincoln: University of Nebraska Press, 1988).

9. Chamberlain's comment appears in William G. McLoughlin, *Cherokees and*

Missionaries, 1789–1839 (New Haven: Yale University Press, 1984), 185. The best, but inadequate, biography of Sequoyah remains Grant Foreman, *Sequoyah* (Norman: University of Oklahoma Press, 1938). Traveller Bird, *Tell Them They Lie: The Sequoyah Myth* (Los Angeles: Westernlore Publishers, 1971) is a work of political mythology. For details concerning Sequoyah's creation of the syllabary, see McLoughlin, 183–186, as well as John K. White, "On the Revival of Printing in the Cherokee Language," *Current Anthropology* 3 (1962), 511.

10. Carolyn Thomas Foreman, *Oklahoma Imprints, 1835–1907: A History of Printing in Oklahoma before Statehood* (Norman: University of Oklahoma Press, 1936), xv, and Lester Hargrett, *Oklahoma Imprints 1835–1890* (New York: R. R. Bowker Company, 1951), ix. Foreman's book remains the best account of nineteenth-century newspaper and magazine publishing in what became Oklahoma but is superseded by Hargrett's work for nonserial publications.

11. Foreman, *Oklahoma Imprints*, xvi. McLoughlin, *Cherokees*, 304. Daniel F. Littlefield, Jr., and James W. Parins, *American Indian and Alaska Native Newspapers and Periodicals, 1826–1924* (Westport, Conn.: Greenwood Press, 1984), 84–90; hereafter referred to as Littlefield & Parins, *Newspapers and Periodicals*.

12. Foreman, *Oklahoma Imprints*, xvi. Hargrett, *Oklahoma Imprints*, ix–x. Hargrett's bibliography remains the most thorough listing of Park Hill imprints.

13. Foreman, *Oklahoma Imprints*, 76–77.

14. Littlefield & Parins, *Newspapers and Periodicals*, xiii–xv, 64.

15. For examples of circulation policies, see masthead notices in the *Cherokee Advocate*, December 9, 1847, August 15, 1877, April 6, 1883, and November 30, 1887 issues. See also Littlefield & Parins, *Newspapers and Periodicals*, 68–69.

16. "Brown Was Disappointed," *Cherokee Advocate*, August 5, 1905, 1, column 1.

17. Untitled essay, *Cherokee Advocate*, February 6, 1906, 2, column 1.

18. Littlefield & Parins, *Newspapers and Periodicals*, xiii, 66.

19. Ibid., 67.

20. Untitled editorial, *Cherokee Advocate*, September 9, 1905, 2, column 1.

21. Foreman, *Oklahoma Imprints*, 83.

22. Ibid., 83–84. Littlefield & Parins, *Newspapers and Periodicals*, 73.

23. Untitled editorial, *Cherokee Advocate*, February 3, 1906, 2, column 3.

24. Ibid., February 10, 1906, 2, column 1.

25. White's efforts are described in his article in *Current Anthropology*, cited above. The anthropologist Jack F. Kilpatrick amassed an extensive collection of Sequoyan medical formulas, most of which are now stored in the Yale Collection of Western Americana at the Beinecke Rare Book and Manuscript Library. Kilpatrick and his wife, Anna G. Kilpatrick, published several major studies from his collections, including *Friends of Thunder: Folktales of the Oklahoma Cherokees* (Dallas: Southern Methodist University Press, 1964), *Run toward the Nightland: Magic of the Oklahoma Cherokees* (Dallas: Southern Methodist University Press, 1967), and *Walk in Your Soul: Love Incantations of the Oklahoma Cherokees* (Dallas: Southern Methodist University Press, 1965).

26. Francis Paul Prucha, *The Great Father: The United States Government and the American Indians* (Lincoln: University of Nebraska Press, 1984), xi.

27. Quoted in Douglas R. Parks, "The Importance of Language Study for the Writing of Plains Indian History," in *New Directions in American Indian History*, edited by Colin G. Calloway (Norman: University of Oklahoma Press, 1987), 154. Boas

first published his exhortation in *Handbook of American Indian Languages*, Part I (Washington, D.C.: Smithsonian Institution, 1911).

28. Quoted in Francis Paul Prucha, ed., *Americanizing the American Indians: Writings by the "Friends of the Indian" 1880–1900* (Lincoln: University of Nebraska Press, 1978), 201. Originally published as *Report of the Commissioner of Indian Affairs to the Secretary of the Interior*, September 21, 1887, House Executive Document No. 1, part 5, vol. II, 50th Congress, 1st session, serial 2542, 18–23.

29. Parks observes: "Ironically, the disregard of language characterizing the work of historians has become progressively more common among anthropologists who are interested in historical study. Coincidentally with the rise of autonomous linguistics in many universities, most anthropology departments no longer insist that their students have minimal competence in descriptive linguistics" (155–56). As a result, Park demonstrates, North American Indian linguistics remains a field full of basic research needs and opportunities. Another valuable consideration of the implications of linguistic studies for Native American history is William L. Leap, "American Indian Languages," in *Language in the USA*, edited by Charles A. Ferguson and Shirley Brice Heath (Cambridge, England: Cambridge University Press, 1981), 116–44.

30. "Brown Was Disappointed," *Cherokee Advocate*, August 5, 1905, 1, column 1.

31. For a discussion of the issues surrounding the "Indianness" of the Civilized Tribes generally, see W. David Baird, "Are the Five Tribes of Oklahoma 'Real' Indians?," *Western Historical Quarterly*, XXI:1 (February 1990), 5–18.

32. Quoted in John W. Lydekker, *The Faithful Mohawks* (Port Washington: Ira J. Friedman, Inc., 1968), 83. See page 73 for information that Paulus is teaching in 1753.

33. *The Morning and Evening Prayer, and God His Message, the Church Catechism, . . . Together with Other Things, in the Mohawk Language*, translated by Lawrence Claesse under the direction of William Andrews (New York: William Bradford, 1715). For discussion of the prayer book's scarcity at mid-century, see Lydekker, *Faithful Mohawks*, 182, and R. W. McLachlan, *The First Mohawk Primer* (Montreal: 1908), 4.

34. *Na Yakawea Yondereanayendaghkwa Oghseragwegouh . . .* (London: C. Buckton, 1787).

35. On the preparation of the third edition of the prayer book, see Lydekker, *Faithful Mohawks*, 183. The quotation describing the school's use of manuscript scraps is from a letter by Daniel Claus, assistant superintendent of Indian affairs, to William Morice dated October 10, 1781, quoted in Lydekker, *Faithful Mohawks*, 166–67.

36. The first edition of the primer was printed in Montreal at the establishment of Fleury Mesplets in 1781. The second edition was printed in London at the firm of C. Buckton in 1786.

37. For examples, see the Claus Papers, 3:13 and 355 and 4:3, 5, 27, 29, and 79. I am indebted to Colin Calloway for this information.

38. Jonathan Edwards, *Observations on the Language of the Muhhekaneew Indians* (New Haven: Josiah Meigs, 1788). Willard Walker, "Native American Writing Systems," in *Language in the USA*, 154, and James C. Pilling, *Proofsheets of the Bibliography of the Languages of the North American Indians* (Washington: Government Printing Office, 1885), 39.

39. Andrew J. Blackbird, *History of the Ottawa and Chippewa Indians of Michigan; a Grammar of Their Language, and Personal Family History of the Author* (Ypsilanti, Mich.: Ypsilanti Job Printing House, 1887), 31.

40. Walker, "Native American Writing Systems," 157.

41. For a discussion of the Winnebago story, see Alice Fletcher, "A Phonetic Alphabet Used by the Winnebago Tribe of Indians," *Journal of American Folklore* 3 (1890), 299–301, and "The Phonetic Alphabet of the Winnebago Indians," *Proceedings of the American Association for the Advancement of Science, 38th Meeting, August, 1889, Toronto* (Salem, Mass.: Salem Press Publishing and Printing Co., 1890), 354–58.

42. Blowsnake's autobiography was first published in *University of California Publications in American Archaeology and Ethnology* XVI:7 (1920), 381–473. The first book form publication was by Appleton and Company of New York in 1926.

43. On the Micmacs, Yaquis, Luiseños, Aleuts, and Eskimos, see Willard Walker, "Native American Writing Systems." For the Sioux, see Parks, "Importance of Language Study," 161–63. The Navajos are discussed in Robert W. Young, "Written Navajo: A Brief History," in *Advances in the Creation and Revision of Writing Systems,* edited by Joshua A. Fishman (The Hague: Mouton & Co., 1977), 459–70. For the Apaches, see Keith Basso and Ned Anderson, "A Western Apache Writing System: The Symbols of Silas John," in *Advances in the Creation and Revision of Writing Systems,* 77–104.

44. The figures are based on Daniel F. Littlefield, Jr., and James W. Parins, *A Biobibliography of Native American Writers, 1772–1924* (Metuchen: Scarecrow Press, 1981) and Daniel F. Littlefield, Jr., and James W. Parins, *A Biobibliography of Native American Writers, 1772–1924: A Supplement* (Metuchen: Scarecrow Press, 1985).

45. The ideas discussed in this paragraph were initially stimulated by this observation of Vine Deloria, Jr., about the Apaches: "Tribal identity is assumed, not defined, by the reservation people. Freedom to choose from a wide variety of paths of progress is characteristic of the Apaches; they don't worry about what type of Indianism is 'real.' " *Custer Died for Your Sins: An Indian Manifesto* (New York: Avon Books, 1972), 89. They also borrow freely from three reappraisals of culture as an analytic tool and human construct: *The Anthropology of Experience,* Eric R. Wolf, *Europe and the People without History* (Berkeley: University of California Press, 1982), and Marshall Sahlins, *Islands of History* (Chicago: University of Chicago Press, 1985). Sahlins presents an especially compelling evaluation of the relationship between the concepts of culture and history as employed by anthropologists and historians. I am indebted to Richard White for bringing his discussion to my attention.

46. Gary Moulton has completed a similar project for another Native American leader. See *The Papers of Chief John Ross,* edited by Gary Moulton (Norman: University of Oklahoma Press, 1985).

47. The authors include William Apes (Pequod), Black Hawk (Sauk), George Copway (Chippewa), Paul Cuffe, father and son of the same name (Wampanoag), David Cusick (Tuscarora), Peter Jacobs (Chippewa), Peter Jones (Missisauga), Eleazar Williams (Mohawk). For summaries of their various publications, see Littlefield and Parins, *A Biobibliography . . .* and H. David Brumble III, *An Annotated Bibliography of American Indian and Eskimo Autobiographies* (Lincoln: University of Nebraska Press, 1981).

48. H. Craig Miner, *The Corporation and the Indian: Tribal Sovereignty and Industrial Civilization in Indian Territory, 1865–1907,* 2d ed. (Norman: University of Oklahoma Press, 1989). The archives of the Civilized Tribes are housed at the Oklahoma Historical Society in Oklahoma City.

49. On the Iroquois, see *The History and Culture of Iroquois Diplomacy: An Inter-*

disciplinary Guide to the Treaties of the Six Nations and Their League, edited by Francis Jennings et al. (Syracuse: Syracuse University Press, 1985). On the Hudson's Bay Company, see Arthur J. Ray, *Indians in the Fur Trade: Their Role as Hunters, Trappers, and Middlemen in the Lands Southwest of Hudson Bay, 1660–1870* (Toronto: University of Toronto Press, 1974) and Arthur J. Ray and Donald Freeman, *"Give Us Good Measure": An Economic Analysis of Relations between the Indians and the Hudson's Bay Company before 1763* (Toronto: University of Toronto Press, 1978).

50. For an example of the way material culture can be analyzed in this fashion, see Victoria Wyatt, *Shapes of Their Thoughts: Reflections of Culture Contact in Northwest Coast Indian Art* (Norman: University of Oklahoma Press, 1984). For a consideration of the way one community of Indians made use of lawyers and lobbyists in the mid-nineteenth century, see James A. Clifton, *The Pokagons, 1683–1983: Catholic Potawatomi Indians of the St. Joseph River Valley* (Lanham, Md.: University Press of America, 1984), especially chap. 7.

ON THE BOUNDARIES OF EMPIRE
Connecting the West to Its Imperial Past

1. Frederick Jackson Turner, "The Significance of the Frontier in American History," *Annual Report of the American Historical Association for the Year 1893* (Washington, D.C.: 1894), reprinted in Turner, *The Frontier in American History* (New York: Henry Holt, 1920), 33–35.

2. Ray Allen Billington and Martin Ridge, *Westward Expansion*, 5th ed. (New York: Macmillan, 1982), Section I, especially chap. 7; also chap. 19 and 30 in Section III.

3. A pivotal statement in this regard was Earl Pomeroy's essay "Toward a Reorientation of Western History: Continuity and Environment," *Mississippi Valley Historical Review* 41 (March 1955).

4. Richard C. Wade, *The Urban Frontier* (Cambridge: Harvard University Press, 1959) was a pioneering work and remains an important study of western urbanism. For an enlightening perspective by an economic geographer, see James E. Vance, Jr., *The Merchant's World: The Geography of Wholesaling* (Englewood Cliffs, N.J.: Prentice Hall, 1970). See also Howard R. Lamar, *The Trader on the American Frontier: Myth's Victim* (College Station: Texas A&M University Press, 1977). This book provides a wonderful introduction to the trader's world in the West. I am, of course, indebted to Professor Lamar for provoking my curiosity about the international West. Professor Lamar has a knack for conveying complex historical landscapes, their intriguing humanity and their scholarly possibilities.

5. Gilbert J. Garraghan, S. J., *Catholic Beginnings in Kansas City, Missouri* (Chicago: Loyola University Press, 1920), 68, 121; for a more recent view of Creole Kansas City, see Charles E. Hoffhaus, *Chez les Canses: The French Foundations of Metropolitan Kansas City* (Kansas City: Lowell Press, 1984).

6. Howard Lamar and Leonard Thompson, eds., *The Frontier in History* (New Haven: Yale University Press, 1981), editors' introductory chapter, 7. For a brief study of the etymology of "frontier," see Lucien Febvre, *"Frontière: The Word and the Concept"* (1928), reprinted in Febvre, *A New Kind of History*, edited by Peter Burke (New York: Harper & Row, 1973).

7. Robin Winks, "A System of Commands: The Infrastructure of Race Contact," in *Studies in British Imperial History*, edited by Gordon Martel (London: Macmillan, 1986), 31.

8. Canadian historians have always considered the role of the metropole to be of primary historical importance. Canadian ethnohistorians have shed much new light on the complex social and economic interactions between European and Indian communities. The fur trade has served as the focus of many of these investigations, for it, in fact, epitomized the international nature of frontier activities.

9. Francis Jennings, *The Invasion of America* (Chapel Hill: University of North Carolina Press for the Institute of Early American History and Culture, 1975). See also Jennings, *The Ambiguous Iroquois Empire* (New York: W. W. Norton, 1984); James Axtell, *The European and the Indian* (New York: Oxford University Press, 1981) and *The Invasion Within* (New York: Oxford University Press, 1985); and Neal Salisbury, *Manitou and Providence: Indians, Europeans, and the Making of New England, 1500–1643* (New York: Oxford University Press, 1982).

10. In his most recent book, *Empire of Fortune* (New York: W. W. Norton, 1988), Jennings has attempted a thorough reinterpretation of the Seven Years War. Taking the traditional interpretation of Lawrence Henry Gipson to task, Jennings shows convincingly that a heterogeneous array of groups opposed each other in this struggle. Neither side had consistent aims, the British group in particular being riddled with crosscutting agendas. Jennings also argues that British objectives were, to some degree, forced upon recalcitrant provincial assemblies. In what can only be described as a Whig interpretation of history, Jennings indicts, among others, the duke of Cumberland, the earl of Halifax, Thomas Penn, George III, and Lord North for being militaristic, repressive, and "hot for empire" (12, 471). One might quibble with Jennings on a number of points. The French were not provoked by the formation of the Ohio Company of Virginia in 1747. They were already well aware of the potential danger in Ohio to their interests when an incident between the Hurons and Ottawas occurred in 1738. As for Pitt, the Great Commoner was every bit as much a believer in the imperial chain of command and the coercive power of the state as his Tory opponents; indeed, a general strengthening of the machinery of empire had been in process for quite some time. On this last point, see Michael Kammen, *Empire and Interest* (Philadelphia: J. B. Lippincott, 1970), chap. 6; John Brewer, *Party Ideology and Popular Politics at the Accession of George III* (Cambridge, England: Cambridge University Press, 1976); Linda Colley, *In Defiance of Oligarchy: The Tory Party 1714–1760* (Cambridge, England: Cambridge University Press, 1982); Sir Charles Grant Robertson, *Chatham and the British Empire* (1946; reprinted, New York: Collier, 1962); and Stephen Saunders Webb, *The Governors-General* (Chapel Hill: University of North Carolina Press for the Institute of Early American History and Culture, 1979).

11. Charles R. Cutter, *The Protector de Indios in Colonial New Mexico, 1659–1821* (Albuquerque: University of New Mexico Press, 1986); see also Ralph E. Twitchell, ed., *The Spanish Archives of New Mexico*, 2 vols. (Cedar Rapids, Iowa: Torch Press, 1914).

12. C. Richard Arena, "Land Settlement Policies and Practices in Spanish Louisiana," in *The Spanish in the Mississippi Valley 1762–1804*, edited by John Francis McDermott (Urbana: University of Illinois Press, 1974).

13. Intertribal slaving was a fact of life in the Spanish Southwest, and Taos was one center of the trade in Indian slaves in the eighteenth century. Attempts were

made to terminate the trade, but profits were high. The trade was justified by arguing that ransoming captives saved them from death. The French in the Mississippi Valley provided one market for Indian slaves and were opposed to Spanish efforts to comply with imperial regulations. Despite the continuing existence of Indian slavery in Spanish Louisiana throughout the eighteenth century, the illegality of the practice made a difference. For more on this subject, see Russell Magnaghi, "The Role of Colonial Indian Slavery in St. Louis," *Bulletin of the Missouri Historical Society* 31 (1975), 264–272, and "Intertribal Slaving on the Great Plains in the Eighteenth Century," in *From the Mississippi to the Pacific: Essays in Honor of John Francis Bannon, S.J.*, edited by Magnaghi (Marquette: Northern Michigan University Press, 1982); Stephen Webre, "The Problem of Indian Slavery in Spanish Louisiana, 1769–1803," *Louisiana History* 25 (1984), 117–35; and Carl J. Ekberg, *Colonial Ste. Genevieve* (Gerald, Mo.: Patrice Press, 1985).

14. There is no recent treatment of this fascinating episode in American colonial history. Many of the documents can be found in the Manuscripts and Archives Collection of the Yale University Library. For an older discussion, see John W. De Forest, *History of the Indians of Connecticut* (Hartford: Wm. J. Hamersley, 1851).

15. W. J. Eccles, *The Canadian Frontier, 1534–1760*, rev. ed. (1969; Albuquerque: University of New Mexico Press, 1983), chap. 1, 4; William E. Foley and Charles David Rice, "Pierre Chouteau, Entrepreneur as Indian Agent," *Missouri Historical Review* 72: 4 (July 1978), 377. For a complicated case of cross-cultural legal problems, see Patricia Galloway, "The Barthelemy Murders: Bienville's Establishment of the *Lex Talionis* as a Principle of Indian Diplomacy," in *Proceedings of the Eighth Annual Meeting of the French Colonial Historical Society, 1982*, edited by E. P. Fitzgerald (Lanham, Md.: University Press of America, 1985).

16. For an in-depth discussion of this issue, see the recent exchange between Immanuel Wallerstein and Steve J. Stern in *American Historial Review* 93:4 (October 1988). The literature on dependency theory and world systems analysis is enormous. The following books provide a useful background for western historians: Richard White, *The Roots of Dependency: Subsistence, Environment, and Social Change among the Choctaws, Pawnees, and Navajos* (Lincoln: University of Nebraska Press, 1983); Eric R. Wolf, *Europe and the People without History* (Berkeley: University of California Press, 1982); Immanuel Wallerstein, *The Modern World-System*, 3 vols. (New York: Academic Press, 1976, 1980, 1989).

17. Daniel H. Usner, Jr., "The Frontier Exchange Economy of the Lower Mississippi Valley in the Eighteenth Century," *William and Mary Quarterly* 44:2 (April 1987).

18. William J. Eccles, "The Fur Trade and Eighteenth-Century Imperialism," *William and Mary Quarterly* 40:3 (July 1983), 82–83.

19. For some of the scattered details of this story, see Richebourg Gaillard McWilliams, ed., *Iberville's Gulf Journals* (University: University of Alabama Press, 1981); Ross Phares, *Cavalier in the Wilderness* (Baton Rouge: Louisiana State University Press, 1952); Jay Higginbotham, *Old Mobile: Fort Louis de la Louisiane, 1702–1711* (Mobile: Museum of the City of Mobile, 1977).

20. For an intriguing essay on the awareness of local actors on an imperial frontier, see Peggy K. Liss, "Creoles, the North American Example and the Spanish American Economy, 1760–1810," in *The North American Role in the Spanish Imperial Economy, 1760–1819*, edited by Jacques A. Barbier and Allan J. Kuethe (Manchester:

Manchester University Press, 1984); see also William S. Coker and Thomas D. Watson, *Indian Traders of the Southeastern Spanish Borderlands: Panton, Leslie and Company and John Forbes and Company, 1783–1847* (Pensacola: University of West Florida Press, 1986).

21. William H. Keating, *Narrative of an Expedition* (1824; reprinted, Minneapolis: Ross & Haines, 1959), 75.

22. John F. Bosher, "Government and Private Interests in New France," *Canadian Public Administration / Administration publique du Canada* 10 (1967), 244–57.

23. For a guide and introduction to this complex Indian-European landscape in this period, see Helen H. Tanner, ed., *Atlas of Great Lakes Indian History* (Norman: University of Oklahoma Press, 1987); Bert Anson, "The Fur Traders in Northern Indiana, 1796–1850" (Ph.D. thesis, Indiana University, 1953); and Anson, *The Miami Indians* (Norman: University of Oklahoma Press, 1970). For a theoretical discussion of such situations, the classic work is Fredrik Barth, ed., *Ethnic Groups and Boundaries: The Social Organization of Cultural Difference* (Boston: Little, Brown and Co., 1969).

24. For Russian Alaska, see the series of documents edited by Lydia Black and Richard Pierce for the Limestone Press (Kingston, Ontario); James R. Gibson, *Imperial Russia in Frontier America* (New York: Oxford University Press, 1976); and Frederick Starr, ed., *Russia's American Colony* (Durham: Duke University Press, 1987). For the French Mississippi Valley and Great Lakes region, see Daniel H. Usner, Jr., *Indians, Settlers, and Slaves in a Frontier Exchange Economy: The Lower Mississippi Valley before 1783* (Chapel Hill: University of North Carolina Press for the Institute of Early American History and Culture, in press) and "Food Marketing and Interethnic Exchange in the 18th-Century Lower Mississippi Valley," *Food and Foodways* 1 (1986); Patricia K. Galloway, ed., *La Salle and His Legacy: Frenchmen and Indians in the Lower Mississippi Valley* (Jackson: University Press of Mississippi, 1982); Richard White, *The Middle Ground: Indians, Empires, and Republics in the Great Lakes Region, 1650–1815* (Cambridge, England: Cambridge University Press, 1991); Tanis Chapman Thorne, "People of the River: Mixed-Blood Families on the Lower Missouri" (Ph.D. thesis, University of California, Los Angeles, 1987); Jacqueline Peterson "The People in Between: Indian-White Marriage and the Genesis of a Métis Society and Culture in the Great Lakes Region, 1680–1830" (Ph.D. thesis, University of Illinois at Chicago Circle, 1981). For the Spanish Gulf, see William S. Coker and Robert R. Rea, eds., *Anglo-Spanish Confrontation on the Gulf Coast during the American Revolution* (Pensacola: Gulf Coast History and Humanities Conference, 1982) and Peter H. Wood, Gregory A. Waselkov, and M. Thomas Hatley, eds., *Powhatan's Mantle: Indians in the Colonial Southeast* (Lincoln: University of Nebraska Press, 1989). See also the following bibliographical essays: Carl A. Brasseaux, "French Louisiana" and Light T. Cummins, "Spanish Louisiana," in *A Guide to the History of Louisiana*. For additional references, see Notes 19 and 22. This is very much a partial list.

25. William Cronon, "Revisiting the Vanishing Frontier: The Legacy of Frederick Jackson Turner," *Western Historical Quarterly* 18:2 (April 1987), 170.

26. Any discussion of imperial frontiers would seem to necessitate a certain amount of chronological dislocation. That may be unavoidable because we cannot be in two places at once.

27. Ignoring, as we usually do, the existence of Mexico, Quebec, and a multitude of tribal polities, "international" or imperial frontiers do indeed retreat. The end point of that narrative seems to be conquest, marginalization, and enclavement. That

is not to say that the interplay between these broadly defined frontiers is not important to the narrative of each one. Nor should we imagine that the cultures forged on our international frontier are without a voice in contemporary American culture. But the problem remains, How do we integrate these different narratives?

28. For a discussion of how the traditional colonial American narrative ought to change in this regard, see James H. Merrell, "Some Thoughts on Colonial Historians and American Indians," *William and Mary Quarterly* 46:1 (January 1989) and *The Indians' New World* (Chapel Hill: University of North Carolina Press for the Institute of Early American History and Culture, 1989).

29. See a marvelous book on this subject, which delivers more than it promises: Dorothy V. Jones, *License for Empire: Colonialism by Treaty in Early America* (Chicago: University of Chicago Press, 1982); also, Jack M. Sosin, "The French Settlements in British Policy for the North American Interior, 1760–1774," *Canadian Historical Review* 39:3 (September 1958); Marjorie G. Reid, "The Quebec Fur-Traders and Western Policy, 1763–1774," *Canadian Historical Review* 6:1 (March 1925); Pierre Tousignant, "The Integration of the Province of Quebec into the British Empire, 1763–91," in *Dictionary of Canadian Biography*, Vol. IV, *1771–1800* (Toronto: University of Toronto Press and Les Presses de L'Université Laval, 1979); Clarence W. Alvord, *The Mississippi Valley in British Politics*, 2 vols. (1916; reprinted, New York: Russell and Russell, 1959); Peter Marshall, "The Government of the Quebec Fur Trade: An Imperial Dilemma, 1761–1775," in *Le Castor Fait Tout: Selected Papers of the Fifth North American Fur Trade Conference, 1985*, edited by Bruce G. Trigger et al. (Montreal: Lake St. Louis Historical Society, 1987); and Colin G. Calloway, *Crown and Calumet: British-Indian Relations, 1783–1815* (Norman: University of Oklahoma Press, 1987). For an enlightening look at the complexities of imperial policymaking and the place of Quebec in British politics in this period, see Philip Lawson, *The Imperial Challenge: Quebec and Britain in the Age of the American Revolution* (Montreal: McGill-Queen's University Press, 1989).

30. See F. Clever Bald, *Detroit's First American Decade, 1796 to 1805* (Ann Arbor: University of Michigan Press, 1948), 29–32; Nelson V. Russell, *The British Regime in Michigan and the Old Northwest, 1760–1796* (1939; reprinted, Philadelphia: Porcupine Press, 1978), chap. 6; Father Christian Denissen, *Genealogy of the French Families of the Detroit River Region*, 2 vols., edited by Harold F. Powell, and revised and edited by Robert L. Pilon (Detroit: Detroit Society for Genealogical Research and Burton Historical Collection of the Detroit Public Library, 1987).

31. Paul LaChance, "Intermarriage and French Cultural Persistence in Late Spanish and Early American New Orleans," *Histoire sociale* 15 (Mai 1982).

32. On this point, see Carl J. Ekberg and William E. Foley, eds., *An Account of Upper Louisiana by Nicolas de Finiels* (Columbia: University of Missouri Press, 1989).

33. Sosin, "French Settlements," 200.

34. R. David Edmunds, " 'Unacquainted with the Laws of the Civilized World': American Attitudes toward the Métis Communities in the Old Northwest," in *The New Peoples: Being and Becoming Métis in North America*, edited by Jacqueline Peterson and Jennifer S. H. Brown (Winnipeg: University of Manitoba Press, 1985), 187.

35. See Notes 22, 23, and 30.

36. The most detailed study of the Louisiana revolt is still Marc de Villiers du Terrage, *Les Dernières Années de la Louisiane française* (1903), recently translated into English and published as *The Last Years of French Louisiana* (Lafayette: Center for Lou-

isiana Studies, 1982). For a review of the historical literature on this event, see the essays by Carl Brasseaux and Light Cummins in *Louisiana*. See also the interesting article by Pierre H. Boulle, "French Reactions to the Louisiana Revolution of 1768," in *The French in the Mississippi Valley*, edited by John F. McDermott (Urbana: University of Illinois Press, 1965).

37. Sosin, "French Settlements," 207. See also *Invitation Sérieuse aux Habitants des Illinois* (Philadelphia: 1772; edited with an introduction by Clarence W. Alvord and Clarence E. Carter in 1908; reprinted, New York: Burt Franklin, 1968).

38. Hamilton to Haldimand, September 22–October 3, 1778, in *Michigan Historical Collections*, IX, 478.

39. Herbert E. Bolton, "Defensive Spanish Expansion and the Significance of the Borderlands" (1930), reprinted in John F. Bannon, ed., *Bolton and the Spanish Borderlands* (Norman: University of Oklahoma Press, 1964), 59.

40. See, for example, Gerald E. Poyo and Gilberto M. Hinojosa, "Spanish Texas and Borderlands Historiography in Transition: Implications for United States History," *Journal of American History* 75:2 (September 1988); Dora P. Crouch, Daniel J. Garr, and Axel I. Mundigo, *Spanish City Planning in North America* (Cambridge: MIT Press, 1982); and John F. McDermott, ed., *The Spanish in the Mississippi Valley, 1762–1804* (Urbana: University of Illinois Press, 1974). For a discussion of the Turnerian influence, or lack thereof, on Bolton, see David J. Weber, "Turner, the Boltonians, and the Borderlands," *American Historical Review* 91:1 (February 1986). For the standard yet valuable Boltonian research and interpretations, see George P. Hammond, ed., *New Spain and the Anglo-American West: Historical Contributions Presented to Herbert Eugene Bolton*, 2 vols. (1932; reprinted, New York: Kraus, 1969); John Francis Bannon, *The Spanish Borderlands Frontier, 1513–1821* (New York: Holt, Rinehart, and Winston, 1970); and Abraham P. Nasatir, *Borderland in Retreat* (Albuquerque: University of New Mexico Press, 1976).

41. Jesus Lorente Miguel, "Commercial Relations between New Orleans and the United States, 1783–1803," in *Spanish Imperial Economy;* Liss, "Creoles"; and C. Richard Arena, "Land Settlement Policies and Practices in Spanish Louisiana," William S. Coker, "The Bruins and the Formulation of Spanish Immigration Policy in the Old Southwest, 1787–88," and John G. Clark, "The Role of the City Government in the Economic Development of New Orleans: Cabildo and City Council, 1783–1812," in *Spanish in the Mississippi Valley*.

42. To gain some idea of Spain's commitment to this frontier, consult Abraham P. Nasatir, "Government Employees and Salaries in Spanish Louisiana," *Louisiana Historical Quarterly* 29 (1946), 885–1040, and Robert R. Archibald, "From 'La Louisiane' to 'Luisiana': The Imposition of Spanish Administration in the Upper Mississippi Valley," *Gateway Heritage* 11:1 (Summer 1990).

43. Morris Arnold, *Unequal Laws unto a Savage Race: European Legal Traditions in Arkansas, 1686–1836* (Fayetteville: University of Arkansas Press, 1985); Edward F. Haas, ed., *Louisiana's Legal Heritage* (Pensacola: Perdido Bay Press for the Louisiana State Museum, 1983); George Dargo, *Jefferson's Louisiana: Politics and the Clash of Legal Traditions* (Cambridge: Harvard University Press, 1975); David J. Langum, *Law and Community on the Mexican California Frontier* (Norman: University of Oklahoma Press, 1987).

44. Langum, *Law and Community*, 132–33, 142; Dargo, *Jefferson's Louisiana*, chap. 1 and 4.

45. Louis Nicolas Fortin to Antoine Marechal, July 25, 1803, Lasselle Papers, Indiana State Library, Indiana Division, Indianapolis.

46. Dargo, *Jefferson's Louisiana*, 13–17.

47. Dargo, "Steamboats, Towboats and Legal Historiography: The Law in Louisiana and the New Nation," in *Legal Heritage*, 138.

48. The first priest to serve in Congress was, after all, Father Richard of Michigan.

49. Irving McKee, ed., *The Trail of Death: Letters of Benjamin Marie Petit*, Indiana Historical Society Publications, 14:1 (1941) (Indianapolis: Bobbs-Merrill, 1944), 102–03.

50. William Barnaby Faherty, S.J., *Dream by the River: Two Centuries of Saint Louis Catholicism, 1766–1980* (St. Louis: River City Publishers, 1973), chap. 3. See also George Paré, *The Catholic Church in Detroit, 1701–1888* (Detroit: Gabriel Richard Press, 1951); Frank B. Woodward and Albert Hyma, *Gabriel Richard, Frontier Ambassador* (Detroit: Wayne State University Press, 1958); Gilbert J. Garraghan, S.J., *The Jesuits of the Middle United States*, 3 vols. (1938; reprinted, Chicago: Loyola University Press, 1983); Charles E. O'Neill, *Church and State in French Colonial Louisiana* (New Haven: Yale University Press, 1966); Thomas J. Schlereth, *The University of Notre Dame* (Notre Dame: University of Notre Dame Press, 1976); Thomas McAvoy, *Catholic Church in Indiana, 1789–1834* (New York: AMS Press, 1940); R. O. Gerow, *Cradle Days of St. Mary's at Natchez* (1941; reprinted, Natchez: n.p., 1985).

51. On this point, see Patricia Nelson Limerick, *The Legacy of Conquest* (New York: W. W. Norton, 1987), especially chap. 6 and 7.

52. One would have to conclude that the Chouteaus, among many others, were masters at subverting the intentions of the Republic to conform with the political culture of the *ancien régime*. Albert Gallatin had warned Jefferson about this, but to no avail.

53. See the editors' introduction in this volume for an attempt at such a narrative framework.

AMERICANS, MEXICANS, MÉTIS
A Community Approach to the Comparative Study
of North American Frontiers

1. Theodore Roosevelt, *The Winning of the West: Selections*, edited by Harvey Wish (New York: Capricorn Books, 1962), 10, 142; Turner quoted, ibid., xxi.

2. William C. Sturtevant, ed., *Handbook of North American Indians* (Washington, D.C.: Smithsonian Institution, 1978–   ), eventually to include twenty volumes, is organized by cultural areas. See also Arlene B. Hirschfelder, Mary Gloyne Byler, and Michael A. Dorris, *Guide to Research on North American Indians* (Chicago: American Library Association, 1983). The classic text on the culture area concept is A. L. Kroeber, *Cultural and Natural Areas of Native North America* (Berkeley: University of California Press, 1939); the limitations of the paradigm are suggested in James H. Howard, "The Culture-Area Concept: Does It Diffract Anthropological Light?," *Indian Historian* 8 (1975), 22–26.

3. Herbert E. Bolton, "The Epic of Greater America," *American Historical Review* 38 (1933), 448–74, remains a key statement concerning the multiple frontiers of the

continent. For introductions to non-Anglo frontiers, see Bolton, *The Spanish Border-lands: A Chronicle of Old Florida and the Southwest* (New Haven: Yale University Press, 1921); John Francis Bannon, *The Spanish Borderlands Frontier, 1513–1821* (New York: Holt, Rinehart and Winston, 1970); David J. Weber, *The Mexican Frontier, 1821–1846: The American Southwest under Mexico* (Albuquerque: University of New Mexico Press, 1982); W. J. Eccles, *The Canadian Frontier, 1534–1760*, rev. ed. (1969; Albuquerque: University of New Mexico Press, 1983); Hector Chevigny, *Russian America: Alaskan Venture, 1741–1867* (1965; reprint ed., n.p.: Binford, 1979); James R. Gibson, *Imperial Russia in Frontier America: The Changing Geography of Supply of Russian America, 1784–1867* (New York: Oxford University Press, 1976); Frederick Luebke, "Ethnic Minority Groups in the American West," in *Historians and the American West*, edited by Michael P. Malone (Lincoln: University of Nebraska Press, 1983), "Ethnic Group Settlement on the Great Plains," *Western Historical Quarterly* 8 (1977), 405–30, and Leubke, ed., *Ethnicity on the Great Plains* (Lincoln: University of Nebraska Press, 1980); and Carlton C. Qualey, "Ethnic Groups and the Frontier," *American Frontier and Western Issues*, edited by Roger L. Nichols (New York: Greenwood Press, 1986).

4. On the frontier as a zone of intercultural contact, see Howard R. Lamar and Leonard Thompson, eds., *The Frontier in History: North America and Southern Africa Compared* (New Haven: Yale University Press, 1981); Ladis K. D. Kristof, "The Nature of Frontiers and Boundaries," *Annals of the Association of American Geographers* 49 (1959), 269–82; and J. R. V. Prescott, *The Geography of Frontiers and Boundaries* (Chicago: Aldine, 1965). The history of distinctive North American regional societies calls for an *Annales* approach: John Opie, "The Environment and the Frontier," in *American Frontier and Western Issues*, 7–25; F. Roy Willis, "The Contribution of the *Annales* School to Agrarian History: A Review Essay," *Agricultural History* 52 (1978), 538–48; and Robert Forster and Orest Ranum, eds., *Biology of Man in History: Selection from the Annales: Economies, Societies, Civilizations* (Baltimore: Johns Hopkins University Press, 1975). James C. Malin pioneered such an approach to the history of the "grasslands of North America"; see selections from his work in *History and Ecology*, edited by Robert P. Swierenga (Lincoln: University of Nebraska Press, 1984), and the evaluation in Robert Galen Bell, "James C. Malin and the Grasslands of North America," *Agricultural History* 46 (1972), 414–24. More recently the work of historical geographer D. W. Meinig has pointed in a similar direction: "The Growth of Agricultural Regions in the Far West, 1850–1910," *Journal of Geography* 54 (1955), 221–32; "The Mormon Culture Region: Strategies and Patterns in the Geography of the American West, 1847–1964," *Annals of the Association of American Geographers* 55 (1965), 191–220; *The Great Columbia Plain: A Historical Geography, 1805–1910* (Seattle: University of Washington Press, 1968); *Imperial Texas: An Interpretive Essay in Cultural Geography* (Austin: University of Texas Press, 1969); *Southwest: Three Peoples in Geographical Change, 1600–1970* (New York: Oxford University Press, 1971); "American Wests: Preface to a Geographical Introduction," *Annals of the Association of American Geographers* 62 (1972), 159–84; and *The Shaping of America: A Geographical Perspective on 500 Years of History*, volume 1, *Atlantic America, 1492–1800* (New Haven: Yale University Press, 1986), and vol. 2 forthcoming.

5. For a discussion of comparative frontier studies, see Marvin W. Mikesell, "Comparative Studies in Frontier History," in *Turner and the Sociology of the Frontier*, edited by Richard Hofstadter and Seymour Martin Lipset (New York: Basic Books,

1968), and the introduction to William W. Savage, Jr., and Stephen I. Thompson, eds., *The Frontier: Comparative Studies* (Norman: University of Oklahoma Press, 1979). Among the more important contributions to comparative frontier history are James Leyburn, *Frontier Folkways* (New Haven: Yale University Press, 1935); Walker D. Wyman and Clifton B. Kroeber, eds., *The Frontier in Perspective* (Madison: University of Wisconsin Press, 1957); and Lamar and Thompson, eds., *The Frontier in History.* Two proposals for the comparison of American frontiers may be found in Bolton, "The Epic of Greater America," and Jerome O. Steffens, *Comparative Frontiers: A Proposal for Studying the American West* (Norman: University of Oklahoma Press, 1980). On the comparative approach in general, very helpful is Marc Bloch, "A Contribution towards a Comparative History of European Societies," in *Land and Work in Medieval Europe: Selected Papers by Marc Bloch* (New York: Harper & Row, 1969).

6. Conrad M. Arensberg, "The Community as Object and as Sample," *American Anthropologist* 63 (1961), 253.

7. Anthony F. C. Wallace, *The Decline and Rebirth of the Seneca* (New York: Alfred A. Knopf, 1969); William G. McLoughlin, *Cherokee Renascence in the New Republic* (Princeton: Princeton University Press, 1986); James Mooney, *The Ghost-Dance Religion and the Sioux Outbreak of 1890* (1892–93; reissued, Chicago: University of Chicago Press, 1965); David I. Bushnell, Jr., "Native Villages and Village Sites East of the Mississippi River," *Bureau of American Ethnology Bulletin 69* (Washington, D.C.: Smithsonian Institution, 1919); Arrell Morgan Gibson, "The Great Plains as a Colonization Zone for Eastern Indians," in *Ethnicity on the Great Plains;* John Mack Faragher, "The Custom of the Country: Cross-Cultural Marriage in the Far Western Fur Trade," in *Western Women: Their Land, Their Lives,* edited by Lillian Schlissel, Vicki L. Ruiz, and Janice Monk (Albuquerque: University of New Mexico Press, 1988).

8. I find the following works on the historical study of community particularly helpful: David J. Russo, *Families and Communities: A New View of American History* (Nashville: American Association for State and Local History, 1974); Robert V. Hine, *Community on the American Frontier: Separate but Not Alone* (Norman: University of Oklahoma Press, 1980); Richard R. Beeman, "The New Social History and the Search for 'Community' in Colonial America," *American Quarterly* 29 (1977), 422–43; Don Harrison Doyle, "Social Theory and New Communities in Nineteenth-Century America," *Western Historical Quarterly* 8 (1977), 151 65; Thomas Bender, *Community and Social Change in America* (New Brunswick: Rutgers University Press, 1978); and Kathleen Neils Conzen, "Community Studies, Urban History, and American Local History," in *The Past before Us: Contemporary Historical Writing in the United States,* edited by Michael Kammen (Ithaca: Cornell University Press, 1980).

9. Kenneth Lockridge, *A New England Town: The First Hundred Years, Dedham, Massachusetts, 1626–1736* (New York: W. W. Norton, 1970), 168, 172, and Kenneth P. Wilkinson, "In Search of the Community in the Changing Countryside," *Rural Sociology* 51 (1986), 1, 5. For the ideal of community in European and American social thought, see Robert Nisbet, *The Sociological Tradition* (New York: Oxford University Press, 1965) and Raymond Plath, *Community and Ideology: An Essay in Applied Social Philosophy* (London: n.p., 1974).

10. Leyburn, *Frontier Folkways* and Steffens, *Comparative Frontiers* discuss the distinctions between camps and communities; see also Kenneth E. Lewis, *The American Frontier: An Archaeological Study of Settlement Pattern and Process* (Orlando: Aca-

demic Press, 1984). On fur trade communities, see Sylvia Van Kirk, *Many Tender Ties: Women in Fur-Trade Society in Western Canada, 1670–1870* (Winnipeg: Watson & Dwyer, 1980).

11. Timothy Flint, *Recollections of the Last Ten Years* (Boston: Cummings, 1826), 76, 204; Frederick Jackson Turner, *The Significance of the Frontier in American History* (New York: Unger, 1963), 51, and *The Frontier in American History* (New York: Henry Holt, 1920), 107, 342, 344.

12. The sources for the discussion in this and subsequent paragraphs may be located in John Mack Faragher, *Sugar Creek: Life on the Illinois Prairie* (New Haven: Yale University Press, 1986).

13. For the tradition of open country settlement see: Faragher, *Sugar Creek*; Faragher, "Open-Country Community: Sugar Creek, Illinois, 1820–1850," in *The Countryside in the Age of Capitalist Transformation: Essays in the Social History of Rural America*, edited by Steven Hahn and Jonathan Prude (Chapel Hill: University of North Carolina Press, 1985); Darrett B. Rutman, "People in Process: The New Hampshire Towns of the Eighteenth Century," *Journal of Urban History* 1 (1975), 268–92; James T. Lemon, "The Weakness of Place and Community in Early Pennsylvania," in *European Settlement and Development in North America: Essays on Geographical Change in Honour and Memory of Andrew Hill Clark*, edited by James R. Gibson (Toronto: University of Toronto Press, 1978); and Richard R. Beeman, *The Evolution of the Southern Backcountry: A Case Study of Lunenburg County, Virginia, 1746–1832* (Philadelphia: University of Pennsylvania Press, 1984). In the early twentieth century rural sociologists pioneered the study of open country settlements. These valuable works are rarely consulted: Charles J. Galpin, *Rural Life* (1915; reprinted, New York: Holt, 1923); Paul S. Peirce, "Social Surveys of Three Rural Townships in Iowa," *University of Iowa Monographs, Studies in the Social Sciences* 5 (1917); J. H. Kolb, "Primary Rural Groups: A Study of Agricultural Neighborhoods," *University of Wisconsin Agricultural Experiment Station Research Bulletin* 51 (1921); Carl C. Taylor and Carle C. Zimmerman, "Rural Organization: A Study of Primary Groups in Wake County, North Carolina," *North Carolina Agricultural Experiment Station Bulletin* 245 (1922); Dwight Sanderson and Warren S. Thompson, "The Social Areas of Oswego County," *Cornell University Agricultural Experiment Station Bulletin* 422 (1923); E. L. Morgan and Owen Howells, "Rural Population Groups," *University of Missouri Agricultural Experiment Station Research Bulletin* 74 (1925); C. E. Liveley and P. G. Beck, "Movement of the Open Country Population in Ohio, I: The Family Aspect," and "II: The Individual Aspect," *Ohio Agricultural Experiment Station Bulletin* 467 (1930) and 489 (1931); and W. A. Anderson, "The Mobility of Rural Families," *Cornell University Agricultural Experiment Station Bulletin* 607 (1934) and 623 (1935). For a brief discussion of this work in the context of community study, see Faragher, "Open-Country Community."

14. Mody C. Boatright, "The Myth of Frontier Individualism," in *Turner and the Sociology of the Frontier*.

15. For a tradition of mobility on the Anglo-American frontier, see W. R. Prest, "Stability and Change in Old and New England: Clayworth and Dedham," *Journal of Interdisciplinary History* 6 (1976), 359–74; Lorena S. Walsh, "Staying Put or Getting Out: Findings for Charles County, Maryland, 1650–1720," *William and Mary Quarterly* 3d series, 44 (1987), 89–103; John W. Adams and Alice Bee Kasakoff, "Migration and the Family in Colonial New England: The View from Genealogies," *Journal*

of *Family History* 9 (1984), 24–44; Georgia C. Villaflor and Kenneth L. Sokoloff, "Migration in Colonial America: Evidence from the Muster Rolls," *Social Science History* 6 (1984), 539–70; Don Harrison Doyle, *The Social Order of a Frontier Community: Jacksonville, Illinois, 1825–1870* (Urbana: University of Illinois Press, 1978), 96, 261, 262, 264; Peter Coleman, "Restless Grant County: Americans on the Move," in *The Old Northwest*, edited by Harry Scheiber (Lincoln: University of Nebraska Press, 1969), 65–77; Mildred Thorne, "Population Study of an Iowa County in 1850," *Iowa Journal of History* 57 (1959), 305–30; James C. Malin, "The Turnover of Farm Population in Kansas," *Kansas Historical Quarterly* 4 (1935), 339–72; Merle Curti, *The Making of an American Community: A Case Study of Democracy in a Frontier County* (Stanford: Stanford University Press, 1959), 65–77; William G. Robbins, "Opportunity and Persistence in the Pacific Northwest: A Quantitative Study of Early Roseburg, Oregon," *Pacific Historical Review* 39 (1970), 279–96; and Richard S. Alcorn, "Leadership and Stability in Mid-Nineteenth Century America: A Case Study of an Illinois Town," *Journal of American History* 61 (1974–75), 685–702. For Canada, see Paul Voisey, *Vulcan: The Making of a Prairie Community* (Toronto: University of Toronto Press, 1988).

16. For studies of the importance of kinship in community formation, see Faragher, *Sugar Creek*, 56–60, 144–45, 150–51, 199–200, and *Women and Men on the Overland Trail* (New Haven: Yale University Press, 1979); Darrett B. Rutman and Anita H. Rutman, *A Place in Time: Middlesex County, Virginia, 1650–1750* (New York: W. W. Norton, 1984); Beeman, *Evolution of the Southern Backcountry*, 202–04; Paula Hathaway Anderson-Green, "The New River Frontier Settlement on the Virginia-North Carolina Border, 1760–1820," *Virginia Magazine of History and Biography* 86 (1978), 413–31; Doyle, *Social Order of a Frontier Community*, 267; Frank Lawrence Owsley, "Patterns of Migration," in *The South: Old and New Frontiers, Selected Essays of Frank Lawrence Owsley*, edited by Harriet Chappell Owsley (Athens, Ga.: University of Georgia Press, 1969); Irene W. D. Hecht, "Kinship and Migration: The Making of an Oregon Isolate Community," *Journal of Interdisciplinary History* 8 (1977), 45–67; Deborah Fink, "Rural Women and Family in Iowa," *International Journal of Women's Studies* 7 (1984), 57–69; Robert A. Riley, "Kinship Patterns in Londonderry, Vermont, 1772–1900: An Intergenerational Perspective of Changing Family Relationships" (Ph.D. dissertation, University of Massachusetts, 1980); Emora Messer Matthews, *Neighbor and Kin: Life in a Tennessee Ridge Community* (Nashville: Vanderbilt University Press, 1965); and F. Carlene Bryan, *We're All Kin: A Cultural Study of a Mountain Neighborhood* (Knoxville: University of Tennessee Press, 1981).

17. In denominating these communities "American," "Mexican," and "métis," I acknowledge numerous problems. The residents of northern Mexico more likely considered themselves *tejanos, neuvomexicanos,* or Californios than Mexicans. Métis peoples went by a number of names, many of them pejorative. All of them were, by some lights, Americans, but following nineteenth-century usage, "American" in this text is reserved for citizens and subjects of the British colonies or the United States. Names always have a political dimension. For illuminating discussions of ethnic names in relation to the métis, see John E. Foster, "The Métis: The People and the Term," in *Riel and the Métis: Riel Mini-Conference Papers*, edited by Antoine Lussier (Winnipeg: Manitoba Métis Federation Press, 1979), 84–92, and Jennifer S. H. Brown, "Linguistic Solitudes and Changing Social Categories," in *Old Trails and New Directions: Papers of the Third North American Fur Trade Conference*, edited by Carol M. Judd and

Arthur J. Ray (Toronto: University of Toronto Press, 1980), 147–59.

18. Josiah Gregg, *Commerce of the Prairies*, edited by Max L. Moorhead (Norman: University of Oklahoma Press, 1954), 103.

19. John Reps, *Town Planning in Frontier America* (Princeton: Princeton University Press, 1970), 68; Stephen F. de Borhegyi, "The Evolution of a Landscape [Chimayo, New Mexico]," *Landscape* 4 (1954), 24–30; Oakah L. Jones, Jr., *Los Paisanos: Spanish Settlers on the Northern Frontier of New Spain* (Norman: University of Oklahoma Press, 1979); Weber, *The Mexican Frontier*; Roxanne Dunbar Ortiz, *Roots of Resistance: Land Tenure in New Mexico, 1680–1980* (Los Angeles: Chicano Studies Research Center Publications, University of California, Los Angeles, 1980); Marc Simmons, "Settlement Patterns and Village Plans in Colonial New Mexico," *Journal of the West* 8 (1968), 7–21; A. W. Conway, "Village Types in the Southwest," *Landscape* 2 (1952), 14–19; Robert J. Rosenbaum, *Mexicano Resistance in the Southwest: "The Sacred Right of Self-Preservation"* (Austin: University of Texas Press, 1981); and John R. Van Ness, "Hispanic Village Organization in Northern New Mexico: Corporate Community Structure in Historical and Comparative Perspective," in *The Survival of Spanish American Villages, Colorado College Studies*, edited by Paul Kutsche, 15 (1979), 21–44. A number of recent excellent community studies have added greatly to our understanding of settlement in far northern Mexico: Albert Camarillo, *Chicanos in a Changing Society: From Mexican Pueblos to American Barrios in Santa Barbara and Southern California, 1848–1930* (Cambridge: Harvard University Press, 1979); Richard Griswold del Castillo, *The Los Angeles Barrio, 1850–1890* (Berkeley: University of California Press, 1979); Mario T. Garcia, *Desert Immigrants: The Mexicans of El Paso, 1880–1920* (New Haven: Yale University Press, 1981); Arnoldo De León, *The Tejano Community, 1836–1900* (Albuquerque: University of New Mexico Press, 1982); Gilberto Miguel Hinojosa, *A Borderlands Town in Transition: Laredo, 1755–1870* (College Station: Texas A&M University Press, 1983); and Thomas E. Sheridan, *Los Tucsonenses: The Mexican Community in Tucson, 1854–1941* (Tucson: University of Arizona Press, 1986).

20. Rosenbaum, *Mexicano Resistance*, 112–13.

21. Jesus F. de la Teja and John Wheat, "Bexar: Profile of a Tejano Community, 1820–1832," *Southwestern Historical Quarterly* 89 (1985), 7–34; Sheridan, *Los Tucsonenses*, 15; Weber, *Mexican Frontier*, 33, 118; Rosenbaum, *Mexicano Resistance*, 11, 112.

22. Simpson quoted in Marcel Giraud, *The Métis in the Canadian West*, translated by George Woodcock, 2 vols. (1945; English translation, Lincoln: University of Nebraska Press, 1986), 2, 555n; John Reynolds, quoted in Faragher, *Sugar Creek*, 143; Richard Colebrook Harris, *The Seigneurial System in Early Canada: A Geographical Study* (Madison: University of Wisconsin Press, 1966); Jacqueline Peterson, "Ethnogenesis: Settlement and Growth of a 'New People,' " *American Indian Culture and Research Journal* 6 (1982), 22–64, and "The People in Between: Indian-White Marriage and the Genesis of a Métis Society and Culture in the Great Lakes Region, 1680–1830" (Ph.D. dissertation, University of Illinois at Chicago Circle, 1981); Jacqueline Peterson and Jennifer S. H. Brown, eds., *The New Peoples: Being and Becoming Métis in North America* (Lincoln: University of Nebraska Press, 1985); Margaret MacLeod and W. L. Morton, *Cuthbert Grant of Grantown: Warden of the Plains of Red River* (Toronto: McClelland & Stewart, 1963); William C. Wonders, "Far Corner of the Strange Empire: Central Alberta on the Eve of Homestead Settlement," *Great Plains Quarterly* 3 (1983), 92–108; and R. Geoffrey Ironside and E. Tomasky, "Agriculture and River Lot Settle-

ment in Western Canada: The Case of Pakan (Victoria), Alberta," *Prairie Forum* 1 (1976), 3–18. The best general history of the métis is Joseph Howard, *Strange Empire: Louis Riel and the Métis People* (1952; reprinted, Toronto: James Lewis & Samuel, 1974).

23. Stevens in *Report of the Commissioner of Indian Affairs* (Washington, D.C.: Government Printing Office, 1854), 399–402. For métis cart trains, see Rhoda R. Gilman, Carolyn Gilman, and Deborah M. Stultz, *The Red River Trails: Oxcart Routes between St. Paul and the Selkirk Settlement, 1820–1870* (St. Paul: Minnesota Historical Society, 1979).

24. G. Herman Sprenger, "The Métis Nation: Buffalo Hunting vs. Agriculture in the Red River Settlement (circa 1810–1870)," in *The Other Natives: The / Les Métis*, edited by Antoine S. Lussier and D. Bruce Sealey, 3 vols. (Winnipeg: Manitoba Metis Federation Press, 1978), 1:115–30; Gilman, Gilman, and Stultz, *The Red River Trails;* Julia D. Harrison, *Métis: People between Two Worlds* (Vancouver: Glenbow-Alberta Institute, 1985), 22.

25. W. L. Morton, *Manitoba: A History* (Toronto: University of Toronto Press, 1957), 79. Both Giraud, *The Métis* and Howard, *Strange Empire* discuss this point at length.

26. Jones, *Los Paisanos*, 130 and passim; Hinojosa, *A Borderlands Town in Transition*, 32; Marcus Hanson, *Mingling of the Canadian and American Peoples* (Toronto: University of Toronto Press, 1940); and D. Wayne Moodie, "The Trading Post Settlement of the Canadian Northwest, 1774–1821," *Journal of Historical Geography* 13 (1987), 360–74.

27. Marvin Mikesell, "Comparative Studies in Frontier History" quoted in Gilman, Gilman, and Stultz, *Red River Trails*, 86. For patterns in northern Mexico, see Teja and Wheat, "Bexar"; De León, *Tejano Community*, 114; Janet Lecompte, "The Independent Women of Hispanic New Mexico, 1821–1846," *Western Historical Quarterly* 12 (1981), 17–35. For the métis, see Van Kirk, *Many Tender Ties;* Jennifer S. H. Brown, *Strangers in Blood: Fur Trade Company Families in Indian Country* (Vancouver: University of British Columbia Press, 1980) and "Women as Centre and Symbol in the Emergence of Métis Communities," *Canadian Journal of Native Studies* 3 (1983); Jacqueline Peterson, "Women Dreaming: The Religiopsychology of Indian-White Marriage and the Rise of Metis Culture," in *Western Women*, 49–68. For a historiographic discussion of women in frontier societies, see Joan M. Jensen and Darlis A. Miller, "The Gentle Tamers Revisited: New Approaches to the History of Women in the American West," *Pacific Historical Review* 49 (1980), 173–213, and John Mack Faragher, "History from the Inside-Out: Writing the History of Women in Rural America," *American Quarterly* 33 (1981), 537–57.

28. Weber, *Mexican Frontier*, 190–95; Rosenbaum, *Mexicano Resistance*, 112–14; Meinig, *Southwest*.

29. Sprenger, "The Métis Nation"; Frits Pannekoek, "A Probe into the Demographic Structure of Nineteenth Century Red River," in *Essays on Western History in Honour of Lewis Gwynne Thomas*, edited by Lewis H. Thomas (Edmonton: University of Alberta Press, 1976), 81–95; and John A. Hussey, *Champoeg: Place of Transition* (n.p.: n.p, 1967).

30. Population figures from *Historical Statistics of the United States, Colonial Times to 1970* (Washington, D.C.: Government Printing Office, 1976), series A6–8, A195–209.

31. Rosenbaum, *Mexicano Resistance*, 42–45, 99–124, and passim, discusses these examples and others and provides further citations.

32. Weber, *Mexican Frontier*, 240. Rosenbaum, *Mexicano Resistance* and De León, *Tejano Community* take approaches that focus respectively on revolutionary and conventional politics, but both their interpretations seem compatible with this perspective.

33. On métis ethnic identity, see John E. Foster, "The Origins of the Mixed Bloods in the Canadian West," in *Essays on Western History*, 69–80; A. S. Morton, "The New Nation, the Métis," *The Other Natives*, 1, 27–37; and Joe Sawchuk, *The Metis of Manitoba: Reformulation of an Ethnic Identity* (Toronto: Peter Martin Associates, 1978).

34. Song quoted in Howard, *Strange Empire*, 202. Howard provides the best discussion of these events, but the literature on the subject is extensive; consult George F. G. Stanley, *The Birth of Western Canada: A History of the Riel Rebellions* (1936; reprinted, Toronto: University of Toronto Press, 1960) and *Louis Riel* (Toronto: Ryerson, 1963); George Woodcock, *Gabriel Dumont: The Métis Chief and His Lost World* (Edmonton: M. G. Hurtig, 1975); Frits Pannekoek, "Some Comments on the Social Origins of the Riel Protest of 1869," *Riel and the Métis*, 66–83; Wonders, "Far Corner of the Strange Empire," 105, 106; and Irene M. Spry, "The Transition from a Nomadic to a Settled Economy in Western Canada, 1856–96," *Transactions of the Royal Society of Canada* 6 (1968), 187–201.

35. Bolton, "The Epic of Greater America," 463.

LANDSCAPE OF ENCLAVES
Race Relations in the West, 1865–1990

The author would like to thank the editors of this volume for remarkably close attention and invaluable advice, the other volume participants—Ann Butler, Richard White, and John Higham—for taking the time to comment on early drafts, and the National Humanities Center for its bibliographic support and collegial stimulation.

1. Interviews collected for Sarah Deutsch, *No Separate Refuge: Culture, Class, and Gender on an Anglo-Hispanic Frontier in the American Southwest* (New York: Oxford University Press, 1987).

2. For recent historiographical essays on race in the American West, see Richard White, "Race Relations in the American West," *American Quarterly* 38 (Bibliography 1986), 397–416; Robert C. Carriker, "The American Indian from the Civil War to the Present," in *Historians and the American West*, edited by Michael P. Malone (Lincoln: University of Nebraska Press, 1983); Roger L. Nichols, "Historians and Indians," in *American Frontier and Western Issues: A Historiographical Review*, edited by Roger L. Nichols (New York: Greenwood Press, 1986); and Patricia Nelson Limerick, *The Legacy of Conquest: The Unbroken Past of the American West* (New York: W. W. Norton & Co., 1987).

3. The Library of Congress houses more material on this battle than on any other. The impact was heightened by the news hitting the East five days after the nation's centennial. The literature on Custer himself is enormous and easily accessible, but two interesting analyses of the meaning of Custer and that battle are Edward T. Linenthal, Department of Religion and American Studies, University of Wiscon-

sin, guest lecture, MIT, November 12, 1986, *Changing Images of the Warrior Hero in America: A History of Popular Symbolism* (Lewiston, N.Y.: Edwin Mellen Press, 1983), and Richard Slotkin, *The Fatal Environment: The Myth of the Frontier in the Age of Industrialization* (Middletown, Conn.: Wesleyan University Press, 1985).

4. Richard White, *The Roots of Dependency: Subsistence, Environment, and Social Change among the Choctaws, Pawnees, and Navajos* (Lincoln: University of Nebraska Press, 1983), 320, and Deutsch, *No Separate Refuge*, 199.

5. See, for example, Slotkin, *Fatal Environment* on race wars.

6. Victor Clark, 1908, quoted in Deutsch, *No Separate Refuge*, 36. It is in this context that Anglo determination to turn other cultures' gender patterns into replicas of relatively new middle-class ideals must be seen. The Dawes Severalty Act, for example, contained no provision for married women's allotments, and the language describing it made constant reference to its bestowal of "manhood" on the allotted men along with their allotted property, now private. Yet Indian men complained that Anglo agents were trying to make them "become like women," by encouraging them to farm. Dolores Janiewski, "Making Women into Farmers' Wives: The Native American Experience in the Inland Northwest," in *Women and Farming: Changing Roles and Changing Structures*, edited by Wava G. Haney and Jane B. Knowles (Boulder: Westview Press, 1988), 35, 37, 44, and see Janiewski, "To Tame and Domesticate Wild Indians: Gender Relations and Indian Policy in the Late Nineteenth Century" (Social Science History Association Annual Conference, Chicago, November 3–5, 1988), throughout; and Robert A. Trennert, "Educating Indian Girls at New Mexico Reservation Boarding Schools, 1878–1920," in *The American Indian Past and Present*, 3d ed., edited by Roger L. Nichols (New York: Alfred A. Knopf, 1986), 218–31. The Six Companies blamed Chinese prostitution for anti-Chinese sentiment, a conclusion no doubt fostered by the competition between the Six Companies and the tongs (which controlled most of the prostitution) over control of the Chinese in California. Lucie Cheng and Edna Bonacich, eds., *Labor Immigration under Capitalism: Asian Workers in the United States before World War II* (Berkeley: University of California Press, 1984), 402–30, point out that the heyday of Chinese prostitution in San Francisco coincided with mounting anti-Chinese labor agitation and that labor leaders accused Chinese prostitutes of taking sewing from white women; in the period of moral reform, codes aimed at suppressing Chinese prostitution and brothels, though white prostitution was at least as prevalent. See also Lucie Cheng Hirata, "Chinese Immigrant Women in Nineteenth-Century California," in *Women of America: A History*, edited by Carol Ruth Berkin and Mary Beth Norton (Boston: Houghton Mifflin Company, 1979), 224–44.

7. Slotkin, *Fatal Environment*, 320, 442.

8. Jack Chen, *The Chinese of America* (San Francisco: Harper & Row, 1980), 65, points out that before 1869 it was cheaper and quicker to get from Canton to San Francisco than from the Missouri River to San Francisco. Sucheng Chan, *This Bittersweet Soil: The Chinese in California Agriculture, 1860–1910* (Berkeley: University of California Press, 1986), 81–88, 90, 103, 193 on "developmental leasing," 203–206 on leasing from corporations in partnerships. Nell Irvin Painter, *Exodusters: Black Migration to Kansas after Reconstruction* (New York: Alfred A. Knopf, 1977); W. Sherman Savage, *Blacks in the West* (Westport, Conn.: Greenwood Press, 1976), 100, 103–04.

9. Allensworth was not founded until the early twentieth century but expressed many of the same motifs as the 1870s and 1880s Kansas colonies did. On black colo-

nies, see Lonnie G. Bunch, "The Allensworth Saga as Public history," *OAH Newsletter* 16 (November 1988), 4–5; William Loren Katz, *The Black West* (Garden City: Doubleday and Co., 1971), 175–77; Marguerite Mitchell Marshall et al., *An Account of Afro-Americans in Southeast Kansas 1884–1984* (Manhattan, Kan: Sunflower University Press, 1984); Glenda Riley, "American Daughters: Black Women in the West," *Montana* 38:2 (Spring 1988), 14, 20–21; and Sue Armitage, Theresa Banfield, and Sarah Jacobus, "Black Women and Their Communities in Colorado," *Frontiers* 2 (1977), 48.

10. Recent historiographical essays on ethnicity in the American West include Frederick C. Luebke, "Ethnic Minority Groups in the American West," in *Historians and the American West*, 387–418; Carlton C. Qualey, "Ethnic Groups and the Frontier," in *American Frontier*, 199–216. Immigration has rivaled the frontier in the theory of American exceptionalism, and the rivals have evolved largely in isolation from, if not in opposition to, each other. Only the studies of German and Scandinavian immigrants to farming communities on prairies and plains have combined ethnic and frontier analyses, encouraged by the juxtaposition of rural West to urban East. See, for example, Frederick C. Luebke, ed., *Ethnicity on the Great Plains* (Lincoln: University of Nebraska Press, 1980), xii, in which Luebke makes a similar complaint about frontier and ethnic history. Historians of multiethnic mining communities and cities in the West have been slower to set their stories in the context of a distinctly western history. These ethnic histories of European groups set in the West seem to point out more similarities than differences, with the exception of Micaela di Leonardo, cited below. Historians of Chicanos, Indians, and Asians, on the other hand, are often too quick to point to the unique qualities of the histories of those groups.

11. To Irish laborers who had rioted against blacks in New York City during the Civil War, Chinese contract labor seemed all too familiar a pattern. Joining with Asian workers would have meant identifying with their status and lack of power. The IWW sought allies across races in the early 1900s, but Denis Kearney's largely Irish Workingmen's party had a different vision of what it meant to be working class in the 1870s. Cheng and Bonacich, *Labor Immigration*, 177; Alexander Saxton, *The Indispensable Enemy: Labor and the Anti-Chinese Movement in California* (Berkeley: University of California Press, 1971). Slotkin, *Fatal Environment*, 487, holds that the 1890s saw the end of the frontier in the sense that no longer could society permit mavericks—people beyond control—because industry had forged a tight interdependence all too horribly revealed in the paralysis wrought by the railroad strike of 1877. Racial hostility, he and Saxton agree, redirected Anglo workers' attention from monopolies to their fellow workers (443). Cf. John Higham, *Strangers in the Land: Patterns of American Nativism 1860–1925* (New York: Atheneum, 1966) on Jack London's interwoven socialism and racism in the light of western salvation mythology (175).

12. More work needs to be done on cross-ethnic and cross-racial cooperation. Japanese and Mexican farm laborers did join together in a California strike in the early twentieth century. See also George Sanchez, "Chicanos among Others: An Exploration of Multi-ethnic Life in Boyle Heights (California), 1920–1960" (paper delivered at the 3d Annual Latin American Studies Conference, Oberlin College, April 19–20, 1990); C. Robert Haywood, " 'No Less a Man': Blacks in Cow Town Dodge City, 1876–1886," *Western Historical Quarterly* 19 (May 1988), 163; White, "Race Relations," 405; Katz, *The Black West*, 245, 251, 252, 299. See John R. Wunder, "Chinese in Trouble: Criminal Law and Race on the Trans-Mississippi Frontier,"

Western Historical Quarterly 17 (January 1986), 25–41, on the entirely Mexican-American jury for a Chinese man accused of murder in East Las Vegas.

Despite interracial interdependence and intimacy on trail drives and between domestic servants and employers, casual racist rhetoric was all-pervasive in the West and reflected continued job inequities. Clarity of inequality and difference can encourage employers to confide intimacies even more readily than equality can. Trail crews consisted of Mexicans, Indians, and blacks as well as whites, however, and there is little material on relations among the first three. See also Chan, *This Bittersweet Soil*, 381, on rural communities as less prone to racial violence than urban; Michael L. Tate, "From Scout to Doughboy: The National Debate over Integrating American Indians into the Military, 1891–1918," *Western Historical Quarterly* 17 (October 1986), 417–437; Evelyn Nakano Glenn, "The Dialectics of Wage Work: Japanese-American Women and Domestic Service, 1905–1940," *Feminist Studies* 6 (Fall 1980), 432–471; Katz, *The Black West*, 145–148, 164. It would be interesting to know why blacks were segregated in the army but Indians were not.

13. Stacy Flaherty, "Boycott in Butte: Organized Labor and the Chinese Community, 1896–1897," *Montana* 37 (Winter 1987), 35–47; David M. Katzman, *Seven Days a Week: Women and Domestic Service in Industrializing America* (Urbana: University of Illinois Press, 1981), 45, 55; Marion S. Goldman, *Gold Diggers and Silver Miners: Prostitution and Social Life on the Comstock Lode* (Ann Arbor: University of Michigan Press, 1981), 97; and Hirata, "Chinese Immigrant Women," 233. Ironically, exclusion laws enhanced attributes already rendering Chinese deeply suspicious in white eyes. They did not eradicate the Chinese presence but limited it to men and simultaneously forbade intermarriage between Chinese and white residents. The overwhelmingly male Chinese population figured in lurid tales of white slavery.

14. Quoted in Slotkin, *Fatal Environment*, 348. And see Note 6.

15. Slotkin, *Fatal Environment*, 402–03.

16. For example, John Modell, describing anti-Japanese sentiment in California in the 1930s, explained that in contrast with stereotypes of Afro-Americans, Japanese-Americans were supposed to be subject not to chaotic, uncontrolled, primitive lust but rather to an overcivilized, imperial, disciplined drive: "Japanese men didn't want white women; Japan wanted California." But, the theory ran, they would get it by getting white women. John Modell, *The Economics and Politics of Racial Accommodation: The Japanese of Los Angeles, 1900–1942* (Urbana: University of Illinois Press, 1977), 6–7. In addition to the above literature on prostitution in the West, see Ann Butler, *Daughters of Joy, Sisters of Misery: Prostitutes in the American West, 1865–1890* (Urbana: University of Illinois Press, 1985) and Paula Petrik, *Women and Family on the Rocky Mountain Mining Frontier, Helena, Montana, 1865–1900* (Helena: Montana Historical Society Press, 1987).

17. See, for example, Sandra L. Myres, *Westering Women and the Frontier Experience 1800–1915* (Albuquerque: University of New Mexico Press, 1982), 75–76, 80, and "Mexican Americans and Westering Anglos: A Feminine Perspective," *New Mexico Historical Review* 57 (October 1982), 326; and Glenda Riley, *Women and Indians on the Frontier, 1825–1915* (Albuquerque: University of New Mexico Press, 1984).

18. Alice Fletcher, "The Indian Woman and Her Problems," Fletcher-LaFlesche papers, National Anthropological Archives, Smithsonian Museum of Natural History, cited in Janiewski, "To Tame and Domesticate," 4–5.

19. Deutsch, *No Separate Refuge*, 63–86; Janiewski, "To Tame and Domesti-

cate," 4, 10–11; Laura F. Klein, "Contending with Colonization: Tlingit Men and Women in Change," in *Women and Colonization*, edited by Mona Etienne and Eleanor Leacock (New York: Praeger Publishers, 1980), 101–102, 104, on resistance to mission and teacher efforts to "domesticate" Tlingit women who saw no reward for taking on Euroamerican sex roles and much to lose in terms of status within their own group and in relations between the groups. See also Peggy Pascoe, "Gender Systems in Conflict: The Marriages of Mission-Educated Chinese American Women, 1874–1939," *Journal of Social History* 22:4 (Summer 1989), 631–52, and *Relations of Rescue: The Search for Female Moral Authority in the American West, 1874–1939* (New York: Oxford University Press, 1990).

20. Robert W. Larson, "The Knights of Labor and Native Protest in New Mexico," in *Labor in New Mexico: Unions, Strikes, and Social History since 1881*, edited by Robert Kern (Albuquerque: University of New Mexico Press, 1983), 31–52; John Thompson, *Crossing the Frontier: Radical Response in Oklahoma, 1887–1923* (Norman: University of Oklahoma Press, 1986); Helen S. Carter, "Legal Aspects of Widowhood and Aging," in *On Their Own: Widows and Widowhood in the American Southwest 1848–1939*, edited by Arlene Scadron (Urbana: University of Illinois Press, 1988), 271–300.

21. Francis Paul Prucha, *The Great Father: The United States Government and the American Indians* (Lincoln: University of Nebraska Press, 1984), II:479–82, 489–500.

22. Savage, *Blacks in the West*, 158–160, 163–164; Katz, *The Black West*, 256–58, 304; and Garcia, "Mexican Americans and the Politics of Citizenship," 187–204. See also Deutsch, *No Separate Refuge*, 109–11.

23. Glenn, "Dialectics of Wage Work," 442, 470 33n; Armitage et al., "Black Women," 45, 46; David Montejano, *Anglos and Mexicans in the Making of Texas, 1836–1986* (Austin: University of Texas Press, 1987), 133–36; Chan, *This Bittersweet Soil*, 210, 386; Katz, *The Black West*, 252.

24. Rodolfo Acuña, *Occupied America: A History of Chicanos*, 3d ed. (New York: Harper & Row, 1988), 96; Deutsch, *No Separate Refuge*, 26.

25. Roger Daniels, *The Politics of Prejudice: The Anti-Japanese Movement in California and the Struggle for Japanese Exclusion* (Berkeley: University of California Press, 1962); Glenn, "Dialectics of Wage Work," 434–35; Deutsch, *No Separate Refuge*, 154–55; Mario T. Garcia, "Mexican Americans and the Politics of Citizenship: The Case of El Paso, 1936," *New Mexico Historical Review* 59 (April 1984), 187–204, and *Mexican-Americans: Leadership, Ideology, and Identity, 1930–1960* (New Haven: Yale University Press, 1989); Armitage et al., "Black Women," 47; and see Josef J. Barton, "Land, Labor, and Community in Nueces: Czech Farmers and Mexican Laborers in South Texas, 1880–1930," in *Ethnicity on the Great Plains*, 199, on institution building in immigrant enclaves as creating artificial families to perform services their home communities would have provided through family networks.

26. Edward H. Spicer, *Cycles of Conquest: The Impact of Spain, Mexico, and the United States on the Indians of the Southwest, 1533–1960* (Tucson: University of Arizona Press, 1962), 209. The Osage found it was their retention of their kinship system, despite allotment, that preserved their integrity as a tribe, as much as their retention of the subsurface mineral rights that garnered them so much wealth; see Terry P. Wilson, *The Underground Reservation: Osage Oil* (Lincoln: University of Nebraska Press, 1985), x, 20, 22, 45, 175. Headrights to subsurface oil did increase the autonomy and status of widows by 1920.

27. See, for example, Deutsch, *No Separate Refuge;* Janiewski, "To Tame and Domesticate"; Trennert, "Educating Indian Girls"; Spicer, *Cycles of Conquest*, 480, found that matrilineal forms tended to survive longer than patrilineal under the strain of the reservation system; Klein, "Contending with Colonization," 88–108; Laila Shukry Hamamsy, "The Role of Women in a Changing Navaho Society," *American Anthropologist* 59 (1957), 101–11; Scadron, ed., *On Their Own*, particularly Sarah M. Nelson, "Widowhood and Autonomy in the Native-American Southwest" and Alice Shlegel, "Hopi Family Structure and the Experience of Widowhood." Such practices represented both continuity of contribution and discontinuity in form and could increase women's autonomy without liberating them from a primary duty to family and possibly oppressive work and family conditions. Armitage et al., "Black Women," 48; Joan Jensen, "New Mexican Farm Women, 1900–1940," in *Labor in New Mexico*, 61, 65; Glenn, "Dialectics of Wage Work," 435–67; Sylvia Junko Yanagisako, *Transforming the Past: Tradition and Kinship among Japanese Americans* (Stanford: Stanford University Press, 1988), 5. Cf. Yuji Ichioka, *"Amerika Nadeshiko:* Japanese Immigrant Women in the United States, 1900–1924," *Pacific Historical Review* 49 (May 1980), 339–57. Japanese women seemed to find it easier to desert their husbands *(kakeochi)* in this country, but more likely the phenomenon owed itself primarily to the absence of sufficient family and community networks that in Japan made it difficult to "disappear," rather than to the ability to work for wages, since these women usually ran off with men. The unique generational structure of Japanese immigrants caused by the idiosyncrasies of American immigration policy fostered a situation in which women's expected economic contribution to the household often took the form of their paid labor outside the home, in part because their older husbands had reached years of declining income.

28. Spicer, *Cycles of Conquest*, 470, 473–80. And see Scadron, ed., *On Their Own*.

29. Cf. Yanagisako, *Transforming the Past*, who insists that it is time to stop talking about the "traditional family" and to recognize its variable construction, past and present. See also Micaela di Leonardo, *The Varieties of Ethnic Experience: Kinship, Class, and Gender among California Italian-Americans* (Ithaca: Cornell University Press, 1984); Pascoe, "Gender Systems in Conflict"; and Glenn, "Dialectics of Wage Work," 432–71. Maxine Hong Kingston, *The Woman Warrior: Memoirs of a Girlhood among Ghosts* (New York: Vintage Books, 1975); see also, for example, Jeanne Wakatsuki Houston and James D. Houston, *Farewell to Manzanar* (Toronto: Bantam Books, 1973 / San Francisco: Houghton Mifflin, 1974); Cleofas Jaramillo, *Romance of a Little Village Girl* (San Antonio: Naylor, 1955) and *Shadows of the Past* (Santa Fe: Seton Village Press, 1941); Riley, *Women and Indians;* and Deutsch, *No Separate Refuge*, e.g., 63–86.

30. Two directions of comparative work in particular bear far more attention: the significance of age structures and family formation in accounting for different kinds of work experience among racial groups in the West, and differences between regions in the experience of women of the same race. Beginnings on such comparative work have been made by Julia Kirk Blackwelder, *Women of the Depression: Caste and Culture in San Antonio, 1929–1939* (College Station: Texas A&M University Press, 1984); Lawrence de Graaf, "Race, Sex, and Region: Black Women in the American West, 1850–1920," *Pacific Historical Review* 49 (May 1980), 289, 291, 296–97; Riley, "American Daughters," 21–24; and Sarah Deutsch, "Regionalism in U.S. Women's History: The West, 1870–1980" (paper delivered at the Western Historical Associa-

tion Annual Conference, Billings, Montana, October 1986), 7–9, 23 3n and 17n. Women's experience in homesteading may have borne many similarities across races, but the differences in women's relation to the larger society had to affect their domestic experiences as well.

31. See di Leonardo, *Varieties of Ethnic Experience* on definitions of ethnicity varying by sex, economic status, family size, and a host of other variables. This individualization of ethnic identity would make it difficult to define, let alone study, groups, unless various levels of experience were simultaneously recognized. External definitions—for example, the Anglos' identification of Spanish Americans as "Mexicans"— affected all Spanish Americans regardless of how each defined his or her own identity. Nonetheless, the problem of reconciling such multitudinous variety and its effects with group-level histories of racial and ethnic dynamics is far from resolved.

32. For example, Margaret Eleanor Rose, "Women in the United Farm Workers: A Study of Chicana and Mexicana Participation in a Labor Union, 1950 to 1980" (Ph.D. dissertation, University of California at Los Angeles, 1988), 25. Not only spatial boundaries between groups but the geography within enclaves intimately bore on power relations within and between communities. Grid-style multiethnic coal-mining towns, reservation agency towns, urban barrios, black utopias, and rural villages all carried different possibilities for community interaction. Their geography also affected and reflected degrees of individual autonomy, female employment, and hierarchy. Who owned the land? Who designed the layout? Did coethnics live close enough to provide essential support in times of illness or unemployment? Was the work site close enough for neighborhood to overlap with the work force? The work of historical geographers on differences between Hispanic, imperial, ordered town plans and seemingly chaotic pueblos needs to be brought forward to the twentieth century, and the implications for race and ethnic dynamics need to be more fully explored. An example of a western urban study that connects spatial change to changes in power, economy, and politics, as well as demography, is Albert Camarillo, *Chicanos in a Changing Society: From Mexican Pueblos to American Barrios in Santa Barbara and Southern California, 1848–1930* (Cambridge: Harvard University Press, 1979). Spicer, *Cycles of Conquest*, 468, on agency towns; di Leonardo, *Varieties of Ethnic Experience*, 93–94, on *campanilismo* as related to density of settlement; Deutsch, *No Separate Refuge*, 37, 85–106, on coal camps. For examples of historical geography, see essays in Paul Kutsche, ed., *The Survival of Spanish American Villages* (Colorado College Studies, no. 15, Colorado Springs, Spring 1979); Spicer, *Cycles of Conquest*, e.g., 463–65; John W. Reps, *Cities of the American West: A History of Urban Planning* (Princeton: Princeton University Press, 1979); and on a regional level Donald W. Meinig, *Southwest: Three Peoples in Geographical Change, 1600–1970* (New York: Oxford University Press, 1971).

33. Di Leonardo, *Varieties of Ethnic Experience*, 136; Victor G. Nee and Brett de Bary Nee, *Longtime Californ': A Documentary Study of an American Chinatown* (New York: Pantheon, 1972), 73; Tate, "From Scout to Doughboy," 429; Limerick, *Legacy of Conquest*, 252; for 1898 suspicions, see Richard Melzer and Phyllis Ann Mingus, "Wild to Fight: The New Mexico Rough Riders in the Spanish-American War," *New Mexico Historical Review* 59 (April 1984), 126.

34. See, for example, Modell, *The Economics and Politics of Racial Accommodation*, 53, 56, 59, on the rise of antiorientalism in Los Angeles at the time when Japanese were marrying, opening new neighborhoods, and building institutions, and coincid-

ing in their expansion with residential invasions of blacks and immigrant renters; Spicer, *Cycles of Conquest*, 549, 555–59.

35. On racial violence in this period, see, for example, Katz, *Black West*, 225–26.

36. On the relation between minority status and small-farmer dreams, see Deutsch, *No Separate Refuge*, 123–26, 140–42 (the quote by Francis Carey, the president of the National Sugar Company, is from U.S. Congress, Senate, Committee on Finance, *Hearings on the Proposed Tariff of 1921*, Schedule 5, 67th Congress, 2d session. Senate Documents 108, 2264).

Boundary setting also occurred between minority groups in this period. Spanish Americans and Mexicans distanced themselves from each other with derogatory terms as well as residential segregation; there were few marriages between them. Chinese also separated into ethnic groups in this country. Little work has been done on this aspect of boundary setting for these groups or for Indians and blacks. According to Mario Garcia's recent article, Mexican-Americans in El Paso were sufficiently horror-struck at the notion of being identified as "coloreds" to reach unprecedented mobilization in protest. They argued less often for the removal of barriers to the polls and segregation from blacks than that Mexicans belonged with whites. Garcia, "Mexican Americans and the Politics."

37. See Patricia Zavella, *Women's Work and Chicano Families: Cannery Workers of the Santa Clara Valley* (Ithaca: Cornell University Press, 1987); Deutsch, *No Separate Refuge*, 168–99; Vicki Lynn Ruiz, *Cannery Women / Cannery Lives: Mexican Women, Unionization, and the California Food Processing Industry, 1930–1950* (Albuquerque: University of New Mexico Press, 1987); David H. Dinwoodie, "Indians, Hispanos, and Land Reform: A New Deal Struggle in New Mexico," *Western Historical Quarterly* 17 (July 1986), 291–323; Prucha, *The Great Father*, 761–62, 944, 956, 964; Kenneth R. Philp, *John Collier's Crusade for Indian Reform* (Tucson: University of Arizona Press, 1977); Janiewski, "Making Women," 47–48; and White, "Race Relations," 403.

38. Leonard Dinnerstein and David M. Reimers, *Ethnic Americans: A History of Immigration and Assimilation* (New York: Harper & Row, 1975), 78, 80; Modell, *The Economics and Politics of Racial Accommodation*, 181–85; Roger Daniels et al., eds., *Japanese Americans: From Relocation to Redress* (Salt Lake City: University of Utah Press, 1986), 4, 6, 132; Yanagisako, *Transforming the Past*, 5, 42, 68, 73–74, 76; Ann Umemoto, "Crisis in the Japanese Family," in *Asian Women* (Los Angeles: Asian American Studies Center, University of California, Los Angeles, 1975), 31–34; and Glenn, "Dialectics of Wage Work," 434–35.

39. Limerick, *Legacy of Conquest*, 209; Kenneth R. Philp, "Dillon S. Myer and the Advent of Temination: 1950–1953," *Western Historical Quarterly*, 19:1 (January 1988), 37–41; Prucha, *The Great Father*, 1047–48; Harvey D. Rosenthal, "Indian Land Claims and the American Conscience: A Brief History of the Indian Claims Commission," in *Irredeemable America: The Indians' Estate and Land Claims*, edited by Imre Sutton et al. (Albuquerque: University of New Mexico Press, 1985), 46, 55, 57; League of Women Voters, "The Menominee: A Case against Termination" in *The American Indian*, 273–74.

40. Limerick, *Legacy of Conquest*, 209; Yanagisako, *Transforming the Past*, 79; Daniels et al., eds., *Japanese Americans*, 4. By this time, too, the United States Supreme Court had declared the Alien Land Act (1913) unconstitutional and the McCarran-Walter

Act of the same year, 1952, had lifted the ban on Asian immigration and citizenship, which could be seen as the result of the same individualist-conformist impulse. Dinnerstein and Reimers, *Ethnic Americans*, 80; Vernon M. Briggs, Jr., *Immigration Policy and the American Labor Force* (Baltimore: Johns Hopkins University Press, 1984), 101; cf. Montejano, *Anglos and Mexicans*, 270–81, on the impact of the war.

41. Peter Wiley and Robert Gottlieb, *Empires in the Sun: The Rise of the New American West* (New York: G. P. Putnam's Sons, 1982); Acuña, *Occupied*, 310 has some convincing theories on why Chicanos did not join in the Watts riot in the same way blacks did, including higher proportion of homeownership; Rose, "Women in the UFW," 129. Henry Gutierrez addresses some of these issues in his work; see, for example, Henry J. Gutierrez, "The Black and Chicano Education Rights Movements in Los Angeles, 1962–1970" (paper delivered at the annual meeting of the Organization of American Historians, Washington, D.C., March 22–25, 1990).

42. Rose, "Women in the UFW"; see, for example, 6: "Their roles as wives and mothers drew more attention than their presence as picketers, organizers, boycotters, and administrators. Thus gender was the defining characteristic in their work and in the union." Rose poses women's participation in the union in terms of "political familism," using Maxine Baca Zinn's term ("Political Familism: Toward Sex Role Equality in Chicano Families," *Aztlan* 6:1 [1976], 13–27). Note that Florencia Mallon's work on Mexican women in revolutionary movements raises the important caveat that such political familism is not neutral but can perpetuate gender inequalities rather than minimize them. According to Rose, women ran the *campesino* centers of the UFW, which provided social welfare and educational aid.

43. Rose, "Women in the UFW," 90. In addition, the United States unilaterally terminated the bracero program, and in 1975 the Voting Rights Act was extended to include Mexican-Americans as well as blacks in the Southwest; Indians had benefited from inclusion in the War on Poverty. Briggs, *Immigration Policy*, 101; Dinnerstein and Reimers, *Ethnic Americans*, 101–03; Montejano, *Anglos and Mexicans*, 289; William T. Hagan, "Tribalism Rejuvenated: The Native American Since the Era of Termination," in *The American Indian*, 299.

44. Montejano, *Anglos and Mexicans*, 298–99, 304; Briggs, *Immigration Policy*; Acuña, *Occupied America*, 369, 375, 418—in 1983 there were seventy-five such representatives.

45. Wiley and Gottlieb, *Empires in the Sun*; Acuña, *Occupied America*, 384, 415–22. Significantly it is a Chicana politician who is trying to buck the machine in Los Angeles, and her tactic is neighborhood organizing.

46. See, for example, Robert J. Thomas, *Citizenship, Gender, and Work: Social Organization of Industrial Agriculture* (Berkeley: University of California Press, 1985); Zavella, *Women, Work, and Family*; Limerick, *Legacy of Conquest*, 339–47; Silvia Pedraza-Bailey, *Political and Economic Migrants in America* (Austin: University of Texas Press, 1985); Acuña, *Occupied America*, 323, 442–43; Briggs, *Immigration Policy*; Wiley and Gottlieb, *Empires in the Sun*; and White, *Roots*, 311.

47. Prucha, *The Great Father*, 1116–17; Alvin M. Josephy, Jr., *Now That the Buffalo's Gone: A Study of Today's American Indians* (New York: Alfred A. Knopf, 1982), 215ff; Linenthal, guest lecture, MIT, November 12, 1986.

48. Arthur Margon, "Indians and Immigrants: A Comparison of Groups New to the City," *Journal of Ethnic Studies* 4 (Winter 1977), 17–25, blames not the interface between two cultures or even structural discrimination, but the structure or lack of

one in Indian urban enclaves. John F. Martin, "From Judgment to Land Restoration: The Havasupai Land Claims Case" in *Irredeemable America*, loc. cit., 272; Prucha, *The Great Father*, 1109.

49. Daniels et al., eds., *Japanese Americans*, 4–5; "This Is America," *Datelines*, 16, n.d.; Acuña, *Occupied America*, 423–24; Josephy, *Now That the Buffalo's Gone*, 237.

50. Cf. Limerick, *Legacy of Conquest*.

51. Montejano, *Anglos and Mexicans*; cf. White, "Race Relations," 397, on Indians; Howard Lamar on Kanakas in "From Bondage to Contract: Ethnic Labor in the American West, 1600–1890," in *The Countryside in the Age of Capitalist Transformation: Essays in the Social History of Rural America*, edited by Steven Hahn and Jonathan Prude (Chapel Hill: University of North Carolina Press, 1985), 310; di Leonardo, *Varieties of Ethnic Experience*; and Garcia, "Mexican Americans and the Politics of Citizenship," 187–204.

52. Quoted in Wilcomb E. Washburn, "Land Claims in the Mainstream of Indian / White Land History," in *Irredeemable America*, 26.

53. For example, Frederick Jackson Turner, "The Significance of the Frontier in American History," *Proceedings of the Forty-first Annual Meeting of the State Historical Society of Wisconsin* (Madison: 1894), 79–112.

ENGENDERING THE WEST

1. Norman Maclean, *A River Runs through It and Other Stories* (Chicago and London: University of Chicago Press, 1976); Maclean, *A River Runs through It*, with photographs by Joel Snyder (Chicago: University of Chicago Press, 1983); Ronald McFarland and Hugh Nichols, eds., *Norman Maclean*, American Authors Series (Lewiston, Idaho: Confluence Press, 1988).

My thanks to Ann Fabian, Valerie Hartouni, Gail Hershatter, Susan Johnson, Regina Kunzel, George Miles, and Mary Murphy for their comments on earlier versions of this essay.

2. Countless studies explore the ideological place of the American West as symbol and myth, as "an invention of cultural myth," and as frontier. See, for example, Henry Nash Smith, *Virgin Land: The American West as Symbol and Myth* (Cambridge: Harvard University Press, 1950) and Alan Trachtenberg, *The Incorporation of America: Culture and Society in the Gilded Age* (New York: Hill & Wang, 1982), 11–37.

The image of the West frequently obscures the story of its past. Rather than define this disjuncture between "image" and "reality," I plan in this essay to examine the dialectic of the ideology and the experience of the West.

3. Maclean, *A River Runs through It*, 62; Maclean, "The Pure and the Good: On Baseball and Backpacking," 79–80, and Maclean, "USFS 1919: The Ranger, the Cook, and a Hole in the Sky," in McFarland and Nichols, eds., *Norman Maclean*, 127.

4. These overlapping questions reveal the complex relation between experience and ideology. Maclean's lived experiences, for example, contribute to his own understanding of the ideologies of the West and of gender. In addition, his writings, as part of the discourse that produces and inscribes that experience, contribute to our cultural understanding of these ideologies. Narratives work here to naturalize ideology, to hide its constructed quality. In thinking about the relation between ideology and experience, I have found useful Peter L. McLaren, "On Ideology and Education:

Critical Pedagogy and the Politics of Empowerment," *Social Text* 19–20 (Fall 1988), 153–85; Clifford Geertz, "Ideology as a Cultural System," *The Interpretation of Cultures* (New York: Basic Books, 1973), 193–233; and Joan Wallach Scott, "The Evidence of Experience," 1991 (unpublished paper).

As noted below, "gender" is defined here as an ongoing construction that shapes identities and the social practices of women and men over time. In this paper I use the term "gendering" to refer to the process of applying these cultural constructions to people, places, objects, activities, or ideas. While "gendering" is often determined by society, "engendering" is a conscious individual act. On definitions of gender, see "Editorial," *Signs* 13 (Spring 1988), 399–402. Other recent works on gender that have influenced my thinking are Linda J. Nicholson, *Gender and History: The Limits of Social Theory in the Age of the Family* (New York: Columbia University Press, 1986); Joan Wallach Scott, *Gender and the Politics of History* (New York: Columbia University Press, 1988); and Sherry B. Ortner and Harriet Whitehead, eds., *Sexual Meanings: The Cultural Construction of Gender and Sexuality* (Cambridge, England: Cambridge University Press, 1981).

5. See, for example, Frederick Jackson Turner, *The Frontier in American History* (New York: H. Holt & Co., 1920); Ray Allen Billington, *Western Expansion: A History of the American Frontier* (New York: Macmillan, 1949); and Frederick Merk, *History of the Westward Movement* (New York: Alfred A. Knopf, 1978).

6. Dee Brown, *The Gentle Tamers: Women of the Old Wild West* (Lincoln: University of Nebraska Press, 1958), 137.

7. T. A. Larson, "Dolls, Vassals, and Drudges: Pioneer Women in the West," *Western Historical Quarterly* III (January 1972), 5–16; Clifford Drury, *First White Women over the Rockies: Diaries, Letters, and Biographical Sketches of the Six Women of the Oregon Mission Who Made the Overland Journey in 1836 and 1838*, 3 vols. (Glendale, Calif.: A. H. Clark Co., 1963–66).

8. The work of the Coalition for Western Women's History and the Southwest Institute for Research on Women is particularly notable. At least two of the recent conferences resulted in publications: Women's West Conference, Sun Valley, Idaho, 1983, in Susan Armitage and Elizabeth Jameson, eds., *The Women's West* (Norman: University of Oklahoma Press, 1987), and Western Women, Their Land, Their Lives Conference, Tucson, Arizona, 1984, in Lillian Schlissel, Vicki L. Ruiz, and Janice Monk, eds., *Western Women: Their Land, Their Lives* (Albuquerque: University of New Mexico Press, 1988).

9. Nancy A. Hewitt, "Beyond the Search for Sisterhood: American Women's History in the 1980s," *Social History* 10 (October 1985), 299–321; Johnny Faragher and Christine Stansell, "Women and Their Families on the Overland Trail, 1842–67," *Feminist Studies* 2–3 (1975), 150–66; Julie Roy Jeffrey, *Frontier Women: The Trans-Mississippi West, 1840–1880* (New York: Hill & Wang, 1979); John Mack Faragher, *Women and Men on the Overland Trail* (New Haven: Yale University Press, 1979); and Lillian Schlissel, *Women's Diaries of the Western Journey* (New York: Schocken, 1982).

Not all writings on western women adopted a feminist perspective. Working within the framework of western history rather than women's studies, Sandra Myres, for example, argued that "women were an important part of the American frontier experience, but they must be viewed within the context of that experience, not isolated in pristine splendor." Myres thus celebrated the ways in which women and men shared the western experience. Sandra L. Myres, *Westering Women and the Frontier*

Experience, 1800–1915 (Albuquerque: University of New Mexico Press, 1982), xv, and *Ho! For California: Women's Diaries from the Huntington Library* (San Marino: Huntington Library Publications, 1980). Myres also criticizes the work of western historians whose discussions of women were "tacked on at the end of a chapter on the winning of the West."

10. Family stories about female westerners inspired Cathy Luchetti, for example, to help remedy "their absence from history as taught in school. At the time we learned only about the men who defended the Alamo, the men who rode roughshod into Mexico to claim more land for the United States, the men who forged across the mountains and opened the Northwest Passage. History seldom tells the stories of the eight hundred thousand women who also came West. . . ." Cathy Luchetti and Carol Olwell, *Women of the West* (St. George, Utah: Antelope Island Press, 1982), 14. See also Beverly Stoeltje, " 'A Helpmate for Man Indeed': The Image of the Frontier Woman," *Journal of American Folklore* 88 (January–March 1975), 25–41, and Annette Kolodny, *The Lay of the Land: Metaphor as Experience and History in American Life and Letters* (Chapel Hill: University of North Carolina Press, 1975) and *The Land before Her: Fantasy and Experience of the American Frontiers, 1630–1860* (Chapel Hill: University of North Carolina Press, 1984).

11. John Faragher, "History from the Inside Out: Writing the History of Women in Rural America," *American Quarterly* 33:5 (1981), 537–77, and Vera Norwood and Janice Monk, eds., *The Desert Is No Lady: Landscapes in Women's Writing and Art* (New Haven: Yale University Press, 1987).

The University of Nebraska Press has republished many of these materials. See also the recent collections and interpretations of western women's writings, such as Christiane Fischer, ed., *Let Them Speak for Themselves: Women in the American West* (New York: E. P. Dutton, 1977); Elizabeth Hampsten, *Read This Only to Yourself: The Private Writings of Midwestern Women, 1880–1910* (Bloomington: Indiana University Press, 1982); Luchetti and Olwell, *Women of the West;* and Lillian Schissel, Byrd Gibbens, and Elizabeth Hampsten, *Far from Home: Families of the Westward Journey* (New York: Random House, 1989).

12. Glenda Riley, *The Female Frontier: A Comparative View of Women on the Prairie and the Plains* (Lawrence: University Press of Kansas, 1988), 197. See also Riley, *Frontierswomen: The Iowa Experience* (Ames: Iowa State University Press, 1981).

13. For a recent overview of some of this literature, see Elizabeth Jameson, "Toward a Multicultural History of Women in the Western United States," *Signs* 13 (1988), 761–91. See also Rosalinda Mendez Gonzalez, "Distinctions in Western Women's Experience: Ethnicity, Class, and Social Change," in Armitage and Jameson, eds., *The Women's West*, 237–51; Sarah Deutsch, *No Separate Refuge: Culture, Class, and Gender on an Anglo-Hispanic Frontier in the American Southwest, 1880–1940* (New York: Oxford University Press, 1987); Vicki L. Ruiz and Susan Tiano, eds., *Women on the U.S.-Mexico Border* (Boston: Allen & Unwin, 1987); Peggy Pascoe, "Gender Systems in Conflict: The Marriages of Mission-Educated Chinese American Women, 1874–1939," *Journal of Social History* 22 (Summer 1989), 631–52, and *Relations of Rescue: The Search for Female Moral Authority in the American West, 1874–1939* (New York: Oxford University Press, 1990); Mary Paik Lee, "A Korean / California Girlhood," edited by Sucheng Chan, *California History* LXVII (March 1988), 43–55; Asian Women United of California, eds., *Making Waves: An Anthology of Writings by and about Asian American Women* (Boston: Beacon Press, 1989); Shirley Geok-Lin Lim,

Mayumi Tsutakawa, and Margarita Donnelly, eds., *The Forbidden Stitch: An Asian American Women's Anthology* (Corvallis, Ore.: Calyx Books, 1989); Nobuya Tsuchida, ed., *Asian and Pacific American Experiences: Women's Perspectives* (Minneapolis: University of Minnesota Press, 1982); and Susan Armitage, Helen Bannan, Katherine G. Morrissey, and Vicki L. Ruiz, eds., *Women in the West: A Guide to Manuscript Sources* (New York: Garland Publishing, forthcoming).

14. For the purposes of this essay I have provided only a brief overview of western women's history. There have been many fine historiographies and interpretative essays on the state of western women's history. For more complete coverage of this field, see Joan Jensen and Darlis Miller, "Gentle Tamers Revisited: New Approaches to the History of Women in the American West," *Pacific Historical Review* 49 (May 1980), 173–213; Susan Armitage, "Women and Men in Western History: A Stereoptical Vision," *Western Historical Quarterly* 16 (October 1985), 381–95; Paula Petrik, "The Gentle Tamers in Transition: Women in the Trans-Mississippi West," *Feminist Studies* 11 (Fall 1985), 677–94; and Elliot West, "Western Women's History: Past Trends and Future Opportunities" and Elizabeth Jameson, "Comment: Western Women's History in Wider Contexts," papers presented at the American Historical Association Convention, December 1986.

15. Patricia Nelson Limerick, *The Legacy of Conquest: The Unbroken Past of the American West* (New York: W. W. Norton, 1987), 52.

16. Brown, *Gentle Tamers*, 297. Brown notes: "It was the males themselves, of course, who brought about the destruction of their lusty frontier hegemony."

17. Julie Roy Jeffrey, *Frontier Women* (New York: Hill & Wang, 1979), xv–xvi.

18. Maclean, *A River Runs through It*, 101.

19. McFarland and Nichols, eds., *Norman Maclean*, 139, 121–22.

20. There have been many fine studies of the western lumber industry, Forest Service, and forest environment. See, for example, William G. Robbins, "The Western Lumber Industry: A Twentieth-Century Perspective," in *The Twentieth-Century West: Historical Interpretations*, edited by Gerard D. Nash and Richard W. Etulain (Albuquerque: University of New Mexico Press, 1989), 233–56; Ralph W. Hidy, Frank Ernest Hill, and Allan Nevins, *Timber and Men: The Weyerhaeuser Story* (New York: Macmillan, 1963); Thomas R. Cox, *Mills and Markets: A History of the Pacific Coast Lumber Industry to 1900* (Seattle: University of Washington Press, 1974); Robert L. Tyler, *Rebels in the Woods: The IWW in the Pacific Northwest* (Eugene: Oregon Press, 1967); and Harold K. Steen, *The U.S. Forest Service: A History* (Seattle: University of Washington Press, 1976).

21. Paula Petrik, *No Step Backwards: Women and Family on the Rocky Mountain Mining Frontier, Helena, Montana, 1865–1900* (Helena: Montana Historical Society Press, 1987); Ralph Mann, *After the Gold Rush: Society in Grass Valley and Nevada City, California, 1849–1870* (Stanford: Stanford University Press, 1982); Elizabeth Jameson, "Imperfect Unions: Class and Gender in Cripple Creek, 1894–1904" in *Class, Sex and the Woman Worker*, edited by Milton Cantor and Bruce Laurie (Westport, Conn.: Greenwood Press, 1977); Elliot West, "Beyond Baby Doe: Child Rearing on the Mining Frontier" and Mary Murphy, "The Private Lives of Public Women: Prostitution in Butte, Montana, 1878–1917," in Armitage and Jameson, eds., *The Women's West*, 179–92, 193–205; and Susan Johnson, " 'Nothing Like Home Comforts and Home Joys': Gold Rush Domestic Life in California's Southern Mines" (1986) and " 'Into

This Vortex': Men and the Meaning of Morality in Gold Rush California" (1987) (unpublished papers).

22. Olive Barber, *The Lady and the Lumberjack* (New York: Thomas Y. Crowell Co., 1952), v.

23. Forestry remains a gender-specific activity. See Elaine Pitt Enarson, *Woods-Working Women: Sexual Integration in the U.S. Forest Service* (Tuscaloosa: University of Alabama Press, 1984); Paula J. Williams, "Women and Forest Resources: A Theoretical Perspective" in *Women in Natural Resources: An International Perspective*, edited by Molly Stock, Jo Ellen Force, and Dixie Ehrenreich (Moscow: University of Idaho, Forest, Wildlife & Range Experiment Station, 1969), 93–130.

24. Barbara Amy Breitmayer Vatter, *A Forest History of Douglas County, Oregon: A Microcosmic Study of Imperialism* (New York: Garland Publishing, 1985); see also William Grover Robbins, "The Far Western Frontier: Economic Opportunity and Social Democracy in Early Roseburg, Oregon" (Ph.D. dissertation, University of Oregon, 1969).

25. For memoirs by women of their lives in forestry and logging, see, for example, Jeanne Kellar Beaty, *Lookout Wife* (New York: Random House, 1953); Roberta McConnell, *Never Marry a Ranger* (New York: Prentice Hall, 1950); Dorothy G. Gluck, "Occupation, Ranger's Wife," *American Forests* 61 (March 1955), 32, 65–66; Anna M. Lind, "Women in Early Logging Camps: A Personal Reminiscence," *Journal of Forest History* 19 (July 1975), 128–35.

26. Emil Engstrom, *The Vanishing Logger* (New York: Vantage Press, 1956), Irma Lee Emmerson with Jean Muir, *The Woods Were Full of Men* (New York: David McKay Co., 1963), 27. See also Barber, *Lady and Lumberjack* and McConnell, *Never Marry a Ranger* on the process of initiation.

27. "The Forest Ranger: Yesterday and Today," *American Forests* 61 (March 1955), 46–47; Gluck, "Occupation, Ranger's Wife," 32. Elaine Tyler May, *Homeward Bound: American Families in the Cold War Era* (New York: Basic Books, 1988); William H. Whyte, Jr., *The Organization Man* (New York: Simon & Schuster, 1956).

28. Abbie Widner to John Weber, March 11, 1905, Abbie Widner papers, MsSc 194, Eastern Washington State Historical Society, Spokane.

29. Christine Stansell, *City of Women: Sex and Class in New York, 1789–1860* (New York: Alfred A. Knopf, 1986); Kathy Peiss, *Cheap Amusements: Working Women and Leisure in Turn-of-the-Century New York* (Philadelphia: Temple University Press, 1986); and Joanne A. Meyerowitz, *Women Adrift: Independent Wage Earners in Chicago, 1880–1930* (Chicago: University of Chicago Press, 1988). On prostitution in the West, see Ann M. Butler, *Daughters of Joy, Sisters of Misery: Prostitutes in the American West, 1865–90* (Urbana and Chicago: University of Illinois Press, 1985) and Marion S. Goldman, *Gold Diggers and Silver Miners: Prostitution and Social Life on the Comstock Lode* (Ann Arbor, University of Michigan Press, 1981).

30. Catharine Burgess Carr to William Carr, April 22, 1914, Hamptonetta Burgess Carr papers, Cage 139, Manuscripts and Special Collections, Washington State University Library, Pullman, Washington. Carr's letters contain many references to the various women she met on the road. By contrast, there are few references to the men she encountered in her travels.

31. Catharine Carr to William Carr, June 17, 1914, Carr papers.

32. For brief syntheses of postmodernism, see Andrew Ross, ed., "Introduc-

tion," *Universal Abandon? The Politics of Postmodernism* (Minneapolis: University of Minnesota Press, 1988), vii–xviii, and Frederic Jameson, "Postmodernism, or the Cultural Logic of Late Capitalism," *New Left Review* 146 (1984), 53–92.

Recent work on the connections between feminism and postmodernism includes: Linda Alcott, "Cultural Feminism versus Post-Structuralism: The Identity Crisis in Feminist Theory," *Signs* 13 (Spring 1988), 405–36; Jane Flax, "Postmodernism and Gender Relations in Feminist Theory," *Signs* 12 (Summer 1987), 621–43; Nancy Fraser and Linda Nicholson, "Social Criticism without Philosophy: An Encounter between Feminism and Postmodernism," in Ross, ed., *Universal Abandon?*, 83–104; Rachel T. Hare-Mustin and Jeanne Marecek, "The Meaning of Difference: Gender Theory, Postmodernism, and Psychology," *American Psychologist* 43 (June 1988), 455–64; Mary Poovey, "Feminism and Deconstruction," Joan W. Scott, "Deconstructing Equality-versus-Difference: Or, The Uses of Poststructuralist Theory for Feminism," *Feminist Studies* 14 (Spring 1988), 51–65, 33–50.

On the role of language in the construction of gender, see Judith Butler, *Gender Trouble: Feminism and the Subversion of Identity* (New York: Routledge, Chapman & Hall, 1990) and Joan Wallach Scott, "On Language, Gender, and Working-Class History" in *Gender and the Politics of History*, 53–67.

RELIGION IN THE AMERICAN WEST

1. Henry K. Carroll, *The Religious Forces of the United States . . .* (New York: Christian Literature Co., 1893), xiv, xliii.

2. Wilbur Zelinsky, "An Approach to the Religious Geography of the United States: Patterns of Church Membership in 1952," *Annals of the Association of American Geographers* 51 (June 1961), 163–64, 193; also, Eldon G. Ernst, "American Religious History from a Pacific Coast Perspective," *Religion and Society in the American West* (Lanham, Md.: University Press of America, 1987), 9–10.

3. James R. Shortridge, "A New Regionalization of American Religion," *Journal for the Scientific Study of Religion* 16 (June 1977), 143–53.

4. Samuel S. Hill, "Religion and Region in America," *Annals of the American Academy of Political and Social Science* 480 (July 1985), 137; also, Roger W. Stump, "Regional Divergence in Religious Affiliation in the United States," *Sociological Analysis* 45 (Winter 1984), 293.

5. U.S. Bureau of the Census, *Religious Bodies: 1926*, 2 vols. (Washington: Government Printing Office, 1926), and *Religious Bodies: 1936*, 3 vols. (Washington: U.S. Government Printing Office, 1941).

6. Raymond Brady Williams, *Religions of Immigrants from India and Pakistan* (Cambridge, England: Cambridge University Press, 1988), 69–73; Charles Lippy and Peter Williams, eds., *Encyclopedia of the American Religious Experience*, 3 vols. (New York: Scribner's, 1988), 2:688; and J. Gordon Melton, ed., *The Encyclopedia of American Religions*, 3d ed. (Detroit: Gale Research, Inc., 1989), 898.

7. Williams, *Religions of Immigrants*, 64.

8. Arvind Sharma, "The Rajneesh Movement," in *Religious Movements* (New York: Paragon House, 1985), 115, 117; Hugh Milne, *Bhagwan: The God That Failed* (New York: St. Martin's Press, 1986); Kate Strelly, *The Ultimate Game* (San Francisco: Harper & Row, 1987).

9. *Religious Bodies: 1936*, 1:7; Williams, *Religions of Immigrants*, 86.

10. Yvonne Y. Haddad and Adair Lummis, *Islamic Values* (New York: Oxford University Press, 1987), 4.

11. M. Arif Ghayur, "Muslims in the United States: Settlers and Visitors," *Annals of the American Academy of Political and Social Science* 454 (March 1981), 151, 159; Williams, *Religions of Immigrants*, 86; U.S. Bureau of the Census, *1980 Census of Population*, vol. 1, chap. B, part 1, 50, table 47.

12. Ghayur, "Muslims," 159; *Harvard Encyclopedia of American Ethnic Groups* (Cambridge: Harvard University Press, 1980), 523.

13. Remarks of the regional director of the National Conference of Christians and Jews, in *Dialogue: A Journal of Mormon Thought* 18 (Summer 1985), 39.

14. Joseph R. Haiek, *Arab American Almanac*, 3d ed. (Glendale, Calif.: New Circle Publishing Co., 1984), 106–07.

15. *Religious Bodies: 1926*, 2:337, 339; *Religious Bodies: 1936*, 1:383.

16. *Harvard Encyclopedia of American Ethnic Groups*, 140–141, 147.

17. Lippy and Williams, *Encyclopedia of the American Religious Experience*, 1:80.

18. *Religious Bodies: 1936*, 1:7, 11.

19. S. W. Kung, *Chinese in American Life* (Seattle: University of Washington Press, 1962), 53–55; Gunther Barth, *Bitter Strength* (Cambridge: Harvard University Press, 1964); Francis L. K. Hsu, *The Challenge of the American Dream* (Belmont, Calif.: Wadsworth Pub. Co., 1971); Jack Chen, *The Chinese of America* (San Francisco: Harper & Row, 1980); Shi-Shan Henry Tsai, *China and the Overseas Chinese in the United States, 1868–1911* (Fayetteville: University of Arkansas Press, 1983); Tsai, *The Chinese Experience in America* (Bloomington: Indiana University Press, 1986), 42–44; and Sucheng Chang, *This Bittersweet Soil* (Berkeley: University of California Press, 1986), 8.

20. Toru Matsumoto, *Beyond Prejudice* (New York: Friendship Press, 1946), 3.

21. Hilary Conroy, *The Japanese Frontier in Hawaii, 1868–1898* (Berkeley: University of California Press, 1953), 95–96, 101–02; Bill Hosokawa, *Nisei* (New York: William Morrow, 1969), 126, 130–31; John Modell, *The Economics and Politics of Racial Accommodation* (Urbana: University of Illinois Press, 1977), 75–76; Sumio Koga, "A Centennial Legacy" (Chicago: Nobart, 1977), 10; Dorothy Ochiai Hazama and Jane Okamoto Komeiji, *Okage same de: The Japanese in Hawaii, 1885–1985* (Honolulu: Bess Press, 1986), 78; and Yuji Ichioka, *Issei* (New York: Free Press, 1988), 16, 176.

22. Yamato Ichihashi, *Japanese in the United States* (Stanford: Stanford University Press, 1932), 224, and Edward K. Strong, Jr., *Japanese in California* (Stanford: Stanford University Press, 1933), 169.

23. Hosokawa, *Nisei*, 128.

24. *Religious Bodies: 1936*, 1:178, 294, 303; Hosokawa, *Nisei*, 130–31.

25. Eliot G. Mears, *Resident Orientals on the American Pacific Coast* (Chicago: University of Chicago Press, 1928), 379.

26. Dennis M. Ogawa, *Kodomo no tame ni: For the Sake of the Children* (Honolulu: University of Hawaii Press, 1978), 194.

27. Kung, *Chinese in American Life*, 55.

28. Lippy and Williams, *Encyclopedia of the American Religious Experience*, 2:705, 708; Gail Law, *Chinese Churches Handbook* (Hong Kong: Chinese Coordination Centre of World Evangelism, 1982), 243.

29. Soon Jung Lee, "The Role of the Korean Immigrant Church in the United States . . ." (M.Th. thesis, Fuller Theological Seminary, 1983), 61, 65; Chun-Il Cho,

"The History and Prospects of Korean Immigrant Churches" (D.M. dissertation, Fuller Theological Seminary, 1984), 9, 15, 182; Kwon Oh-Dal, "The Growth of the Korean Church in America" (M.Th. thesis, Fuller Theological Seminary, 1986), 62; Marion Dearman, "Structure and Function of Religion in the Los Angeles Korean Community," in Evi-Young Yu, Earl H. Phillips, Eun Sik Yang, eds., *Koreans in Los Angeles* (Los Angeles: California State University, 1982), 168–70.

30. Leonard Dinnerstein and David M. Reimers, *Ethnic Americans*, 3d ed. (New York: Dodd, Mead, 1988), 97.

31. U.S. Bureau of the Census, *Statistical Abstract of the United States: 1990* (Washington: U.S. Government Printing Office, 1990), 10.

32. Nguyen Manh Hung, "Vietnamese," in *Refugees in the United States*, (Westport, Conn.: Greenwood Press, 1985), 203.

33. *Harvard Encyclopedia of American Ethnic Groups*, 510.

34. Chang Duc Vu, "Strategy of Evangelism . . ." (D.M. dissertation, California Graduate School of Theology, 1985), 29–38, and Hung, "Vietnamese," 202.

35. Timothy Dunnigan and Douglas Olney, "Hmong," in *Refugees in the United States*, 112, 117–18, 121.

36. May Ebihara, "Khmer," in *Refugees in the United States*, 131, 135, 138.

37. Paul J. Strand and Woodrow Jones, Jr., *Indochinese Refugees in America* (Durham: Duke University Press, 1985) and Robert M. Jiobu, *Ethnicity and Assimilation* (Albany: State University of New York Press, 1988).

38. George M. Scott, Jr. "A New Year in a New Land: Religious Change among the Lao Hmong Refugees in San Diego," in *The Hmong in the West* (Minneapolis: University of Minnesota Press, 1982), 67–70.

39. William M. Kramer and Norton B. Stern, "The Layman as Rabbinic Officiant in the 19th Century," *Western States Jewish Historical Quarterly* 16 (October 1983), 49–53.

40. Harriet and Fred Rochlin, *Pioneer Jews* (Boston: Houghton Mifflin, 1984), 203–05.

41. Bernard Quinn et al., *Churches and Church Membership in the United States, 1980* (Atlanta: Glenmary Research Center, 1982), 2, 5–9. For contradictory figures, see Jack Wertheimer, "Recent Trends in American Judaism," *American Jewish Yearbook, 1989* (New York: American Jewish Committee, 1989), 84.

42. Robert E. Levinson, *The Jews in the California Gold Rush* (New York: Ktav Publishing House, 1978), 88, and "American Jews in the West," *Western Historical Quarterly* 5 (July 1974), 291–92; Rochlin and Rochlin, *Pioneer Jews*, 208.

43. Peter R. Decker, "Jewish Merchants in San Francisco: Social Mobility on the Urban Frontier" and Mitchell Gelfand, "Progress and Prosperity," *American Jewish Historical Quarterly* 68 (March 1979), 396–407 and 408–23.

44. Lippy and Williams, *Encyclopedia of the American Religious Experience*, 1:295.

45. Neil C. Sandberg, *Jewish Life in Los Angeles* (Lanham, Md.: University Press of America, 1986), 71.

46. Max Vorspan and Lloyd Gartner, *History of the Jews of Los Angeles* (San Marino: Huntington Library, 1970), 283.

47. Dinnerstein and Reimers, *Ethnic Americans*, 180.

48. Wertheimer, "Recent Trends in American Judaism," 83.

49. *Los Angeles Times*, May 18, 1989, part V, 16.

50. F. Patrick Nichelson, "Non-Protestants in Southern California," in William

M. Kramer, ed., *The American West and the Religious Experience* (Los Angeles: Will Kramer, 1974), 138.

51. Eugene L. Fevold, "The Norwegian Immigrant and His Church," *Norwegian-American Studies* 23 (1967), 51, and Lars Ljungmark, *Swedish Exodus* (Carbondale, Ill.: Southern Illinois University Press, 1979), 116.

52. Ljungmark, *Swedish Exodus*, 116–17.

53. Ibid., 117; Abdel Ross Wentz, *A Basic History of Lutheranism in America* (Philadelphia: Muhlenberg Press, 1955), 194; Adolph B. Benson and Naboth Hedin, *Americans from Sweden* (Philadelphia: Lippincott, 1950), 199, 207; and George M. Stephenson, *The Religious Aspects of Swedish Immigration* (Minneapolis: University of Minnesota Press, 1932).

54. Mario S. DePillis, "Cleng Peerson and the Communitarian Background of Norwegian Immigration," *Norwegian-American Studies* 21 (1962), 136–57.

55. Laurence M. Larson, *The Changing West and Other Essays* (Northfield, Minn.: Norwegian-American Historical Association, 1937), 168, and Fevold, "The Norwegian Immigrant and His Church," 4, 25–27.

56. Theodore C. Blegen, *Norwegian Migration to America: The American Transition* (Northfield, Minn.: Norwegian-American Historical Association, 1940), 173.

57. Arlow W. Andersen, *The Norwegian-Americans* (Boston: Twayne Publishers, 1975), 112.

58. Frederick Hale, ed., *Danes in North America* (Seattle: University of Washington Press, 1984), 164, 166, and George R. Nielsen, *The Danish Americans* (Boston: Twayne Publishers, 1981), 59–69, 79, 82, 88.

59. Johannes Knudsen, *The Formation of the Lutheran Church in America* (Philadelphia: Fortress Press, 1978), 17; also, E. Clifford Nelson, ed., *The Lutherans in North America* (Philadelphia: Fortress Press, 1975), 272–75.

60. Wentz, *Basic History of Lutheranism*.

61. Terry G. Jordan, "A Religious Geography of the Hill Country Germans of Texas," in *Ethnicity on the Great Plains*, edited by Frederick C. Luebke (Lincoln: University of Nebraska Press, 1980), 116.

62. Linda K. Prichard, "A Comparative Approach to Western Religious History. . . ," *Western Historical Quarterly* 19 (November 1988), 416–19.

63. Ann Crittenden, *Sanctuary* (New York: Weidenfeld and Nicholson, 1988) and Ignatius Bau, *This Ground Is Holy* (New York, 1985).

64. James S. Slotkin, *The Peyote Religion* (Glencoe, Ill.: Free Press, 1956; reprinted, New York: Free Press, 1975); Robert S. Michaelsen, " 'We Also Have a Religion': The Free Exercise of Religion among Native Americans," *American Indian Quarterly* 7 (Summer 1983), 111–42; and *New York Times*, April 18, 1990, A-10.

65. *1980 Census*, vol. 1, chap. B, part 1, 50, table 47, 115, table 58.

66. Clyde A. Milner II and Floyd A. O'Neil, eds., *Churchmen and the Western Indians, 1820–1920* (Norman: University of Oklahoma Press, 1985).

67. Alvin M. Josephy, *Now That the Buffalo's Gone* (New York: Alfred A. Knopf, 1982), 78, 81.

68. David Ross Scates, "Religious Change among the Navajo" (D.M. dissertation, Fuller Theological Seminary, 1979), 144.

69. Åke Hultkrantz, *The Study of American Indian Religions* (New York and Chico, Calif.: Crossroad Publishing Co., 1983), 110.

70. Lippy and Williams, *Encyclopedia of the American Religious Experience*, 1:149–

50; Åke Hultkrantz, *Native Religions of North America* (San Francisco: Harper & Row, 1987), 84, 127; Josephy, *Now That the Buffalo's Gone*, 91.

71. *Salt Lake Tribune*, September 2, 1989, 2, and *New York Times*, September 3, 1989, 29.

72. Sam Gill, *Native American Religious Action* (Columbia, S.C.: University of South Carolina Press, 1987), 177.

73. Sarah Deutsch, *No Separate Refuge* (New York: Oxford University Press, 1987); Arnoldo De León, *The Tejano Community, 1836–1900* (Albuquerque: University of New Mexico Press, 1982).

74. Richard G. del Castillo, *The Los Angeles Barrio, 1850–1890* (Berkeley: University of California Press, 1979); Albert Camarillo, *Chicanos in a Changing Society* (Cambridge: Harvard University Press, 1979); Mario T. Garcia, *Desert Immigrants* (New Haven: Yale University Press, 1981); Ricardo Romo, *East Los Angeles* (Austin: University of Texas Press, 1983); Gilberto M. Hinojosa, *A Borderlands Town in Transition, Laredo, 1755–1870* (College Station: Texas A&M University Press, 1983); David Montejano, *Anglos and Mexicans in the Making of Texas, 1836–1986* (Austin: University of Texas Press, 1987).

75. Leo Grebler et al., *The Mexican-American People* (New York: Free Press, 1970), 443.

76. Alfredo Mirande, *The Chicano Experience* (Notre Dame: University of Notre Dame Press, 1985), 132–34.

77. Ibid., 134, 141 and Rodolfo Acuña, *Occupied America: A History of Chicanos*, 2d ed. (New York: Harper & Row, 1981), 55, 114, 124, 304, 314.

78. David J. Weber, "Failure of a Frontier Institution: The Secular Church in the Borderlands under Independent Mexico, 1821–1846," *Western Historical Quarterly* 12 (April 1981), 125–43.

79. Acuña, *Occupied America*, 121.

80. Thomas Muller and Thomas J. Espenshade, *The Fourth Wave: California's Newest Immigrants* (Washington, D.C.: Urban Institute Press, 1985), e.g., 59.

81. Mirande, *Chicano Experience*, 133.

82. Jeffrey M. Burns, "The Mexican-American Catholic Community in California, 1850–1980," in *Religion and Society in the American West*, 261–64; Matt S. Meier and Feliciano Rivera, *Dictionary of Mexican American History* (Westport, Conn.: Greenwood Press, 1981), 299.

83. Burns, "Mexican-American Catholic Community," 263.

84. Carroll, *Religious Forces*, 378–79, and J. Russell Hale, *The Unchurched: Who They Are and Why They Stay Away* (San Francisco: Harper & Row, 1980), 41.

85. On the data, see Kevin J. Christiano, *Religious Diversity and Social Change: American Cities, 1890–1906* (Cambridge, England: Cambridge University Press, 1987), 30–41.

86. Quoted in Eldon G. Ernst, "Religion in California," *Pacific Theological Review* 19 (Winter 1986), 46.

87. Carroll V. West, "Montana's Self-Confessed Elite," *Montana* 33 (Autumn 1983), 39.

88. Rodney Stark and William Sims Bainbridge, *The Future of Religion: Secularization, Revival and Cult Formation* (Berkeley: University of California Press, 1985), 69.

89. *Statistical Abstract of the United States, 1990*, 58; *Yearbook of American & Cana-*

dian Churches, 1990 (Nashville: Abingdon Press, 1990), 293.

90. B. Quinn et al., *Churches and Church Membership*, 10–310.

91. Stark and Bainbridge, *Future of Religion*, 70–72, 77, 79, and Barry A. Kosmin, *Research Report: The National Survey of Religious Identification, 1989–90* (New York: City University of New York, 1991), 10–11.

92. Ferenc Morton Szasz, *The Protestant Clergy in the Great Plains and Mountain West, 1865–1915* (Albuquerque: University of New Mexico Press, 1988), 211.

93. D. F. Anderson, "San Francisco Evangelicalism, Regional Religious Identity, and the Revivalism of D. L. Moody," *Fides et Historia* 15 (Spring–Summer 1983), 60.

94. Wade Clark Roof and William McKinney, *American Mainline Religion: Its Changing Shape and Future* (New Brunswick, N.J.: Rutgers University Press, 1987), 131.

95. Roger W. Stump, "Regional Migration and Religious Commitment in the United States," *Journal for the Scientific Study of Religion* 23 (September 1984), 295, and Robert Wuthnow, *Experimentation in American Religion* (Berkeley: University of California Press, 1978), 11.

96. Stark and Bainbridge, *Future of Religion*, 74–75.

97. Jeffrey K. Hadden and Charles E. Swann, *Prime Time Preachers: The Rising Power of Televangelism* (Reading, Mass.: Addison-Wesley, 1981), 59–61.

98. William Martin, "Television: The Birth of a Media Myth," *Atlantic* (June 1981), 11–13, and Jeffrey K. Hadden and Anson Shupe, *Televangelism* (New York: H. Holt, 1988), 147–57.

99. George Gallup, Jr., and David Poling, *The Search for America's Faith* (Nashville: Abingdon Press, 1980), 79.

100. W. Sherman Savage, *Blacks in the West* (Westport, Conn.: Greenwood Press, 1976) and William L. Katz, *The Black West*, 3d ed. (Seattle: Open Hand Publishing, 1987).

101. Stump, "Regional Migration and Religious Commitment," 295, 298–99.

102. Hill, "Religion and Region in America," 135.

103. Carroll, *Religious Forces*, xliii.

104. B. Quinn et al., *Churches and Church Membership*, 10–27, and Kosmin, *Research Report*, 10–11.

105. Stark and Bainbridge, *Future of Religion*, 70.

106. B. Quinn et al., *Churches and Church Membership*, 10–11, 13–14, 18–21, 23, 25–27, and LDS Church statistical report for December 31, 1990. Kosmin's *Research Report* does not itemize denominations (such as Baptists) by their separate churches and therefore shows a different pattern.

107. Rodney Stark, "The Rise of a New World Faith," *Review of Religious Research* 26 (September 1984), 22; remarks of Stark at annual meeting of the Society for the Scientific Study of Religion, Salt Lake City, Utah, October 27, 1989; B. Quinn et al., *Churches and Church Membership*, 80; Klaus J. Hansen, *Mormonism and the American Experience* (Chicago: University of Chicago Press, 1981); Robert Gottlieb and Peter Wiley, *America's Saints* (New York: Putnam, 1984); Jan Shipps, *Mormonism* (Urbana: University of Illinois Press, 1985); Edward Leo Lyman, *Political Deliverance* (Urbana: University of Illinois Press, 1986); Thomas G. Alexander, *Mormonism in Transition* (Urbana: University of Illinois Press, 1986); Eugene E. Campbell, *Establishing Zion* (Salt Lake City: Signature Books, 1988); Edwin Brown Firmage and R. Collin Man-

grum, *Zion in the Courts* (Urbana: University of Illinois Press, 1988); and Marvin S. Hill, *Quest for Refuge* (Salt Lake City: Signature Books, 1989).

108. Lawrence Foster, *Religion and Sexuality* (New York: Oxford University Press, 1981) and Jessie L. Embry, *Mormon Polygamous Families* (Salt Lake City: University of Utah Press, 1987). See also D. Michael Quinn, "Plural Marriage and Mormon Fundamentalism," in *Remaking the World: Fundamentalist Impact*, edited by Martin Marty and R. Scott Appleby (Chicago: University of Chicago Press, 1992).

109. Dean May, "A Demographic Portrait of the Mormons, 1830–1980," in *After 150 Years* edited by Thomas Alexander and Jessie Embry (Provo: Brigham Young University Press, 1983), 37–70; Thomas Martin, Tim Heaton and Stephen Bahr, eds., *Utah in Demographic Perspective* (Salt Lake City: Signature Books, 1986); and Larry Logue, *Sermon in the Desert: Belief and Behavior in Early St. George, Utah* (Urbana: University of Illinois Press, 1988).

110. Boyd K. Packer, "The Mantle Is Far, Far Greater than the Intellect," *BYU Studies* 21 (Summer 1981), 259–78; "Apostles versus Historians," *Newsweek* (February 15, 1982), 77; "Access to the Archives," *Sunstone Review* (September 1983), 7; Davis Bitton, "Ten Years in Camelot: A Personal Memoir," *Dialogue* 16 (Autumn 1983), 9–20; Shipps, *Mormonism*, 41–65.

111. Stark and Bainbridge, *Future of Religion*, 95.

112. Sandra S. Frankiel, *California's Spiritual Frontiers* (Berkeley: University of California Press, 1988).

113. Christiano, *Religious Diversity and Social Change*, 68, 181–84.

114. Sydney Ahlstrom, "From Sinai to the Golden Gate," in *Understanding the New Religions*, edited by Jacob Needleman and George Baker (New York: Seabury Press, 1978), 21–22.

115. Nichelson, "Non-Protestants in Southern California," 131–32.

116. Winthrop Hudson, *Religion in America*, 4th ed. (New York: Macmillan Publishing Co., 1987), 5.

117. Gregory H. Singleton, *Religion in the City of Angels* (Ann Arbor: UMI Research Press, 1979), 147, and Robert S. Ellwood, Jr., and Donald E. Miller, "Eastern Religions and New Spiritual Movements," in *The Religious Heritage of Southern California*, edited by Msgr. Francis J. Weber (Los Angeles, 1976), 99.

118. Singleton, *Religion in the City of Angels*, 159, and Melton, *Encyclopedia of American Religions*, 987–1025.

119. Ernst, "Religion in California," 46.

120. Robert Wuthnow, "The New Religions in Social Context," in *The New Religious Consciousness*, edited by Charles Y. Glock and Robert N. Bellah (Berkeley: University of California Press, 1976), 292.

121. Charles A. Fracchia, "The Western Context: Its Impact on Our Religious Consciousness," *Lutheran Quarterly* 29 (February 1977), 14.

122. John R. Hall, *Gone from the Promised Land: Jonestown in American Cultural History* (New Brunswick, N.J.: Transaction Books, 1987), especially 61–201 on California.

123. David Chidester, *Salvation and Suicide* (Bloomington: Indiana University Press, 1988), xi.

124. *New Consciousness Sourcebook* (Berkeley: Spiritual Community, 1982), 175–215.

125. J. Gordon Melton, ed., *Encyclopedic Handbook of Cults in America* (New York: Garland Publishing, 1986), 72, 85, 88–91; Lippy and Williams, *Encyclopedia of the American Religious Experience*, 720, and Melton, *Encyclopedia of American Religions*, 717–18, 726–27, 731, 773–74, 976.

126. Randall H. Alfred, "The Church of Satan," in *New Religious Consciousness*, 183, 194; Melton, *Encyclopedic Handbook of Cults*, 77, 215, and Melton, *Encyclopedia of American Religions*, 785–87, 803–04.

127. Lippy and Williams, *Encyclopedia of the American Religious Experience* 1:143–45, 2:1257.

128. Steven M. Tipton, "Making the World Work. . . ," in *Of Gods and Men: New Religious Movements in the West*, edited by Eileen Barker (Macon, Ga.: Mercer University Press, 1983), 267.

129. Donald Stone, "The Human Potential Movement," in *New Religious Consciousness*, 93–115, and Roy Wallis, "The Dynamics of Change in the Human Potential Movement," in *Religious Movements*, 129–56.

130. Lippy and Williams, *Encyclopedia of the American Religious Experience*, 2:704, and Melton, *Encyclopedia of American Religions*, 966.

131. Fracchia, "The Western Context," 16, and Emma McCloy Layman, *Buddhism in America* (Chicago: Nelson-Hall Publishers, 1976), 124, 280, and Melton, *Encyclopedia of American Religions*, 915–16.

132. Lippy and Williams, *Encyclopedia of the American Religious Experience*, 1:676. Kosmin's *Research Report*, 8, shows what percentage of various ethnic groups are Buddhist but does not say what percentage of Buddhists are members of any ethnic group.

133. Lippy and Williams, *Encyclopedia of the American Religious Experience*, 2:690–91.

134. Ibid., 2:692–93; E. Burke Rochford, Jr., *Hare Krishna in America* (New Brunswick, N.J.: Rutgers University Press, 1984), 287 2n; Francine Jeanne Daner, *The American Children of Krsna* (New York: Holt, Rinehart, and Winston, 1974), 110, and Melton, *Encyclopedia of American Religions*, 867–68.

135. Williams, *Religions of Immigrants*, 145, 147; Lippy and Williams, *Encyclopedia of the American Religious Experience*, 2:697; Alan Tobey, "The Summer Solstice of the Healthy-Happy-Holy Organization," in *New Religious Consciousness*, 5–30, and Melton, *Encyclopedia of American Religions*, 898–99.

136. Jeanne Messer, "Guru Maharaj Ji and the Divine Light Mission," in *New Religious Consciousness*, 63; Lippy and Williams, *Encyclopedia of the American Religious Experience*, 2:695, and Melton, *Encyclopedia of American Religions*, 901–02.

137. Lippy and Williams, *Encyclopedia of the American Religious Experience*, 2:693; Harold H. Bloomfield et al., *TM . . .* (New York: Delacorte Press, 1975), 229–30, and Melton, *Encyclopedia of American Religions*, 889–90.

138. Fracchia, "The Western Context," 17. Examples in *New Religious Movements*, edited by Eileen Barker (New York: Edwin Mellen Press, 1982), 69–85; Melton, *Encyclopedia of American Religions*, and Melton, *Encyclopedic Handbook of Cults in America*.

139. *Los Angeles Times*, February 21, 1989, part II, 3.

140. Martin E. Marty, *Pilgrims in Their Own Land: 500 Years of Religion in America* (Boston: Little, Brown, 1984), 457.

141. Gerald F. Kreyche, "Introduction: Religion and the American West," *Lis-*

tening: Journal of Religion and Culture, 19 (Autumn 1984), 175.

142. Ferenc M. Szasz, "Religion in the American West: An Introduction," *Journal of the West* 23 (January 1984), 3.

143. Anderson, "San Francisco Evangelicalism," 45.

144. D. Michael Quinn, *Early Mormonism and the Magic World View* (Salt Lake City: Signature Books, 1987).

145. Ernst, "Religion in California," 51.

MAKING THE MOST OF WORDS
Verbal Activity and Western America

1. For comments and suggestions on this essay, I am indebted to Rolena Adorno of the University of Michigan, Gordon Bakken of California State University at Fullerton, Mary Cayton of Miami University, Charles Rankin of *Montana—The Magazine of Western History,* Steven Siporin of Utah State University, and George Cheney, Phillip Tompkins, and John Bowers of the University of Colorado communications department.

2. Milo Milton Quaife, ed., *Kit Carson's Autobiography* (Lincoln: University of Nebraska Press, 1966), 135.

3. Ibid., 135.

4. In an earlier draft of this paper I overstated the differences between print cultures and oral cultures; my understanding of the continued predominance of oral experience was much deepened by Professor Steven Siporin at Utah State, who provided me with assigned readings in western folklore, and by Professor Rolena Adorno at the University of Michigan, who called my attention to the illuminating collection "Selections from the Symposium on 'Literacy, Reading, and Power,' " *Yale University Journal of Criticism* 2:1 (1988) and to the work of Jack Goody, especially *The Interface between the Written and the Oral* (Cambridge, England: Cambridge University Press, 1987). Goody lists three aspects of the written-oral interface: "There is the meeting of cultures with and without writing, historically and geographically. There is the interface of written and oral traditions in societies that employ writing to varying degrees in various contexts. And there is the interface between the use of writing and speech in the linguistic life of any individual" (ix). Goody's work on these aspects is perfectly set up for applications to western America.

5. Reading a first draft of this essay, my colleague at the University of Colorado Phillip Tompkins pointed out that I had unknowingly adopted a key term, "verbal behavior," from B. F. Skinner. Since I did not intend the essay to carry any "behavioralist" implications, I have accordingly shifted to the word "activity."

6. Much of my approach here was inspired by my reading, fifteen years ago, the works of Kenneth Burke, especially *A Grammar of Motives* (1945; reprinted, Berkeley: University of California Press, 1969) and *A Rhetoric of Motives* (1950; reprinted, Berkeley: University of California Press, 1969). Phillip Tompkins and George Cheney of the University of Colorado reminded me of my debt to Burke by calling my attention to Burke's essays "Definition of Man" and "Terministic Screens," in *Language as Symbolic Action: Essays on Life, Literature, and Method* (Berkeley: University of California Press, 1966). Susanne K. Langer, *Philosophy in a New Key: A Study in the Symbolism of Reason, Rite, and Art* (1942; reprinted; Cambridge: Harvard University

Press, 1976) was another useful source of ways of thinking about language. The work of folklorists is also an inspiration in ways of analyzing verbal activity; see Barre Toelken's essays "Northwest Regional Folklore" in *Northwest Perspectives: Essays on the Culture of the Pacific Northwest*, edited by Edwin R. Bingham and Glen A. Love (Seattle: University of Washington Press, 1979), 21–42, and "Folklore in the American West," in *A Literary History of the American West* (Fort Worth: Texas Christian University Press, 1987), 29–67. Also worth noting is J. Sanford Rikoon, "The Narrative of 'Chief Bigfoot': A Study in Folklore, History and World View," in *Idaho Folklife: Homesteads to Headstones*, edited by Louis W. Attebery (Salt Lake City: University of Utah Press, 1985), 199–215.

7. Henry Nash Smith, *Virgin Land: The American West as Symbol and Myth* (1950; reprinted, Cambridge: Harvard University Press, 1970), xi.

8. Ibid, 251.

9. Ibid., 74.

10. Ibid., 257.

11. Richard Henry Dana, Jr., *Two Years before the Mast* (New York: New American Library, 1964), 151, 142–43.

12. Keith H. Basso, *Portraits of "The Whiteman": Linguistic Play and Cultural Symbols among the Western Apache* (Cambridge, England: Cambridge University Press, 1979).

13. George Gibbs, *Dictionary of the Chinook Jargon, or Trade Language of Oregon* (New York: Cramoisy Press, 1863).

14. Phoebe Goodell Judson, *A Pioneer's Search for an Ideal Home* (Lincoln: University of Nebraska Press, 1984), 111.

15. I have found Kenneth Haltman's Yale seminar paper " 'Sober and Obedient': Preliminary Notes to a Biographical Index of Nineteenth Century Indian-White Linguistic Interpreters on the North American Frontier" to be very useful; Haltman plans a book-length study in the future.

16. Dana, *Two Years*, 151.

17. See David Fridtjof Halaas, *Boom Town Newspapers: Journalism on the Rocky Mountain Mining Frontier, 1850–1881* (Albuquerque: University of New Mexico Press, 1981). Charles Rankin, the editor of *Montana—The Magazine of Western History*, is presently completing a very insightful, comprehensive study of western journalism.

18. Quoted in Glenn S. Dumke, *The Boom of the Eighties in Southern California* (San Marino, Calif.: Huntington Library, 1944), 138.

19. See David Emmons, *Garden in the Grasslands: Boomer Literature of the Central Great Plains* (Lincoln: University of Nebraska Press, 1971) and Jan Blodgett, *Land of Bright Promise: Advertising and the Texas Panhandle and South Plains, 1870–1917* (Austin: University of Texas Press, 1988).

20. Rankin points out additional aspects of change "from pioneer to modern journalism": "replacement of informal fraternity" among editors "with more formal professionalism"; "the transition from overt political dependence to increased political independence"; "economic consolidation"; "increased divisions of labor." Letter to the author, December 4, 1989.

21. Ibid.

22. J. S. Holliday, *The World Rushed In: The California Gold Rush Experience* (New York: Simon & Schuster, 1981), 239–40.

23. Mark Twain, *Roughing It* (New York: New American Library, 1962), 148–49.

24. James Boyd White, *When Words Lose Their Meaning: Constitutions and Reconstitutions of Language, Character, and Community* (Chicago: University of Chicago Press, 1984) is a key book for the study of law and literature and, indeed, for the study of verbal activity altogether. White's definition of rhetoric asks to be applied to western history: "the study of the ways in which character and community—and motive, value, reason, social structure, everything, in short, that makes a culture—are defined and made real in performances of language" (xi).

25. Western legal history is presently thriving. See, for instance, the special issue ("Law in the West," edited by David Langum) of *Journal of the West* XXIV:1 (January 1985), and the newly created journal *Western Legal History* (first issue Winter–Spring 1988).

26. Alvin Josephy, *Now That the Buffalo's Gone: A Study of Today's Indians* (New York: Alfred A. Knopf, 1982), chap. 6.

27. Rodman Wilson Paul, *Mining Frontiers of the Far West, 1848–1880* (Albuquerque: University of New Mexico Press, 1963), 173–75; Alfred Runte, *National Parks: The American Experience* (Lincoln: University of Nebraska Press, 1979), 104; and Christopher Stone, *Should Trees Have Standing? Toward Legal Rights for Natural Objects* (New York: Avon Books, 1974).

28. John Phillip Reid, *Law for the Elephant: Property and Social Behavior on the Overland Trail* (San Marino: Huntington Library, 1980) and David J. Langum, *Law and Community on the Mexican California Frontier: Anglo-American Expatriates and the Clash of Legal Traditions, 1821–1846* (Norman: University of Oklahoma Press, 1987).

29. John R. Wunder's work on the standing of the Chinese in western American law is on the forefront of ethnic and legal history; see his "Chinese in Trouble: Criminal Law and Race on the Trans-Mississippi West Frontier," *Western Historical Quarterly* XVII:1 (January 1986), 25–41.

30. Charles Wilkinson, *American Indians, Time, and the Law: Native Societies in a Modern Constitutional Democracy* (New Haven: Yale University Press, 1986).

31. Richard Slotkin has been the most prominent successor to Smith, in *Regeneration through Violence: The Mythology of the American Frontier, 1600–1860* (Middletown, Conn.: Wesleyan University Press, 1973) and *The Fatal Environment: The Myth of the Frontier in the Age of Industrialization, 1800–1890* (New York: Atheneum, 1985). Edwin Fussell's *Frontier: American Literature and the American West* (Princeton: Princeton University Press, 1965) focuses the inquiry on frontier thinking in "classic" American literature.

32. Despite revised editions, Roderick Nash's *Wilderness and the American Mind*, 3d ed. (New Haven: Yale University Press, 1982) has provided the most consistent example of an emphasis on nature that barely acknowledges the existence of Indians.

33. Francis Jennings, *The Invasion of America: Indians, Colonialism, and the Cant of Conquest* (Chapel Hill: University of North Carolina, 1975); Richard Drinnon, *Facing West: The Metaphysics of Indian-Hating and Empire-Building* (Minneapolis: University of Minnesota Press, 1980); and Frederick Turner, *Beyond Geography: The Western Spirit against the Wilderness* (New York: Viking Press, 1980).

34. William Goetzmann, *Exploration and Empire: The Explorer and the Scientist in the Winning of the American West* (New York: Alfred A. Knopf, 1966).

VIEWS AND REVIEWS
Western Art and Western History

1. This image appears as View 10 in *Photographs Showing Landscape, Geological and Other Features, of Portions of the Western Territory of the United States, Obtained in Connection with Geographical and Geological Explorations and Surveys West of the 100th Meridian Seasons of 1871, 1872, 1873 and 1874, 1st Lieut. Geo. M. Wheeler, Corps of Engineers, U.S. Army in Charge* (Washington, D.C.: War Department, Corps of Engineers, ca. 1876). The stereographic version of the image appears as View 20 in the set of stereographs published for the survey's 1873 season. Both prints may be found in the Western Americana Collection, Beinecke Library, Yale University.

2. Engineer Department, U.S. Army, *Report upon United States Geological Surveys West of the One Hundredth Meridian in Charge of Captain George M. Wheeler* I, Geographical Report (Washington, D.C.: Government Printing Office, 1889), 75 and plate IX.

3. Francis Parkman, *The Oregon Trail: Sketches of Prairie and Rocky-Mountain Life* (Toronto: George N. Morang & Company, 1900); "Preface to the Edition of 1892," cited in Brian W. Dippie, *Looking at Russell* (Fort Worth: Amon Carter Museum, 1987), 84.

4. Statement by Gordon Snidow in *The Cowboy Artists of America: Sixth Annual Exhibition, 1971*, exhibition catalog published for the show at the National Cowboy Hall of Fame and Western Heritage Center, 1971.

5. John C. Ewers, "Fact and Fiction in the Documentary Art of the American West," in *The Frontier Reexamined*, edited by John Francis McDermott (Urbana: University of Illinois Press, 1967), 79–95.

6. Ewers speaks to this point in "Fact and Fiction," and Brian W. Dippie updates Ewers's comments in "Of Documents and Myths: Richard Kern and Western Art. A Review Essay," *New Mexico Historical Review* 61 (April 1986), 147–58.

7. The organizers of the Remington exhibition made their point and betrayed their bias in the very title they chose for their exhibition and book, "Frederic Remington: The Masterworks." See Michael Edward Shapiro and Peter H. Hassrick, *Federic Remington: The Masterworks* (New York: St. Louis Art Museum and Buffalo Bill Historical Center / Harry N. Abrams, Inc., 1988). Elizabeth Johns's remarks appear in "La Farge and Remington," *Art Journal* 47 (Fall 1988), 243.

8. Wanda M. Corn, "Coming of Age: Historical Scholarship in American Art," *Art Bulletin* LXX:2 (June 1988), 188–207.

9. See, for example, William H. Goetzmann and William N. Goetzmann, *The West of the Imagination* (New York: W. W. Norton & Co., 1986).

10. Joel Snyder, *American Frontiers: The Photographs of Timothy H. O'Sullivan, 1867–1874* (Philadelphia: Philadelphia Museum of Art, 1981), 37, and Weston J. Naef in collaboration with James N. Wood, *Era of Exploration: The Rise of Landscape Photography in the American West, 1860–1885* (New York: Albright-Knox Art Gallery and the Metropolitan Museum of Art, 1975), 130.

11. The first extensive study of western art and patronage is the impressive new text Brian W. Dippie, *Catlin and His Contemporaries: The Politics of Patronage* (Lincoln: University of Nebraska Press, 1990).

12. The largest surviving collection of Hime's views are in the National Archives

of Canada. These and other images are reproduced in Richard J. Huyda, *Camera in the Interior: 1858, H. L. Hime, Photographer, the Assiniboine and Saskatchewan Exploring Expedition* (Toronto: Coach House Press, 1975).

13. H. Y. Hind, *Narrative of the Canadian Red River Exploring Expedition of 1857 and of the Assiniboine and Saskatchewan Exploring Expedition of 1858* (London: Longman, Green, Longman and Roberts, 1860), I, plate opposite 135. For a study of selected American images and their printed transformations in government reports, see David J. Weber, "The Artist, the Lithographer, and the Desert Southwest," *Gateway Heritage* 5 (Winter 1984–85), 32–41, and the similar discussion of this point in Weber, *Richard H. Kern: Expeditionary Artist in the Far Southwest, 1848–1853* (Albuquerque: University of New Mexico Press, 1985), 245–81.

14. For general information on Catlin's Indian Gallery, see William H. Truettner, *The Natural Man Observed: A Study of Catlin's Indian Gallery* (Washington, D.C.: Smithsonian Institution Press, 1979); for Kane, see J. Russell Harper, *Paul Kane's Frontier* (Austin: University of Texas Press, 1971); for Stanley, see Julie Schimmel, "John Mix Stanley and Imagery of the West in Nineteenth-Century American Art" (Ph.D. dissertation, New York University, 1983).

15. The best overview of the gold rush panoramas is John Francis McDermott, "Gold Rush Movies," *California Historical Society Quarterly* 33 (March 1954), 29–38. For more specific information on individual western panoramas, see Joseph Earl Arrington, "Skirving's Moving Panorama: Colonel Frémont's Western Expeditions Pictorialized," *Oregon Historical Society Quarterly* LXV (June 1964), 133–72; John Francis McDermott, ed., *An Artist on the Overland Trail: The 1849 Diary and Sketches of James F. Wilkins* (Pasadena: Huntington Library, 1968); and the wonderfully rich text of John Banvard, *Banvard's Geographical Panorama of the Mississippi River, with the Adventures of the Artist* (Boston: John Putnam Printer, 1847). The connections between panorama painters and early western photographers is explored in my essay "Undecisive Moments: The Narrative Tradition in Western Photography," in *Photography in Nineteenth Century America*, edited by Martha A. Sandweiss (New York: Harry N. Abrams, Inc., and Amon Carter Museum, 1991).

16. For general biographical information on Vance, see Peter E. Palmquist, "Robert Vance, Pioneer in Western Landscape Photography," *American West* (September–October 1981), 22–27. Palmquist is at work on a full-length biography of this important figure. I am working on an extended study of Jones and his Daguerrean project. In the meantime, the basic (if somewhat exaggerated) information on Jones and his project may be found in John Ross Dix (pseud.), *Amusing and Thrilling Adventures of a California Artist while Daguerreotyping a Continent* (Boston: published for the author, 1854) and in "Jones' Pantoscope of California," *California Historical Society Quarterly* VI (June 1927), 109–29; (September 1927), 238–53.

17. Terry Wm. Mangan, *Colorado on Glass: Colorado's First Half-Century as Seen by the Camera* (Denver: Sundance Ltd., 1975), 86, and William D. Pattison, "Westward by Rail with Professor Sedgwick: A Lantern Journey of 1873," *Historical Society of Southern California Quarterly* 42 (December 1960), 335–49. Monsen's lectures may be found in the Photographic Collections, Henry E. Huntington Library; McClintock's lectures are in the Western Americana Collection, Beinecke Library; Gilpin's are in the Photographic Collections, Amon Carter Museum.

18. The legend that Jackson's photographs *themselves* persuaded Congress to make Yellowstone a national park is effectively debunked in Howard Bossen, "A Tall Tale

Retold: The Influence of the Photographs of William Henry Jackson on the Passage of the Yellowstone Park Act of 1872," *Studies in Visual Communications* 8:1 (Winter 1982), 98–109. Bossen nonetheless agrees that Jackson's photographs were seen by congressmen along with other materials from the Hayden survey and accepted as factual items of evidence. A moving account of Jackson's later years is in Peter Bacon Hales, *William Henry Jackson and the Transformation of the American Landscape* (Philadelphia: Temple University Press, 1988), 283–95. A similarly ironic transformation may be traced in the photographic collages or "paste-ups" later assembled from Jackson's images and reproduced in booklets of scenic western views compiled by William H. Crane in the 1910s and 1920s. Here bits and pieces of nineteenth-century views have been pasted together, with new details, including people, added by hand. Again, photographs that once informed the public were transformed to suit the public taste for images of a mythical West. A collection of these views is in the Amon Carter Museum, Fort Worth.

19. There is a voluminous bibliography on Russell. For a recent critique of Russell's work that considers the issue of outside influences on his painting, see Dippie, *Looking at Russell*.

20. John C. Ewers, "Early White Influence upon Plains Indian Painting: George Catlin and Carl Bodmer among the Mandan, 1832–1834," *Smithsonian Miscellaneous Collections* 134:7 (1957), 1–11; Victoria Wyatt, *Shapes of Their Thoughts: Reflections of Culture Contact in Northwest Coast Indian Art* (New Haven and Norman: Peabody Museum of Natural History and University of Oklahoma Press, 1984), and J. J. Brody, *Indian Painters and White Patrons* (Albuquerque: University of New Mexico Press, 1971).

21. For these Northwest Coast examples I am indebted to the following papers delivered at a session entitled "American Indians, Photography, and Western History" held at the Western History Association meeting in Wichita, Kansas in October 1988: Carolyn Marr, "Photography on the Southern Northwest Coast: Responses, Adaptations, and Uses by Native Americans" and Rod Slemmons, "Photography and the Native American: 1890–1920."

22. See John E. Carter's essay on Trager and the Wounded Knee photographs in Richard E. Jensen, R. Eli Paul, and John Carter, *Eyewitness at Wounded Knee* (Lincoln: University of Nebraska Press, 1991). An early metaphoric use of the photographs may be found in Leo J. Ryan, "Long Lost Pictures of Last Indian Battle in Nebraska," [Lincoln?] *Sunday World Herald*, July 10, 1921.

23. Annette Kolodny, *The Lay of the Land: Metaphor as Experience and History in American Life and Letters* (Chapel Hill: University of North Carolina Press, 1975) suggests how literary material may be mined for evidence of gender-specific responses to the western landscape. For further information on Gilpin, see Martha A. Sandweiss, *Laura Gilpin: An Enduring Grace* (Fort Worth: Amon Carter Museum, 1986) and "The Historical Landscape: Laura Gilpin and the Tradition of American Landscape Photography," in *The Desert Is No Lady: Southwestern Landscapes in Women's Writing and Art*, edited by Vera Norwood and Janice Monk (New Haven: Yale University Press, 1987), 62–73. The essays gathered together in *The Desert Is No Lady* form the broadest investigation of how art may reflect gender-specific responses to the western landscape.

24. Cited in *The Desert Is No Lady*, loc. cit., 231.

25. R. A. C., "Photography in California," *Photography and Fine Art Journal* (April 1857), 112.

THE VIEW FROM WISDOM
Four Layers of History and Regional Identity

1. The author thanks Ona Siporin, Barre Toelken, Carol O'Connor, Anne M. Butler, Dave Walter, and Richard Maxwell Brown for their aid and advice on this essay.

2. Carroll Van West, *A Traveler's Companion to Montana History* (Helena: Montana Historical Society Press, 1986), 209–10, and Roberta Carkeek Cheney, *Names on the Face of Montana: The Story of Montana's Place Names* (Missoula: Mountain Press, 1983), 282–83.

3. Clastic rock: "A sedimentary rock composed principally of fragments derived from pre-existing rocks and transported mechanically to their places of deposition; e.g. a sandstone, conglomerate, or shale, or a limestone consisting of particles derived from a pre-existing limestone." Robert L. Bates and Julia A. Jackson, eds., *Dictionary of Geological Terms*, 3d ed. (New York: Anchor Press, 1984), 91.

4. Silas B. Gray Reminiscence, Small Collection (SC) 766, Montana Historical Society Archives (MHSA), Helena. This copy is a forty-page typescript. The original manuscript is not in the archives, although internal evidence in the typescript, such as correction of spelling in parentheses next to a word, indicates that one did exist. All quotations of Gray's words are from the typescript in the archives. An introductory paragraph tells of Gray's life up to 1879.

5. My thoughts on the process of "life review" come from conversations with Ona Siporin and a reading of Steve Siporin's essay "The Fruit Jobber's Tales," *International Folklore Review* 7 (1990), 30–34. Major studies of life review include Barbara Myerhoff, *Number Our Days* (New York: E. P. Dutton, 1978); Simon Bronner, *Chain Carvers: Old Men Crafting Meaning* (Lexington: University Press of Kentucky, 1985); and Mary Hufford, Marjorie Hunt, and Steven Zeitlin, *The Grand Generation: Memory, Mastery, Legacy* (Washington, D.C.: Smithsonian Institution Traveling Exhibition Service / Seattle: University of Washington Press, 1987).

6. "Silas B. Gray, Well-Known Resident of Helena, Passes," *Helena Independent*, March 4, 1940. I am grateful to Dave Walter of the Montana Historical Society Library for sending me this obituary.

7. Psychologist Erik Erikson has maintained that "the term identity points to an individual's link to the unique values, fostered by a unique history of his people." Erikson's assertion presents a "uniqueness" assumed by a people with a shared identity. This "uniqueness" also may be recognized by people who do not claim the same identity. Erik H. Erikson, "The Problem of Ego Identity," in *Identity and Anxiety*, edited by Maurice R. Stein et al. (Glencoe, Ill.: Free Press, 1960), 38. In Si Gray's case, his stories express familiar *western* themes that the local audiences in his own time would accept in an *esoteric* context. These stories also capture familiar *western* themes that other audiences in an *exoteric* context would recognize. These other audiences would include many people today who might read Gray's memoir and believe that his stories are distinctly *western*.

8. Robert N. Bellah et al., *Habits of the Heart: Individualism and Commitment in American Life* (Berkeley: University of California Press, 1985), 153–54. Bellah and his coauthors also state, "We live in a society that encourages us to cut free from the past, to define our own selves, to choose the groups with which we wish to identify." In

other words, the community of memory is not the only community with which an individual may choose to identify.

9. George Lubick, "Cornelius Hedges: Frontier Educator," *Montana—The Magazine of Western History* 28 (April 1978), 28, and Wyllys A. Hedges, "Cornelius Hedges," *Contributions to the Historical Society of Montana* 7 (1910; reprinted, Boston: J. S. Canner and Co., 1966), 181–85.

10. Hedges may have given the same public talk several times. His fellow Masons kept a penciled manuscript of his presentation in the archives of the Grand Lodge Library in Helena. For an edited version, see Cornelius Hedges, "Reminiscences of Early Days in Helena," *Montana Masonic News*, April 1967, May 1967, October 1967, January 1968, and March 1968 in Manuscript File 598, Special Collections, Renne Library, Montana State University, Bozeman. A typescript with the same title was edited by Hedges's granddaughter Mrs. Helen Brazier. It contains some longer accounts and many identical passages to the Masonic publication. This typescript may be found in Manuscript File 554, Special Collections, Renne Library. All quotations in this essay are from Brazier's edited typescript. A note in that file stated that this version may have been a speech for the Unity Club. A third version in typescript, titled "Excerpts from a Manuscript of Cornelius Hedges Entitled Reminiscences of Early Days in Helena," is retained in Manuscript Collection 33, Box 4, Folder 38, MHSA, with an identical copy in Small Collections 209, Toole Archives, Mansfield Library, University of Montana, Missoula.

11. A note in the typescript added by its editor, Helen Brazier, reads, "C.H. was a Vigilante." Historian George Lubick states, "The New Englander strongly supported the vigilante committee, although he probably was not an actual member." Lubick, "Cornelius Hedges: Frontier Educator," 28.

12. For more elaboration on these matters, see Clyde A. Milner II, "The Shared Memory of Montana's Pioneers," *Montana—The Magazine of Western History* 37 (Winter 1987), 2–13.

13. See, for example, Glenda Riley, "The Specter of a Savage: Rumors and Alarmism on the Overland Trail," *Western Historical Quarterly* 15 (October 1984), 427–44; Lillian Schlissel, *Women's Diaries of the Westward Journey* (New York: Schocken Books, 1982), 14–15, 154; and John D. Unruh, Jr., *The Plains Across: The Overland Emigrants and the Trans-Mississippi West, 1840–60* (Urbana: University of Illinois Press, 1979), 175–77, 185. An examination of eight emigrant trains that traveled from Minnesota to the Montana gold camps between 1862 and 1867 revealed that only the 1864 expedition suffered a serious Indian attack. All eight of these trains, except the first one in 1862, received some protection from the army. Helen McCann White, ed., *Ho! For the Gold Fields: Northern Overland Wagon Trains of the 1860s* (St. Paul: Minnesota Historical Society, 1966), 115–17, 143–53.

14. *Fergus County* (Lewistown, Montana) *Argus*, August 22, 1928, in Manuscript File 420, Special Collections, Renne Library, Montana State University, Bozeman.

15. Both quotations are from Barre Toelken, *The Dynamics of Folklore* (Boston: Houghton Mifflin, 1979), 106.

16. Unruh, *The Plains Across*, 382–85 and 510, 17n.

17. *Constitution and By-Laws of Pioneers of Eastern Montana*, (Billings: McFarlin Printing, 1916), vertical files, Parmley Billings Public Library, Billings, Montana.

18. A recent study of festivals in the three Wyoming towns of Lusk, Thermop-

olis, and Newcastle indicated that the exclusion of Indians as pioneers continues. See Audrey C. Shalinsky, "Indian-White Relations as Reflected in Twentieth Century Wyoming Town Celebrations," *Heritage of the Great Plains* 21 (Spring 1988), 21–34. This article concludes that the festivals "celebrate the American ideal of progress. . . . The Indian is in all cases relegated to the past as a symbol of static time which is condemned in the American value system."

19. Arthur Fisher, "Montana: Land of the Copper Collar," in *These United States*, edited by Ernest Gruening (New York: Boni & Liveright, 1924), 40, quoted in Clark C. Spence, *Montana: A Bicentennial History* (New York: W. W. Norton, 1978), 191.

20. Wilbur Zelinsky, *The Cultural Geography of the United States* (Englewood Cliffs, N.J.: Prentice-Hall, 1973), 23. Zelinsky's Doctrine of First Effective Settlement presupposes an erasure of native peoples beginning in the colonial era that is akin to the ethnocentric view that American Indians are not "westerners."

21. Bertha Josephson Anderson Reminiscence, SC 360 MHSA. This typescript consists of excerpts selected from the original memoir by Camilla May Anderson. This daughter is listed in volume 21 of *Who's Who in America* (1940–41) as a psychiatrist in Philadelphia with a private practice and teaching appointments at Temple University and the University of Pennsylvania medical schools. Her birth in 1904 may explain why the narrative emphasized events up to 1907, the time of the Andersons' silver wedding anniversary. Camilla's mother probably wished to explain her life up to the time her youngest daughter became part of the family. This process of reminiscence may have fitted some of Camilla Anderson's professional interests. *Who's Who* indicates that her one major book bore the title *Emotional Hygiene: The Art of Understanding* (1937). All quotations are from this fifty-two-page typescript.

22. In a telephone conversation on March 21, 1991, Camilla May Anderson said about her mother, "Oh, of course she would have called herself a westerner." Dr. Anderson emphasized to me that her parents became Americans "fast" and that "They were westerners, you bet."

23. For individuals within the West, this process of accepting a regional identity is akin to the appropriation of a hyphenated identity on the part of some immigrant populations. For example, in the case of Mexican-Americans or Italian-Americans, some assimilation of a national identity occurs, but a cultural identity remains to support an individual's self-definition. Westerners may see themselves as a special group of Americans, not so much in cultural terms through language and custom as in terms of their distinct location and "unique" history. Demographic trends indicate that today great numbers of first-generation residents have the opportunity to establish a western identity. Between 1940 and 1970 the population of the Mountain and Pacific states (excluding Alaska and Hawaii) jumped from over thirteen million to over thirty-three million. Migration explains much of this growth, and these newcomers headed overwhelmingly for western cities. By 1970 83 percent of the population in these states lived in metropolitan areas. (See John M. Findlay, "Far Western Cityscapes and American Culture Since 1940," *Western Historical Quarterly* 22 [February 1991], 19–43.) Now, more than two decades later in the 1990s, many of these largely urban residents may accept a regional identity that celebrates the national epic of migration and settlement and expresses a sense of locale through shared memory.

24. For a recent assessment of De Voto's ideas, as well as of the general theme of economic colonialism in the West, see William G. Robbins, "The 'Plundered Prov-

ince' Thesis and Recent Historiography of the American West," *Pacific Historical Review* 55 (November 1986), 577–97.

25. Jules A. Karlin, *Joseph M. Dixon of Montana*, Part 2, *Governor versus the Anaconda, 1917–1934* (Missoula: University of Montana Publications in History, 1974).

26. Richard Roeder, "Joseph Kinsey Howard and *Montana: High, Wide and Handsome*," in *Montana Myths*, edited by Richard Allen Chapman, (a booklet in typescript prepared for a conference sponsored by the Montana Committee for the Humanities, "Montana Myths: Sacred Stories, Sacred Cows" in Helena, Montana, May 11–12, 1984), 31–36, and Harry W. Fritz, "The Best Books about Montana: A Reader's Guide to the Treasure State," *Montana—The Magazine of Western History* 32 (Winter 1982), 60–61. My interpretation of Howard's book follows Roeder's ideas.

27. Roeder in *Montana Myths*, 32.

28. Joseph Kinsey Howard, *Montana: High, Wide, and Handsome* (1959; reprinted, Lincoln: University of Nebraska Press, 1983), 196, 192–95.

29. Wallace Stegner, *The American West as Living Space* (Ann Arbor: University of Michigan Press, 1987), especially 25 and 85. Stegner also stresses the mobility of westerners within their own region, but I wonder if the pattern is migrations in childhood or early adulthood with eventual settlement in one place. This fits the lives of Gray, Hedges, Anderson, and Howard in this essay.

30. Howard, *Montana: High, Wide, and Handsome*, 275 and 313–14.

31. Rodman W. Paul and Michael P. Malone, "Tradition and Challenge in Western Historiography," *Western Historical Quarterly* 16 (January 1985), 30.

32. In 1949 Carey McWilliams explained that the intermountain West was "A colony in a two-fold sense: a colony of the East *and* a colony of California." McWilliams, *California: The Great Exception* (New York: Current Books, 1949), 343, quoted in Robbins, "The 'Plundered Province' Thesis," 585.

HISTORY FOR THE MASSES
Commercializing the Western Past

1. I would like to thank the editors and Marni Sandweiss for their help on this essay. On the World's Columbian Exposition, see Reid Badger, *The Great American Fair: The World's Columbian Exposition & American Culture* (Chicago: N. Hall, 1979). Badger mentions Buffalo Bill on pages 88 and 120. See also Robert W. Rydell, *All the World's a Fair: Visions of Empire at American International Expositions, 1876–1916* (Chicago: University of Chicago Press, 1984), 38–71. Turner's paper is available in many forms. It can be found in *The Frontier in American History* (Huntington, N.Y.: R. E. Krieger Publishing Co., 1976). On Buffalo Bill, see the essays collected in *Buffalo Bill and the Wild West* (Brooklyn: Brooklyn Museum, 1981).

2. For a useful reading of Turner and the writing of history, see Richard Hofstadter, *The Progressive Historians: Turner, Beard, Parrington* (New York: Alfred A. Knopf, 1968). See also Ray Allen Billington, *Frederick Jackson Turner: Historian, Scholar, Teacher* (New York: Oxford University Press, 1973). For insights into the early ideological appropriation of frontier history and frontier imagery, see Warren I. Susman, "The Frontier Thesis and the American Intellectual," *Culture as History: The Transfor-*

mation of American Society in the Twentieth Century (New York: Pantheon Books, 1984), 27–38.

3. A study of the historiography of the West casts light on aspects of the discipline and practice of history. In the American West professional historians have often witnessed the complicity of their craft in the production of acknowledged fictions and in the explanations offered for territorial conquest. In the West the popular has also challenged the scholarly for control of the past and sometimes exposed the folly of intellectual claims to a monopoly on "truth." Both Turner and his popular colleagues tried to cut the frontier past off from the present, to establish the discontinuities necessary for writing history. If life on the frontier had been about interracial contests, life in the history of the frontier has been about contested representations. Buffalo Bill, Professor Turner, along with many others struggled for control of the frontier metaphor. See Michel Foucault, "History, Discourse, and Discontinuity," translated by Anthony M. Nazzaro, *Salmagundi* 20 (Summer–Fall, 1972), 229–33.

4. Did professional historians elevate their own versions of the past at the expense of the popular? Recent work in cultural history suggests they did. By putting Turner alongside Cody, we might, as Lawrence Levine put it, "risk eroding the hierarchy, though in fact we might learn a great deal in the process." *Highbrow / Lowbrow: The Emergence of Cultural Hierarchy in America* (Cambridge: Harvard University Press, 1988), 2. On questions in the textuality of history, see Hayden White, "The Historical Text as Literary Artifact" and "The Fictions of Factual Representation," *Tropics of Discourse: Essays in Cultural Criticism* (Baltimore: Johns Hopkins University Press, 1978); Frederic Jameson, *The Political Unconscious: Narrative as a Socially Symbolic Act* (Ithaca: Cornell University Press, 1981), 82; and Dominick LaCapra, "Rhetoric and History" and "History and the Novel," *History and Criticism* (Ithaca: Cornell University Press, 1985), 15–44 and 115–34.

5. On professional intellectuals and the university, see Burton J. Bledstein, *The Culture of Professionalism: The Middle Class and the Development of Higher Education in America* (New York: W. W. Norton, 1976) and Thomas Bender, *New York Intellect: A History of Intellectual Life in New York City, from 1750 to the Beginnings of Our Own Time* (New York: Alfred A. Knopf, 1987), 265–318.

6. Gene M. Gressley, "The West: Past, Present, and Future," *Western Historical Quarterly* XVII (January 1986), 6–7.

7. When a man named Dr. Dolbeare printed the story of the captivity of a Virginia woman named Dolly Webster who had lived among the Comanches in the 1840s, he began by attesting to the veracity and authenticity of Mrs. Webster's story. Dolbeare seemed to have written the first few paragraphs and then dropped out of the text as the pronoun for the heroine changes from third person to first. The story was then related by Webster, but Dolbeare better understood literary property, for noted prominently on the title page was "copy-right secured by law." Mrs. Webster experienced the captivity; Dr. Dolbeare turned her captivity to a profit. Benjamin Dolbeare, *A Narrative and Suffering of Dolly Webster among the Comanche Indians in Texas with an Account of the Massacre of John Webster and His Party, as Related by Mrs. Webster* (Clarksburg, Va.: M'Granaghan & M'Carty Printer, 1843).

8. John Filson, *The Discovery, Settlement and Present State of Kentuck* (Wilmington, Del.: James Adams, 1784). Richard Slotkin made marvelous use of Filson and Boone in his *Regeneration through Violence: The Mythology of the American Frontier, 1600–1860* (Middletown, Conn.: Wesleyan University Press, 1973), 268–354. Slotkin also dis-

cusses the religious interpretation given to narratives of war and captivity on pages 83–85 and 94–115. Among the best of moralized narratives is Mary Rowlandson, *A True History of the Captivity & Restoration of Mrs. Mary Rowlandson* (Cambridge, England: J. Wilson and Son, 1903).

9. James T. Lloyd, *Lloyd's Steamboat Directory and Disasters on Western Waters* (Philadelphia and Cincinnati: Jas. T. Lloyd and Co., [1856]). Lloyd also published a newspaper and timetable, *Lloyd's American Weekly*, as well as "Lloyd's Topographical Map of the Hudson River" (1864), "Lloyd's List of Post Offices" (1863), and "Lloyd's Map of the Lower Mississippi" (1862). Lloyd took many of his maps and descriptions from Zadok Cramer, *The Navigator, Containing Directions for Navigating the Monongahela, Allegheny, Ohio and Mississippi Rivers*, which was published in Pittsburgh in 1802 by John Scull and then revised and reissued numerous times through 1824. He also took descriptions from the sources used by S. A. Howland in his *Steamboat Disasters and Railroad Accidents in the United States to Which Is Appended Accounts of Recent Shipwrecks, Fires at Sea, Thrilling Incidents &c.* (Worcester, Mass.: W. Lazell, 1846). Howland, however sensational his descriptions, did not peddle his book to the travelers who might soon wind up on his lists of the dead, nor did he sell space on his pages to advertisers whose profits depended on still-risky forms of transportation. See also James Hall, *The West: Its Commerce and Navigation* (Cincinnati: H. W. Derby and Co., 1848) and Leo Marx, *The Machine in the Garden: Technology and the Pastoral Ideal in America* (New York: Oxford University Press, 1964). In *The Social Context of Innovation* (Princeton: Princeton University Press, 1982), Anthony Wallace argues that disasters had to be put in a cultural context: "[I]n certain domains—the high pressure steam engine and the coal mine, at least—the Industrial Revolution would appear to be a game played by technological gamblers who liked to bet their own and others' lives and money against disaster, in the hope in part of the noneconomic reward of the industrial hero's accolade." The quotation appears on page 150, but see also pages 140–41.

10. Lloyd, *Steamboat and Railroad Directory*, 141–43; Howland, *Steamboat Disasters*, 97–98.

11. Reports of Indian aversion to steam travel and Gardiner's letter are reprinted in *Senate Executive Document*, 512, 23d Congress, 1st Session, 591, 687–88. Edward Said, "Opponents, Audiences, Constituencies, and Community," *Critical Inquiry* 9 (September 1982), 1–26.

12. Howard Lamar, *The Trader on the American Frontier: Myth's Victim* (College Station: Texas A&M University Press, 1977), 17. Warren Susman pointed out that "only in the late 1920s did any systematic critique appear that questioned the truth and the efficacy of the Turner thesis itself" and that it was the Great Depression that "stimulated thinking anew of the problems of our history." "The Frontier Thesis and the American Intellectual," 36. The recent literature on the social history of the West is vast. See, for instance, Robert R. Dykstra, *The Cattle Towns: A Social History of the Kansas Cattle Trading Centers Abilene, Ellsworth, Wichita, Dodge City and Caldwell, 1867–1885* (New York: Alfred A. Knopf, 1976); Mark Wyman, *Hard-Rock Epic: Western Miners and the Industrial Revolution, 1860–1910* (Berkeley: University of California Press, 1979); Michael Malone, *The Battle for Butte: Mining and Politics on the Northern Frontier, 1864–1906* (Seattle: University of Washington Press, 1981); David M. Emmons, *The Butte Irish: Class and Ethnicity in an American Mining Town, 1875–1925* (Urbana: University of Illinois Press, 1989); Sarah Deutsch, *No Separate Refuge: Culture, Class, and*

Gender on an Anglo-Hispanic Frontier in the American Southwest, 1880–1940 (New York: Oxford University Press, 1987); and Sandra L. Myres, *Westering Women and the Frontier Experience: 1800–1915* (Albuquerque: University of New Mexico Press, 1982).

13. See, for example, Ann M. Butler, *Daughters of Joy, Sisters of Misery: Prostitutes in the American West, 1865–1890* (Urbana: University of Illinois Press, 1985); Paula Petrik, *No Step Backward: Women and Family in the Rocky Mountain Mining Frontier, Helena, Montana, 1865–1900* (Helena: Montana Historical Society Press, 1987); and Gary Cunningham, "Chance, Culture, and Compulsion: The Gambling Games of the Kansas Cattle Towns," *Nevada Historical Society Quarterly* 26 (Winter 1983), 255–71.

14. See Robert M. Utley, *Billy the Kid: A Short and Violent Life* (Lincoln: University of Nebraska Press, 1989) and Stephen Tatum, *Inventing Billy the Kid: Visions of the Outlaw in America, 1881–1891* (Albuquerque: University of New Mexico Press, 1982). Eric J. Hobsbawm, *Social Bandits and Primitive Rebels* (Glencoe, Ill.: Free Press, 1959) changed the outlaw history of the West. See, for example, Richard White, "Outlaw Gangs of the Middle Border: American Social Bandits," *Western Historical Quarterly* 12 (October 1981), 387–408. In his recent novel *Anything for Billy* (New York: Simon & Schuster, 1989), Larry McMurtry exploited just the imagery historians had abandoned and drew a portrait of eastern image maker (a dime novelist on the lam from genteel Philadelphia) befriended by tough westerner. Once in the West, the dime novelist also moves deftly between his own imagined fictions and his author's imagined "reality."

15. The phrase is from Dominick LaCapra, "History and the Novel," 133. Jane Tompkins began *Sensational Designs: The Cultural Work of American Fiction, 1790–1869* (New York: Oxford University Press, 1985) with a plea to read literary texts of the past as "attempts to redefine the social order." She continued: "In this view, novels and stories should be studied not because they manage to escape the limitations of their particular time and place, but because they offer powerful examples of the way a culture thinks about itself, articulating and proposing solutions for the problems that shape a particular historical moment" (xi). Tompkins concentrated on the sensational and sentimental projects of popular fiction, but perhaps the popular histories of the West offered meditations on social problems as well.

16. Lee Clark Mitchell, *Witness to a Vanishing America: The Nineteenth-Century Response* (Princeton: Princeton University Press, 1981); Roderick Nash, *Wilderness and the American Mind* (New Haven: Yale University Press, 1973); and Peter J. Schmitt, *Back to Nature: The Arcadian Myth in Urban America* (New York: Oxford University Press, 1969).

17. Renato Rosaldo, "Imperialist Nostalgia," *Representations* 26 (Spring 1989), 109, 121. Rosaldo includes Slotkin among his demystifiers, but he cites *Regeneration through Violence*, not Slotkin's later *The Fatal Environment: The Myth of the Frontier in the Age of Industrialization, 1800–1890* (New York: Atheneum, 1985), in which Slotkin confronts many of the limits of the process of demystification. For a fascinating reading of the play of race and party politics in popular versions of the West, see Alexander Saxton, *The Rise and Fall of the White Republic: Class Politics and Mass Culture in Nineteenth-Century America* (London: Verso, 1990).

18. Michael Denning, *Mechanic Accents: Dime Novels and Working-Class Culture in America* (London: Verso, 1987), 157–66. Alan Trachtenberg began *The Incorporation of America: Culture and Society in the Gilded Age* (New York: Hill & Wang, 1982) with

a discussion of the production of the popular imagery of the West and with the role of images in reshaping the real West. See "The Westward Route," 11–37. For an astute discussion of popular readership, see Cathy N. Davidson, *Revolution and the Word: The Rise of the Novel in America* (New York: Oxford University Press, 1986).

19. Turner, "The Significance of the Frontier," 37.

20. Robert Athearn, *The Mythic West in Twentieth Century America* (Lawrence, Kan.: University Press of Kansas, 1986), 45, 70–77. Gerald D. Nash makes a similar argument in his concluding essay, "Epilogue: Sharpening the Image," in *The Twentieth-Century West: Historical Interpretations*, edited by Gerald D. Nash and Richard W. Etulain (Albuquerque: University of New Mexico Press, 1989), 407–19.

21. Slotkin, *The Fatal Environment* contains a long and detailed discussion of the physical consequences of cultural beliefs.

22. Robert Sklar, *Movie-Made America: A Cultural History of American Movies* (New York: Vintage Books, 1975), 77–85.

23. Richard Brodhead, "Country Matters" will appear in the third volume of the *Cambridge History of American Literature* (New York: Cambridge University Press, forthcoming).

24. In *The Condition of Postmodernity: An Enquiry into the Origins of Cultural Change* (Oxford: Blackwell, 1989), David Harvey lists certain characteristics of postmodernity that capture Ralph Lauren's skills as a fashionable *bricoleur:* "It is hardly surprising that the artist's relation to history (the peculiar historicism we have already noted) has shifted, that in the era of mass television there has emerged an attachment to surfaces rather than roots, to collage rather than in-depth work, to super-imposed quoted images rather than worked surfaces, to a collapsed sense of time and space rather than solidly achieved cultural artefact. And these are all vital aspects of artistic practice in the post-modern condition" (61).

25. For a description of one group of Lauren's models, see G. Edward White, *The Eastern Establishment and the Western Experience: The West of Frederic Remington, Theodore Roosevelt, and Owen Wister* (New Haven: Yale University Press, 1968).

26. It helps here, I think, to bring the big guns of interpretation into the world of fashion. Lauren looks pretty innocuous, but as Roland Barthes learned studying French bourgeois culture as France's empire dissolved in the 1950s, the most banal of cultural expressions are also often forms of cultural power. See *Mythologies* (1957; reprinted, New York: Hill & Wang, 1972) and *The Fashion System* (1967; reprinted, New York: Hill & Wang, 1983). Lauren has also made a great deal of money. Some of the French sociologist Pierre Bourdieu's insights help us make sense of Lauren's project. Describing the "aesthetic disposition," Bourdieu has written, "objective distance from necessity and from those trapped within it combines with a conscious distance which doubles freedom by exhibiting it. As the objective distance from necessity grows, life-style increasingly becomes the product of what Weber calls a 'stylization of life,' a systematic commitment which orients and organizes the most diverse practices—the choice of a vintage or a cheese or the decoration of a holiday home in the country. This affirmation of power over a dominated necessity always implies a claim to a legitimate superiority over those who, because they cannot assert the same contempt for contingencies in gratuitous luxury and conspicuous consumption, remain dominated by ordinary interests and urgencies." *Distinction: A Social Critique of the Judgement of Taste* (Cambridge: Harvard University Press, 1984 [1979]), 55–56. In part Bourdieu was anticipated by Thorstein Veblen, *The Theory of the Lei-*

sure Class: An Economic Study of Institutions (New York: The Modern Library, 1934). Christopher Lasch also described the western transformations of Theodore Roosevelt and argued that the American upper class preserved its "distinction" by refusing to become a leisure class. See his "Moral and Intellectual Rehabilitation of the Ruling Class," *The World of Nations* (New York: Alfred A. Knopf, 1973), 80–91. Roosevelt, of course, could not foresee Lauren's full articulation of the worlds of style and consumption.

27. Brooke Hayward, "Home on the Range," *Vanity Fair* (February 1988), 102–08, 142–44, and Patricia Leigh Brown, "Lauren's Wink at the Wild Side," *New York Times* (February 8, 1990), C1, C6.

IS THERE A TWENTIETH-CENTURY WEST?

1. Gene M. Gressley, "Whither Western American History? Speculations on a Direction," *Pacific Historical Review* 53 (August 1984), 493–501, and "The West: Past, Present, and Future," *Western Historical Quarterly* 17 (January 1986), 5–23; Spencer C. Olin, Jr., "Toward a Synthesis of the Political and Social History of the American West," ibid. 55 (November 1986), 599–611; Rodman W. Paul and Michael P. Malone, "Tradition and Challenge in Western Historiography," *Western Historical Quarterly* 16 (January 1985), 27–53, especially 51. For a more optimistic view, see Howard R. Lamar, "Persistent Frontier: The West in the Twentieth Century," *Western Historical Quarterly* 4 (January 1973), 5–25, and "Much to Celebrate: The Western History Association's Twenty-Fifth Birthday," *Western Historical Quarterly* 17 (October 1986), 397–416.

2. For the organizational approach, see Louis Galambos, "The Emerging Organizational Synthesis in Modern American History," *Business History Review* 44 (Autumn 1970), 279–90, and "Technology, Political Economy, and Professionalization: Central Themes of the Organizational Synthesis," ibid. 57 (Winter 1983), 471–93; Robert F. Berkhofer, Jr., "The Organizational Interpretation of American History: A New Synthesis," *Prospects* 4 (1979), 611–29; and Robert D. Cuff, "American Historians and the 'Organizational Factor,' " *Canadian Review of American Studies* 4 (Spring 1973), 19–31. Leading works of the genre include Samuel P. Hays, *The Response to Industrialism, 1885–1914* (Chicago: University of Chicago Press, 1957); Hays, *American Political History as Social History: Essays by Samuel P. Hays* (Knoxville: University of Tennessee Press, 1980); Ellis W. Hawley, *The Great War and the Search for a Modern Order: A History of the American People and Their Institutions, 1917–1933* (New York: St. Martin's Press, 1979); Robert H. Wiebe, *The Search for Order, 1877–1920* (New York: Hill & Wang, 1967); and William Appleman Williams, *The Contours of American History* (1961; reprinted, New York: New Viewpoints, 1973).

3. On the issues of southern identity, see C. Vann Woodward, *The Burden of Southern History*, rev. ed. (Baton Rouge: Louisiana State University Press, 1968).

4. Howard R. Lamar, "From Bondage to Contract: Ethnic Labor in the American West, 1600–1890," in *The Countryside in the Era of Capitalist Transformation*, edited by Stephen Hahn and Jonathan Prude (Chapel Hill: University of North Carolina Press, 1985), 293–324.

5. Walter Prescott Webb, *Divided We Stand: The Crisis of a Frontierless Democracy* (New York: Farrar, Rinehart, Inc., 1937), especially 157–58. Webb, of course, was

not being entirely fair to historians, particularly Frederick Jackson Turner, the architect of the frontier thesis. Turner, as we will see, clearly believed that the demise of the frontier would imperil individualism and democracy.

6. For a sense of the diversity and some of the implications of western social history, see Paul and Malone, "Tradition and Challenge," 46–49; Lamar, "Much to Celebrate," 401–04; and the essays in Gerald D. Nash and Richard W. Etulain, eds., *The Twentieth-Century West: Historical Interpretations* (Albuquerque: University of New Mexico Press, 1989).

7. Bernard De Voto, "The Anxious West," *Harper's* 193 (December 1946), 481–91 (quotation on 481), "The West against Itself," ibid. 194 (January 1947), 1–13, and "The West: A Plundered Province," ibid. 169 (August 1934), 355–64; Webb, *Divided We Stand*, 51 and 87; A. G. Mezerik, *The Revolt of the South and West* (New York: Duell, Sloan and Pearce, 1946), 4, 9, and 26. Interestingly Webb's publisher, not Webb himself, came up with the title for *Divided We Stand;* Webb's first choice was *Should the South and West Secede?*. See Walter Rundell, Jr., "W. P. Webb's *Divided We Stand:* A Publishing Crisis," *Western Historical Quarterly* 13 (October 1982), 395. On the colonialist literature, see also "Colonialism and the American West," in Gene M. Gressley, *The Twentieth-Century American West: A Potpourri* (Columbia, Mo.: University of Missouri Press, 1977), 31–47, and Gressley's earlier essay "Colonialism: A Western Complaint," *Pacific Northwest Quarterly* 54 (January 1963), 1–8.

8. Webb, *Divided We Stand*, 221–22; John W. Caughey, *The American West: Frontier and Region*, edited by Norris Hundley, Jr., and John A. Schutz (Los Angeles: Ward Ritchie Press, 1969), 24–25; Caughey, "Editorial Remarks," *Pacific Historical Review* 16 (May 1947), 228–31.

9. De Voto, "Anxious West," 2, and "West against Itself," 1–13; William G. Robbins, "The 'Plundered Province' Thesis and the Recent Historiography of the American West," *Pacific Historical Review* 55 (Nov. 1986), 577–97; Peter Wiley and Robert Gottlieb, *Empires in the Sun: The Rise of the New American West* (New York: Putnam, 1982).

10. Kevin Phillips, *The Emerging Republican Majority* (New Rochelle, N.Y.: Arlington House, 1969); Kirkpatrick Sale, *Power Shift: The Rise of the Southern Rim and Its Challenge to the Eastern Establishment* (New York: Random House, 1975); and Carl Oglesby, *The Yankee and Cowboy War: Conspiracies from Dallas to Watergate* (Mission, Kan.: Sheed, Andrews and McMeel, 1976).

11. Webb, *The Great Plains* (Boston: Ginn and Company, 1931) and "The American West: Perpetual Mirage," *Harper's* 214 (May 1957), 25–31.

12. Donald Worster, *Rivers of Empire: Water, Aridity, and the Growth of the American West* (New York: Pantheon Books, 1985), 7, and Gerald D. Nash, *The American West in the Twentieth Century: A Short History of an Urban Oasis* (Englewood Cliffs, N.J.: Prentice-Hall, 1973).

13. For instance, Norris Hundley, Jr., *Dividing the Waters: A Century of Controversy between the United States and Mexico* (Berkeley: University of California Press, 1966) and *Water and the West: The Colorado River Compact and the Politics of Water in the American West* (Berkeley: University of California Press, 1975); Elmo Richardson, *The Politics of Conservation: Crusades and Controversies, 1897–1913* (Berkeley: University of California Press, 1962) and *Dams, Parks, and Politics: Resource Development and Preservation in the Truman-Eisenhower Era* (Lexington, Ky.: Lexington University Press of Kentucky, 1973); Donald C. Swain, *Federal Conservation Policy, 1921–1933* (Berkeley:

University of California Press, 1963); Donald Worster, *Dust Bowl: The Southern Plains in the 1930s* (New York: Oxford University Press, 1970); and Wiley and Gottlieb, *Empires in the Sun.*

14. Donald Meinig, "American Wests: Preface to a Geographical Introduction," *Annals of the Association of American Geographers* 62 (June 1972), 159–84; Paul and Malone, "Tradition and Challenge," 28–29; Gene M. Gressley, "Regionalism and the Twentieth-Century West," in *The American West: New Perspectives, New Dimensions*, edited by Jerome O. Steffen (Norman: University of Oklahoma Press, 1979), 197–234; Raymond D. Gastil, *Cultural Regions of the United States* (Seattle: University of Washington Press, 1975); and Frederick C. Luebke, "Regionalism and the Great Plains: Problems of Concept and Method," *Western Historical Quarterly* 15 (January 1984), 19–38.

15. Webb, "American West," 30.

16. Kenneth N. Owens, "Pattern and Structure in Western Territorial Politics," *Western Historical Quarterly* 1 (October 1970), 373–92; Martin Shefter, "Regional Receptivity to Reform: The Legacy of the Progressive Era," *Political Science Quarterly* 98 (Fall 1983), 459–83; Paul Kleppner, "Voters and Parties in the Western States, 1876–1900," *Western Historical Quarterly* 14 (January 1983), 49–68, and "Politics without Parties: The Western States, 1900–1984," in Nash and Etulain, eds., *Twentieth-Century West*, 295–338; David R. Mayhew, *Placing Parties in American Politics: Organization, Electoral Settings, and Government Activity in the Twentieth Century* (Princeton: Princeton University Press, 1986).

17. Eleanor Flexner, *Century of Struggle: The Woman's Rights Movement in the United States*, rev. ed. (Cambridge: Harvard University Press, 1975), especially 159–66; Robert Westbrook, "Politics as Consumption: Managing the Modern American Election," in *The Culture of Consumption: Critical Essays in American History, 1880–1980*, edited by Richard Wightman Fox and T. J. Jackson Lears (New York: Pantheon Books, 1983), 153–54; Michael E. McGerr, *The Decline of Popular Politics: The American North, 1865–1928* (New York: Oxford University Press, 1986); and Kleppner, "Politics without Parties," 301–04.

18. Gerald D. Nash, "Bureaucracy and Reform in the West: Notes on the Influence of a Neglected Interest Group," *Western Historical Quarterly* 2 (July 1971), 295–305. On the federal role in the territorial period, see Earl S. Pomeroy, *The Territories and the United States, 1861–1890: Studies in Colonial Administration* (Philadelphia: University of Pennsylvania Press, 1947); Lewis L. Gould, *Wyoming: A Political History, 1868–1896* (New Haven: Yale University Press, 1968); and Howard Roberts Lamar, *Dakota Territory, 1861–1889: A Study of Frontier Politics* (New Haven: Yale University Press, 1956) and *The Far Southwest, 1846–1912: A Territorial History* (New Haven: Yale University Press, 1966). On the impact of the federal government in the twentieth century, see Leonard J. Arrington, *The Changing Structure of the Mountain West, 1850–1950* (Logan, Utah: Utah State University Press, 1963) and James L. Clayton, "Defense Spending: Key to California's Economic Growth," *Western Political Quarterly* 15 (June 1962), 280–93 and "The Impact of the Cold War on the Economies of California and Utah, 1946–1965," *Pacific Historical Review* 36 (November 1967), 449–73.

19. F. Alan Coombs, "Twentieth-Century Western Politics," in *Historians and the American West*, edited by Michael P. Malone (Lincoln: University of Nebraska Press, 1983), 300–22, nicely summarizes the evidence on this point. See also Richard

Franklin Bensel, *Sectionalism and American Political Development: 1880–1980* (Madison: University of Wisconsin Press, 1984).

20. Kleppner, "Politics without Parties."

21. Lamar, "Persistent Frontier," 6; Frank J. Popper, "The Strange Case of the Contemporary American Frontier," *Yale Review* 76 (December 1986), 101–21.

22. On modern conservatism generally, see Paul Gottfried and Thomas Fleming, *The Conservative Movement* (Boston: Twayne Publishers, 1988).

23. Barry Goldwater with Jack Casserly, *Goldwater* (New York: Doubleday, 1988), xi, 35, and 45. See also Edwin McDowell, *Barry Goldwater: Portrait of an Arizonan* (Chicago: H. Regnery Co., 1964), 69–86.

24. Goldwater, *Goldwater*, 67 and 96.

25. Ibid., 144 and 114–21.

26. Ibid., 121 and 213.

27. Ibid., 67, 96, and 400.

28. Lou Cannon, *Reagan* (New York: Putnam, 1982), especially 349–70.

29. In addition to the works cited in Note 2, see, for instance, James Weinstein, *The Corporate Ideal in the Liberal State, 1900–1918* (Boston: Monthly Review Press, 1968); Robert Griffith, "Dwight D. and the Corporate Commonwealth," *American Historical Review* 87 (February 1982), 87–122; and Allen J. Matusow, *The Unraveling of America: A History of Liberalism in the 1960s* (New York: Harper & Row, 1984).

30. Frederick Jackson Turner, *Frontier and Section: Selected Essays of Frederick Jackson Turner*, edited by Ray Allan Billington (Englewood Cliffs, N.J.: Prentice-Hall, 1961), 88–89, 109–11, and 161–62.

31. Gressley, "West," 23; Henry Nash Smith, *Virgin Land: The American West as Symbol and Myth* (Cambridge: Harvard University Press, 1950); Kevin Starr, *Americans and the California Dream, 1850–1915* (New York: Oxford University Press, 1973) and *Inventing the Dream: California through the Progressive Era* (New York: Oxford University Press, 1985); John G. Cawelti, *The Six-Gun Mystique* (Bowling Green: Bowling Green University Popular Press, 1971); John H. Lenihan, *Showdown: Confronting Modern America in the Western Film* (Urbana: University of Illinois Press, 1980); Richard W. Etulain, "The American Literary West and Its Interpreters," *Pacific Historical Review* 45 (August 1976), 311–48; Ray Allen Billington, *America's Frontier Heritage* (New York: Holt, Rinehart & Winston, 1966); Robert G. Athearn, *The Mythic West in Twentieth-Century America* (Lawrence, Kan.: University of Kansas Press, 1986); Robert N. Bellah, *Habits of the Heart* (New York: Perennial Library, 1986); and Christopher Lasch, *The Culture of Narcissism: American Life in an Age of Diminishing Expectations* (New York: W. W. Norton, 1978). Obviously the comparison of the United States with other industrial nations is a large issue. For some suggestive discussion of the matter, see George C. Lodge and Ezra F. Vogel, eds., *Ideology and National International Economic Competitiveness: An Analysis of Nine Countries* (Boston: Harvard Business School Press, 1987).

32. Worster, *Rivers of Empire*, 14 and 260.

33. For an introduction to the historical and philosophical connotations of individualism, see Steven Lukes, *Individualism* (Oxford: Blackwell, 1973).

34. Nash, *American West in the Twentieth Century*, 6 and 262.

WESTERING IN
THE TWENTY-FIRST CENTURY
Speculations on the Future of the Western Past

1. John Steinbeck, *The Red Pony*, in *The Short Novels of John Steinbeck* (New York: Viking Press, 1971), 199.

2. Henry David Thoreau, "Walking," *Selected Works of Thoreau*, rev. ed. (Boston: Houghton Mifflin, 1975), 668.

3. C. P. Cavafy, "Waiting for the Barbarians," in *The Poems of C. P. Cavafy*, translated by John Mavrogordato (London: Hogarth Press, 1951), p. 28.

4. Richard Slotkin, *Regeneration through Violence: The Mythology of the American Frontier, 1600–1860* (Middletown, Conn.: Wesleyan University Press, 1973) and Patricia Nelson Limerick, *The Legacy of Conquest: The Unbroken Past of the American West* (New York: W. W. Norton, 1987).

5. See especially Limerick, ibid.; Gerald D. Nash, *The American West in the Twentieth Century: A Short History of an Urban Oasis* (Englewood Cliffs, N.J.: Prentice-Hall, 1973); Richard Lowitt, *The New Deal and the West* (Bloomington: Indiana University Press, 1984); Michael P. Malone and Richard W. Etulain, *The American West: A Twentieth-Century History* (Lincoln: University of Nebraska Press, 1989).

The April 26–29, 1989 conference was sponsored by the Beinecke Library, Yale University. In addition to the twelve paper givers, Richard Maxwell Brown, Ann Butler, David Thelen, David Weber, and Richard White served as commentators.

6. Frederick Jackson Turner, "The Significance of the Frontier in American History," American Historical Association *Annual Report*, 1893 (Washington, D.C.: 1894).

7. Alfred W. Crosby, "Reassessing 1492," *American Quarterly* 41 (December 1989), 661–69.

8. A new generation of scholars seems more appreciative of the significance of the territorial system. See, for example, a special issue of the *Indiana Magazine of History* 84 (March 1988), 1–116, which includes essays by W. W. Abbot, Robert V. Remini, Rowland Berthoff, Malcolm J. Rohrbough, Carl F. Kaestle, David Brion Davis, Robert F. Berkhofer, Jr., and George W. Geib. See also Peter S. Onuf, *Statehood and Union: A History of the Northwest Ordinance* (Bloomington: Indiana University Press, 1987).

The territorial and admission experiences of the Omnibus states have been reassessed in "The Centennial West," a series of articles in *Montana—The Magazine of Western History*, 37–40 (Fall 1987, 1988, 1990), and in *South Dakota History* 19 (Spring, Summer, Fall, and Winter 1989); also Howard R. Lamar, "Statehood for Washington: Symbol of a New Era," in *Washington Statehood*, edited by David H. Stratton (Pullman: Washington State University Press, 1991).

9. John Thompson, *Closing the Frontier: Radical Response in Oklahoma, 1889–1923* (Norman: University of Oklahoma Press, 1986) and Howard R. Lamar, *The Far Southwest: A Territorial History* (New York: W. W. Norton, 1976).

10. Ernest R. May, *Imperial Democracy: The Emergence of America as a Great Power* (New York: Harcourt Brace Jovanovich, 1961); John Ericson Eblen, *The First and Second United States Empires: Governors and Territorial Government, 1784–1912* (Pitts-

burgh: University of Pittsburgh Press, 1968); Stuart Creighton Miller, *"Benevolent Assimilation": The American Conquest of the Philippines, 1899–1903* (New Haven: Yale University Press, 1983); Russell Roth, *Muddy Glory: American Indian Wars in the Philippines, 1899–1935* (West Hanover, Mass.: Christopher Publishing House, 1981); Roland I. Perusse, *The United States and Puerto Rico: Decolonization Options and Prospects* (Lanham, Md.: University Press of America, 1987); and George B. Tindall, *America: A Narrative History* (New York: W. W. Norton, 1984), 887–88. The unbelievably racist politics characterizing American rule in Puerto Rico, the Virgin Islands, and Hawaii are detailed in T. H. Watkins, *Righteous Pilgrim: The Life and Times of Harold L. Ickes, 1874–1952* (New York: Henry Holt and Co., 1990), 495–529.

11. John S. Whitehead, "Completing the Union: The Alaska and Hawaii Statehood Movement: Research Report for the Alaska Historical Commission Studies in History," No. 198, June 1986; also Whitehead, "Alaska Statehood: The Memory of the Battle and the Evaluation of the Present by Those who Lived It—An Oral History of the Remaining Actors in the Alaska Statehood Movement," Alaska Statehood Commission, Fairbanks, September 1981.

12. Roger J. Bell, *Last among Equals: Hawaiian Statehood and American Politics* (Honolulu: University of Hawaii Press, 1984).

13. Ronald Takaki, *Pau Hana: Plantation Life and Labor in Hawaii, 1835–1920* (Honolulu: University of Hawaii Press, 1983); Lawrence H. Fuchs, *Hawaii Pono: A Social History* (San Diego, New York, London: Harcourt Brace Jovanovich, 1961); and Thomas R. Berger, *Village Journey: The Report of the Alaska Native Review Commission* (New York: Hill and Wang, 1985).

14. "In Search of the 51st Star on the U.S. Flag," Interview with Paul Gewirtz, *Yale Weekly Bulletin and Calendar*, April 30–May 7, 1990 (New Haven: Yale University), 1–9; also "Testimony of Paul Gewirtz before the Committee on Energy and National Resources of the United States Senate on S.710, S.711 and S.712, June 2, 1989," typescript, 1–36; Lamar, *Far Southwest*, 491, 497; and Jack E. Holmes, *Politics in New Mexico* (Albuquerque: University of New Mexico Press, 1967), 47–54.

15. Robert Athearn, *The Mythic West in Twentieth-Century America* (Lawrence: University Press of Kansas, 1986), 105–30, 150–51.

16. James W. Fesler and Donald F. Kettl, *The Politics of the Administrative Process* (Chatham, N.J.: Chatham Press, 1990); Francis de Baecque et Jean-Louis Quernonne, eds., *Administration et politique sous la Cinquième République* rev. ed. (Paris: Presses de la Fondation Nationale des Sciences Politiques, 1982); and Ezra N. Suleiman, *Politics, Power and Bureaucracy in France* (Princeton: Princeton University Press, 1974).

17. Interview with Jan Deutsch, professor of law, Yale Law School, Summer 1984.

18. Donald Worster, *Rivers of Empire: Water, Aridity and the Growth of the American West* (New York: Pantheon Books, 1985), 19–60.

19. Watkins, *Righteous Pilgrim*.

20. Malone and Etulain, *The American West*, chap. 6 and 7, 219–94; Gerald D. Nash, *The American West Transformed: The Impact of the Second World War* (Bloomington: Indiana University Press, 1985). See also "Henry J. Kaiser" in Howard R. Lamar, *Reader's Encyclopedia of the American West* (New York: Crowell, 1977), 606–07; Harold Mansfield, *Vision, the Story of Boeing* (New York: Duell, Sloan and Pearce, 1966); Peter M. Bowers, *Boeing Aircraft since 1916* (New York: Funk & Wagnalls, 1968); and Julian Dana, *A. P. Gianinni, Giant in the West: A Biography* (New York: Prentice Hall, 1947).

21. The reference is to current contemporary debates in newspapers and magazines concerning oil spills and marine life, the spotted owl and the lumber industry, wolves, coyotes and livestock growers, federal pollution laws and industry, and pollution and human health. A useful discussion of the role of the environmental historian in this debate is "A Round Table: Environmental History," essays by Donald Worster, Alfred W. Crosby, Richard White, Carolyn Merchant, William Cronon, and Stephen J. Pyne, *Journal of American History* 76 (March 1990), 1087–1147.

22. The litigious nature of Americans is a theme in Limerick, *Legacy of Conquest*, 54ff, but see also James Willard Hurst, *Law and Economic Growth: The Legal History of the Lumber Industry in Wisconsin, 1831–1915* (Cambridge: Harvard University Press, 1964) and *Law and Social Order in the United States* (Ithaca: Cornell University Press, 1977).

23. See essay by George Miles in this volume.

24. Arrell Gibson, *Oklahoma: A History of Five Centuries* (Oklahoma City: Harlow Publishing Company, 1965), 292–295, and Danney Goble, *Progressive Oklahoma: The Making of a New Kind of State* (Norman: University of Oklahoma Press, 1980), 7, 127–28.

25. John Thompson, *Closing the Frontier*, 28–30; William McLoughlin, *Cherokee Renascence in the New Republic* (Princeton: Princeton University Press, 1986); J. Leitch Wright, Jr., *Creeks and Seminoles: The Destruction and Regeneration of the Muscogulge People* (Lincoln: University of Nebraska Press, 1986); and Michael Green, *The Politics of Indian Removal* (Lincoln: University of Nebraska Press, 1982).

26. Thompson, *Closing the Frontier*, 22–24, 41.

27. Edwin C. McReynolds, *Oklahoma: A History of the Sooner State* (Norman: University of Oklahoma Press, 1964), 250–65, 266–69, 270–77.

28. *Chicasaw Petition to the U.S. Congress, 1899*, 4–5. Yale Western Americana Collection.

29. Pleasant Porter, "Chief P. Porter's Message Delivered to the Creek Council, October 1900" (Muskogee, Indian Territory, 1900). Copy in Yale Western Americana Collection.

30. Ibid., 20.

31. Worth Robert Miller, *Oklahoma Populism: A History of the People's Party in Oklahoma Territory* (Norman: University of Oklahoma Press, 1987).

32. Angie Debo's writings, for example, *And Still the Waters Run: The Betrayal of the Five Civilized Tribes* (1940; reprinted Princeton: Princeton University Press, 1972), are critical of white treatment of Indians, as is Thompson, *Closing the Frontier*, 22.

33. Keith L. Bryant, *Alfalfa Bill Murray* (Norman: University of Oklahoma Press, 1968). Goble, *Progressive Oklahoma*, 192–94, 206–22.

34. Goble, *Progressive Oklahoma*, 219, 223–24.

35. Red Bird Investment Company, *Red Bird, Creek Nation, I.T. Opening of New Town. An Opportunity for the Colored Man* (Fort Smith, Ark.: 1905) 1–15. Yale Western Americana Collection.

36. Ibid.

37. Laurie Maffley-Kipp, "The Cause of the West: Home Missions in California, 1848–1870" (Ph.D. dissertation, Yale University, 1990). The great promise of religious history studies is suggested by Ferenc Morton Szasz, *The Protestant Clergy in the Great Plains and Mountain West, 1865–1915* (Albuquerque: University of New Mexico Press, 1988).

38. The outpouring of serious scholarship on women's experiences in the West is both wonderful and astounding. See studies or edited accounts by Susan Armitage, John M. Faragher, Christiane Fischer Dichamp, Susan S. Harjo, Elizabeth Jameson, Annette Kolodny, Ruth Moynihan, Sandra L. Myres, Paula Petrik, Glenda Riley, Lillian Schlissel, Mary Lee Spence, Sylvia Van Kirk, and many, many others.

39. See E. H. Thomas, *Chinook: A History and Dictionary of the Northwest Coast Trade Jargon* (Portland, Ore.: Metropolitan Press, 1935) and Elizabeth D. Carr, *Da Kine Talk: From Pidgin to Standard English in Hawaii* (Honolulu: University Press of Hawaii, 1972).

40. The value of children's testimony is amply demonstrated in Elliott West, *Growing Up with the Country: Childhood on the Far Western Frontier* (Albuquerque: University of New Mexico Press, 1989).

41. Ronald Takaki, *Strangers from a Different Shore: A History of Asian Americans* (Boston: Little, Brown, 1989) and Arlene Lum, ed., *Sailing for the Sun: The Chinese in Hawaii, 1789–1989* (Honolulu: University of Hawaii Center for Chinese Studies, 1988).

42. While scholars continue to study and praise Mark Twain as a true master of the American vernacular and see contemporary writers like Wallace Stegner, Wright Morris, Ivan Doig, Frederick Manfred, Joan Didion, Rudolfo Anaya, Larry McMurtry, among others, as capturing aspects of the western vernacular, folkloric studies sometimes seem very local or very theoretical. Rosemary Levy Zumwalt, *American Folklore Scholarship* (Bloomington: Indiana University Press, 1988) and Simon J. Bronner, *American Folklore Studies: An Intellectual History* (Lawrence: University of Kansas Press, 1986) do not mention J. Frank Dobie. Allen Tullos, *Habits of Industry: White Culture and the Transformation of the Carolina Piedmont* (Chapel Hill: University of North Carolina Press, 1989) finds the voices of the textile millworkers of the piedmont and could serve as a model for finding the voices of particular western communities. One of the most impressive volumes to appear in decades is the Western Literature Association, *A Literary History of the American West* (Fort Worth: Texas Christian University Press, 1987), which not only discusses oral traditions and folklore but is a gold mine of sources and suggestions for the historian interested in the western voice.

43. If Frederick Jackson Turner, Frederick Merk, and Josiah Royce seemed to represent the West at Harvard, so did George Lyman Kittredge, who pursued the study of American folklore and balladry with great intensity, an activity manifested not only by his leadership in the American Folklore Society and his speeches before the Texas Folklore Society but by the correspondence in the Kittredge Papers at Harvard.

44. Charles Wilson and William Ferris, eds., *Encyclopedia of Southern Culture* (Chapel Hill: University of North Carolina Press, 1989).

45. James M. Gregory, *American Exodus: The Dust Bowl Migration and Okie Culture in California* (Berkeley: University of California Press, 1989). See also Thomas D. Norris, "Southern Baptists and the 'Okie' Migration: A Sectarian Rebirth in California, 1930s–1940s," *Locus: A Historical Journal of Regional Perspectives* 2 (Fall 1989), 35–48.

46. Walter Prescott Webb, *The Great Plains* (Boston: Ginn and Company, 1931).

47. Athearn, *The Mythic West in Twentieth-Century America*.

48. Two excellent retrospectives of local Nebraska and Texas artists illustrate how they used European styles. See Norman A. Geske, *Art and Artists in Nebraska*

(Lincoln: University of Nebraska Press, 1983) and Becky Duvall Reese, *Texas Images and Visions* (Austin: University of Texas Press, 1983).

49. Payton Boswell, Jr., *Varnum Poor* (New York: Hyperion Press, Harper and Brothers, 1941), 23.

50. Emory Lindquist, "Birger Sandzén: A Painter and His Two Worlds," *Great Plains Quarterly* 5 (Winter, 1985), 57; Jon Nelson, "European Influence on the Visual Art of the Great Plains," ibid., 4; and Howard R. Lamar, "Seeing More than Earth and Sky: The Rise of a Great Plains Aesthetic," ibid. 9 (Spring 1989), 69–77, esp. 70.

51. Gibson, *Oklahoma*, 471–75, and *The Santa Fe and Taos Colonies: Age of the Muses, 1900–1942* (Norman: University of Oklahoma Press, 1983), especially 87–178; Charles L. Briggs, *The Wood Carvers of Cordova, New Mexico: Social Dimensions of an Artistic "Revival"* (Albuquerque: University of New Mexico Press, 1989); and Ralph Coe, *Lost and Found Traditions: Native American Art, 1885–1985* (New York: University of Washington Press, in association with American Federation of Arts, 1986).

Contributors

WILLIAM CRONON is a professor of history at Yale University. He is the author of *Changes in the Land: Indians, Colonists, and the Ecology of New England* and *Nature's Metropolis: Chicago and the Great West*.

SARAH DEUTSCH is a professor of history at Clark University. She is the author of *No Separate Refuge: Culture, Class, and Gender on an Anglo-Hispanic Frontier in the American Southwest, 1880–1940*.

ANN FABIAN is an associate professor of history at Yale University. She is the author of *Card Sharps, Dream Books, & Bucket Shops: Gambling in 19th-Century America*.

JOHN MACK FARAGHER is a professor of history at Mount Holyoke College. He is the author of *Women and Men on the Overland Trail* and *Sugar Creek: Life on the Illinois Prairie*.

JAY GITLIN serves as a lecturer in history at Yale University and is completing a study of the French in the Mississippi Valley, "The Bourgeois Frontier: French Creole Communities in the American Midwest, 1770–1840."

HOWARD LAMAR is Sterling Professor of History at Yale University. He is the author of many books and articles, including *Dakota Territory*, *Far Southwest*, and *The Reader's Encyclopedia of the American West*.

PATRICIA NELSON LIMERICK is a professor of history at the University of Colorado, Boulder. She is the author of *Desert Passages* and *Legacy of Conquest: The Unbroken Past of the American West*.

343

MICHAEL MCGERR is a professor of history at Indiana University. He is the author of *The Decline of Popular Politics: The American North, 1865–1928* and is completing *The Gospel of Wealth: The United States, 1900–1932*, a volume in *The Oxford History of the United States*.

GEORGE MILES is the curator of the Western Americana Collection at the Beinecke Rare Book and Manuscript Library at Yale University.

CLYDE MILNER II is a professor of history at Utah State University. He is the author of *With Good Intentions: Quaker Work among the Pawnees, Otos, and Omahas in the 1870s*, the author and editor of *Churchmen and the Western Indians, 1820–1920*, and editor of the *Western Historical Quarterly*.

KATHERINE MORRISSEY is an assistant professor of history at the University of Arizona. She is the author of *Mental Territories: The Creation of a Western Region*.

D. MICHAEL QUINN is an independent historian living in New Orleans. He is the author of *Early Mormonism and the Magic World View* and *J. Reuben Clark: The Church Years*.

MARTHA A. SANDWEISS is the director of the Mead Art Museum and an adjunct associate professor of fine arts and American studies at Amherst College. She is the author of *Laura Gilpin: An Enduring Grace* and the author and editor of *Photography in Nineteenth-Century America*.

DAVID WEBER is Dedman Professor of History at Southern Methodist University. He is the author of numerous books, including *The Mexican Frontier 1821–1846: The American Southwest under Mexico*, *Richard H. Kern: Expeditionary Artist in the Far Southwest, 1848–1853*, and *New Spain's Far Northern Frontier: Essays on Spain in the American West, 1540–1821*.

INDEX